21ST CENTURY LITERACY FOR MIDDLE & SECONDARY STUDENTS

21ST CENTURY LITERACY FOR MIDDLE & SECONDARY STUDENTS

FIRST EDITION

Edited by Suzanne Rose

Slippery Rock University

SAN DIEGO

Bassim Hamadeh, CEO and Publisher
Mazin Hassan, Acquisitions Editor
Tony Paese, Project Editor
Alia Bales, Production Editor
Emely Villavicencio, Senior Graphic Designer
Michael Skinner, Senior Licensing Specialist
Natalie Piccotti, Director of Marketing
Kassie Graves, Vice President of Editorial
Jamie Giganti, Director of Academic Publishing

Cover image Copyright © 2014 Depositphotos/SergeyNivens.

Printed in the United States of America.

3970 Sorrento Valley Blvd., Ste. 500, San Diego, CA 92121

CONTENTS

INTRODUCTION

This text, *21st Century Literacy for Middle and Secondary Students*, is designed as an introduction to instructional ideas and approaches that have been shown to be effective in supporting the literacy development of students in grades 5 through 12.

Chapter 1, Assessing Text Difficulty, reviews the methods used by publishers to assign a "grade level" to a text. An article by Edward Fry, one of the major researchers in the field of readability, is provided.

Chapter 2, Textbooks and Collateral Readings, introduces the idea that, while textbooks are a major source of reading material for middle and secondary readers, there is a need to supplement textbooks with fiction, nonfiction, magazine articles, poetry, and other genre of literature. This chapter also introduces resources related to censorship and banned books.

Chapter 3, Matching Readers with Texts, explores factors that motivate and interest tweens and adolescents and introduces ideas for bringing students together with texts that they actually will want to read.

Close Reading and Study Skills are the focus of Chapter 4. Also included in this chapter is a pertinent article by Fisher, Frey, and Lapp, which provides an overview of the use of 'learning cycles' as a method for enhancing students' text interactions.

Chapter 5, Vocabulary Development, provides ideas for the development of students' vocabulary, both while reading literature and academic texts. The chapter also provides an article highlighting the importance of background knowledge for reading comprehension.

Comprehension and Text Structure, two areas that are extremely important in adolescent literacy instruction, are the focus of Chapter 6. These ideas are further developed in Chapter 7, Academic Literacy, and Chapter 8, Aesthetic Reading.

Chapter 9, Text-Based Lessons, pulls together information from the preceding chapters to provide guidance in designing curriculum that supports adolescents' literacy development. The use of multiple texts is also explored.

Chapter 10, Writing in the Content Areas, presents three articles related to incorporating writing activities within the content areas and to support close reading of text.

The final chapter, Chapter 11, provides useful information related to supporting students with literacy challenges in middle and secondary school classrooms, both literacy-focused classes and content-area classes.

Each chapter provides pertinent readings by experts in the field. In addition, there are related pre- and post-reading questions, as well as application and hands-on activities to help future and in-service teachers utilize their newly acquired information in their own classrooms.

Assessing Text Difficulty

One of the best ways to support students' literacy development is to assure that students are reading text at an appropriate level of difficulty. In order to do this, teachers need to understand what factors impact the readability of text as well as the methods that are used by publishers to determine text difficulty.

Chapter Focus Questions

Before beginning the chapter, consider these questions. Keep these in mind and try to answer them as you continue through the chapter.

1. What are some factors that make one text more difficult to read than another?
2. Why is it important to determine the difficulty of a text before using it in the classroom?
3. What are some ways that the difficulty of text can be determined?
4. Why is it important to consider both text factors and reader characteristics when determining text difficulty?

Factors that Contribute to Text Difficulty

Many aspects of a written text can contribute to the difficulty that a reader has when trying to read and comprehend that text. Each factor contributes to the overall text difficulty, so each must be examined in terms of its impact on the reader. In general, factors that contribute to text difficulty fall in one of these categories: book and print features, sentence complexity, content/themes/ideas, and language/literary features.

Book and Print Features

Book and print features that impact the difficulty level of the text include the length of the text, including the number of pages and words and the number of lines on a page. The print on the page itself also impacts the text difficulty. Print factors include the type and size of the font and the amount of space used between words and between lines on a page. The layout of text on a page also impacts its readability. The consistency of the layout from page to page, the use of organizational features such as headings, and the actual placement of the words and pictures on the page contribute to the difficulty of the text. The range of punctuation included, the use of illustrations, and the match between illustrations and the text are also features that can impact the reading difficulty of a text.

Sentence Complexity

The complexity of the sentences in the text greatly influences the difficulty of the text. For example, longer sentences are often more difficult than shorter ones because they tend to be complex or compound sentences. The use of more uncommon punctuation, such as the ellipsis and semi-colon can create text that is at a higher level of difficulty.

Content

The content of a text greatly impacts its readability. The reader's familiarity with the subject matter and prior knowledge about the topic can make a text easier. Technical or complex content is more difficult, as is text that relates to sophisticated ideas and themes.

Language Features

The author's use of figurative language, such as similes, metaphors, personification, and allusions will impact the difficulty level of a text. Dialogue can also be challenging for students to follow and comprehend. Texts with unexpected or uncommon points-of-view or which are written in an unexpected style, such as stream of consciousness, can increase text difficulty.

Vocabulary

The use of high-frequency, simple, and commonly-used words decreases text difficulty. Vocabulary specific to a particular content area, multisyllabic words, words with multiple meanings, and the use of foreign words or phrases increases text difficulty.

Readability

Readability generally refers to the difficulty or ease with which a text can be read. Most often, readability is determined using *readability formulae*, which consider text factors such as sentence length and vocabulary difficulty in order to determine a readability score for the text. In theory, the readability score indicates the reading level at which a student should be reading before s/he would be able to effectively interact with the text. These formulae are widely used by publishers of textbooks and instructional materials.

One problem with readability formulae are that they only consider *text characteristics*, not *reader characteristics*. A reader's prior knowledge, vocabulary knowledge, reading fluency, motivation, interest level, and other reader characteristics are not considered in the determination of the readability score. Reading teachers know that these reader characteristics are very important when matching students with appropriate texts. Since readability formulae do not consider reader characteristics, the readability level provided by the formulae should be looked at as only a rough estimate or a guide as you attempt to match students with texts or materials on appropriate reading levels.

Common Readability Formulae

Fry Readability Graph

The Fry Readability Graph was first developed by well-known reading researcher Edward Fry in 1963. It has been revised numerous times and is still one of the most commonly used readability formulae. The Fry Readability Graph uses measures of sentence length and word difficulty (measured by number of syllables in each word) to determine an estimate of the readability of the text. The Fry Readability Chart provides an estimate of the instructional reading level on which a student should be reading in order to be able to effectively interact with the given text.

Steps:

1. Select 3, 100-word passages from the text to be evaluated. Ideally, one sample should come from the beginning of the text, one from the middle of the text, and one from the end of the text.
2. Count the number of sentences in each of the 100-word passages. If the 100-word sample ends in the middle of a sentence, estimate the part of the final sentence that is included, to the nearest tenth. For example, if the 100-word passage ends after the fourth word of a ten-word sentence, the fraction of that sentence included in the passage would be .4 (4 out of 10 words).
3. Count the number of syllables in each of the 100-word samples. Pronounce any numbers in the passage as if they are words. For example, if the passage includes the number 103, you would say "one hundred three," not "one-oh-three."

Create a chart that shows the data you gathered from the three passages:

Passage	# sentences	# syllables
1 (1st 100 words)		
2 (2nd 100 words)		
3 (3rd 100 words)		
Total for all 3 passages:		
Average (Total divided by 3)		

The average number of sentences and the average number of syllables from the three passages are then plotted on the Fry Readability Graph.

Place a dot at the intersection of the average sentence length and average number of syllables per 100 words. The number in the circle in that section of the graph indicates the approximate instructional reading level of the text that was assessed. For example, if the dot falls in the "8" section, a student who can read eighth grade material on an instructional level should be able to read the text during a lesson with the teacher.

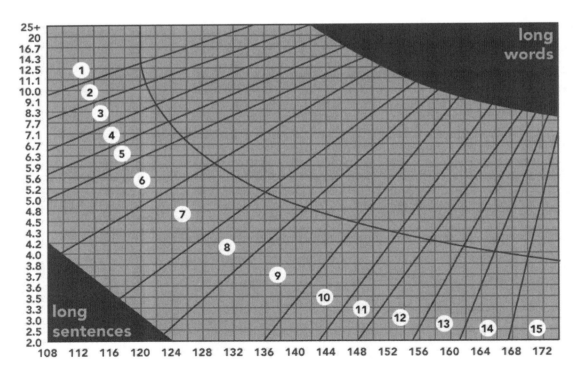

FIGURE 1.1   Fry Readability Graph.

If the dot would fall into one of the dark blue sections of the chart, where there are no lines or grade levels indicated, the text cannot be accurately assessed using the Fry Readability Graph because it has unusually long words or unusually long sentences.

The Fry Readability Graph only works with "typical" text—for example, novels and textbooks. It does not work with poetry or any other text that is not typical prose. Texts written by authors with an unusual style of writing, such as those written in stream of consciousness by James Joyce or math word problems will not be accurately assessed with the Fry Readability Graph.

SMOG Readability Formula

The SMOG Readability Formula was developed by G. Harry McLaughlin in 1969. Like the Fry Readability Graph, the SMOG is also based on measures of sentence length and word difficulty; however, the analysis is conducted in a different manner. In contrast to the Fry Readability Graph, which provides the instructional reading level needed to adequately understand the text, the SMOG formula provides an estimate of the *independent reading level*. Therefore, it is useful to use the SMOG for materials that students will be reading for homework or independent practice.

Steps:

1. Select 10 consecutive sentences from the front of the text, 10 consecutive sentences from the middle of the text, and 10 consecutive sentences from near the end of the text, for a total of 30 sentences that will be analyzed. Hyphenated words are considered to be one word.
2. Circle or highlight each word of three or more syllables that appears in the 30-sentences. Circle every word of three or more syllables, even if the same word is repeated numerous times in the text. As with the Fry Graph, pronounce numbers that appear in the text as if they were written as words. Any abbreviated words should be read as if they are not abbreviated.
3. Count the number of three syllable words that you have identified in the entire 30 sentence sample.
4. Round off the number of three or more syllable words to the nearest perfect square. For example, if there are 98 words with three or more syllables, round up to 100, which is a perfect square. If there are 30 words with three or more syllables, round down to 25, which is the nearest perfect square. After you have rounded off the word count, determine the square root. In the given examples, the square root of 100 would be 10 and the square root of 25 would be 5.
5. Add three to the square root to determine the reading level of the text. Using the given examples, 10 + 3 would mean the text is on a Grade 13 independent reading level (college freshman), and 5 + 3 would mean the text is on a Grade 8 independent reading level.

The Lexile Framework

The Lexile Framework was developed in the late 1980's by Stenner & Smith. Like other measures of readability, the Lexile Framework utilizes measures of sentence length and word difficulty to determine the readability level of a given text. Lexile scores range from the lowest score of "BR" (Beginning Reader) to the highest score of "2000L."

Lexile measures are commonly reported for packaged reading programs, such as the Accelerated Reader program. In addition, the developers of the Lexile Framework advocate using a comprehension test to assess students so that the students' "Lexile reader level" can be determined, to facilitate the matching of students to texts at an appropriate difficulty level.

Readability

Insights, Sidelights, and Hindsights

Edward Fry

In this article by Edward Fry, he reviews some criticisms of commonly used readability formulas. As the developer of the Fry Readability Graph, his insights are based from the viewpoint of one who is in favor of using these formulae to assess texts.

LEARNING OBJECTIVES

1. Define "readability" in your own words.
2. What are some issues with readability formulae with which you are already familiar?

Readability

Insights, Sidelights, and Hindsights

Edward Fry

Once upon a time many years ago in the middle of Africa (Uganda, 1961) I found a need for readability. I was assigned by the university to improve the reading of a group of community college instructors who were in turn going to improve the reading skills of their students. The practical problem was that the students had difficulty reading manuals for autos and other machinery. I knew, from some years running a reading clinic in the United States, that you can make more progress if you start the students out in relatively easy reading material so the students can read the materials with some comprehension and success. But how do you tell these African instructors how to select "relatively easy" reading materials in technical English? The answer, I deduced, was to use a readability formula. There not being any easily accessible readability formulas lying around in Uganda, I decided to make one. It worked for the Uganda context and, with modification and much more supporting research, it has served many thousands of teachers removed in both time and distance from that small group of community college instructors in the early 1960s.

Readability Defined

Harris and Hodges (1995) defined readability in *The Literacy Dictionary* as "the ease of comprehension because of style of writing." For the purposes of this chapter, I will focus on readability formulas that objectively assign difficulty levels to books and other written passages. Brenda Weaver, in another International Reading Association (IRA) publication *Leveling Books K–6* (2000), defines *leveling* as "selecting books to match the competencies of a reader or writer." Both definitions are correct.

At a very practical level, readability usually means the application of readability formulas. True readability does have a more general meaning found in popular dictionaries such as "easy or interesting to read—capable of being read" (The Random House Dictionary of the English Language, 1983). But in classrooms and publishing houses readability is often thought of as an objective numerical score obtained by applying a readability formula. Leveling, on the other hand, also yields a score of difficulty, but it is less objective and takes into account additional subjective factors not included in traditional readability formula. Readability formulas typically assign a grade level or some other numerical designation to a book. Readability designations have been applied to almost every kind of prose including laws, newspaper articles, test passages, military manuals, and advertising. It is not surprising that readability scores are most often found for textbooks and literature books used in the schools since most of the early research was done by university-based educational psychologists and much of the later work by or for educational publishers.

To put it in broad prospective, readability is really part of the scientific movement in education, which began in the 1920s when schools started using standardized tests to measure students' achievement and word counts to aid in curriculum development. Before that and continuing to the present, many educators use more subjective judgment with statements such as, "I think this book would be about right for my third graders." Most readability formulas, on the other hand, are so objective that they can be done by computers—simply type in a passage or scan in a whole book and a computer software program will give you an estimate of the difficulty level of the text's score (e.g, 3.0 grade level).

Most computer formulas are based on two inputs, which have been verified by many research studies (see Klare, 1988): (1) a measure of syntactic difficulty (grammatical complexity), usually measured by sentence length; and, (2) a measure of semantic difficulty (meaning or word meaning). A common measure of semantic difficulty is word length measured in syllables or number of letters. Alternatively, semantic difficulty is judged by frequency, either an actual frequency count of the word or the fact that the word does or does not appear on a list of familiar words. These two basic factors have been supplemented, and occasionally replaced, by a number of other input factors such as book length and other forms of subjective judgment of difficulty.

In fact, any readability formula must be used along with subjective judgment because formulas do not take many important factors into account, such as:

- **Motivation**—is the student really interested in the subject and/or are there other incentives?
- **Appropriateness**—adult novels might not be appropriate for junior high, though some of them have eighth grade readability scores.
- **Reader's background**—readers all have different cultural background and educative experiences (e.g., membership in some ethnic group, some social class, some geographical region).

To further clarify the nature and use of readability formula, it is helpful to consider some basic questions that surround readability.

What is the Purpose of a Readability Formula?

Certainly one of readability formulas' most common purposes is to help students learn to read better. Teachers have long known that giving the student a book at the right level will both cause him or her (1) to really read it, (2) to comprehend it, and (3) to enjoy it. Give the student a book that has too high a readability level, and one or all of those three things is apt to be missing.

Aiding comprehensibility, or the transfer of information, is certainly one of the major purposes of readability. A readability formula attempts to predict the reader's understanding of the written passage. This is certainly important in selecting textbooks. Much education is expected to take place by reading the textbook in many subjects at every level from elementary school through college. Comprehensibility is also very important in many areas outside of school; it is no accident that General Motors, the Army, and the Navy have all done extensive work in readability as have all major publishing organizations whose output of manuals, correspondence, directives, and advertisements rival many traditional publishing houses.

An interesting use of readability can be found in the field of law. A number of states have Plain Language Laws, which state that various documents such as loan contracts or insurance policies must be readable. At least 27 states required plain language in insurance policies sold in their state. In practice this often means written at about the eighth grade level. President Carter signed a directive to federal government agencies that they should produce readable documents, but there is some doubt if this well-intentioned order has had much effect on such agencies as the IRS or the Department of Justice.

Readability formulas have fared rather well when tested in court. I was an expert witness in a class action suit brought against the Medicare system for informing users of their appeal rights in a difficult-to-read letter (Readability Grade Level 16). Judge Weinstein in the New York federal appellate court case found readability formulas appropriate and ordered the U.S. Dept. of Health and Welfare to rewrite a Medicare appeal letter (David v. Heckler 1984).

Some law professors have tried to get their students and the legal profession to write more clearly and drop "legalese." But considering how many lawsuits pivot on the understanding of a written document, readability has barely scratched the legal surface.

How Do We Know If Readability Formulas Are Any Good?

Readability is one of the most widely researched areas in education. Klare (1988) stated that there are over 1,000 published articles on readability. A more recent look (2006) in the ERIC system under the entry term *readability* yielded 2,692 documents. The overwhelming majority say readability works in fields as diverse as adult basic education and horticulture. The demonstration of validity is most often found in the correlation with a comprehension test. The student understands less as the readability score increases. The proof of student comprehension is often a multiple choice comprehension test but sometimes it is a written or oral response.

A somewhat unique comprehension proof is the use of a *cloze test* in which the student is asked to fill in blanks where words were omitted. One advantage of a cloze score is that it is very objective; for example, every fifth word can be omitted and only exact word replacement is counted. Cloze thus eliminates the subjectiveness of writing or selecting comprehension test items.

Another demonstration of the validity of readability formulas is the correlation with oral reading errors. As readability score increases so do oral reading errors. This interestingly enough substantiates the three levels, *frustration, instructional*, and *basic*, suggested by Emmett Betts in 1946. He proposed that a student read a passage and that one oral reading error in every 20 words would place that reading material on the student's *instructional level*, more errors would place the material on the student's *frustrational level*, and fewer errors on the *independent level*. But teachers have long known that too difficult material shouldn't be used. Readability formulas simply refine and objectify this concept.

Readership is a concept borrowed from library science and journalism. Basically it is concerned with how many people are reading their materials. Studies have shown that by lowering the readability score, readership increases.

Readability can also be shown by eye–voice span. Turn off the light in the middle of a student reading aloud and see how many words he continues to say. The more words he continues the easier the readability of the passage. In other words, the greater the distance between where the eye is fixating and where the voice is saying them, the easier the reading material.

A similar objective demonstration, or proof, is found in levels of subvocalization. *Subvocalization* is often thought of as the little voice you hear inside your head while reading silently. More objectively it can be measured by electrodes placed on the lips to monitor tiny muscle movements. The greater the subtle muscle movement the more difficult the passage.

Subjective judgment has also been used to validate formulas. A group simply reads a number of passages then ranks them. This ranking is greatly facilitated (made more reliable) if judgment is aided by comparisons with a set passage of known standard difficulty. This is the basis of the Singer (1975) readability procedure. Singer assigned readability grade levels by having the teacher or editor compare graded paragraphs with the text sample. Subjective judgment is part of the Reading Recovery book leveling procedure.

Finally, most formulas agree fairly well on ranking a set of books. We could say they have concurrent validity or good correlation. However, there is less agreement on giving the level. For example, one formula might place a book at fifth grade and another place the same book at sixth grade. Grade level scores are usually within a year difference. Lately readability measures have used a variety of types of scores, such as Level K or Lexile 370. See Table 1.1.1 for some comparisons of different types of scores.

Are Readability Formulas Criticized?

Yes, they certainly are. Some of the major criticisms are partly philosophical; namely, there are still many educators who oppose the scientific method. To them classifying literature prose into a numerical score of difficulty is abhorrent. These same people frequently oppose standardized test scores. They prefer subjective judgment to objective scores. Flying under such banners as *whole language, literature based*, or earlier *progressive education*, they point out the flaws of readability formulas. Here are some of them:

TABLE 1.1.1 Comparison of Reading Levels Among Systems

Grade Level	Reading Recovery	DRP	Lexile	Fountas Pinnell*	Wright Group*
.5	3–5	27	70	B	B
1	10–11	35	170	F	G
2	16–17	42	370	K	L
3		46	508	)	Q

ATOS = Advantage TASA Open Standard (Similar to Flesch Kincaid); DRP = Degrees of Reading Power (TASA, 1999); Reading Recovery (Clay, 1991); Lexile (Meta Metrics, 1995); Fountas & Pinnell (1999); Wright Group (publishers Bothel, WA).

*Indicates scores from *leveling*. The others are readability formulas. Source: https://commons.wikimedia.org/wiki/File:Fry_Graph.png.

Formulas and tests are sometimes wrong. Correct, there is a *standard error of measurement* in all prediction or assessment scores. There is no standard error of measurement in subjective judgment because there is no way of quantifying it. To take it out of measurement terms, readability formulas are sometimes wrong, but subjective judgment is sometimes "wronger." It is difficult to have a standard error if you don't use objective measures or understand or don't wish to use the applications of probability inherent in the normal distribution curve.

Readability formulas are also criticized for causing bad writing, sometimes called *formula writing* or "dumbing down" textbooks. The criticism goes something like this: "The reason many elementary textbooks and some children's trade books are so bad is because the writer had to write them to a certain grade level." While there is some truth in this, the formula didn't cause the bad writing, the formula is meant to estimate (predict) readability after a piece is already written. It is not the formula's fault if the publisher has a bad editor and a bad writer. For some comments on how to simplify and clarify writing, see Fry's article on writeability (in Zakaluk & Samuels, 1988, or ERIC ED 220 799). In brief, readability formulas are not writers' guides; there is much more to good writing than two simple inputs such as word and sentence length.

The critics are correct in pointing out that readability formulas do not take into account all of the more cognitive factors that make reading difficult. The formula-makers simply point out that the formulas are useful in doing what they are supposed to do, and that is in predicting comprehension and reading ease by a number of traditional and experimental measures.

Readability is not the same thing as *legibility*. Legibility has to do with type size, spacing, and the quality of letter formation (in handwriting for example). Publishers sometimes take an old children's story and set it in large type. This might increase sales to parents but it really does not change the true readability much and the readability score not at all.

How Old is the Readability Field?

The first readability formula was published in 1923 by Lively and Pressey. However, before that there have been numerous discussions of literary criticism, rhetoric, and writing style and they date back to Aristotle and continue to the present. William Holmes McGuffey is credited with writing the first series of graded readers in the mid-1800s. The McGuffey Readers sold over 130 million copies between the 1850s and the early 1900s. Considering that the total population of the United States was 23 million in 1850 and only 76 million in 1900, that means a very high percentage of the school population used McGuffey's graded readers. This is interesting proof that graded reading textbooks had wide acceptance.

There are several rather detailed histories of readability (Chall, 1958; Klare, 1984; Gilliland, 1972; Harris & Jacobson, 1979). Discussions of readability also occur in many major reading methods textbooks used in teacher training, such as Harris and Sipay (1985), Ruddell (1999), Manzo and Manzo (1995), and Vacca, Vacca, and Gove (1995).

The most widely used formula in schools and with educational publishers in the 1950s, 1960s and 1970s was the Dale Chall formula (Dale & Chall, 1948). Businesses tended to use the Flesch formula (1948), or its slight modification known as the *Flesch Kincaid*.

The original Dale Chall formula graded books from grade 4–12, so for grades 1–4 in the 1960s, the Spache formula (1953) became popular for grading books below fourth grade. Both used a list of familiar words, sentence length, and required a numerical calculation.

In the 1980s popularity shifted, as Klare (1988) writes:

> Another significant move toward the ease of usage is the Readability Graph developed by Fry (1963). The Graph permits a direct estimate of reading grade level on entering with syllable length and number of sentences per 100 word sample, thus providing another way of avoiding the manual use of a formula. It seems safe to say that in its most recent version (1977), Fry's Graph is the most widely used of all readability methods.

By 2000, readability had become less dependent on one or a few formulas and much more diverse. The readability grading of books is now largely done by publishers and large companies often using formulas which require their computers. For example, Advantage Learning Systems has a graded list of 25,000 books, which contains most of the trade books used in schools. They use their own formula, known as *ATOS* (Advantage TASA Open Standard), which uses the inputs of sentence length, average grade level of words, and length of book. This formula uses a computer and the entire content of the book, not just samples of text. The formula yields grade-level scores that are coordinated with their own STAR reading achievement test (Standardized Test for Achievement of Reading).

Another company that has analyzed 15,000 books is TASA (Touchstone Applied Science Associates) using their own computerized readability formula, which yields DRP units (Degrees of Reading Power). Their inputs are sentence length, word length, and proportion of common words. These readability levels coordinate with their own reading test, which yields DRP units.

A third company that is doing computerized readability on large amounts of materials (26,000 trade books) is Meta Metrics. This program output is in units called *Lexiles*. Lexiles can be translated into grade levels. A student can take their achievement test that yields Lexiles, or any well-known standardized test like the Stanford 9 Achievement Test.

Traditional readability formulas like the Dale Chall and Fry Graph are also available in computer format for individual use. One company providing these is Micro Power & Light Co. Lexiles, DRP, and ATOS are not available for individual computers.

What is "Leveling"?

Leveling refers to various systems of grading books for difficulty using a larger number of subjective and objective factors than most readability formulas. Leveling sometimes incorporates more traditional readability formulas or the inputs of traditional formulas. It is used much more at the primary levels than upper levels. The goal of leveling is often fluency, rather than strictly comprehension. Some of the factors taken into account by some of the leveling procedures are:

- **Content**—is it appropriate or familiar to that age group?
- **Illustrations**—do pictures tell the story or explain vocabulary?
- **Length**—are there two words on a page? how many pages in the book?
- **Levels**—(scores) are not necessarily grade levels, often finer grading.
- **Curriculum**—levels related to teaching methods and/or framework.
- **Language structure**—includes repetitious words or phrases, flow.
- **Experience**—levels can be adjusted using subjective judgment from teaching experience.
- **Format**—type size, spacing, page layout.

The modern use of leveling is due in no small part to the work of the New Zealand Department of Education. It was partly popularized in the United States by Marie Clay (1991) and her Reading Recovery system, which used early intervention of reading tutoring for children who had a high probability of failure. The Reading Recovery system found a need to find books with closely spaced difficulty level, particularly at the first and second grade levels. Most traditional readability formulas are not particularly sensitive at those levels. Traditional wide range readability formulas such as the Dale Chall and Fry Graph only give whole grade designations at grades 1 and 2. Large company book readability formulas such as Lexiles, DRP, and ATOS do have finer unit designations but usually lack the more subjective text support factors.

Readability formulas aimed at the primary level, grades 1–4, like the Spache (1953) and Gunning (1998) do give tenths of a year designations. However, the Spache and Gunning, like the other traditional formulas, still use only the two traditional inputs of sentence length and vocabulary.

Several leveling systems have book lists of a number of leveled books. Fountas and Pinnell (1999) have over 7,000 books, Weaver (2000) has over 2,000 books and Gunning (1998) over 1,000 books. Gunning's leveling incorporates his own primary readability formula, and Weaver's leveling incorporates the Fry Graph, Dale Chall formula, or DRP. Book leveling can be done by classroom teachers.

Book leveling is also a major part of the Reading Recovery system of reading teaching (Clay, 1991). She discusses *text support*, which includes text features that are predictive, repetitive, and close to a student's natural language.

Are Readability Formulas Available for Other Languages?

Klare (1988) reported that there are readability formulas for 14 languages ranging from Afrikaans to Vietnamese. Most of the languages are alphabetic and use the two major inputs of syntax and semantics, which in practice is sentence length and vocabulary. An interesting problem occurs in nonalphabetic languages like Chinese, which is written in ideographs (characters). The inputs for Chinese are vocabulary (proportion of words on a 5,600-word list) and brush strokes per character. Other languages have unique problems; for example, Spanish has many longer polysyllabic words than English. Gilliam, Pena, and Mountain (1980) found that in using the Fry Graph for the first three grades you need to subtract 67 from the average syllable count.

A readability formula developed in Sweden and that is used in Europe is the *lix*, which is short for "lasbarhetsindex" (which translated means readability index), and is simply sentence length plus word length. A later modification is called *Rix* and it is the number of long words divided by sentence length.

What do Readability Formulas Actually Look Like?
Since there are over 100 readability formulas it would be difficult to show them all, but here are a few to give you a more concrete idea of what they look like. The original readability formula developed by Lively and Pressey (1923) used five inputs and six numerical constants in their formula to yield an average comprehension score:

$$x1 = .01029x2 + .009012x5 - .02094x6 - .03313x7 - .01485x8 + 3.77$$

x1 = average comprehension score

x2 = number of hard words not on Dale List of 769

x5 = number of personal pronouns

x6 = average number of words per sentence

x7 = percentage of different words

x8 = number of prepositional phrases

Readability formulas have since been greatly simplified. The New Dale Chall Readability Formula (Chall & Dale, 1995) has only two inputs to get grade level but is necessary to have the manual, which includes a 3,000-word vocabulary of familiar words and tables to yield grade level or cloze scores.

The Fry Graph, used widely in schools and by educational publishers, requires two inputs: sentence length and word length in number of syllables. These are entered into a graph to yield grade level.

To get Lexiles, DRP units, or ATOS Grade level you pretty well need a large computer—which in practice means that it is usually done by the company which developed those formulas.

The Flesch Kincaid Reading Ease Formula is used widely in industry and is fairly easy to calculate:

Grade Level =.4 (words/sentence) + 12 (syllables/word) − 16

Leveling requires specific directions according to which leveling system you wish to use. As was mentioned earlier, leveling often requires a number of subjective judgment factors such as content appropriateness, format, language structure, and illustration use.

What are Some Other Applications of Readability Formula (Outside of Education)?

The concept of readability, and more specifically readability formulas, has had an important influence on American education and the selection of school reading materials. To a lesser extent readability has influenced written communication in the armed services, industry, government, and law. Some important practical uses of readability outside of textbooks are:

- **Newspapers**—Rudolf Flesch was hired by the Associated Press to bring down the readability of front page news stories—he did (from Grade 16 to Grade 12).
- **Public health**—schools of nursing found the need for materials on illness prevention and correction so they include readability formulas in some of their textbooks.
- **Insurance**—a number of state insurance commissioners demand that policies issued in their state be readable. In practice that means about Grade 8.
- **Banks**—in some states, such as New York, plain language laws state that consumer loan documents be readable. The banks resisted, saying that the legal language was necessary because it had been tested in the courts. Yet when the banks rewrote the loan documents in plain language they had fewer lawsuits—maybe because the customers understood what they were signing.

Conclusion

The fundamental purpose of readability is to improve reading comprehension. This is particularly important in selecting textbooks and trade books for school use, but it is important to consider readability in any type of written communication. Other important uses of readability are in selecting materials for successful reading instruction and for increasing the readership of library books and periodicals. Leveling is a variation of readability more often used along with instruction methods at the primary levels. It uses a number of subjective factors and has the related goals of fluency and teachability

Research has shown that most readability formulas are based on the two factors of syntax (often sentence length) and semantics (word difficulty). Furthermore, most formulas will rank a set of materials in the same difficulty order but there is less agreement on obtaining the same grade level for any one piece of writing. There is even less agreement on the way the readability score is reported. A grade level score is widely used, but difficulty is also reported in a variety of scores, such as alphabet (A, B, C, etc.), Lexiles, and DRP units. Readability is an active field under continuous development. The more than 2,500 references to readability in the ERIC system testify to its widespread uses and interest.

References

Anderson, J. (1983). Lix and Rix: Variations on a little known readability index. *Journal of Reading, 26*, 490–496.

Benson, R.W. (1985). The end of legalese: The game is over. *New York University Review of Law and Social Change, 13*, 519–573.

Betts, E.A. (1946). *Foundations of reading instruction.* New York: American Book Co.

Chall, J. (1958). *Readability: An appraisal of research and application.* Columbus, OH: Bureau of Educational Research, Ohio State University.

Chall, J., Bissex, C., Conrad, S.S., & Harris-Sharples, S.H. (1996). *Holistic assessment of texts, scales for estimating the difficulty of literature, social studies and science materials.* Cambridge MA: Brookline.

Chall, J.S. & Dale, E. (1995). *Manual for the new Dale-Chall Readability Formula.* Cambridge, MA: Brookline Books.

Clay, M. (1991). *Becoming literate: The construction of inner control.* Portsmith, NH: Heinemann.

Dale, E. & Chall, J.S. (1948). A formula for predicting readability. *Educational Research Bulletin,* Ohio State University, 27, 11–20.

David v. Heckler (1984), Appellate Court Case No. 79C2813, U.S. District Court, E.D. New York.

DRP Program: The Readability Standard. (1999). Brewster, NY: Touchstone Applied Science Associates (TASA).

Flesch, R.F. (1948). A new readability yardstick. *Journal of Applied Psychology, 32*, 221–233.

Fountas, I. & Pinnell, G.S. (1999). *Matching books to readers: Using leveled books in guided reading.* Portsmith, NH: Heinemann.

Fry, E.B. (1977). Fry's readability graph: Clarifications, validity, and extensions to Level 17. *Journal of Reading, 21*, 242–252.

Fry, E.B. (1988). Writeability: The principles of writing for increased comprehension. In B. Zakaluk & S.J. Samuels (Eds.), *Readability It's past, present, and future,* pp. 77–97. Newark, DE: International Reading Association. (ERIC ED 220 799).

Fry, E.B. (1989). *Legal aspects of readability.* ERIC System No. ED 322 489.

Fry, E.B. (2001). Readability. In B. Guzzetti (Ed.), *Literacy in America: An encyclopedia.* Denver, CO: ABC-CLIO.

Fry, E.B. (2002). Readability versus leveling. *The Reading Teacher, 56*, 3, 286–291.

Gilliam, B., Pena, S.C., & Mountain, L. (1980). The Fry Graph applied to Spanish readability. *The Reading Teacher, 33*, 426–430.

Gilliland, J. (1972). *Readability.* London: University of London Press.

Gunning, T.G. (1998). *Best books for beginning readers*. Boston, MA: Allyn & Bacon.

Harris, A.J. & Jacobson, M.D. (1979). A framework for readability research: Moving beyond Herbert Spencer, *Journal of Reading, 22*, 390–398.

Harris, A.J. & Sipay, E. (1985). *How to increase reading ability* (8th ed.). New York & London: Longman.

Harris, T.L. & Hodges, R.E. (1995). *The literacy dictionary: The vocabulary of reading and writing*. Newark, DE: International Reading Association.

Klare, G.R. (1984) "Readability." In Pearson, P.D. (Ed.) Handbook of reading research. New York: Longman.

Klare, G.R. (1988). The formative years. In B. Zakaluk & S.J. Samuels (Eds.), *Readability: It's past, present, and future* (pp. 14–35). Newark, DE: International Reading Association. (ERIC ED 220 799).

The Lexile framework for reading. (1995). Durham, NC: Meta Metrics Inc.

Lively, B.A. & Pressey, S.L. (1923). A method of measuring vocabulary burden of textbooks. *Educational Administration and Supervision, 9*, 389–398.

Manzo, A.V. & Manzo, U.C. (1995). *Teaching children to be literate*. Fort Worth, TX: Harcourt Brace.

New Breakthrough in Measuring Readability: the ATOS Readability Formula for Books. (2000). Wisconsin Rapids, WI: Advantage Learning Systems Inc.

Rabin, A.T. (1988). Determining difficulty levels in test written in languages other than English. In B. Zakaluk & S.J. Samuels (Eds.), *Readability: It's past, present, and future* (pp. 46–76). Newark, DE: International Reading Association. (ERIC ED 220 799).

Readability calculations. (1999). (Manual for computer disk). Dallas, TX: Micro Power & Light Co.

Ruddell, R.B. (1999). *Teaching children to read and write*. Boston, MA: Allyn and Bacon.

Simply Stated. (1983). Washington, DC: American Institute for Research.

Singer, H. (1975). A non-computational procedure for quickly estimating readability level. *Journal of Reading Behavior, 7*, 255–267.

Spache, G. (1953). A new readability formula for primary grade reading material. *Elementary School Journal, 53*, 410–413.

Thorndyke, E.L. (1921) *The teachers wordbook*. New York: Teachers College, Columbia University.

Vacca, J.A., Vacca, R., & Gove, M.K. (1995). *Reading and learning to read*. New York: Harper Collins.

Venezky, R.L (1984). The history of reading. In P.D. Pearson (Ed.), *The Handbook of Reading Research* (pp. 3–38). New York and London: Longman.

Vygotsky, L. (1978). *Mind and society*. Cambridge, MA: Harvard University Press.

Weaver, B.M. (2000). *Leveling books K–8: Matching readers to text*. Newark, DE: International Reading Association.

Zakaluk, B. & Samuels, S.J. (1988). *Readability: It's past, present, and future*. Newark, DE: International Reading Association (ERIC ED 292 058).

Discussion Questions

1. In your own words, explain how Edward Fry defines readability in the article. What purposes do readability formulas fill?
2. What are some of the reasons that readability formulas are criticized?
3. What is leveling and how is it different from using readability formulas to determine text difficulty?
4. What is your opinion about the use of readability formulas to match students with texts? Provide support for your response using information from the Fry article and the other information presented in this chapter.
5. Which do you think is more effective for determining text difficulty—readability formulas or leveling? Provide a rationale for your response.

Conclusion

Chapter Activities

Activity 1.1

Use the list of text factors in this chapter to assess the difficulty of a text meant for students in grades 5–12. Give the citation for the text.

Write one paragraph to address each of the main areas of text factors: book and print features, sentence complexity, content, language features, and vocabulary.

For each listed area, indicate what features of the assessed text might make this text easier or more difficult for students.

Activity 1.2

Practice using the Fry Readability Graph using a content area textbook written for grades 4–8. Follow the steps given in this chapter and complete the chart, like the one in this chapter, showing the sentence lengths and syllable counts for each of the 100-word passages you select from the text. Make sure that you select your three 100-word passages from the beginning, middle, and end of the text.

After you have completed your calculations and have the average number of sentences per 100 words and the average number of syllables per 100 words, plot your data on the chart.

Identify the difficulty level of the text.

Activity 1.3

Practice using the SMOG Readability formula using the same passages you used for Activity 1.2. You may need to go back to the original text to add more sentences if your text samples do not have ten sentences in each one. Identify the estimated reading level of the text according to the SMOG. Compare the Fry and SMOG scores. Are they different? Explain why you think this is the case.

Activity 1.4

View the video at this link: https://www.youtube.com/watch?v=CRs9sqZVPNg to learn how to determine the Lexile level of a particular text. Then practice the process by determining the Lexile level of a textbook used in your classroom.

Activity 1.5

In the chapter reading by Edward Fry, he mentions the following literacy-focused topics and researchers. Select one of the topics and one of the researchers. Do some research about that topic/researcher and write a paragraph about each one describing what you have learned and how it relates to literacy instruction in middle- or secondary-level literacy instruction.

Topics	**Researchers**
Cloze	Edward Fry
Three reading levels	Emmett Betts
Eye-voice span	Marie Clay

Chapter 1 Online Resources

Online Fry Readability Calculator
http://www.readabilityformulas.com/free-fry-graph-test.php

Online SMOG Readability Calculator
http://www.readabilityformulas.com/smog-readability-formula.php

Online New Dale-Chall Readability Formula Calculator
http://www.readabilityformulas.com/free-dale-chall-test.php

Locate Lexile Levels for Published Books
www.Lexile.com/findabook

Lexile- to Grade-Level Correspondences
https://www.lexile.com/about-lexile/grade-equivalent/grade-equivalent-chart/

Textbooks and Collateral Readings

Although digital content is becoming more prevalent, most classrooms in middle and secondary schools still rely on a textbook for a large portion of the course instruction. There are both positive and negative aspects of textbook usage. Supplementing textbooks with collateral or supplemental readings is an important way to overcome the limitations of traditional texts. Adding e-books, children's picture books, and other collateral texts to the curriculum can provide many advantages.

Chapter Focus Questions

Consider these questions before you begin reading the chapter. Keep them in mind as you continue your reading.

1. What are some benefits of using textbooks in a middle or secondary classroom?
2. What are some drawbacks or difficulties of using textbooks?
3. As a high school student, what were some sources of information that you preferred to use instead of textbooks?

Pros and Cons of Using Textbooks

Pros of Using Textbooks

- Textbooks provide an outline that the teacher can follow for planning lessons and units. They also provide ideas for activities related to the text content.
- Textbooks provide students with a great deal of information about a topic in a relatively brief format.
- Textbooks are portable and can be easily taken home by students to share with families or for additional study.
- When students have the same textbook, it becomes a *touchstone text*—a common ground of information that all the students share and can use for discussion and for lesson activities.
- Many textbooks provide visual aids, such as photos, maps, or charts, which can support students' content learning by providing information in a visual format.

Cons of Using Textbooks

- Because the goal of a textbook is to provide a lot of information in a brief format, the information is often presented in a dry and boring manner, with the colorful and interesting aspects of a topic omitted to save space. Many tend to be essentially lists of facts.
- The reading level of the textbook, often provided by the publisher, is an average of the difficulty of the entire book; individual chapters or sections may vary greatly in difficulty. In other words, Chapter 6 of a text may be written on a fourth-grade reading level, while Chapter 9 may be on a ninth-grade reading level, as long as the overall difficulty level hits the target grade for the textbook.
- Because textbook authors are aiming for a particular readability level (for example, sixth grade level or seventh grade level), they may manipulate sentence length in order to decrease the readability score. To do this, authors use shorter sentences, which results in a lower readability level obtained by a readability formula.
- Unfortunately, in order to create shorter sentences, the words that are often omitted are words that indicate relationships, so the relationships among the concepts presented in the edited text may be unclear. For example, the complex sentence, "Abraham Lincoln was under great pressure to abolish slavery in the southern states, but since he was a supporter of states' rights, he did not wish to do so." could be divided into these two sentences: "Abraham Lincoln was under great pressure to abolish slavery in the southern states." and "He was a supporter of states' rights." By splitting the complex sentence into two shorter sentences, the calculated readability of the passage would decrease; however, the relationship between the two presented ideas is made much less clear in the revised version.
- Vocabulary terms are often made less precise as authors attempt to use easier words in order to lower the calculated readability of the text. For example, instead of using the

three-syllable word "enormous," the author can substitute the word "large." This decreases the syllable count by two and will help to reduce the calculated readability level.

- In any class, students will vary widely in reading ability and in conceptual background; however, a textbook cannot account for this variability. All students receive the same textbook, regardless of its appropriateness for them.
- Because textbooks are expensive, they are often not replaced for extended periods of time. This can result in books that do not contain current information, especially in the areas of social studies and science.
- Despite extensive editing, many textbooks have both conceptual and grammatical errors.
- Textbooks are often biased. The greatest biases result from choices of omission and inclusion—what the authors determine to be important or unimportant for students to know. This is often due to requirements placed on publishers by the states of Texas, California, and New York, because they are the largest textbook purchasers. Textbooks tend to closely reflect the curriculum of these states because publishers want their books to be selected for adoption by their statewide textbook adoption committees.
- The reading and conceptual levels of textbooks are often inappropriate for the students who are supposed to read them.

Pros and Cons of Using Collateral Readings

Pros of Using Collateral Readings

- Collateral readings can pique students' interest about a topic. They can be used effectively to introduce units or to supplement the information provided in the textbook so that the "bare bones" information in the textbook can be expanded.
- Collateral readings can provide students with a variety of viewpoints about a certain topic. For example, consider the differences that might be found in textbook chapters about the Civil War if the textbooks were printed in the North or in the South! This encourages students to make text-to-text connections.
- Since collateral readings often come from nonbook sources, such as newspapers, magazines, or websites, they are often more current. This also can help students make text-to-world connections about the information they are learning, which makes the information more relevant to them.
- Collateral readings can be on a variety of reading levels, so students who are not able to effectively read and comprehend the textbook can still learn the same material.
- Collateral readings can be used to build or correct students' background knowledge about a topic that will be introduced in the course textbook.
- Students with reading difficulties often are more motivated to read magazines, websites, and picture books than they are to read the course textbook.
- Many collateral readings are in narrative form, which is easier for most students to read than expository (informational) text.

Cons of Using Collateral Readings

- It takes time for teachers to gather a variety of collateral resource materials for all the units they teach.
- Storing collateral resource materials takes space if they are kept in printed form.
- The teacher must read each of the collateral resources to make sure the information is accurate, appropriate for the students, and to determine that the resource provides essential content information.
- Locating appropriate collateral readings on some content-related topics can be challenging.

Picture Books in Middle and Secondary School Classrooms

Although many picture books are written for young children, a large number of them are useful for content area instruction in middle and secondary school classrooms. Because they are short and contain many illustrations, the information provided in picture books is often more accessible for students.

Picture books are useful for:

- introducing new topics,
- building and correcting students' background knowledge on a topic,
- building a common body of knowledge about the topic for all students,
- appealing to visual learners,
- supplementing information briefly mentioned in the textbook, and
- introducing vocabulary related to the topic.

Incorporating 21st-Century Literacies in the Classroom

Due to the increasing popularity and availability of various forms of media in the classroom, electronic texts, video, and other multimedia resources are gradually replacing many printed texts in school "libraries," which are now often referred to as "media centers."

These resources are often referred to as *electronic resources or e-resources*. Many, though not all, middle and high school classrooms have Internet access, interactive whiteboards, and computers, which can be used to provide students with access to collateral readings and media to support the textbook.

Benefits of utilizing e-resources in the classroom include the following:

- *Motivation*—Students live in a technology-driven world and are often much more motivated to read text that is presented on a computer or using other electronic devices.
- *Currency*—E-resources are often more up-to-date than printed textbooks because it is less expensive and quicker to edit and revise their content.
- *Engagement*—Many e-resources capture students' interest more than printed textbooks because they can utilize animations, videos, and interactive activities. Many also contain colored illustrations and a more appealing layout.

- *Relevance*—Content included in e-resources often seems more relevant to students because it is more like the texts that they interact with outside of school.
- *Interactivity*—Students can interact with e-resources in ways that they cannot with a printed textbook; e-texts can be manipulated by the students and many e-texts can support students' reading by providing definitions, examples, or additional information about the topic. E-texts can support English Language Learners, for example, by providing instant translations from English to their home language.
- *Multimodalities*—Since e-resources may include audio and video components, they provide a multimodal experience that appeals to students' various learning styles and which can provide support for special needs students.

Challenged and Banned Books

Books for young adults often include situations, language, and topics that relate to the psychological, social, and physiological changes facing students of this age group. Because of this content, many books for middle and secondary students are challenged by parents or teachers and some have been banned from certain schools.

When selecting trade books, which are any books that are not textbooks, be sure to consider the appropriateness of their content for the students in your classroom. Issues related to content, language, themes, and violence are commonly cited as concerns that may lead to book challenges.

Even classics that have been read for generations are not immune from complaints; commonly banned classics include *The Catcher in the Rye, 1984*, and *The Lord of the Rings*, among many, many others. The American Library Association (ALA) maintains records of these book challenges and provides support for teachers whose book choices have been challenged by parents or others in the community.

According to the ALA, there are hundreds of attempts to ban books each year, a clear challenge to intellectual freedom and the first amendment. The ALA sponsors a "Banned Book Week," providing materials that can be used to raise awareness about the "right to read," and encouraging teachers to get involved.

Using Authentic Literature to Develop Challenging and Integrated Curriculum

Lisa M. Ciecierski and William P. Bintz

In this article, the authors introduce the idea of using literature in place of and to supplement textbooks in the middle-level classroom.

LEARNING OBJECTIVES

1. Predict what you think the term "authentic literature" will mean. Give some examples of what you would classify as "authentic literature."
2. Would you use picture books in a middle- or secondary-level classroom? Why or why not?

Using Authentic Literature to Develop Challenging and Integrated Curriculum[1]

Lisa M. Ciecierski and William P. Bintz

D r. William Alexander, a noted curriculum authority and a central founder of the middle school movement, shared in a presentation in 1963 that teachers must have a goal of stimulating a "love for learning, an attitude of inquiry, a passion for truth and beauty, a questioning of mind" (National Middle School Association, 2010, pp. 3–4). He asserted, "Learning the right answers is not enough … beyond answers alone, we must help children ask the right questions, and discover their answers through creative thinking, reasoning, judging, and understanding." (NMSA, 2010, pp. 3–4). Although Alexander was quoting a belief statement from Winnetka Public Schools in Illinois where he was a superintendent, his words remain inspirational today to middle grades teachers across the country—including those of us who read the pages of this journal—and Alexander's ideals have been influential in the development of the Association for Middle Level Education (AMLE) position paper, *This We Believe*.

We know that developing challenging and integrated curriculum so foundational to successful middle school is not easy; it is messy and in and of itself, challenging. What makes it even more challenging is that the Common Core State Standards (CCSS) emphasize that students must be given opportunities to grapple with "works of exceptional craft and thought" (National Governors Association Center for Best Practices and Council of Chief State School Officers, 2010, p. 35). The range of these

---

1   This article acknowledges the difficulties in using authentic literature instead of predictable and linear textbooks, while articulating methods for developing an alternative practice that promises the nurturing of lifelong literacy as a spillover benefit.

works must not only extend across genres but also across culture and across time. Both challenges must be accepted.

This article responds to *This We Believe* by describing one attempt to develop challenging and integrated curriculum. It also responds to CCSS by describing how authentic literature can be used with instructional strategies to support learning across the curriculum.

This article shares a brief review of related literature. Next, instructional strategies to use with authentic literature are shared. The article concludes with final thoughts about using authentic literature to develop challenging and integrated curriculum.

Authentic Literature's Scholarly Context

While no single, simple definition for authentic literature exists in the *Literacy Dictionary* (Harris & Hodges, 1995), we know that authentic texts are published for a wide audience beyond schools (i.e., the general public) and includes varied forms such as picture books, novels, and informational text. Much professional literature indicates that when teachers use authentic literature in the classroom, good things happen. For example, when teachers use authentic literature, student motivation, enthusiasm, and interest increases (Billman, 2002; Broemmel & Rearden, 2006; Chick, 2006; Lindquist, 2002; Soalt, 2005; Zambo, 2005). Students are highly engaged and often extend learning opportunities on their own. Students' vocabulary increases significantly when teachers use authentic literature (Fang & Wei, 2010; Gareis, Allard, & Saindon, 2009). This is due to the fact that authentic literature includes rich language, both figurative and informational. Teachers can use this rich language to help students analyze, among other things, word families, study prefixes, suffixes, and roots; learn synonyms, antonyms, and paraphrases; and explore idioms, collocations, and registers (Gareis, et al., 2009). In short, the language of authentic literature has keen relevance to the everyday language used by young adolescents in the communities where they reside.

In addition, when teachers use authentic literature, students learn content area material more efficiently and effectively. George & Stix (2000) refer to this as helping content area material come alive. Moreover, authentic literature engages students' in higher order thinking skills (George & Stix, 2000; Villano, 2005) and maximizes students' understanding of the specific content being studied (Atkinson, Matusevich, & Huber, 2009; Shelley, 2007; Taliaferro, 2009; Villano, 2005). In sum, when teachers use authentic literature, good things happen not only in language arts, but also across the curriculum.

Authentic Literature Across the Curriculum

When using authentic literature across the curriculum, teachers should consider building a classroom library that includes narrative and informational texts written at various levels that reflect wide interests. Many types of authentic literature can be used as instructional tools in the content areas. Picture books (Albright, 2002; Murphy, 2009), young adult literature (Bean, 2003), and nonfiction trade books (Palmer & Stewart, 1997) all contain multiple rich concepts to assist teachers and young adolescents in building relevance and understanding.

Many examples of authentic literature can be used across the curriculum. Here, several criteria were used to share specific pieces of literature. For example, only newly published literature was considered because the goal was to introduce new literature to the content area classroom. Second, particular attention was paid to award-winning literature. The International Reading Association (IRA), National Council of English Teachers (NCTE), National Council of Social Studies (NCSS), National Council of Teachers of Mathematics (NCTM), and National Science Teachers Association (NSTA) are just a few of many organizations that recognize and honor award-winning literature. Finally, literature that stood out as being outstanding or unique in some way was considered. For instance, some literature is unique in the way it integrates content with the story line, and others are unique in the presentation style or design format. Based on these criteria, three categories of authentic literature emerged: picture books, novels, and nonfiction trade books. Each category discussed in the pages that follow identifies two high-quality, even award winning, pieces of literature, a synopsis of each, instructional strategies linked to the CCSS, and other recommended examples of authentic literature. The CCSS emphasize that students should be able to analyze multiple texts connected by theme or topic in order to increase content knowledge as

Abdul-Jabbar, K. & Obstfeld, R. (2012). *What color is my world: The lost history of African-American inventors.* Somersville, MA: Candlewick Press.

Bartoletti, S.C. (2008). *The boy who dared.* New York: Scholastic.

Buyea, R. (2010). *Because of Mr. Terupt.* New York: Delacorte Press.

Coombs, K. (2012). *Water sings blue.* San Francisco, CA: Chronicle Books.

Kamkwamba, W., Mealer, B., & Zunon, E. (2012). *The boy who harnessed the wind.* New York: Dial.

Kadohata, C. (2006). *Weedflower.* New York: Atheneum Books for Young Readers.

Lewis, J.P. (2012). *National Geographic book of animal poetry: 200 poems with photographs that squeak, soar, and roar.* Des Moines, IA: National Geographic Children's Books.

Novesky, A. (2012). *Georgia in Hawaii: When Georgia O'Keeffe painted what she pleased.* Boston: Harcourt Children's Books.

Park, L.S. (2002). *When my name was Keoko.* Boston: Sandpiper.

Palacio, R.J. (2012). *Wonder.* New York: Alfred A. Knopf.

Rodriguez, R.V. (2006). *Through Georgia's eyes.* New York: Henry Holt & Company.

Sepetys, R. (2011). *Between shades of gray.* New York: Speak.

Smith, L. (2012). *Abe Lincoln's dream.* New York: Roaring Book Press.

Smith, L. (2006). *John, Paul, George, and Ben.* New York: Hyperion.

Van Drannen, W. (2001). *Flipped.* New York: Random House.

Winter, J. (2003). *My name is Georgia: A portrait by Jeanette Winter.* New York: Sandpiper Press.

FIGURE 2.1.1   Authentic Literature Exemplars.

well as compare approaches that authors take. Recommending books to pair with the showcased books may provide ideas for additional resources.

Picture Books

Integrating picture books into the content areas is a way to bring texts of various levels and genres into the classroom. With an average of 32 pages in length, picture books captivate visual learners with illustrations on every page or every page spread. Picture books appeal to readers of all ages and, while they are shorter than a novel, many are highly sophisticated due to their compacted language combined with rich aesthetic displays. They bring the content alive and enable a middle level teacher to emphasize concepts, thereby potentially building relevance in multiple ways. According to Murphy (2009), picture books can lead students to a greater understanding of the world around them. Not only are they entertaining and informative, picture books may also captivate those students who are not interested in academic learning in general or the specific content being studied. Picture books provide students an opportunity to connect to the material being studied in a meaningful way (Taliaferro, 2009; Villano, 2005), and they can build curiosity in middle level students, true to the important emphasis on exploratory education that successful middle schools should embrace. The connection-making that picture books create so easily and so profusely may increase diffident or recalcitrant students' motivation to learn, as well.

Picture books may be used by teachers to explore other forms or genres of literature (Murphy, 2009) by demonstrating the way that rich relationships can be built between books. Through these demonstrations, common barriers that interrupt learning may be overcome. Routman (2000) recommends using picture books as an ice breaker to engage students' sensibilities and capture their attention. Picture books also provide a necessary outlet for students to share their feelings and emotions about the topic they are studying. It gives teachers an avenue to engage students in constructing their own meaning of what they are learning through their thinking and their conversations.

Picture books may also be used as "way-in" books (Keene & Zimmermann, 1997). According to Bintz (2011), "way-in books are high-quality, often award-winning texts that provide students a 'way-in'—an unexpected entry into a world of topics they might find interesting to explore" (pp. 34–35). These books are tools for exploration. They give students a way to inquire as well as an opportunity to pose questions and arouse curiosities. Because picture books are short in length but rich in appeal, they may be used as "way-in" books frequently and with great benefits. Here are a few.

What Color is My World? The Lost History of African-American Inventors (Abdul-Jabbar, & Obstfeld, 2012) is unique in its construction and holds multiple instructional opportunities. The story begins with a mother telling her two adolescent twins they will have to use their imagination to appreciate the dilapidated house they have just moved into. While mother goes to get supplies, the twins help a handyman who was hired to help with the renovations. The handyman tells the twins that the house has exquisite craftsmanship and is a culmination of human progress. He shares that it is a "celebration of humankind, the history of America, and the history of African

Americans" (Abdul-Jabbar & Obstfeld, 2012, p. 3). Interesting facts about African-American inventors are interwoven throughout the story of the twins working with the handyman. Even though the twins were far from thrilled about the prospect of working with the handyman at the beginning, they convince him to spend more than his allotted time sharing information about the famous inventors.

According to Broemmel and Rearden (2006), books need to be more than just interesting; they also need to have visual features to motivate the student. The format of this book is not only appealing, but it provides teachers with a valuable tool for reading instruction. This mulitgenre book has interesting facts and information interwoven with page flaps, diagrams, and comic-like formats. This format is consistent with the CCSS (National Governors Association Center for Best Practices and Council of Chief State School Officers, 2010) in that students must be able to "integrate and evaluate content presented in diverse formats" (p. 35). Because the type of text is intermixed, readers will need to be cognizant of what type of text solicits what type of reading in order to be read proficiently. Students may make their thinking evident by reflecting on their reading practices while collaborating with fellow students. They may also record their thought processes in an interactive notebook (Lent, 2012; Marcarelli, 2010). Partner reading, where two students read together, is one more technique that may be used by students to model their reading practices and make their thinking visible, emergent, and exploratory.

The main character of the book, which is told in first person, documents what he learns and thinks in a journal extending on his more than 400 previously composed journal entries documenting his life. Journal writing is an experience often met with mixed emotions. However, the main character writes with great enthusiasm. Using journals as a tool to document learning and thinking in inquiry-based learning is a practice students may embrace after reading this book. When used appropriately, journal writing like this is consistent with CCSS in that students should be able to "write informative/explanatory texts to examine and convey complex ideas and information clearly and accurately through the effective selection, organization, and analysis of content" (National Governors Association Center for Best Practices and Council of Chief State School Officers, p. 41). By writing with this premise in mind, students will stretch to interpreting and analyzing the ideas they are studying. Making journal writing part of the instructional routine is consistent with the CCSS in that students should "write routinely over extended time frames and shorter time frames for a range of tasks, purposes, and audiences" (National Governors Association Center for Best Practices and Council of Chief State School Officers, p. 41). Writing can take many forms; this is one recommendation among many of how to integrate writing into the curriculum.

The beauty of this book lies below the surface. The book, told in a format that is creative and innovative, integrates factual information in a unique fashion, and encourages teachers to incorporate writing into their instructional practices. However, it also shows how these African American individuals overcame significant struggles to become successful and resilient. Because middle level students are developing their own identities, they can connect with the individuals in the book as role models who overcame various struggles to achieve what may have seemed impossible. This helps educators to engage their students in respectful conversations about diverse populations and their ability to aspire to greater things and achieve their dreams.

One book that connects nicely with *What Color is My World? The Lost History of African-American Inventors is The Boy Who Harnessed the Wind* (Kamkwamba, Mealer, & Zunon, 2012). This book could be used as a cornerstone book to introduce the concept of inventions using common, everyday materials. In this nonfiction picture book, 14-year-old William Kamkwamba uses junkyard scraps to build a functioning windmill. His creation brought electricity to his Malawi village that had been hit by drought and saved the crops of those in the village. He became known as the local hero who harnessed the wind. This lyrical story introduces the concept of creating with everyday materials and has the potential of integrating science, social studies, math, and language arts instruction.

Another favorite picture book to address the CCSS is *Abe Lincoln's Dream* (Smith, 2012). It is a stellar example of a picture book that may be used for interdisciplinary instruction because it holds the potential for both social studies and language arts instruction. According to Libresco, Balantic, and Kipling (2011), picture books provide young readers with visual images that make social studies concepts more concrete. This notion is beautifully illustrated in this picture book. The book begins by naming various dogs throughout time that would not enter a particular room in the White House because of fear of ghosts. The book centers on the conversation between Quincy, a young girl, and Abraham Lincoln's ghost. Various facts are interwoven through the text and reinforced with intriguing illustrations. Typical to Smith's works is the inclusion of humor. The book is delightful with many opportunities for extensions.

The CCSS communicate the importance of research in classrooms. Lincoln's ghost poses many questions throughout the book. These questions provide opportunities for students to conduct their own research. While specific and detailed answers are not provided in this book, they are present in a variety of other resources. Teachers may choose to have students find the answers to many of the ghost's questions while composing questions of their own, which serves as a crucial foundation for writing. Researching the answers to these questions would give students the opportunity to employ research skills meaningfully, collaborate with others, and increase their reading of nonfiction text.

The CCSS state that students should "interpret words and phrases as they are used in text" as well as "determine the technical, figurative, and connotative meanings and analyze how specific word choices shape the meaning or tone" (National Governors Association Center for Best Practices and Council of Chief State School Officers, 2010, p. 35). Lane Smith, the author of *Abe Lincoln's Dream*, is a master at communicating a distinguished tone characteristic of his writing. This book is laden with phrases and even jokes that will give students a variety of opportunities to interpret technical, figurative, and connotative meanings. These phrases and jokes truly add to the unique tone of the book. Teachers may choose to reinforce this tone or use this tone to teach voice by connecting *Abe Lincoln's Dream* with *John, Paul, George, and Ben* (2006) also written by Lane Smith.

Novels

Of course young adolescents enjoy reading about other youth (George & Stix, 2000). When students are given the opportunity to read novels in the classroom, they benefit from the instructional opportunities while also enjoying reading about others. Oftentimes, novels feature characters who are about the same age as student readers. This is one characteristic teachers may want to consider before choosing novels to share with their students. Teachers may also want to consider how their students will connect with the characters of the book. Will they find the characters and the plot relevant?

Novels are generally arranged into chapters and are often narrative in nature. This narrative quality does not take away from their instructional value. Actually, the opposite is true. Because novels are written in a variety of genres, the potential for their use as instructional tools is extensive. While reading historical fiction novels, students are able to live through the characters' lives in a vicarious experience. They are far more likely to connect with the identity and emotions of the individuals in novels than they would by trudging through a textbook. Historical fiction novels are not alone in the potential to provide opportunities for interdisciplinary instruction. Science fiction, realistic fiction, fantasy, and many other genres are also worthy contenders.

Title	CCSS	Instructional Strategies	Paired Texts
Between Shades of Gray (Septeys, 2011)	**CCSS.R.2** Determine central ideas or themes of a text and analyze their development; summarize the key supporting details and ideas.	Inquiry Circles	*The Boy Who Dared* (Bartoletti, 2008) *When My Name Was Keoko* (Park, 2002) *Weedflower* (Kadohata, 2006)
	CCSS.R.9 Analyze how two or more texts address similar themes or topics in order to build knowledge or to compare the approaches authors take.		
Wonder (Palacio, 2012)	**CCSS.R.6** Assess how point of view or purpose shapes the content and style of a text.	Student writing	*because of Mr. Terupt* (Buyea, 2010) *Flipped* (Van Drannen, 2001)

FIGURE 2.1.2   Novels.

A favorite novel is *Between Shades of Gray* (Sepetys, 2011). It tells the story of Lithuanians persecuted under Stalin's rule. The story centers on Lina who is a 15-year-old girl with characteristics common to other 15-year-old adolescents. Her life and her world change when she is taken in the middle of the night by Soviet soldiers. She is taken along with her brother and mother by cattle car to Siberia and separated from her father. This harrowing account tells the story of the time she spent while under police arrest.

This book is an excellent choice for many reasons. First, Lina is easy to connect to. Although she is sentenced to living in deplorable conditions and to manual labor, her story is also a love story. The question of her love being enough to help her survive is one that is central and one that adolescents can identify with. According to the CCSS, students need to analyze the development of central ideas and themes and summarize supporting details to support their conclusions. *Between Shades of Gray* provides opportunities for this type of analysis.

Books written about this time period are often based on the Holocaust and focus on Jewish people. However, there were many more groups of people affected during this time period. As shared previously, the CCSS state that students need to "analyze how two or more texts address similar themes or topics in order to build knowledge or to compare the approaches the authors take" (National Governors Association Center for Best Practices and Council of Chief State School Officers, 2010, p. 35). This book could serve as a starting point for an exploration on other groups of people who were affected and how they were the same and different from the Lithuanians. Exploring actions during the time of the Holocaust and the bombing of Pearl Harbor or making connections to current war-torn regions may help to engage students in understanding that historical moments have resounding relevance in the present.

The Boy Who Dared (Bartoletti, 2008) connects readily to *Between Shades of Gray*. It is the story of Helmuth Hubener who is imprisoned for treason after creating and distributing leaflets communicating the truth about Hitler and his actions. Helmuth learns this information by illegally listening to the BBC news on a shortwave radio and shares the information with his friends. All three boys are imprisoned and put on trial.

This book could be one of several used when creating literature circles to analyze how multiple texts address similar themes while also building knowledge. Wood, Pilonieta, and Blanton (2009) recommend using literature circles to teach and reinforce students' understanding on literacy skills and tasks. A literature circle format could be used for students to learn about themes through multiple texts. Traditionally, each literature circle group would read a different book focusing on the treatment of individuals during the time period of World War II. An alternative may be to implement inquiry circles (Daniels & Harvey, 2009) to acknowledge what we know about the research process, thinking, and collaboration to create a structure that supports students in building knowledge. The inquiry circle groups might consist of groups of four and have each group member read one of the following: *Between Shades of Gray* (Sepetys, 2011), *The Boy Who Dared* (Bartoletti, 2008), *When My Name Was Keoko* (Park, 2002), and *Weedflower* (Kadohata, 2006), where individuals who are Lithuanian, German, Korean, and Japanese-American would be represented. Students can deconstruct their individual novel and bring their analyses to their group meeting. Together, the group can create a Category Map to represent the common themes found in each of the books. They could also extend their learning by researching others affected by the leaders of this time period as well as the underlying and stated reasons for the actions taken. Students may take their newly learned knowledge to create a video highlighting the themes discovered and the knowledge learned.

Another favorite novel is *Wonder* (Palacio, 2012). It is an exquisite novel about a young boy born with an extreme facial deformity. Until his fifth grade year, Auggie Pullman did not attend school because of all of the surgeries he had. His challenge in beginning school at Beecher Prep is to convince the students he is really just like them even if he does have an extraordinary face. The book tells a story of fear, tenacity, friendship, and kindness.

According to the CCSS, students need to assess point of view and how point of view shapes the content and style of the text. Because this book is told in the varying points of view of the characters, students are able to see how many of the characters feel and act toward Auggie. The story is told from the point of view of Auggie, his classmates, his sister, and her boyfriend; the book can serve as a foundation for many talking points. It brings the individual identity and adolescent perceptions to the forefront.

This book illustrates the concept of point of view in a manner that is real and relevant to readers. Students could extend this notion by writing their own point of view accounts on a variety of topics that have differing importance in all subject areas. Since writers need options for writing, and options open windows for interest in writing, teachers can invite students to choose from a variety of short passages and write a short story from another point of view. Other examples of realistic fiction using varying points of view may also be shared and analyzed in the classroom as mentor texts. *Because of Mr. Terupt* (Buyea, 2010) and *Flipped* (Van Drannen, 2001) are just a few among many that may be considered.

Title	CCSS	Instructional Strategies	Paired Texts
National Geographic Book of Animal Poetry (Lewis, 2012)	**CCSS.W.6** Use technology, including the Internet, to produce and publish writing and to interact and collaborate with others.	Informational-based Poem Composition & Digital Publication	*Water Sings Blue* (Coombs, 2012)
Georgia in Hawaii (Novesky, 2012)	**CCSS.R.1.** Read closely to determine what the text says explicitly and to make logical inferences from it; cite specific textual evidence when writing or speaking to support conclusions drawn from the text.	One Word	*Through Georgia's Eyes* (Rodriguez, 2006) *My Name is Georgia* (Winter, 2003)

FIGURE 2.1.3   Nonfiction.

Nonfiction

Nonfiction can be a catalyst for learning and curiosity (Johnson & Small, 2008). The term non-fiction is often used interchangeably with the terms *informational text, nonnarative text,* and *nonfiction trade books*. Rather than being sold by textbook publishers, these factual books are sold in book format by booksellers (Atkinson, et al., 2009). While nonfiction text includes biographies, it also includes procedural text as well as other true stories (Duke & Bennett-Armistead, 2003). Appealing to all ages, this genre has made great gains in quality and choice throughout the years.

National Geographic Book of Animal Poetry: 200 Poems with Photographs That Squeak, Soar, and Roar (Lewis, 2012) is a favorite nonfiction piece of literature. It is an amazing book that is sure to capture the interest of many. One of the subjects that students love to read about most is animals. This book is filled with poems written by authors who are well-known as well as new authors, too. The poems are filled with interesting facts and accompanied by real-life photographs.

Students can creatively represent their ideas and knowledge in the content areas in ways other than traditional written and spoken responses (Ciecierski & Bintz, 2012). This book is a good example and may be one to be considered by the teacher to show how a book may be used as a mentor text (Dorfman & Capelli, 2007; Fletcher, 2011; Gallagher, 2011). The goal is for students to refer to an exemplary text to improve themselves as writers, which may be accomplished while students craft their own poems integrating content area material. While there are many other mentor texts teachers may make available to their students as mentor texts, another book in particular that may be considered in conjunction is *Water Sings Blue* (Coombs, 2012). While the format of this book differs from *National Geographic Book of Animal Poetry: 200 Poems with Photographs That Squeak, Soar, and Roar*, it is a wonderful example of integrating facts in a poetic way. Ciecierski and Bintz (2012) provide examples of rhymes connecting to social studies, science, math, and language arts. These examples illustrate the potential of having students craft rhyming text to demonstrate their knowledge in the content areas. The CCSS share the importance of using technology to produce and publish writing. Digitally enhancing and publishing students' creations may be particularly fitting to meet this standard. Furthermore, students may be given the opportunity to collaborate and interact with other students by presenting their finished poems electronically.

One last favorite is *Georgia in Hawaii: When Georgia O'Keefe Painted What She Pleased* (Novesky, 2012). It is a beautifully illustrated book about Georgia O'Keefe and her initial trip to Hawaii. According to the CCSS (National Governors Association Center for Best Practices and Council of Chief State School Officers, 2010), students should be able to "read closely to determine what the text says explicitly and to make logical inferences from it; cite specific textual evidence when writing or speaking to support conclusions drawn from the text" (p. 35). This book provides great opportunities to make inferences using both the illustrations and the text. Both invite readers to explore the type of person Georgia O'Keefe was. They may approach this exploration by reading other books about O'Keefe such as *Through Georgia's Eyes* (Rodriguez, 2006) or *My Name is Georgia: A Portrait by Jeanette Winter* (Winter, 2003).

One way students may use their inferences is to participate in a *One Word* learning experience. While students read the story, they should decide on *one word* to describe O'Keefe. This word may change as students read. While reading, they should pay particular attention to the illustrations as they truly have a symbiotic relationship with the text and add meaning to what is written. Once students have chosen their *one word*, they should write it on the front of an index card. On the back of the index card, they should cite textual evidence to support the conclusions they have drawn from the text. They should do this quietly and on their own because it is a secret! Next, the teacher will pair students up. The first person will share her/his word with her/his partner. The partner then has the job to consult the text to provide evidence for why the person may have chosen this word. After the partner has guessed reasons that support this one word, the first person will share her/his actual reasons for choosing the word. The roles are reversed and repeated.

This type of learning experience directly links to the requirements outlined in the CCSS because it engages students in citing evidence to support their response. Students often have a difficult time with the concept of identifying character traits. This learning experience provides the guided support students sometimes need to not only identify character traits but also document the reasons for their choices. It gives students the opportunity to cite evidence from the text and practice making inferences, which can also be a challenge. In addition, students are preparing and participating in conversation and collaboration as they build on each other's ideas while presenting their thinking clearly and persuasively. This practice gives teachers and students opportunities to address speaking and listening anchor standards.

Final Thoughts

Authentic literature provides learners with opportunities to grapple with high quality pieces of literature including picture books, novels, and nonfiction texts. These opportunities do more than just provide enjoyment and information. Authentic literature helps create passion for reading. According to Kittle (2013), "passions are peculiar, but passions drive readers to devour books" (p. 19). We hope this article will help teachers and students create new passions for authentic literature because when students have passion to read, they have passion to learn.

With this said, we recognize that increasing students' interests and engagement is not easy; it requires teachers to step forward with bravery as they utilize authentic literatures as an instructional tool that encourages students to learn in ways that are creative and innovative. This is unique because it invites educators to stretch beyond the use of traditional literature, which is more commonly used for instruction. It also invites teachers to consider that this type of instruction may create tension. However, in this instance, tension is a good thing. Short and Burke share that tension is not uncommon in learning because knowledge is tentative (1991). This tension in learning is what keeps us "alert, monitoring possibilities, taking new risks, stretching ourselves and our capabilities" (p. 28). These practices and ways of thinking are a transition from learning only for today to learning for today and for tomorrow.

Gallagher (2009) advises us to "never lose sight that our highest priority is to raise students who become lifelong readers. What our students read in school is important; what they read the rest of their lives is more important" (p. 117). Creating lifelong readers and learners should be our greatest mission. When teachers use authentic literature to teach the Common Core State Standards, they are a step closer to accomplishing this goal.

References

Albright, L. (2002). Bringing the Ice Maiden to life: Engaging adolescents in learning through picture book read-alouds in the content areas. *Journal of Adolescent & Adult Literacy, 45*(5), 418–428. Retrieved from: www.reading.org

Atkinson, T.S., Matusevich, M.N., & Huber, L. (2009). Making science trade book choices for elementary classrooms. *The Reading Teacher, 62*, 487–497. doi: 10.1598/RT.62.6.3

Bean, T. (2003). *Using young-adult literature to enhance comprehension in the content areas.* Naperville, IL: Learning Point Associates.

Billman, L. (2002). Aren't these books for little kids? *Educational Leadership, 60*(3), 48–51. Retrieved from: www.ascd.org

Bintz, W.P. (2011). "Way-In" books encourage exploration in middle grades classrooms. *Middle School Journal, 42*(3), 34–45. Retrieved from: www.amle.org

Broemmel, A.D. & Rearden, K.T. (2006). Should teachers use the Teachers' Choices books in science classes? *The Reading Teacher, 60*, 254–265. doi: 10.1598/RT.60.3.5

Chick, K. (2006). Fostering student collaboration through the use of historical picture books. *The Social Studies, 97*(4), 152–157. doi: 10.3200/TSSS.97.4.152-157

Ciecierski, L. & Bintz, W.P. (2012). Using chants and cadences across the curriculum. *Middle School Journal, 44*(2), 20–27.

Dorfman, L.R. & Cappelli, R. (2007). *Mentor texts: Teaching writing through children's literature, K–6.* Portland, ME: Stenhouse Publishers.

Duke, N.K. & Bennett-Armistead, V.S. (2003). *Reading and writing informational text in the primary grades: Research-based practices.* New York: Scholastic.

Fang, Z. & Wei, Y. (2010). Improving middle school students' science literacy through reading infusion. *The Journal of Educational Research, 103*, 262–273. doi:10.1080/00220670903383051

Fletcher, R. (2011). *Mentor author, mentor texts.* Portsmouth, NH: Heinemann.

Gallagher, K. (2009). *Readacide.* Portland, ME: Stenhouse Publishers.

Gallagher, K. (2011). *Write like this: Teaching real-world writing through modeling and mentor texts.* Portland, ME: Stenhouse Publishers.

Gareis, E., Allard, M., & Saindon, J. (2009). The novel as textbook. *TESL Canada Journal, 26*, 136–147. Retrieved from: www.teslcanadajournal.ca

George, M.A. & Stix, A. (2000). Using multilevel young adult literature in middle school American studies. *The Social Studies, 91*(1), 25–31. Retrieved from: http://www.tandfonline.com

Harris, T.L. & Hodges, R.E. (ed). (1995). *The literacy dictionary: The vocabulary of reading and writing.* Newark, DE: International Reading Association.

Johnson, J.C. & Small, D. (2008). Sparking students' interests (and meeting their needs): Nonfiction, content areas and collaboration. *Journal of Content Area Reading, 7*(1), 131–148. Retrieved from: http://www.content-reading.org

Keene, E.O. & Zimmermann, S. (1997). *Mosaic of thought: Teaching comprehension in a reader's workshop.* Portsmouth, NH: Heinemann.

Kittle, P. (2013). *Book love: Developing depth, stamina, and passion in adolescent readers.* Portsmouth, NH: Heinemann.

Lent, R.C. (2012). *Overcoming textbook fatigue: 21st century tools to revitalize teaching and learning.* Alexandria, VA: Association for Supervision and Curriculum Development.

Lindquist, T. (2002). *Why and how I teach with historical fiction.* Available: http://teacher.scholastic .com/lessonsrepro/lessonplans/instructor/social1.htm

Libresco, A.S., Balantic, J., & Kipling, J.C. (2011). *Every book is a social studies book: How to meet standards with picture books, K–6.* Santa Barbara, CA: Libraries Unlimited.

Marcarelli, K. (2010). *Teaching science with interactive notebooks.* Thousand Oaks, CA: Corwin Publishers.

Murphy, P. (2009). Using picture books to engage middle school students. *Middle School Journal, 40,* 20–24. Retrieved from: http:/nmsa.org

National Middle School Association. (2010). *This we believe: Keys to educating young adolescents.* Westerville, OH: Author.

National Governors Association Center for Best Practices and Council of Chief State School Officers. (2010). *Common Core State Standards.* Washington, D.C.: NGA Center and CCSSO.

Palmer, R.G. & Stewart, R.A. (1997). Nonfiction trade books in content area instruction: Realities and potential. *Journal of Adolescent and Adult Literacy, 40,* 630–641. Retrieved from: www.reading.org

Routman, R. (2000). *Conversations.* Portsmouth, NH: Heinemann.

Shelley, W. (2007). Using trade books to improve science education. *Science Scope, 31*(1), 69–71. Retrieved from: www.nsta.org

Short, K. & Burke, C. (1991). *Creating curriculum: Teachers and students as a community of learners.* Portsmouth, NH: Heinemann.

Soalt, J. (2005). Bringing together fictional and informational texts to improve comprehension. *The Reading Teacher, 58*(7), 680–683. doi: 10.1598/RT/58.7.8

Taliaferro, C. (2009). Using picture books to expand adolescents' imaginings of themselves and others. *English Journal, 99*(2), 30–36. Retrieved from: www.ncte.org

Villano, T.L. (2005). Should social studies textbooks become history? A look at alternative methods to activate schema in the intermediate classroom. *The Reading Teacher, 59,* 122–130. doi:10.1598/RT.59.2.2

Wood, K.D., Pilonieta, P., & Blanton, W.E. (2009). Teaching content and skills through integrated literacy circles. *Middle School Journal, 41*(1), 56–62. Retrieved from: www.amle.org

Zambo, D. (2009). Using visual literacy to help adolescents understand how images influence their lives. *TEACHING Exceptional Children, 41*(6), 60–67. Retrieved from: http://www.cec.sped .org/AM/Template.cfm?Section=Publications1

Discussion Questions

1. What is authentic literature? What are some benefits of using authentic literature in the classroom, according to the authors? What are three criteria that can be used for selecting literature for use in the classroom?
2. What are the benefits of using picture books in the classroom? Novels? Nonfiction?
3. Using Figure 2.1.3 in the article as a guide, identify a nonfiction text that could be used effectively in a middle- or secondary-level science or social studies classroom. Identify an appropriate Common Core State Standard, instructional strategy, and at least one text that could be paired with the nonfiction text you selected. Write a rationale to support your choices.

The Art of Learning to Be Critically Literate

Jerome C. Harste

Jerome Harste's approach to teaching literacy is based on the premise that in today's society, students need to learn to "read" a variety of "texts." He defines texts as any medium that portrays a message, such as a song, a dance, a painting, or a traditional text.

LEARNING OBJECTIVES

1. The article describes an approach called "transmediation." Predict what you think this word means.
2. Brainstorm a list of ways that the arts could be used to enhance literacy instruction in middle- and secondary-level classrooms.

The Art of Learning to Be Critically Literate

Jerome C. Harste

Every now and then, we really do have breakthroughs in our understanding of literacy and literacy learning. Two of the more recent insights are "multiple literacies" and "literacy as social practice." Instead of one literacy, there are multiple literacies (Street, 1995). In addition to language, humans have developed a variety of ways to mean (art, music, movement, etc.). This is what the humanities are all about as well as why movies have sound tracks, textbooks have pictures, and why malls select what music they play very carefully. It is also why Kress (2003) can make the case that the screen is overtaking the page in terms of its communicative potential.

The notion of multiple literacies has several important implications for how we think about literacy. Different cultural groups have different ways of making meaning. Even further, different cultural groups induct their children into literacy in different ways. Literacy means different things to different groups depending on their contexts, cultures, and schooling. Closer to home, school literacy may be very different from "everyday literacy," or even literacy as the parents and students in your class may be thinking about it. As James Gee (2007) said, children are learning more literacy outside of school than inside. I tend to agree with him.

Instead of thinking about literacy as a commodity (something you either have or don't have), thinking about literacy as a *social practice* can be revolutionary. When coupled with the notion of multiple literacies, literacy can be thought of as a particular set of social practices that a particular set of people value. In order to change anyone's definition of literacy, the social practices that keep a particular definition of literacy in place have to change. This goes for changing school curricula, too. In order to value new forms of literacy, our social practices—what we have often called *methods*—need to change.

I find it generative to think of curriculum as a set of social practices and then to begin to ask questions: What kinds of social practices are in place and, as a result, what kinds of literacies are valued? Who benefits from the social practices that are currently in place? Who is put in jeopardy? How might I better prepare students to become both visually and critically literate? What social practices would I put in place to demonstrate that I value visual literacy just as much as I value print literacy?

This is not a matter of walking away from what we already know. A good language arts program for the 21st century continues to be comprised of three components: meaning making, "language" study, and inquiry-based learning, *but* (and this is a big *but*) the emphasis is different. In this article, I discuss these three components, followed by four arguments as to why I believe the arts must be included in all aspects of a critically informed literacy curriculum. I also discuss how to create a strong critical language arts program that critically positions *languages* as important to becoming a critically literate being.

Three Components of a Good Language Arts Program

Meaning Making
M. A. K. Halliday (1975) taught us that language did not develop because of one language user but rather because of two, and they wanted to communicate. What is true about language is also true about other sign systems. Sign systems are first and foremost social meaning-making processes. While Wells (1986) made this argument in relationship to language, I think it is inclusive of all sign systems: most of what we know we have learned from interacting with sign systems and being in the presence of others messing around with sign systems in an effort to mean. What this means for today's and future classrooms is that students are going to continue to need lots and lots of opportunities to mean, not only in the form of reading and writing, but also in the form of nonprint-based literacies.

One of the ways to talk about this is through a process called transmediation (see sidebar), or the movement of meaning in one sign system to another. Moving across sign systems (from language to art, video to art, art to language, for example) has been shown to generate new ideas and new insights. Many teachers find that transmediation enlivens their reading program, while it also supports students' comprehension. One of the strategies that supports transmediation and that I have used with students and teachers is Sketch-to-Stretch. After reading a story, students are asked to sketch what they think a text means (e.g., story, video, poem, image). Sketch does not necessarily mean pencil to paper drawings; learners can and should be encouraged to use a range of different media (like tempera, markers, and clay) to sketch and stretch their ideas.

Figure 2.2.1 is a Sketch-to-Stretch by a student after we watched a YouTube video titled *The Power of Words* (https://www.youtube.com/watch?v=CNhYbJbqg-Y). In short, the video features a blind man sitting and listening to the passersby. Next to him is a sign, "I'm blind. Please help," which elicits a few coins from passersby. A sighted person comes along and rewrites his sign to read, "It's a beautiful day, but I can't see it," after which more and larger donations are given by passersby. The message of the video ends with "Change Your Words, Change Your World." This video signals to me the importance of *languages*—written,

FIGURE 2.2.1 A Student Drew This Sketch-to-Stretch After Watching a YouTube Video Titled *The Power of Words*.

TRANSMEDIATION

Transmediation (Leland & Harste, 1994; Siegel, 1984, 1995; Suhor, 1984) involves taking something that you know in language and moving that knowing to another sign system such as art, music, mathematics, dance, or drama. Moving across sign systems (from language to art, for example) has been shown to generate new ideas and new insights. Many teachers find that transmediation enlivens their reading program while also supporting students' comprehension.

MATERIALS & PROCEDURES

- A piece of literature
- Musical instruments, audiotapes of musical selections
- Scarves or other props to support interpretive dance and drama (optional)

Read the story aloud to everyone or form small groups and give each a copy to read together.

Form four groups. After reviewing the text, students discuss the messages they think the author wanted to convey. Group 1 expresses these messages through music, Group 2 expresses them through mathematics, Group 3 through interpretive dance, and Group 4 through drama.

Each group presents their interpretation using as few words as possible. Students in other groups try to explain what was expressed and how it connected to the book. Once these arguments have been made, members of each group talk about their interpretation of the story and how it relates to their presentation.

OTHER NOTES

Sketch to Stretch asks students to symbolize what the story means through a sketch. (This is different from drawing a picture of a favorite scene and entails deeper thinking.) Typically students meet in small groups to talk about what the story means to them before drawing. Sketches are shared with the entire class using the procedure described above.

It is important to vary the medium to keep an edge on learning. Introducing new forms of expression like clay, collage, or puppets helps to achieve this goal. In addition, students might choose which sign system they want to use in subsequent experiences.

FIGURE 2.2.2 Students Use Jacob Lawrence's Technique to Make Critical Statements About Literacy.

visual, gestural—to encourage action. After viewing this video, the student in Figure 2.2.1 used *languages* to situate his meaning critically, and moved it into a critical literacy statement about "help" as a collective and social endeavor.

Another arts-based strategy that has proven successful over the years is "Save the Last Word for the Artist" (Short, Harste, & Burke, 1995); it prepares learners to talk and act critically through art. The visual meanings that get produced are powerful ways to talk about issues and situate learners to become social actors in the world. Figure 2.2.2 represents an engagement that I designed that invites students to make critical statements about literacy by using an artist's technique to support their meaning making. Students watch a documentary on Harlem Renaissance painter Jacob Lawrence, *The Glory of Expression* (Freeman, 1994), and mimic his techniques in painting to create a critical statement of their own about literacy. This strategy provides space by first having participants hypothesize what they think the artist was trying to say and then hearing from the artist him- or herself. More often than not, the use of art will generate and often invigorate the discussion and the story by introducing new meanings. Dramatizing—adding music, movement, and dialogue—will do the same thing. In essence, transmediation is a powerful way to think about the complex meanings that are designed and created within, between, and among sign systems.

"Language" Study

I have put quotation marks around the word *language* to highlight that I am using the word metaphorically. I see all of the various ways we have to mean (art, music, mathematics, movement, etc.) as *languages*. Language study, therefore, not only includes the study of language as a sign system, but includes other sign systems as well: art, music, movement, and others.

Too often in the past, we have reduced the study of language to phonics in reading and spelling and grammar in the area of writing. I would argue that that approach has never been good enough, but it is even less effective when it comes to preparing 21st-century literate beings. Rather than think in terms of phonics, spelling, and grammar, I believe it is helpful to think about what kinds of literacy one needs in order to read things critically. Bill Green (in Comber & Green, 1998) calls this "instrumental literacy." Instrumental literacy is made up of all of those proficiencies one needs in order to be able to access a text and understand what it is doing to you as a reader.

I think most of what is exciting about language falls well above the phoneme and grapheme level of text, and yet we do very little to help students understand how "language" works. Students need to be invited to become linguistic and visual detectives as well as encouraged to create texts that do different kinds of work. It is especially important that "everyday texts" be an integral part of our language arts program, as this is where literacy is occurring in the lives of our students. Gee (2007), in fact, argues that today's youth learn more about literacy and what it means to be literate *outside* of school than they do in school. In school, students can learn to examine the literacies that operate on them outside of school and how they might position and reposition themselves differently in the outside world. Critical literacy, Hilary Janks says (2000, 2008, 2013), is about sign systems and power, including dominance, access, diversity, and redesign. No matter how it is said, literacy in the 21st century is not a spectator sport.

To support language learners, we (Lewison, Leland, & Harste, 2007, 2014) have developed strategies that acquaint them with Fairclough's discourse analysis strategies (1989), Gee's notion of "cultural models" (1989), and Luke and Freebody's (1997) "Four Resources Model" (see Strategy Lessons sidebar). We begin by using such things as birthday cards and newspaper headlines before moving on to more complex texts.

We also introduce students to Kress and van Leeuwen's (2006) grammar of visual design. Students learn how to deconstruct visual images by parsing pictures into quadrants for purposes of identifying what is new information as opposed to what is given, assumed, or taken-for-granted. Students become aware of focal points and how artists get pictures to do the work they want by directing the eye using vectors and color. We have found that while students learn much by studying commercial ads, they learn even more about the grammar of visual design by creating counter ads for the ads they have studied.

By providing space for students to explore and create through a number of engagements, we emphasize the use of languages and the study of languages to encourage deeper and critical understandings of how languages work on us to act, believe, and reproduce culture. These influences, of course, have the potential to serve some more than others.

Inquiry-Based Learning

We can be sure that there continue to be critical issues of concern that we're attempting to address—poverty, homelessness, pollution, over-utilization of our natural resources ... the list goes on. However, there are no magic answers to these problems, nor is it likely that such problems will be solved simply or single-handedly; we need to study these complex issues, and support learning that is collaborative and generative. Given this "reading" of our times, it should surprise no one that I am an advocate of inquiry-based collaborative learning (Harste, 1990, 1993).

> *Most of what is exciting about language falls well above the phoneme and grapheme level of text, and yet we do very little to help students understand how "language" works.*

What I want to see in curriculum is lots and lots of opportunities for students to explore their own inquiry questions using reading, writing, and other sign systems as tools and toys for learning. For today's students and those in the future, I want to produce learners who know how to use art, music, drama, etc., to reposition themselves, gather information, change perspectives, re-theorize issues, and take thoughtful new social action.

STRATEGY LESSONS

LANGUAGE AT WORK

Norman Fairclough's discourse analysis strategies (1989) are a way for students to begin to pay attention to language, the work it does in the world, and how it can shape our perceptions. This is best done a few times as a whole class and then students can break up in partners and small groups to do this analysis.

Materials and Procedures

Newspaper headlines on a common issue ("*Gaddafi Strikes at Rebels,*" "*Rebels Are Attacked,*" "*Gaddafi Is Dangerous,*" "*War Erupts in the Middle East,*" "*May Peace Reign,*" "*Peace Might Come after Talks,*" "*Followers Bowed as Gaddafi Passed*")

Examining *words*:

> What formal or polite language is used? (*May Peace Reign*)
>
> How is respect for status or position shown? (*Gaddafi* as opposed to *Rebels; Followers Bowed as Gaddafi Passed*)
>
> Do words express positive or negative values to readers? (*Gaddafi* is dangerous; *Rebels* signals nonconformists)

Examining *grammatical features*:

> How are grammatical forms used to express certain messages?
>
> Active voice (taking responsibility): (*Gaddafi Strikes at Rebels*)
>
> Passive voice (concealing responsibility): (*War Erupts*)
>
> How are *conditionals* used—may, might, should, could, can, can't, ought? (*Peace Might Come after Talk*—the key agents needed to create the state of peace are not named or being considered)

What types of *agency* predominate?

> Direct Action: (*Gaddafi Strikes at Rebels*)—an agent acts on something
>
> Non-directed Action: (*Rebels Are Attacked*)—they just happened to be there with no part in this action
>
> What attributions are given agents?: (*Gaddafi Is Dangerous*)
>
> Is agency unclear?: (*War Erupts*)—no agent; it just happened
>
> Is the agent an inanimate object?: (*War, Peace*)
>
> What is the authority of one character in relation to other?: (*Gaddafi* is singled out as a leader; the *Rebels* as a mass of nonconformists)

DISCOURSE ANALYSIS FOR KIDS

Jim Gee's discourse analysis strategies (1999) can be simplified and used with all students. It's a way for students to begin to pay attention to language, the work it does in the world, and how it can shape perception. This is best done a few times as a whole class and then students can work in small groups to do an analysis. We start with a greeting card because it has brief text; we then move to picturebooks and poems.

Materials and Procedures

Greeting cards for a particular holiday (Valentine's Day, Halloween, Birthdays). Cards that are designed specifically for boys, for girls, or that respond to a topic of interest like Barbie, NASCAR, etc. work especially well.

Examine the *situated meanings* of the card:

> What words are key?

> What message do these words convey?

> How does the font impact the meaning?

Examine the *social languages* of the card:

> Whose language is this?

> Where do people speak in this way?

Examine the *cultural models* of the card:

> What story world is set up by this card?

> What would you have to believe for this card to make sense?

> What symbols are important to the meaning of the card?

Examine the card's *discourses* by looking at the situated meanings, social languages, and cultural models together:

> What is this card trying to make you think?

> How does this thinking match with your own thinking?

Other Notes

Once students have become proficient in analyzing greeting cards, we move on to examining the discourses in children's literature. Picturebooks are a good place to start because of their length and the careful use of language.

BECOMING A TEXT ANALYST

Allan Luke and Peter Freebody (1997) believe that readers need to go beyond being proficient code breakers, meaning makers, and text users and also become text analysts. Text analysts not only gain personal and social meanings from texts but also examine how the text is trying to position them.

Materials and Procedures

Any work of children's or adult literature can be used. (There are a number of questions that can be asked of any text being read.)

For characters and perspectives:

> Whose voices are represented and whose are missing in this text?

> Why is _____ (character) so prominent in this text?

> What would _____ (missing character) say if he/she had a voice in this text?

For plot and meanings:

> Which stories are privileged and which are marginalized in this text?

> How would this story be different if it were told from the perspective of _____ rather than _____?

> What views are represented in this text? Not represented?

For positioning:

In what ways am I positioned within this text?

What did the author want me to believe after reading the text?

What are the ways this text could be rewritten to reposition the reader?

Curriculum has historically been organized around the disciplines. Students move through the school day by going from English to social studies to science to any number of other disciplinary studies. Donald Graves (1994) called this "the cha-cha-cha curriculum." Students tick off subjects like they are on a checklist: "I've taken science; done with that." Even in college, they say, "I've taken women's studies; done with that." Rather than invite students to use earth science or gender as a lens to examine their world, we have inadvertently reinforced the notion that they are "done with that." This is why, in part, the redesign of curriculum begins with reflexivity—the self-reflective interrogation and critique of what it is we have been doing. Rest assured, we all have had our hand in the cookie jar.

Don't get me wrong. I think the disciplines are important. But they are only important in relationship to the inquiry questions of learners. It is for this reason that I want curriculum to begin with what is on students' minds; with what makes them itch; with what questions they have. Disciplines can and should be introduced as perspectives that students can take in unpacking and understanding issues. The same is true of the arts. Curricular invitations to explore what something looks like in art or music (say "Indianapolis," for example) can be absolutely illuminating.

As part of a summer institute that I teach, inservice teachers study how to make content area studies critical. This past summer, we invited Ryan Kerr to talk about his book, *On Growin' Up* (2010). After reading the book and listening to the author, students working in groups were asked to have a written conversation about the book on a big piece of paper (see Fig. 2.2.3). Students began by jotting down their first reactions. To bring closure to the first part of this lesson, students were also asked to use the "big pages" we had placed on their tables to record themes, passages, and questions they had about the book. One group was so motivated, they conducted their own Internet search of groups being targeted worldwide and shared this information with the group. Afterwards, students created a gallery of their big pages and then returned to discuss how other groups had responded in comparison to how their own group had responded.

Next, students were invited to think about times when they had been marginalized and to respond by creating their own 4- to 6-page "growing up" book in the style that Ryan Kerr had used. An appealing alternative, although it never occurred to us at the time, would have been to have students respond in art on top of or using the very pages of the touchstone text itself (Simon, 2014). To culminate our study, students created an art gallery featuring their work, celebrating what they had learned about "group think" and minority targeting and inviting the viewing public to keep vigil.

FIGURE 2.2.3   Ryan Kerr Presents his Book *On Growin' Up* (2010); Afterward, Participants Engage in Written Conversation on a Big Page.

Four Arguments for Inclusion of Art in Curriculum

As an artist and a literacy scholar (including studying my own artistic process), I want to make four arguments for the inclusion of art in every aspect of the school curriculum. First, art encourages learners to see more differently, more aesthetically, more emotionally, more parsimoniously. White (2011) argues that "artists assimilate a whole range of psychological, aesthetic, political, and emotional data points, and they then make forms to organize and give meaning to them" (p. 2). Art renders back to us not simply what we see, but how we react to what we see and what we know as a consequence of that seeing.

As an artist, I firmly believe in the value of close observation, in slowing down to take note of our world. Drawing, sculpting, or putting together a collage are more than tools for rendering and capturing likenesses. These processes transform perception and thought into images and teach us how both to see and to think with our eyes. While art is interested in elaborating, art invites, if not demands, the removal of excess. Art, like poetry, has the power to sum up, to capture what is new long after the event itself (Fredrich, 1996).

Second, art affords critical expression, the questioning of taken-for-granted values. While art is often associated with aesthetics, the advancement of art as a discipline accents talking back. I have found that my best works of art are transgressive; that is, they speak back to what has simply been assumed or taken for granted. In "Casting a Long Shadow," for example (see Fig. 2.2.4), graffiti is positioned as a beautiful form of expression, reminding me of a message I saw painted on a brick wall in Toronto that read: "Billboards for the Rich; Spray Cans for the Poor."

Third, art affords abduction—the exploration of possibility, creativity, and imagination. According to Deely (2004), there are three forms of logic: Induction, which is reaching conclusions based on

FIGURE 2.2.4   "Casting a Long Shadow" (Mixed Watermedia, Harste, 2012).

a series of individual observations; Deduction, which is hypothesizing a conclusion based on a theory; and Abduction, which is the jumping to conclusions intuitively without an explicit set of arguments to follow. Art highlights abduction—the jumping to a new conclusion without any clear path as to how the abductor got there. Because abduction supports intuition, it is the only form of logic that allows newness into the system. Abduction means the focus of art is on insight, whereas in induction and deduction, the focus is on the logical conclusion of facts, data, and information.

Fourth, art affords agency—the ability to impose a different order on experience. Halliday (1975) tells us that it is person-to-person interactions that allow us to develop a personality. Alone we are just a person. Through interaction with others, we come to see how we are alike as well as how we are different. Art allows us to explore who we are, how we are different, what makes us unique, what contributions we might make to the ongoing conversation, even if our contribution differs drastically from current thought. It is this difference that endows us with personality and imprints the art we produce with a unique signature.

What is Critical about the Arts in Curriculum?

Across this writing, I have emphasized what comprises a strong language arts program, and the importance of art as a way to communicate. I now turn to what is critical about the arts in curriculum, an intentional play on words. At once, this subheading signals that the arts position curriculum as a way to learn to read texts and the world critically through our understanding of languages, and it also identifies the critical importance of the arts in curriculum. I have always said, "In order to be literate, you have to see yourself in literacy," not just in reading and writing, but in all meaning-making experiences. I believe that languages should be a part of a critical curriculum, and just as we ask our students to learn to read and write, so too should we ask them to understand how other languages work when designing, creating, and interpreting texts. We need to open up what constitutes writing and reading and begin to reimagine these experiences as ways to change the social practices around language arts curriculum and learning.

Writing

As I see it, art should be seen as an integral part of the writing process. Writing, like art, is about a search for voice. I maintain that if you can get students to write "what is on their minds," the rest may not take care of itself, but you *will* have come a long way toward creating a potentially great literacy program. It starts, of course, with students being free to say or illustrate what is on their mind after reading a text, and to say it in different ways. My experience says that if you have a restrictive reading environment, you have a restrictive writing environment. There is not a separate part of the brain that handles writing, another that handles reading, and a third that handles art. Together the sign systems create a communication potential that language learners must freely move within and across in an effort to mean in writing, reading, and in all communicative events and practices that occur in the classroom. The figures in this article show the significance of meaning making when it is reimagined, extended, and written visually.

To make our writing programs critical, we first need to free children up to write, and then we need to follow through by inviting them to unpack what they have written in terms of the social, historical, and cultural factors that have been at play to position their voices in certain ways. While no one can write from nowhere, similarly no writing is innocent. We grow by interrogating and understanding our own positionality.

In our work with teachers in Toronto, we asked them to bring in a cultural artifact that was important to them. Regardless of what teachers brought in—a teapot, a fine writing pen, a beaded coin purse—we asked teachers to explore the historical, political, and cultural significance of the object by answering these questions: What significance does this object have to you? How does this object relate to your identity as a person and as a culture? How does possession of this object position you in relationship to other groups, historically as well as in the present? Teachers wrote in response to these questions as well as used dramatic play to share their conclusions and insights. The owner of the fine writing pen, for example, began to see her artifact as coinciding with the values of the culture in which she found herself, and with it, access to privileges that other immigrant groups did not have.

Reading

In reading, we must continue to have "grand conversations" (Peterson & Eeds, 1990) across all sorts of texts including literature, image, music, drama, and so on. Discussions around texts, for example, are cultural practices that an important segment of our society values and that we, as English language arts educators, are mandated to pass on to future generations. Most likely, these are literature discussions, as literature is valued in our society. Yet, these same discussions are left unsaid in many classrooms when children bring objects and music, or produce art and dramas in response to a topic. Nonetheless, it is now obvious that we need to expand the canon so that all participants can see themselves in literature, not as "other" but as the main character, and to see how image, music, drama, and so on also present characters and traits through which readers *and viewers* see themselves.

This is why the use of literature, art, music, drama, and so on must be centered on multicultural artists; we can then use these texts to raise important social issues, the key to making reading relevant (Leland, Lewison, & Harste, 2013). I think it is important that students understand that they have not read a book or a text until they have had a conversation about it with someone else, emphasizing Halliday's (1975) point about the development of language and the desire to communicate. I also think it is important that students walk away feeling some social obligation to share their growing insights with the rest of the world. For this to become a regular part of curriculum, I am obligated as a teacher to set certain social practices in place.

To exemplify grand conversations across texts, let me describe our classroom approach to picturebooks. When we discuss picturebooks, we pay special attention to the images that the illustrator has created. Although this is not a novel idea, discussing in depth both the art and the written text as *languages* is. A favorite of mine (which really gets the conversation going) is *I'm Glad I'm a Boy! I'm Glad I'm a Girl!* by Whitney Darrow (1970). Students read the written text alongside the illustrations, carefully noting the juxtaposition of image/words to engage in discussions about gender, literacy, picturebooks, illustrations, and so on.

This allows us to extend the conversation to visual texts. Advertisements, commercials, and public service announcements (among others) need to be "read" as well as interrogated. By having students collect advertisements from teen magazines as well as from the magazines their parents typically read, larger systems of meaning are often exposed. Teachers in Toronto found that McDonalds advertised their green salads in parent magazines, but in teen magazines, their Big Mac sandwiches have the slogan, "Have you had your hands on any buns lately?"

Social Practices

While what materials we read is an issue, even more of an issue is what social practices we institute around our discussion of texts. I like to think of these social practices in terms of opening up new spaces in the classroom for having some critical conversations as well as much-needed *new* conversations. We need to teach in such a way that students enjoy a range of texts, but at the same time come to see that languages are never innocent. Whose story is this? What would this story be like if it had been written by someone very different from the current author? What is this image showing us? How are we implicated in these images? What is being taken for granted? What other ways are there to think about what is being discussed?

Discussions of this sort represent a new set of practices around what it means to be a reader, writer, and producer of text. Today's students and those in the future are going to have to be able to interrogate texts for purposes of understanding how authors and artists position readers. To be literate is to be able to elect what identity one wants to take on. Our goal needs to be to create agents rather than consumers of text.

GRAMMAR OF VISUAL DESIGN

VISUAL LITERACY[2]

Kress and van Leeuwen's (2006) grammar of visual design is intended to assist viewers in understanding ways to analyze art, photography, and advertisements. Viewers learn to identify the ideal and the real, the now and the new, the use of color, and the work that vectors and gaze can do in a graphic image.

Materials & Procedures

Use any two pieces of art including text book images, posters, or professional photography.

1. Ask students to look at the photo and mentally divide it into quadrants. Tell them:
   a. The top half of the picture is called the "ideal."
   b. The bottom half of the picture is called the "real."
   c. The left hand two quadrants are called the "here & now."
   d. The right hand two quadrants are called the "new."

2. With this framework in mind, ask students to analyze the art and to share what they think is being said.

3. Ask students to identify:
   a. The "center," or the place where the eye falls when someone first looks at the picture.
   b. The "vectors" (often called lines or alignments) that carry the eye up, down, or sideways across the picture. Typically "vectors" go from "the real" to "the ideal" or from "the here & now" to "the new."
   c. The "colors" being used. Colors are often used to set moods.
   d. The "gaze." In pictures or photographs containing characters, the direction of the gaze often creates a vector that moves the eye from one point to another. A gaze upward and off the page may suggest the future (an idealized perfect state); a gaze downwards anchors the picture in "the real" or "the here & now."
   e. Any "exaggerations"—items drawn out of proportion to the rest of the items in the picture.

4. With this additional information in mind, ask student to revise as well as share their new interpretation of the piece of art being analyzed.

5. To support students in further gaining confidence in analyzing visual texts, have them select a second piece of art to first "read" and then share with the class what they think the art is trying to say.

6. As a culminating activity, students can be asked to make suggestions as to how the text they have been studying might be redesigned to be more effective as a visual text.

---

2   More elaborated versions of these strategy lessons are available in Leland, Lewison, & Harste (2013) and in Lewison, Leland, & Harste, 2007, 2014.

Conclusion

If asked to critique education, I would argue that too often in the past, our English language arts curricula have focused on meaning making with a half hour of phonics thrown in for good measure. For the most part, studying language and other sign systems in terms of the work they do and how they do it has been left out, as has providing daily opportunities to inquire into problems of personal and social relevance to learners. No wonder, then, that students learn more about literacy on the streets than they do in the classroom. This has to change. The real question that each of us has to ask is, "What kind of literate being should inhabit the 21st century?" Asked differently, "What kinds of lives do we want to live and what kind of people do we want to be?" For my part, I want critically literate beings who know how language and other sign systems work and can use them to make meaning and reposition themselves in the world in a more democratically thoughtful and equitable manner. Infusing the curriculum with art as seamlessly as possible, I believe, is a first, but critical, step.

References

Comber, B., & Green, B. (1998). *Information technology, literacy, and educational disadvantage.* Adelaide: South Australia Department of Education, Training, & Employment.

Darrow, W. (1970). *I'm glad I'm a boy! I'm glad I'm a girl!* New York, NY: Windmill Books.

Deely, J. (2004). *Basics of seimotics.* South Bend, IN: St. Augustine's Press.

Fairclough, N. (1989). *Language and power.* Toronto, ONT: Pearson.

Fredrich, P. (1996). The culture of poetry and the poetry of culture. In E. V. Daniel & J. M. Peck (Eds.), *Culture/contexture: Explorations in anthropology and literary studies* (pp. 37–57). Berkeley, CA: University of California Press.

Freeman, L. (Producer). (1994). *Jacob Lawrence: The glory of expression* [DVD]. Available from http://landsvideo.com/vf-lawrence.shtml.

Gee, J. P. (1999). *An introduction to discourse analysis: Theory and method.* New York, NY: Routledge.

Gee, J. P. (2007). *What videogames have to teach us about learning and literacy* (2nd ed.). New York, NY: Macmillan.

Graves, D. (1994, July). *Inviting diversity through writing.* Keynote address given at the 4th annual meeting of the Whole Language Umbrella [audiotapes], San Diego, CA.

Halliday, M. A. K. (1975). *Learning to mean: Explorations in the development of language.* London, England: Edward Arnold.

Harste, J. C. (1990). Inquiry-based instruction. *Primary Voices, K–6, 1*(1), 3–8.

Harste, J. C. (1993). Literacy as curricular conversations about knowledge, inquiry, and morality. In M. Ruddell & R. Ruddell (Eds.), *Theoretical models and processes of reading* (4th ed., pp. 1220–1242). Newark, DE: International Reading Association.

Harste, J. C. (2003). What do we mean by literacy now? *Voices from the Middle, 10*(3), 8–13.

Janks, H. (2000). Domination, access, diversity, and design: A synthesis for critical literacy education. *Educational Review, 52*(1), 15–30.

Janks, H. (2008). *Language and power.* New York, NY: Routledge.

Janks, H. (2013). *Rethinking the literacy curriculum.* New York, NY: Routledge.

Kerr, R. (2010). *On growin' up.* Toronto, ONT: Cormorant Books.

Kress, G. (2003). *Literacy in the new media age.* London, England: Routledge.

Kress, G., & van Leeuwen, T. (2006). *Visual images: The grammar of visual design* (2nd ed.). New York, NY: Routledge.

Leland, H., & Harste, J. (1994). Multiple ways of knowing: Curriculum in a new key. *Language Arts, 71,* 337–345.

Leland, C., Lewison, M., & Harste, J. C. (2013). *Teaching children's literature: It's critical!* New York, NY: Routledge.

Lewison, M., Leland, C., & Harste, J. C. (2007). *Creating critical classrooms: K-8 reading and writing with an edge.* New York, NY: Routledge.

Lewison, M., Leland, C., & Harste, J. C. (2014). *Creating critical classrooms: K-8 reading and writing with an edge.* (2nd ed.). New York, NY: Routledge.

Luke, A., & Freebody, P. (1997). Shaping the social practices of reading. In S. Muspratt, A. Luke, & P. Freebody (Eds.), *Constructing critical literacies* (pp. 185–223). Cresskill, NJ: Hampton Press.

Peterson, R., & Eeds, M. (1990). *Grand conversations.* New York, NY: Scholastic.

Short, K. G., Harste, J. C., & Burke, C. (1995). *Creating classrooms for authors and inquirers* (2nd ed.). Portsmouth, NH: Heinemann.

Siegel, M. (1984). *Reading as signification.* Unpublished doctoral dissertation, Indiana University, Bloomington, IN.

Siegel, M. (1995). More than words: The generative power of transmediation for learning. *Canadian Journal of Education, 20,* 455–475

Simon, R. (2014). Collaborative inquiry using *Night: An interview with Professor Rob Simon.* Retreived from http://onnetwork.facinghistory.org/collaborative-inquiry-using-night-an-interview-with-professor-rob-simon/.

Street, B. (1995). *Social literacies: Critical approaches to literacy in development, ethnography, and education.* London, England: Longman.

Suhor, C. (1984). Towards a semiotics-based curriculum. *Journal of Curriculum Studies, 16,* 247–257.

Wells, G. (1986). *The meaning makers: Children learning language and using language to learn.* Portsmouth, NH: Heinemann.

White, K. (2011). *101 things to learn in art school.* Cambridge, MA: MIT Press.

Discussion Questions

1. Summarize why Harste believes that the arts need to be included in all aspects of a critically informed literacy curriculum.
2. How is Harste's definition of language different from the traditional definition?
3. Define transmediation. Give an example of an original transmediation task that you could have students complete in the classroom.

New Angles on Differentiating Reading Instruction

Five Best Practices That Deserve a New Chapter in the Common Core Era

Laura Robb

In this article, Laura Robb introduces ideas for differentiating instruction in literacy classrooms. She also relates the practice of differentiation to the Common Core and increasing independent reading by students.

LEARNING OBJECTIVES

1. What comes to mind when you think of "differentiated reading instruction"? Draw a concept map outlining your ideas related to this term.
2. Why do you think independent reading is important for students' reading growth?

New Angles on Differentiating Reading Instruction

Five Best Practices that Deserve a New Chapter in the Common Core Era

Laura Robb

One of my favorite New Yorker cartoons, by Robert Mankoff (1987), is of two men, one a writer, talking at a cocktail party. The caption reads, *"We're still pretty far apart. I'm looking for a six-figure advance and they're refusing to read my manuscript."* It brilliantly captures sky-high expectations that don't match up to reality.

When I think about the expectations of the Common Core State Standards (CCSS) for reading, it seems to me "we're pretty far apart." In saying this, I am not dissenting from the standards' reading and writing goals, but like many educators, I am concerned that the imminence of the CCSS tests puts pressure on schools that may undermine the goals of the CCSS. Teachers need time. They need time to marry their current practices with those of the Common Core, such as close reading and providing text-based responses. They need quality professional development. The space between many teachers' abilities to help readers make sufficient progress and the requirements for reading proficiency expected by the Common Core is still pretty vast. To some extent teachers are innocent victims of the pendulum swings in education. For example, before the CCSS was adopted by New Jersey, students had been required to add a personal connection when writing about reading on the state exam. But with the CCSS, personal connections are out and text-dependent comprehension is in; only effective, ongoing professional development can help teachers and students transition to a new way of thinking. Indeed, the best professional development experiences will empower teachers to examine the "what works" of their own teaching, and realize that readers make personal connections as they read, and they can continue to, *along with* reckoning with the text's meaning.

Students themselves are far apart from the CCSS requirement that all students read complex grade-level texts by the end of the school year. I recently coached a seventh grade teacher in a middle school close to my home. In September, the range of instructional reading levels among the twenty-eight students was from *third to twelfth grade*! Like many teachers, the teacher thought she could not deviate from the district requirement that each and every student *read* the selections in the seventh grade anthology and take the unit tests. To accommodate the sixteen students reading two to four years below grade level, the teacher read aloud the selections to them. Thus, the very students who should be reading *more* every day—more than proficient and advanced readers in order to move forward, aren't reading. Compelling all students to read the same text frustrates these struggling students and lowers their self-confidence and self-efficacy (Guthrie, Wigfield, Metsala, & Cox, 1999; Guthrie, Wigfield, & Klauda, 2012). This teacher is a committed, capable teacher—but she needs training and coaching to deepen her expertise in meeting the needs of a vast range of readers.

So our challenge is this: If we are ever to close the achievement gap, either via the CCSS or whatever is next generating change in education, we have to help classroom teachers at all grade levels embrace and "own" their professional development, and allow them to shake off the notion many across the nation express: that with the Common Core in town, everything they've been doing is wrong. Teachers need to know of, lean on, and cite the strong research base of instructional and independent reading practices that have worked for their students. However, they need to look at their current practices and be open to improvements that the CCSS has brought to the professional discussion. Students ultimately suffer when educators go along with "out with the old, in with the new" swings in pedagogy; so what I advocate here is to marry the old with the new.

In this article, I want to focus on differentiation in reading, and use it as an example of how to stay true to best practices that have a strong research base, and yet bring fresh methods to them in light of the Common Core. As you read about how I change up differentiation for today's standards, I want you to see the professional development power of an article, and to see that effective professional development can be—and maybe should be—small, measurable forays, such as trying the ideas you come across in professional books and articles and discussing them with colleagues. How do we meet the CCSS? *Bird by bird,* as writer Ann Lamott's father advised (1994).

So with that in mind, let's focus on differentiation, and how we can use it to meet Common Core State Standards for Reading by staying true to five best practices that need to play a bigger role:

1. **Use anchor texts to teach reading.** An anchor text provides a common read aloud text for instruction, and this enables students to have choices with instructional reading. Later in this article I provide sample anchor text lessons you can use to model making logical inferences, discovering the author's purpose and tone, and what it means to read a text closely. The lessons illustrate that teaching with an anchor text offers the freedom to meet students where they are and have them read and learn at their instructional levels so they can improve their reading skills (Allison, 2009; Robb, 2008, 2013).

2. **Use formative assessments to inform teaching decisions.** Formative assessments place differentiated reading instruction on a rock-solid foundation because they consider the child's work, behaviors, and attitudes on a daily basis, and thus decisions about learning,

placement, and support emerge from performance-based data, and needn't wait for late-in-the-year standardized tests, when it's too late for the current teacher to act on the data. If schools revalue formative assessment, they stand a far better chance of meeting end-of-year CCSS benchmarks; formative assessments help teachers become more diagnostic in their teaching day to day, and in turn assure students are making sufficient progress week to week, month to month. When students receive frequent, qualitative feedback through formative assessments (conferences, written conversations in reading notebooks, peer feedback, quizzes, and so on) the benefits to the learner accrue quickly (Serravallo, 2010, 2012).

3. **Amplify writing about reading.** English novelist E.M. Forster wrote: "How do I know what I think until I see what I say?" Forster's question captures the point that we can write what we know and understand. Now with the Common Core, there is urgency around students' writing about reading and I think this is a good thing. I encourage you to read the research of Steve Graham and Michael Hebert (2010) in *Write to Read,* which demonstrates that writing that unveils students understandings of a text, his/her thinking with the ideas of the text, improves comprehension. How do we bring writing about reading out of the shadows in order to deepen students' reading experience? I recommend students write something daily—even if it's just a few sentences. In addition, especially beginning in grade three, we can help students to write analytical paragraphs and move to essays in grade five and up.

4. **Recognize that independent reading is the big accelerator.** Students who read voluminously become avid, lifelong readers (Allison, 2009; Allington, 2002, 2011; Krashen, 1993; Miller, 2009; Robb, 2010, 2013). Students want choice in what they read. The more teachers know about fiction and nonfiction books the quicker they can make great text to student suggestions. We need to help teachers rally around independent reading and toward showing students how to choose texts that they *can* read. We can do that by enhancing teachers' abilities to: (1) understand text complexity; (2) assess students' interests, (3) extend discussion of texts, beginning with the routine of book talks, and (4) guide eBook reading at home and at school.

5. **Acquire and select books for instructional reading.** Teachers perceive finding books that meet each student's instructional needs a challenge because school funding is limited or there are no funds available. Here are suggestions that work! Raid your school's book room and your class library. Ask your school and local public librarians to select books that link to your unit's genre or theme and organize them by instructional reading level. Gather enough books to give students choices, and keep the books in your classroom to prevent loss. Offering students choice with instructional books is crucial because if a book doesn't motivate a student or if the student finds it too difficult, having other books at students' instructional levels readily available makes changing books easy.

Before delving into best practices in more detail and how they can work in concert, let's review some basic elements of differentiated instruction.

What is Differentiated Instruction?

Differentiation is a method of teaching that asks teachers to know their students so well that they can respond to individual needs and provide tasks and learning experiences that move each student forward. By using formative assessment to observe and understand the differences and similarities among students, teachers can use this information to plan instruction. Here are three key principles that form the foundation of differentiating reading instruction.

Learners reading levels are diverse. The students in our classes have a wide range of expertise with reading, writing, problem solving, and speaking and require differentiated instruction that takes them where they are and moves them forward (Snow & Biancarosa, 2004). Organizing reading around one textbook or one novel is what Carol Ann Tomlinson calls teaching to the middle (1999). This means that only the group reading at grade level has opportunities to improve their reading skill.

Formative assessment. Teachers study and monitor all of students' work and behaviors to determine what students do and don't grasp in order to design scaffolds, reteach, and adjust curriculum.

Tiered instruction helps students' progress. This means that the books students read and the assignments they complete match their learning needs and levels of expertise. The learning experience is the same but the level of complexity differs (Tomlinson, 1999; Sousa, 2001). For example, the class will study historical fiction. Instead of one book for all, the teacher has each student read historical fiction at his or her instructional level.

If the task is to plan and write an analytical essay that cites text evidence to argue for or against a claim or position, tiering means all students will work on analytical writing. However, the teacher adjusts the level of complexity of the writing task by considering students' writing skill. ELL students and those who struggle with writing might plan and write an analytical paragraph and confer often with the teacher who scaffolds the task. Proficient and advanced writers might complete a fully developed essay. Tiering allows teachers to adjust the amount of structure and support they offer students through teacher led conferences as well as the time students require to complete the writing (Dodge, 2005; Tomlinson, 1995, 1999; Sousa, 2001; Robb, 2008).

How the Five Practices Provide New Angles on Differentiating

Historically, teachers applauded the whole class book and/or grade level anthology because it provided them with a common text for modeling how to infer, pinpoint themes and central ideas, complete journal entries, and study literary elements or nonfiction text structures. One-book-for-all can decelerate the achievement of students who can't read and learn in English language arts and content classes. Instead of progressing, they slowly and steadily slide backwards (Allington, 2002; Robb, 2008; Tomlinson, 1999). Does this mean never-ever read anthology selections together, or a whole class novel or work of nonfiction? Not necessarily, but in the course of the year, it cannot be the sole way teachers address literature and reading.

The five angles of differentiation are the antidote to the same-text-for-all: anchor text, formative assessment, writing about reading, independent reading, and acquiring and selecting books at diverse instructional levels.

The Anchor Text: Teaching the How-to of Reading

The anchor text is a common text that the teacher reads aloud modeling how to apply the CCSS. Lessons are brief—three to five minutes. An eighth grade social studies teacher told me: "I use my textbook and newspaper and magazine articles as anchor texts to introduce vocabulary and show students how to identify big ideas and themes."

A picture book, an excerpt from a novel, informational text, or content textbook, a short story, myth, or legend, or an article from a magazine or newspaper make ideal anchor texts. Match the genre and theme of the anchor text to your reading unit and read aloud one to two paragraphs a day. With this versatile teaching tool, you can make visible how you analyze texts or organize thinking into a journal entry. And because the texts are short and the lessons brief, it's easy to review an anchor text and the lesson in other instructional moments, either while conferring with a student or in another small-group setting.

The series of anchor text lessons that follow apply key Common Core standards to reading an excerpt from a memoir by Frederick Douglass, published in 1845: *Memoir, Narrative of the Life of Frederick Douglass.*

Teaching the Anchor Text Lesson

Anchor text lessons open the door to analytical reading for students who see snapshots of your thinking and writing about reading. Flash the anchor text onto a whiteboard or use a document camera to display it. To heighten students' listening abilities, you might have to read a selection twice or even recap key

> I lived with Mr. Covey one year. During the first six months, of that year, scarce a week passed without his whipping me. I was seldom free from a sore back. My awkwardness was almost always his excuse for whipping me. We were worked fully up to the point of endurance. Long before day we were up, our horses fed, and by the first approach of day we were off to the field with our hoes and ploughing teams. Mr. Covey gave us enough to eat, but scarce time to eat it. We were often less than five minutes taking our meals. We were often in the field from the first approach of day till its last lingering ray had left us; and at saving-fodder time, midnight often caught us in the field binding blades.
>
> If at any one time of my life more than another, I was made to drink the bitterest dregs of slavery, that time was during the first six months of my stay with Mr. Covey. We were worked in all weathers. It was never too hot or too cold; it could never rain, blow, hail, or snow, too hard for us to work in the field. Work, work, work, was scarcely more the order of the day than of the night. The longest days were too short for him, and the shortest nights too long for him. I was somewhat unmanageable when I first went there, but a few months of this discipline tamed me. Mr. Covey succeeded in breaking me. I was broken in body, soul, and spirit. My natural elasticity was crushed, my intellect languished, the disposition to read departed, the cheerful spark that lingered about my eye died; the dark night of slavery closed in upon me; and behold a man transformed into a brute!

details for English language learners and developing readers. Bring students into the lessons once you've modeled a process.

First day. This lesson shows students how to use specific text details to make logical inferences.

1. I say something like this: Today I will read aloud two paragraphs from Frederick Douglass's Memoir, *Narrative of the Life of Frederick Douglass, an American Slave.* This excerpt discusses Douglass's experiences working as a slave for Mr. Covey. While enslaved, Douglass secretly taught himself to read and write believing that knowledge was the path from slavery to freedom. In 1838, Douglass successfully escaped slavery and worked to abolish it; he also supported woman's suffrage. Listen carefully to the selection, and how I use text details to make logical inferences, find unstated text meanings.

2. Read the selection out loud, then present your think aloud. Here's what I say: Details about how Mr. Covey worked his slaves—in all weathers and long, long days—lets me infer that Covey viewed slaves as his property and cared only for producing crops, for making money. I can infer that Covey's slaves had no human rights because Douglass says that he was whipped every week, his spirit broken, his work hours extremely long with only five minutes to eat and gain renewed energy. Notice what I did: I used details from the text to find unstated meanings called inferences.

3. Invite students to turn to a partner to make [find] another inference, telling them to cite text evidence to support their thinking. Two seventh graders explained that they inferred that Covey's treatment of Douglass violated basic human rights and transformed Douglass from cheerful to angry and that Douglass no longer felt human.

Next, show students how to organize their inferences into a double entry journal response. This type of journal is an easy to implement writing about reading device that greatly improves comprehension. Here's the example that I write on chart paper:

Second day. This lesson shows how to discover the author's tone and purpose by selecting ten to fifteen key words and/or phrases from both paragraphs and then linking the words to tone and author's purpose.

1. Here are the words I write on chart paper (or project onto a whiteboard): *sore back, eat—five minutes, whipping, bitterest dregs of slavery, broken in body, soul, spirit, dark night of slavery, brute.*

2. Read the words and phrases out loud, and then tell students the tone I feel they convey, pointing out that it's the

NARRATIVE OF THE LIFE OF FREDERICK DOUGLASS, AN AMERICAN SLAVE

Inference	Evidence from Douglass's Memoir
Covey is a brutal slaver	Covey whips Douglass; gave slaves less than 5 minutes to eat; broke Douglass's body, soul, & spirit; slaves worked late in all kinds of weather

author's choice of words that creates tone. Here's what I say: The tone is anger, anguish, and pain from long, unreasonable work hours, lack of food, and weekly whippings.

The frustrating tone comes from Douglass's inability to control his life and decisions. There is also a sad tone with Douglass losing his humanity and feeling brutish. Knowing the tone helps me figure out the author's purpose because the tone contains ideas that signal the meaning of both paragraphs. Douglass's purpose is to show the evils of slavery and what happens when slaves are victims of inhumane masters like Mr. Covey.

3. Invite students to pair-share and use tone to figure out another author's purpose: A pair of seventh graders explained that a second purpose is to show that when a human being is treated worse than an animal, such treatment can turn a person into a brute who loses his humanity.

Third day. This lesson will help students observe how a close reading can enable them to figure out the meaning of a confusing word or phrase. Here's what I say: In the phrase "My natural elasticity was crushed, my intellect languished, the disposition to read departed, the cheerful spark that lingered about my eye died; the dark night of slavery closed in upon me; and behold a man transformed into a brute!" the words "languished" and "disposition" are unfamiliar. Douglass was transformed into a brute, and he writes that the "dark night of slavery" closed in on him. If reading brings light then disposition could mean desire to read and the word "departed" confirms this hunch. "Languished" refers to intellect or mind. If the desire to read departed, then languished could mean that Douglass didn't use his intellect or mind. He placed his energy on dealing with "the dark night of slavery."

For students who don't experience visualizing, thinking, and feeling about a text, anchor text lessons show them what expert readers do. And these lessons can develop students' in-the-head thinking voices and in-the-heart feelings, bonding them to texts.

Anchor Text Lesson Framework

I've listed the structure of the anchor text lesson so you can plan your own:

- provide background knowledge if necessary;
- tell students what you will model;
- read the passage aloud;
- think aloud, citing details and inferences from the text;
- recap what you did and show students how you used text evidence to support thinking; and
- engage students in the thinking part of the lesson by asking them to infer, determine the author's purpose, etc., with a partner.

When partners discuss ideas and share them with classmates, students can learn from one another and observe the critical thinking process. After you present anchor text lessons, students read their instructional books at school where you are available for scaffolding that can improve comprehension.

Formative Assessments: The Data for Targeted Teaching

Assessment informs instruction (Afflerbach, 2011; Tomlinson, 1999). I'd say the most effective teachers go to class wondering, what am I going to learn from students as much as thinking about what they need to cover. And they understand students' needs by evaluating observational notes, conducting conferences, reading students' written work, and listening during discussions. But the formative assessment that I think is most valuable to students and teachers is the brief conference. You can achieve it every day as you make the rounds and continually circulate among students, responding to questions, helping them solve problems, offering suggestions, and helping them set goals for next steps (Allison, 2009; Serravallo, 2012; Robb, 2008). By making the rounds I feel the pulse of every student's needs, and it's this continual observation that points to topics for five-to-six-minute scheduled conferences for individuals, pairs, and small groups.

Short conferences while making the rounds form the foundation of differentiated reading instruction. I carry a clipboard with dated sticky notes as I circulate to observe students and listen to their conversations. During this time I am providing immediate scaffolding. Often, I jot the main points of our brief conversation on a sticky note and give it to the student for a reminder so they can revise or complete a task with confidence. After helping Tony, a seventh grader, make logical inferences from several pages of *The Great Fire* by Jim Murphy, I jot suggestions onto a sticky note; *inference is an unstated meaning; reread a paragraph or passage to find details; to infer, think about what you can conclude using details; ask what do these details mean? What do they tell you?*

Other times, while making the rounds, I notice that a student requires a longer conference, and I jot on a sticky note the student's name and the topic for our meeting. If there's time, I will confer with the student during class that day; otherwise I schedule the conference for the next time class meets.

Some Possible Reading Conference Topics

Instead of a prepared list of topics, it's best to use your observations of how students apply anchor text lessons to their instructional text as topics. Below are five reading and five writing topics that align with the CCSS and best practices; use these as a starting point until you collect enough data to tap into students' needs.

Five Writing Conference Topics

1. Literary elements: showing understanding by connecting these to a specific text
2. How and why a person or character changes
3. Summarizing
4. Writing about reading (I cut the word "informal" because it's out of favor)
5. Analytical essays

Five Reading Conference Topics

1. Informational text structures: analyzing the organization of nonfiction using these
2. Logical inferences, themes, central ideas
3. Comparing two or more texts to analyze themes, characters, settings, etc.
4. Tone or mood; author's purposes
5. Close reading confusing passages

Recently, I coached a sixth grade teacher who taught four sections of English. She assessed where her students were using completed essays about reading. While it's better than the once-a-year test results, it's not good enough because several weeks passed between each essay—weeks when students received little help.

Clipboard in hand, the teacher made the rounds for a week in each section, and then we met to debrief. "I observed needs every day," she said, "even from my better readers. I polled my students, and they wanted me to continue supporting them every day. The sticky-note reminders got high ratings because on the next day, they had suggestions for inferring or using context clues to figure out the meanings of unfamiliar words." What this teacher experienced is that by making the rounds throughout a class, students had opportunities to learn and to revise their work, avoiding frustrating feelings that the task was an obstacle to learning.

Writing About Reading: Thinking on Paper

Evaluating what student readers put on the page about texts is the most personal, powerful window on a student's life as a reader. We don't want to overdo it by compelling students to write about every book they read—far from it—but as a profession we require it too little. Graham and Hebert (2010) in their landmark report, *Writing to Read* call for extra writing time in all subjects. Yet, a study completed by Arthur N. Applebee and Judith A. Langer in 2006 points to the fact that students in middle and high school ELA classes don't spend enough time writing. Applebee and Langer state: "Overall, this study leaves us with some disturbing findings about how little time many students are spending on writing … ." (p. ii).

Applebee and Langer call for extended writing across the curriculum, especially in English class. The Common Core also calls for extended writing in English and in content subjects. However, middle and high school teachers with 100 to 150 students avoid extended writing tasks due to the grading demands. Again, ongoing professional development can ease the grading problems as teachers come to see the benefits of forming writing partnerships among students and teaching students how to self and peer evaluate their work using a rubric. Teachers provide support while students plan and draft essays and narratives by conferring but ask the students to revise and edit those messy first drafts. And as I point out in *Smart Writing,* teachers who read and grade much improved second drafts do little red marking and rewriting because the students are doing the work of revision and editing and moving toward independence with these tasks (Robb, 2012).

Extended writing tasks are not enough. Graham and Hebert (2010) state: "Writing about a text proved to be better than just reading it, reading and rereading it, reading and studying it, reading and discussing it, and receiving reading instruction" (p. 12). Why? Back to E.M. Forster's statement: "How do I know what I think until I see what I say?" I'm suggesting that in addition to extended writing, students complete brief responses to teachers read alouds and to their instructional and independent reading.

However, the Common Core suggests that students reread a text they don't understand several times to get the text's meaning. One point I've learned from teaching is that if a student can't read and comprehend a text, he or she can't learn from it. Offer students complex texts via your read alouds because students' listening capacity is greater than their instructional reading level (Woods & Moe, 1998). But for instructional reading, offer students materials they can read and learn from.

Clearly, writing about texts is essential if we want our students to improve comprehension. Writing includes drawing and writing about the illustration as well as jotting notes, making lists of ideas, and writing short paragraphs. Informal responses to reading occur every day, and students record their responses in readers notebooks. All learners, including ELL, learning disabled and special education students can complete responses that are short and where the focus is on ideas. As students enter class, have four to five distribute readers notebooks; students immediately head a page with their name and date. Now the notebook is poised and ready to receive hunches, emotional reactions, inferences, drawing, etc. based on the teacher's read aloud.

Short responses are also part of instructional and independent reading. Notebooks are with students while they read at school so they can close write, that is zoom in on applying a skill or strategy to their reading. Even *informal* writing can be differentiated. Some students summarize a paragraph, section, or chapter of a text while others make an inference or pinpoint a theme from a chunk of text, supporting their thoughts with detailed text evidence. I encourage students to talk to a partner before writing because talk clarifies thinking and reclaims ideas. Students use their responses to develop claims or explain a position in an extended essay or a paragraph. Like entries in writers' notebooks, *informal* responses to reading contain idea seeds for more extended writing. And teachers need to differentiate extended writing tasks as this literacy story illustrates.

It was my first day observing in the eighth grade class of a teacher who had invited me in as a coach. While making the rounds, I noticed a girl with her head on her desk. Bending down so I could make eye contact, I gently tapped her shoulder and asked, "Can I help you?" She shrugged her shoulders, and kept her head face down on the desk. Again, I asked, "Can I help you?" No response. After class, I asked the teacher to tell me about her student.

"She's from the Ukraine, been in the U.S. for two years, and she dislikes writing—sometimes, like today, she won't write. She'd rather draw than write, but this is writing class." The teacher and I brainstormed how to differentiate the assignment of writing a narrative. I suggested she let the student draw the events of the story and use her illustrations to write. Asking every student to complete the same writing task, especially when the task is at their frustration level, might satisfy a school's requirements, but it won't result in improving thinking and writing skill.

Independent Reading: The Achievement Accelerator

Read. Four letters. One short word. Powerful skill. Reading is powerful because when students have a rich independent reading life, they can accelerate their reading achievement, enlarge their vocabulary, build prior knowledge, and increase their reading stamina, and ultimately become productive and thoughtful citizens (Allington, 2011; Allison, 2009; Gambrell, Marinak, Brooker, & McCrea-Andrews, 2011; Krashen, 1993; Robb 2010). Independent reading should be easy (99–100% accuracy), enjoyable, and on topics and genres that interest learners. So how do teachers motivate students to read thirty to fifty books a year at an appropriate level? Here are four ways:

Understand text complexity. Insights into text complexity can help you guide students to selecting readable books. The Common Core identifies three aspects of text complexity: quantitative, qualitative, and the reader and the task. Here is a summary of each one:

Quantitative measures examine characteristics of a text best analyzed by computer, such as sentence length and word frequency. School districts latch onto Lexiles because it's a number and easy to use. Lexiles provide readability and not grade level. So a seventh grade ELL student might be able to comprehend texts at a Lexile linked to third grade, while an advanced reader in that same class can comprehend texts Lexiled for tenth grade.

Qualitative measures examine a book's content and concepts: knowledge demands (prior knowledge), levels of meaning, text structure, language conventionality, and clarity. This is the area that is the heart and soul of text complexity. Fifth graders can read *The Giver* by Lois Lowry, but should they read it? This dystopian novel deals with complex issues of euthanasia and inhibiting sexual yearnings, concepts appropriate for seventh and eight graders, not fifth graders—concepts that make the book's text complexity more appropriate to middle schoolers and above. So as we rush students toward texts of increasing complexity, continue to ask yourself, "But is this book's content right for this particular child?"

The reader and the task consider students' motivation, knowledge, and experience to determine whether a book is "just right," giving teachers the flexibility to match students to texts so learning can occur. The Common Core asks teachers to make the final decision about what students can read. This is important because you don't have to place students reading three or more years below grade level in texts they can't read. Developing readers will need more than one year to meet the goal of reading complex grade-level texts.

My point is this: we can differentiate instruction and ramp up independent reading if we are aware of what readers can do and keep independent reading a joyful experience (Allington, 2002; Allison, 2009; Miller, 2009; Krashen, 1993; Snow & Biancarosa, 2004; Robb, 2008). If we "do" Common Core without ever really unpacking its terms, such as text complexity, we probably aren't going to move the needle on achievement very far.

Give an interest inventory and tap into students' interests. When you know students' interests, you can find books that engage them (Allison, 2009; Miller, 2009; Robb, 2010). An eighth grade girl wrote on her interest inventory that she only likes books about vampires. Off I went to the school library, and the public library, and I found ten books about vampires that would be acceptable in an eighth grade classroom. She devoured the books and through book talks inspired classmates to read about vampires. Book talks by her peers and the teacher hooked her onto the Chicken Soup books and then graphic novels. By the end of the year this student had read thirty books! *Read* is a powerful word!

Put book talking on center stage. Book talks introduce students to hundreds of books in the course of a school year. Teachers should book talk all new additions to their class libraries, books by a featured author, and a genre or theme that's spotlighted. Invite students to complete a book talk each month. If a class of twenty-five students presents book talks from September to June, students hear about 250 books. Peer recommendations matter and can transform reluctant readers into book lovers!

Encourage eBook reading at home and at school. The statistics are here: Scholastic's *Kids and Reading Report* (2012). Ten percent more boys read and enjoy eBooks than girls. Half of children age 9–17 say they would read more books for fun if they had greater access to eBooks—a 50% increase since 2010.

Lobby for eBook readers at school, and encourage students to check out eBooks from their public library and read eBooks at home. For today's students, technology can make a huge difference in developing personal reading lives.

Finding Appropriate Texts for Instructional Reading

I organize reading units by genre, a literary category such as historical fiction, biography, or informational texts. This frees me to find books of the same genre that meet students' diverse instructional reading levels. All instructional reading occurs at school so teachers can support students, and meaningful partner and small groups discussions can occur.

Your school and public librarian are the best resources for helping you gather books of the same genre for your students. Use them! About two weeks prior to beginning a unit, ask these librarians to pull books that relate to the genre or theme on the instructional level range in your classes, ask them to identify the readability of each book. If you have a classroom library, mine that for books.

Collect enough books so students at each reading level have choices. Have students put their names on a sticky-note on the cover of the book as students from different sections will choose the same book. You'll find that developing readers select shorter texts than proficient and advanced readers.

Next, give students four to five sticky notes and have them print their name at the top and under that write "Stop to Think;" I call this chunking a book. Divide books into four to five chunks making sure each chunk is at the end of a chapter; this means that skilled readers who select long books will read larger chunks of texts. Place a sticky note at the end of the book, and help students divide their books in chunks of two or more chapters, depending on the book's length.

Since I recommend that instructional reading occur at school, students from different class sections can read the same book. Determine how much class time students need to finish each chunk of text. Those who finish early can complete independent reading. If some students require more time to read a chunk, give it to them. The "stop to think" is students' reminder that they will spend part of two or more classes discussing and writing about a chunk of text before going on to the next chunk. Frequently, I have several students beg: "Can we finish the whole book? Please, please, can we?" Let them; you'll maintain their enthusiasm for reading. I add one caveat: if students finish the book early, they must reread each chunk to refresh their recall of details, but they cannot reveal the book's outcome to peers.

Pair students so partners are no more than one year apart in instructional reading levels and have something to offer each other. Developing readers can pair-up but you need to support them.

Discussing Diverse Texts with Small Groups of Students

Even though students read different books, you can lead small group discussions—just focus them on genre and theme (Serravallo, 2012; Robb, 2008). After students complete their second chunk, schedule two small groups about three times a week to meet for about fifteen minutes during independent work time. Here is a list of topics that students can discuss and compare referring to specific text evidence:

- text structure;
- themes and central ideas;
- author's purposes;
- character's or person's goals, obstacles faced, personality traits;
- significance of information presented; and
- literary elements: setting, plot, conflicts, problems, outcomes, protagonist, antagonistic forces

You can select a focus for the discussion or refer students to the list and ask the group to select a focus. I find that discussions have greater depth if students can prepare for them by jotting notes related to the topic in their readers' notebooks. Students can document their discussions by writing a summary.

Closing Thoughts

A strange disconnect exists in our educational system. We want our students to read, write, think, and speak well; we want them to excel and be the best. We want students to be creative thinkers and problem solvers. To reach this goal, we continually change programs from The Reading First Initiative to No Child Left Behind, to State Standards, and now the Common Core. Programs are not educational solutions; if they were we'd be number one on the PISA (Program for International Student Assessment); but in 2009 we were number 17. In addition, among the 34 nations in the Organization for Economic Cooperation and Development (OECD), the United States ranks 14th in reading (Schleicher, 2011).

The first big takeaway from this article is that it's the teacher who makes the difference in students' progress and learning (Allington & Johnston, 2001), and investing in ongoing professional study is one way to grow great teachers. The second big takeaway is to integrate the five best practices into your curriculum.

Snow and Biancarosa (2004) noted in *Reading Next,* page 8: "A full 70 percent of U.S. middle and high school students require differentiated instruction, which is instruction targeted to their individual strengths and weaknesses." Struggling readers and writers, whether English is their first or second language, deserve opportunities to improve their skills so they can read and comprehend and write and communicate well. Using formative assessments to differentiate reading instruction, to tier writing tasks, and to develop a rich independent reading curriculum provide an efficient pathway to accelerating students' achievement.

References

Afflerbach, P. (2011). *Understanding and using reading assessment, k-12, 2nd edition.* Newark, DE: International Reading Association.

Allington, R.L., & Johnston, P.H. (2001). In Roller, C. (Ed.), *Learning to teach reading: Setting the research agenda.* Newark, DE: International Reading Association.

Allington, R.L., (2002). What I've learned about effective readin instruction. *Phi Delta Kappan, 83*(10), 740–747.

Allington, R.L. (2011). *What really matters for struggling readers: Designing research-based programs, 3rd edition.* Boston, MA: Allyn & Bacon.

Allison, N. (2009). *Middle school readers: Helping them read widely, helping them read well.* Portsmouth, NH: Heinemann.

Applebee, A.N., & Langer, J.A. (2006). A collaboration among the National Writing Project, the College Board, and the Center on English Learning and Achievement, http://www.albany.edu/aire/news/State%20of%20Writing%20Instruction.pdf

Dodge, J. (2005). *Differentiation in action.* New York: Scholastic.

Douglass, F. (1845). *Narrative life of Frederick Douglass, an American slave,* http://en.wikipedia.org/wiki/Narrative_of_the_Life_of_Frederick_Douglass,_an_American_Slave.

Gambrell, L.B., Marinak, B.A., Brooker, H.R., & McCrea-Andrews, H.J. (2011). The importance of independent reading. In S.J. Samuels and A.E. Farstrup (Eds.), *What research has to say about reading instruction, 4th ed.* (pp. 143–158). Newark, DE: The International Reading Association.

Graham, S., & Hebert, M. (2010). *Writing to read: Evidence for how writing can improve reading.* New York: Carnegie Corporation.

Guthrie, J.T., Wigfield, A., Metsala, J., & Cox, K. (1999). Motivational and cognitive predictors of text comprehension and reading amount. *Scientific Studies of Reading, 3*(3), 231–256.

Guthrie, J.T., Wigfield, A., & Klauda, S.L. (2012). *Adolescents' engagement in academic literacy* (Report No. 7). Retrieved from: www.corilearning.com/research-publications

Krashen, S. (1993). *The power of reading: Insights from the research.* Englewood, CO: Libraries Unlimited.

Lamott, A. (1994). *Bird by bird: Some instructions on writing and life.* New York: Anchor Books.

Mankoff, R. (1987, March 30). *New Yorker Magazine.*

Miller, D. (2009). *The book whisperer.* San Francisco, CA: Jossey-Bass.

Murphy, J. (2006). *The great fire.* New York: Scholastic.

PISA, Program for International Student Assessment (2009). U.S. Department of Education, http://nces.ed.gov/pubs2011/2011004.pdf

Robb, L. (2008). *Differentiating reading instruction: How to teach reading to meet the needs of each student.* New York: Scholastic.

Robb, L. (2010). *Teaching reading in middle school: A strategic approach to teaching reading that improves comprehension and thinking.* New York: Scholastic.

Robb, L. (2012). *Smart writing: Practical units for teaching middle school writers.* Portsmouth, NH: Heinemann.

Robb, L. (2013). *Unlocking complex text: A systematic framework for building adolescents comprehension.* New York: Scholastic.

Schleicher, A. (2011). Is the sky the limit to education improvement? *Phi Delta Kappan, 93*(2), 58–63.

Scholastic. (2012). *Kids & Family Reading Report.*

Serravallo, J. (2010). *Teaching reading in small groups: Differentiated instruction for building strategic, independent readers.* Portsmouth, NH: Heinemann.

Serravallo, J. (2012). *Independent reading assessment: Fiction.* New York: Scholastic.

Snow, C.E., & Biancarosa, G. (2004). *A report from the Carnegie Institute of New York: Reading next: A vision for action and research in middle and high school literacy.* Washington, D.C.: Alliance for Excellent Education.

Sousa, D.A. (2001). *How the brain learns.* Newbury Park, CA: Corwin Press.

Tomlinson, C.A. (1995). *How to differentiate instruction in a mixed ability classroom.* Alexandria, VA: ASCD.

Tomlinson, C.A. (1999). *The differentiated classroom: Responding to the needs of all learners.* Alexandria, VA: ASCD.

Woods, M.L., & Moe, A.J. (1998). *Analytical reading inventory, 6th edition.* New York: Prentice Hall.

Discussion Questions

1. Define these terms as used in the article and explain how each contributes to differentiated reading instruction:

   anchor text
   formative assessment
   differentiated instruction
   tiered instruction

2. Explain how writing about reading can support students' literacy development. What are some ways this can be implemented in the classroom?
3. What are four ways to motivate students to do more independent reading?
4. How does the Robb article support the concepts presented in this chapter and in the other articles? Use specific examples from the text and articles to support your conclusions.

Conclusion

Chapter Activities

Activity 2.1

Select one of the books on the most frequently challenged books list at the ALA website. Research this book to identify the basis of the challenges. Write a paragraph explaining why this book has been challenged. Add an additional paragraph giving your opinion about this book. Would you use it with students in middle or secondary school? Why or why not?

Activity 2.2

Select a chapter from a science or social studies textbook marketed for use in one of the middle-level grades, 5–8. Provide the complete citation for the chapter you select.

After reading the chapter, identify five children's picture books that you could use to supplement this chapter for middle-level students. Look for picture books that will provide additional elaboration on the content in the chapter, help teach critical vocabulary needed for the chapter, or provide prior knowledge that is necessary for enhancing comprehension of the text.

List the selected children's books with complete citations. For each book, provide a written rationale of at least one paragraph, which explains how this book will supplement the selected chapter.

Activity 2.3

Read the executive summary of AMLE's *This We Believe* and review the chart at these websites:

http://www.amle.org/portals/0/pdf/twb/TWB_colorchart_Oct2013.pdf
https://www.uww.edu/Documents/colleges/.../This_We_Believe_Exec_Summary.pdf

How do the ideas espoused in this chapter of the text support the essential attributes of education for young adolescents? Use all the readings and the chapter materials to form your response.

Activity 2.4

Complete the 'Discourse Analysis for Kids' activity described on pages 58–59 in the Harste article, using a greeting card of your choice. Complete the analysis yourself, then ask a middle- or secondary-level student to do it. Compare the two responses. Submit both responses and a brief analysis of the differences.

Activity 2.5

Read the Kress and van Leeuwen "'Grammar of Visual Design" activity in the box on page 65 of the Harste article. Select a well-known painting and complete the activity yourself. Submit your responses along with the name of the painting, the artist, and a link to the image online.

Online Resources

Finding Excellent Trade Books to Use as Collateral Readings

The Horn Book
http://www.hbook.com/horn-book-magazine-2/#_

The Horn Book magazine prints reviews of literature for children and young adults. In addition, the articles often focus on books related to specific topics. The website provides information related to choosing and using books in the classroom, as well as ideas to recommend to parents.

International Literacy Association "Young Adults' Choices"
http://literacyworldwide.org/get-resources/reading-lists/young-adults-choices-reading-list

The "Young Adults' Choices" lists on the ILA website are books selected by adolescent readers. These are also available for the years 1998 to the present. A new list is distributed each April. This is one of the few book awards that are presented to books selected by students rather than adults.

National Science Teachers Association "Outstanding Science Trade Books for Students K–12"
http://www.nsta.org/publications/ostb/

Each year, the National Science Teachers Association (NSTA), in conjunction with the Children's Book Council, publishes a list of outstanding science trade books for children in grades K–12. The NSTA website provides free copies of the lists from 1996 to the present. The lists include a brief synopsis of each book and, for lists from 2010 to the present, links to related activities are also included.

The School Library Journal
http://www.slj.com/best-books-2014/

The *School Library Journal* publishes a "Best of …" list for books, apps, and technology each year. Included in the list are best adult books for teens, graphic novels, audiobooks, cool tech tools, apps, tech trends, and DVDs, as well as children's books. A printed version of the current year's list can be downloaded from their website, or it can be viewed in a multimedia presentation. The book list is divided into picture books, middle grades, young adult, and nonfiction.

National Council for the Social Studies (NCSS)
Notable Trade Books for Young People
https://www.socialstudies.org/publications/notables

The National Council for the Social Studies publishes their annual "Notable Tradebooks for Young People" list in the May/June issue of its journal *Social Education*. These books represent the highest quality social studies related books for students in grades K–8. Lists for the years 2000–2013 are available on the NCSS website for everyone to use; however, the most current list is only available to members. (Note: For this link, copy and paste the URL into the browser if the link will not open.)

E-Book Resources

Project Gutenberg
www.gutenberg.org

Project Gutenberg is a website that provides free access to over 46,000 e-books. Many are classic books, but the collection includes textbooks and trade books as well.

Classic Bookshelf
www.classicbookshelf.com

Classic Bookshelf provides free access to thousands of classic books in e-book format. Some classics included their collection are works by Dickens, Shakespeare, Bronte, Alcott, and many, many other authors.

International Children's Digital Library
http://en.childrenslibrary.org/

The International Children's Digital Library provides access to a wide variety of literature for children of all ages. Their mission, as stated on the website, is to "promote tolerance and respect for diverse cultures by providing access to the best children's literature from around the world." This site is an excellent resource for teachers working with English Language Learners.

Children's Books Online
http://www.childrensbooksonline.org/library.htm

This website provides free access to a variety of e-books for children, adolescents, and adults, indexed by age/interest/reading level.

Books for young adults often include situations, language, and topics that relate to the psychological, social, and physiological changes facing students of this age group. Because of this content, many books for middle and secondary students are challenged by parents or teachers and some have been banned from certain schools. Even classics that have been read for generations are not immune from complaints, commonly E-Book Resources.

Banned Books Resources

American Library Association Banned Books Information
http://www.ala.org/bbooks/

The Top Ten Most Frequently Challenged Books (by year)
http://www.ala.org/bbooks/frequentlychallengedbooks/top10#2015

Matching Readers with Texts

One of the most critical jobs of a reading specialist or classroom teacher is to ensure that students are matched with texts that are of an appropriate difficulty level and of interest to the students. Some ways that this can be accomplished are through the use of a systematic deletion cloze, interest surveys, and by analyzing textbooks.

Chapter Focus Questions

Read and think about these questions before you start to read the chapter. As you complete the readings and activities, revisit the questions to see whether you can now answer them.

1. Why is it critical to match students with text that is on an appropriate level?
2. What are some ways that you can determine students' reading levels so that you can match each student with an appropriate text?
3. Why is motivation so important for adolescent readers?
4. What are some ways to motivate readers in middle- and secondary-level classrooms?

CLOZE Procedure

The *CLOZE Procedure*, usually just called the *CLOZE*, is an informal assessment that can be used for a variety of purposes. The process was first described in print by researcher W. L. Taylor in the 1950s, and the approach is still widely used today because it is a quick method for estimating the difficulty of a text for a particular student.

At its most basic level, a cloze procedure is simply a passage taken from a text in which several words have been deleted. The reader's task is to try to identify the missing words. The score is determined by the percentage of correct responses given by the student. There are two main types of CLOZE activities—systematic deletion cloze and selective deletion cloze. The difference between the two is the process by which the words are selected for deletion.

In the *systematic deletion cloze*, the words to be deleted are selected by counting each word and deleting every "*n*th" word. For example, for young children every tenth word might be deleted and for older students every fifth word might be deleted. The first and last sentences in the passage should remain intact, with no blanks. Beginning with the second sentence, the teacher would count and delete the identified words from the passage, replacing them with a blank line.

When creating a *selective deletion cloze*, however, the teacher selectively chooses specific words to delete from the passage. The first and final sentences are still left intact, with no blanks. The teacher chooses words based on the goal for the activity—in general, the selective deletion cloze is most often used to practice target vocabulary words or to provide practice in identifying words using context clues.

When matching readers with appropriate text, the *systematic deletion cloze* can be used. Teachers often create a cloze passage for each unit of the textbook to make sure the students have the necessary background knowledge and vocabulary knowledge to effectively comprehend the text.

Steps for Creating a Systematic Deletion Cloze

1. Select a representative passage from the text to be read. For middle school students, the passage should be between 200 and 250 words, up to a passage of 450–500 words for high school students.
2. Decide on the number you will use to determine the words to be deleted. Middle school students should be able to handle the deletion of every seventh or eighth word; high school students should be able to effectively deal with the deletion of every fifth or sixth word.
3. Always leave the first and last sentences in the passage intact, with no blanks. This is to provide some basis to start the student's comprehension of the passage. Then, beginning with the first word in the second sentence, count every *n*th word, and delete it. It is best to retype the entire passage so that the length of the lines can be made equal; do not vary the line length according to the length of the deleted word. For example, you should make the lines seven spaces long, not two spaces long for the word "it" and twelve spaces long for the word "independence." Delete all the identified words, regardless of

whether they are basic words, such as "the" or "an," or words that have already been deleted earlier in the passage.

4. Do NOT provide a word bank to the students. The analysis of the scores is based on the students' having to determine the words on their own, with no words from which to choose.

5. Ask the students to complete the cloze activity. As a formative assessment, it should not be used for a grade, unless students are given credit for completing the assignment.

6. Assess each completed cloze. Unless the word provided by the student is exactly the word deleted from the text, do not give the student credit for the word. For example, if the word in the text was "large" and the student wrote "big," the student would NOT get credit for that item. This is considered in the percentages used in the analysis of the scores, given in step #7. (This can also upset students, so I recommend that the cloze not be returned to the students following its analysis by the teacher; it should be used as a formative assessment to inform instruction and should then be discarded.)

7. Evaluate the student's comprehension level of the text based on the standard cloze procedure percentages:

Below 44%	Frustration level
44%–57%	Instructional level
58% and above	Independent level

If students score at the frustration level, the textbook you are assessing is probably too difficult for them to read. These students should be given alternative texts on an appropriate reading level. If students score at the instructional level, the text is appropriate for use during classroom activities when the teacher is available to provide support, as needed.

If students score at the independent level, the text is appropriate for the student to read independently—for homework, for example. Students who score at this level may also be provided with alternative texts on a more challenging level.

Textbook Readability Checklist

Another informal assessment that can be used to determine the suitability of a text for a particular group of students is a textbook readability checklist. There are a large number of textbook readability checklists available on the Internet, so there is no need for teachers to create one from scratch. The available checklists can be modified to suit the specific needs of each teacher, subject, or class.

The following links provide usable examples of textbook readability checklists that can be printed or copied for school use:

Irwin-Davis Textbook Readability Checklist
http://shcplainville.org/documents/school/teachers/grade-1/19-textbook-review/file

General Textbook Readability Checklist
http://www.triciajoy.com/subject/general+textbook+readability+checklist/

Motivating Adolescents to Read

Determining that the textbook is of an appropriate difficulty level is just the first step in matching students to texts. While the required local and state curriculum guides and standards must be followed, teachers should strive to motivate students to read collateral texts that complement the content provided by the required textbook and mandated curriculum.

Ways to motivate adolescents to read include the following:

- Providing choices among texts
- Providing alternative texts, especially collateral readings and other non-textbook resources
- Allowing students to work in cooperative groups to discuss their reading
- Avoiding round-robin oral reading in the classroom
- Incorporating multimedia and other 21st-century literacies in addition to paper-based texts
- Providing texts on appropriate levels of difficulty for all students
- Providing texts that reflect content and issues of interest to adolescents

In an article in *Time* magazine, Gayle Forman explained why adolescents tend to like books about "dark" topics. According to Forman (2015), "New brain mapping research suggests that adolescence is a time when teens are capable of engaging deeply with material, both on an intellectual level as well as an emotional one. Some research suggests that during adolescence, the parts of the brain that processes emotion are even more online with teens than with adults ... so, developmentally, teens are hungry for more provocative grist while emotionally they're thirsty for the catharsis these books offer. Of course, teens are drawn to darker, meatier fare. The only surprise about this is that it's a surprise."

The emphasis of young adult literature on what parents and teachers consider "dark" topics is often why many books for adolescents are so frequently included on lists of banned or challenged books.

An Urban School Shapes Young Adolescents' Motivation to Read

Chantal Francois

In the article, "An Urban School Shapes Young Adolescents' Motivation to Read," Chantal Francois describes the way that a "reading school" can make an impact on individual students' motivation and growth as readers.

LEARNING OBJECTIVES

1. Motivating middle and secondary school students can be a challenge. How do you think the school principal can play a role in motivation?
2. Some schools use programs that rely on extrinsic motivation rewards to entice students to read. What are the pros and cons of these approaches?

An Urban School Shapes Young Adolescents' Motivation to Read

Chantal Francois

When I started teaching, I could easily place my students into two categories related to reading—motivated or unmotivated. Those I saw as motivated to read seemed capable of mining my skimpy bookshelf in the corner of the room for something appealing during our silent reading time. They saw themselves as good readers and were ready for a challenge. It was easy to categorize these students as "hardworking" and "capable."

In contrast, the students I believed were unmotivated readers couldn't be bothered with improving their reading skills. I observed these students engaging in habits during our silent reading time that characterized what I believed was a lack of motivation: they chose any book off the shelves—each day a different one—and would sit down, sometimes holding it upside down or sometimes falling asleep. Not only did they struggle with reading independently, they struggled with literacy tasks in general. They told me that reading was "wack" and "boring." It was easy to label those students as "struggling" and "lazy."

I was frustrated that many of my students expressed such a vocal disdain for reading. At the same time, neither I nor my colleagues at my New York City public school knew how to help students become more motivated to read. I also did not know that our collective lack of capacity in supporting students' reading motivation was not only hindering their potential to be successful in most domains of school, it was also setting students on a course for underachievement in and disengagement from reading in the future.

Unfortunately, what I experienced in one urban middle school can be extrapolated to young adolescents across the country; researchers observe a pattern of declining reading motivation among this age group, both in comparison to younger students and, more notably, in longitudinal inquiries of the same population from year to year (Wolters, Denton, York, & Francis, 2014). Researchers also hypothesize that the reason for declining motivation can be attributed to schools' tendency to carry a fixed view of literacy incompatible with middle level students' experiences (del Valle & Lewis, 2009). But I wanted to know, is that the only reality possible in urban public schools?

How Does a School Influence Reading Motivation?

I spent a year at Grant Street Secondary School (school and participants' names are pseudonyms), another New York City public school where I had also taught, interviewing students and teachers and observing school spaces to be able to describe what reading looked like in this context. Further, I also administered a survey on students' reading motivation and a standardized reading assessment. Findings from this study counter what I first believed about reading motivation; that as much as it is intrinsic, it is also contextual. I learned that a school can shape students' motivation to read in the classroom in ways that have positive effects on their reading identity, efficacy in reading, and ability to read well.

Grant Street's student body mirrored most small urban schools in New York City. At the time of the study, the 2009–10 school year, 82 percent of the 560 students were economically disadvantaged, 59 percent were Latina/o students, and 27 percent of the students were Black. About a third of students were designated special education.

I chose to conduct my research on literacy at Grant Street because of its past efforts in literacy instruction and because of its present accomplishments. The principal, Jack Steinberg, led the staff in professional development initiatives that targeted students' literacy growth. For example, the school partnered with the Teachers College Reading and Writing Project, and teachers read professional texts about the teaching of reading together. Steinberg also arranged time in the school's weekly schedule for teachers to plan their curriculum. As a result, the staff learned that the problems with literacy weren't about students' lack of reading motivation but instead were about the staff's shared lack of capacity in incorporating what students' interests were with what was expected of them in school.

Grant Street was also an ideal site for this research because of students' accomplishments in reading during the time of the study. In one year, students outpaced the national sample of the Gates MacGinitie Reading Test, a standardized assessment. Furthermore, Grant Street students displayed higher levels of reading motivation on the Adolescent Motivation Reading Profile (Pitcher et al., 2007) than students in other studies that used the same survey. Equally important, school members and visitors often described Grant Street as having a "culture of reading."

I interviewed a sample of twenty-three students who varied in grade level, academic status, ethnicity, and gender to understand more about their motivation to read and about the school's culture of reading. When I asked students to name what made them want to read in school, their responses illuminated the role the school had in shaping their reading motivation: 75 percent of the sample said that they believed that Grant Street was a "reading school." Another 72 percent said that the constant opportunities to talk about books throughout the school made them want to read, and 42 percent of the sample discussed the role of Steinberg's book club. The students' responses, along with observations that I made during the school year, suggest that young adolescents have clear ideas about what they need to be motivated to read in school, and these ideas affirm the idea that reading is a social, participative activity.

Grant Street is a "Reading School"

Seventh grader Latressa explained that she became more motivated to read when she entered Grant Street because she recognized that the school was "big on reading" in that "they're always talking about it … . They think books are important. They put it out there … . They have posters, the teachers are always reading stuff, the morning announcements have it, they have meetings on it." Latressa believed that these activities made her believe, "maybe it is important to read more." Grant Street's independent reading program appeared to shape students' view of Grant Street as a "reading school" and in turn influenced their willingness to read every day in school.

Notable patterns permeated independent reading, a time that lasted 30 minutes daily in the double-period English classes in sixth to tenth grades and 30 minutes weekly in single-period English classes in the eleventh and twelfth grades. During independent reading, students silently read in the company of other students and their teacher. They chose books from their classroom libraries or visited the school library. They maintained a record of the pages that they read at home and in school, along with a list of books they'd read across the year. Students read books of their choosing, and teachers expected them to read at home each night for at least 30 minutes for a total of twenty-five to forty-five books each year. Teachers read too; otherwise they spent the time conferring with students on reading strategies that they taught in whole-class lessons or on students' reading habits. For teachers and students alike, independent reading took on a nonnegotiable status; it was one of the few activities that everyone had in common during the school day, regardless of grade level or classroom role. These features of the school's independent reading program rendered it meaningful enough to encourage students—even ones who were labeled "struggling"—to become motivated to read in school.

Students and Teachers Talk about Books

School members constantly talked informally and formally about the books they read for independent reading, and students told me that these conversations also motivated them to participate in Grant Street's reading culture. They appreciated the times when teachers carved out a few moments at the end of independent reading to share books with one another and with the whole class. But equally important as the planned moments were the spontaneous ones that took place near a classroom library, in the hallway, or in the school library. Martin, a ninth grader new to Grant Street, said, "In junior high school, we had independent reading. I never liked it …

Here, a teacher recommends a book, and that really helps me. They know my taste. Sometimes I don't know so many titles, and they help me ... ." The appreciation of book recommendations ex tended to students' peers as well. Stephen, an eighth grader, said his classmates knew him well enough to put good books in his hands: "They just come up to me and say, 'You've read this? You have to read this.'" In turn, Stephen often recommended books to his classmates.

While these informal interactions may have come across as arbitrary, they were intentional in the role they played to distribute the expectation that each student could find something that they would want to read at Grant Street. These conversations illuminate what it looked like to be a reading school in the eyes of its students; at any time during the day, and in any space in the school, students could have a meaningful interaction with someone else about a book. These interactions provided an opportunity for the students who might not have appeared to be enthusiastic about the reading culture to become engaged; they came to know that at Grant Street, their interests could be cultivated with a book that they would enjoy.

Teachers can consider different ways to start conversations with students about books. Teachers can set aside a few minutes several times a week to give book talks about titles they think may appeal to students. These book talks—no more than a few minutes per book—can include a quick and captivating summary of the text, major themes, and suggestions for the kinds of readers who might enjoy the plot. At the same time, teachers can confer with individual students during independent reading to make suggestions about titles they plan to read next. By examining students' reading logs or asking them about their most recently beloved titles, teachers can gain insight on the topics and genres that appeal to any student. Teachers can then recommend a few titles that students might enjoy, and students can even set goals for titles that they can read next. Put together, book talks and conferences appeal to both the collective and individual dimensions of independent reading. Book talks allow the teacher and students to publicly celebrate texts that students may enjoy. Meanwhile, conferences enable teachers to develop a deeper understanding of each student's personal interests and be attuned to students' reading trajectory across the year.

The Principal Has a Library and Runs a Book Club

Students also discussed the role their principal had in their reading lives. When Steinberg became Grant Street's principal in 2001, although he appreciated the intimate academic setting that the school provided its students, he recognized that beyond whole-class novels, the school did not do enough to prepare its students to read voluminously and meaningfully. Just as he expected the staff to rethink their instructional practices, he took on practices of his own to motivate students to read more. For example, he rearranged his office to make room for a library of about 800 titles that students could access throughout the day (see Figure 3.1.1). Mario, an eighth grader, observed, "To see the principal get involved with students' reading instead of just straight business is key." The interactions that I observed Steinberg having about books in his office and

FIGURE 3.1.1   The Principal's Office Library Arranged in Bins by Genre. Some
Bin Labels Included Sports Nonfiction, Graphic Novels, Quick Reads With
Female Main Characters, Principal's Book Club, Romance, and Life in the City.

throughout the school upended the traditional interactions we might assume that principals have
with their students and ultimately encouraged many students to want to read more in school.

In addition to his own library and conversations with students about books, Steinberg hosted
book clubs throughout the year for his students. He identified up to ten fiction and nonfiction
titles that would appeal to his students. For example, in the spring of 2014, titles included
Zombie Baseball Beatdown by Paolo Bacigalupi, Veronica Draper's *Out of My Mind*, and "The Best
Report on Bullying I've Ever Read," Emily Bazelon's commentary about the NFL's investigation of
the Miami Dolphins released earlier that year. Steinberg posted fliers in the hallway advertising
the books and purchased several copies of each title to distribute to any student who wanted
to sign up. Those copies became a part of each English teacher's classroom libraries or part of
the school library. Steinberg then hosted a lunch with pizza and drinks for each featured title,
open to any student who had read the text.

Each book club brought together between eight and twenty-five students from different
grades. Together with their principal, students discussed character development, authors'
messages, and new insights into their own lives and society as a result of reading the text. Students in interviews appreciated the book clubs because of their unique multigrade interaction.
Clarence, a seventh grader, told me that he enjoyed participating in book clubs because they
made him go on in books just at the moment when he wanted to quit: "I was reading *Spanking*

Shakespeare. I thought the book was boring towards the beginning, but then kids at the book club were telling me other parts of the book that were interesting, and I said I wanted to get to that part so I finished the book and I liked it."

Grant Street students suggest that school leaders can play a vital role in their reading lives. Principals, assistant principals, literacy coaches, and librarians can consider advertising popular titles in and around the school building to spark interest and momentum for independent reading. School leaders can use bestseller lists and recommendations from students and teachers to identify titles that students may enjoy. School leaders can nurture the interest and momentum for independent reading by hosting periodic book clubs for titles that appeal to students. These actions have the power to shape a schoolwide reading culture that is more sustainable than the impact an individual class or grade can provide.

Redefining School Literacy

Grant Street students taught me more about reading motivation than I knew before I taught them and studied their school; in fact, they helped me to redefine school literacy. The fact that students named schoolwide rituals that were important to their motivation to read shows the importance of coordinated efforts across the school instead of the sometimes temporary impact that an individual classroom can offer. Students articulated that, although the school contexts surrounding young people tend to maintain narrow conceptualizations of reading success that place a premium on standardized tests, textbooks, and worksheets, students at Grant Street understood that encouraging their motivation to read was about cultivating their *joy* of reading. The factors that students named in interviews and that I saw as patterns in observations— nonnegotiable independent reading, constant opportunities to talk about books, and the principal's involvement in their reading at school—affirmed the long-held idea that reading, and the motivation to do it, is mediated by its surrounding context.

References

del Valle, A., & Lewis, C. (2009). Literacy and identity: Implications for research and practice. In L. Christenbury, R. Bomer, & P. Smagorinsky (Eds.), *Handbook of adolescent literacy research* (pp. 307–322). New York, NY: The Guilford Press.

Pitcher, S. M., et al. (2007). Assessing adolescents' motivation to read. *Journal of Adolescent & Adult Literacy, 50*(5), 378–396.

Wolters, C. A., Denton, C. A., York, M. J., & Francis, D. J. (2014). Adolescents' motivation for reading: Group differences in relation to standardized achievement. *Reading and Writing, 27*(3), 503–533.

Discussion Questions

1. What are some of the characteristics that make Grant Street a "reading school"? Why do you think these characteristics are effective with middle- and secondary-level students?

2. How is the participation of the principal crucial to the success of the Grant Street approach? Why do you think this does not happen in more schools?

3. Find an article that describes a successful project for enhancing middle- or secondary-level students' motivation to read. Compare and contrast this project with the Grant Street approach described in the article. What characteristics do they have in common?

Asking the Experts

What Children Have to Say about Their Reading Preferences

Denise Davila and Lisa Patrick

In this article, Davila and Patrick recommend asking the "experts" about what children like to read. By experts, they mean the children themselves. What better source of information than to ask the students directly?

LEARNING OBJECTIVES

1. Think back to your years in middle and secondary school. Brainstorm a list of topics you and your friends were interested in reading about.
2. What are some sources that can be used to find books related to particular topics?

Asking the Experts

What Children Have to Say about Their Reading Preferences

Denise Davila and Lisa Patrick

Good Masters! Sweet Ladies! by Laura Amy Schlitz	Harry Potter series, by J. K. Rowling
The Higher Power of Lucky, by Susan Patron	Captain Underpants series, by Dav Pilkey
Criss Cross, by Lynne Rae Perkins	Goosebumps series, by R. L. Stein
Kira-Kira, by Cynthia Kadohata	Scary Stories series, by Alvin Schwartz

B efore you begin reading this article, take a few moments to examine the two different lists of books in the above chart. Which list reflects the kinds of texts that young audiences most prefer? It's a question worth exploring.

For the most part, adults control the world of children's literature: adults write the books; adults choose which books to publish; adults review the books; adults bestow the awards on books; and adults purchase the books for their homes, bookstores, and libraries. In the midst of all this adult control, children's opinions are often overlooked. This article reviews some of the major research on children's reading preferences, with the intent of understanding the intersection of three constituencies: children, adults, and publishers. Based on the research, we will make recommendations for helping teachers choose literacy materials that will be more consistent with children's reading preferences.

What are children reading? Adults may be surprised to learn that the cannon of children's literature may not be entirely effective in engaging today's young readers. The studies reviewed in this article indicate that children currently prefer to read magazines, comics, and websites, none of which are representative of the traditional cannon. (A brief overview of some of these studies is provided in Appendix A.) This shift away from the cannon has occurred during a time in which children can simultaneously play virtual world video games, text their friends, and engage in social networking. Books are being published with multi-modal capacities, allowing digitally enabled youth to extend their reading experiences via technology. In light of these trends, adult perspectives about what makes an appealing read for kids may need to evolve. Thus, this review of the literature highlights the dichotomy between *authorized* reading materials and *actual* reading materials preferred by children.

Background

According to Barbara Kiefer (2010), the Charlotte S. Huck Professor of Children's Literature at The Ohio State University, "To have a successful literature program, teachers and librarians must know books well, but that is only half the task. It is also necessary to understand children's interests, their growth patterns over time, and the changing patterns of their responses to literature" (p. 33). Moreover, Boltz (2007) argues that there is a distinct difference between the concepts of reading interest and reading preference. A preference infers a "forced choice" (p. 3), in which one selects a book option from a defined collection found in a library or bookstore, for example. In contrast, an interest reflects one's personal curiosity and imagination. Thus, it is possible that one's interest may not be represented by any of the books within a defined collection.

In the best-case scenario, a child's interests inform his or her reading preferences. Alternately, a child's reading preferences could indicate his or her interests, but this is dependent on the range of options in the collection accessible to the child. Thus, when considering the research on children's reading preferences, it is important to note that some reading interests may not be included or accurately reflected in the survey instruments that are employed to measure reading preferences. For example, a child's specific genre interests may not even be listed on the survey. This factor must be taken into account when making generalizations based on the results of reading preference surveys.

Worthy, Moorman, and Turner (1999) speak to this gap that can exist between student interests and the reading materials that schools provide. In surveying 356 sixth graders and 12 teachers across 3 schools in an economically and ethnically diverse district in Texas, the researchers found that while most teachers were aware of students' reading interests, "fewer than one third of the classrooms contained more than a handful of such materials" (p. 22). They observe that when reading options are limited, students are left "with three choices: reading something outside of their interests, obtaining their preferred materials themselves, or not reading at all. Students who cannot afford to buy their preferred materials are more dependent on school sources and, thus, their choices are even more limited" (p. 23). More about students' access to reading materials and libraries will be discussed later in this article. The next section will discuss the connection between students' choices of reading materials and their attitudes toward reading.

Reading Attitudes and Choices

Children are generally positive toward reading, and value it as a lifelong skill, according to a survey of 8,206 British students in grades K–12 (Clark & Foster, 2005). When students' choices for reading materials are limited, however, their attitudes toward reading could be impacted. For example, in surveying 151 sixth and ninth graders in the vicinity of a major northeastern U.S. city, Strommen and Mates (2004) found that many "non-readers" became ambivalent toward reading between the ages of 9 and 11 because they could no longer find reading material that interested them. On a related note, the results of the 2008 Scholastic Kids and Family Reading Report, which surveyed 501 children between the ages of 5 and 17 from across the US, revealed that 55% of the children agree with the statement: "There aren't enough really good books for boys/girls my age" (Scholastic, 2008, p. 14). Additionally, among the participants between the ages of 9 and 17: "'[H]aving trouble finding books that I like' is among the top reasons for not reading more books for fun" (Scholastic, p. 15). Experiencing difficulty in locating books they like may impact how frequently children read.

Congruently, Kim and Krashen (2000) surveyed 103 sixth graders with low standardized test scores from a California school in an area of high poverty. Of the small number of students who reported that they did not like to read, most said that they disliked reading because "it is boring" (p. 1). Thus, Kim and Krashen argue that students who are ambivalent toward reading might have yet to encounter material that could pique their interests, thereby shifting their attitudes toward reading. These scholars believe that students greatly benefit from having an expanded range of options from which to choose reading materials that are relevant to their interests.

What is also noteworthy of Kim and Krashen's (2000) research is the finding that 84% of the students indicated positive attitudes toward reading, and most attributed their interest in reading to specific books, which they named on their survey questionnaires. This finding is consistent with the research of Schatz, Pierce, Ghalambor, & Krashen (2008). Upon querying a culturally and economically diverse group of 2,822 public school children across six states in grades four through six, Schatz and colleagues found not only that the students' responses reflected "considerable enthusiasm for reading," but also that most had a favorite book, and many had also "gotten lost" in a book (p. 70). Similarly, Worthy et al. (1999), whose study was described earlier, observed that nearly every sixth-grade student they surveyed named a preferred author, book, or genre, providing "evidence that middle school students' attitudes toward reading are not as negative as research has shown" (p. 23).

Some research (Iyengar & Ball, 2007; McKenna, Kear, & Ellsworth, 1995) has shown that as children grow older, they become uninterested in reading. In contrast, Krashen (2006) posits that while older children and teens experience more constraints on their time, their "interest in reading remains strong" (p. 5). Moreover, the studies presented in this section provide evidence that adolescents' attitudes toward reading are positive, especially to the extent that many study participants voluntarily named their favorite authors and reading materials on the survey instruments. The studies also indicate that children's favorite books are often those that the children personally selected to read. Thus, it is no surprise that first and foremost, young people want to choose reading materials from options that match their interests (Beers, 1996a, 1996b; Boltz, 2007; Boraks, Hoffman, & Bauer, 1997; Clark & Foster, 2005; Kim & Krashen, 2000; Krashen, 1993; Scholastic, 2008; Strommen & Mates, 2004; Worthy, et al., 1999). For example, Scholastic found that almost 90% of the children surveyed for the 2008 Scholastic Kids and

Family Reading Report said that they liked to choose their own reading materials. Given that children choose books according to their personal interests, what kinds of books and reading materials do children think are really good?

What Kids Say Makes a "Good Read"

Generally speaking, we can be assured that stories that are described as being "scary, funny, and action-packed" will appeal to most children in grades three to five (Boraks et al., 1997, p. 335). Clark and Foster (2005) offer an even broader forecast, finding that overall, British children between the ages of 6 and 16 prefer adventure, comedy, and horror/ghost stories more than other genres of fiction. Similarly, Worthy et al. (1999) found that among more than 400 sixth graders in a highly diverse school district of Texas, scary books and stories were most preferred by boys and girls equally, with more than half of the students naming R. L. Stine, author of the Goosebumps series, as their favorite author. In fact, scary books were the most preferred genre across gender, achievement, attitude, and income level. (While Worthy et al. conducted their study ten years ago, R. L. Stine is still a popular author with the latest Goosebumps Horrorland series, Goosebumps Graphix [graphic novel] series, video games, television programs, and an interactive website.)

Perhaps it is the merging of adventure, humor, and horror with a solid plot and appealing main character that makes for an irresistible "emotional impact" (Boraks et al., 1997, p. 332) among young readers. This may account for the popularity of J. K. Rowling's Harry Potter series, which according to Scholastic's 2008 Kids and Family Reading Report, has been read by more than 6 out of 10 children ages 9 and older. What also may account for the cross-gender popularity of the Harry Potter series is the fact that the protagonist, Harry, is male. According to Boraks et al., while boys prefer books with male protagonists, girls will read stories with either heroes or heroines (p. 324). Thus, stories that feature a male lead character and facilitate a scary adventure that is interspersed with comic relief will more likely appeal to a broad audience of both boys and girls.

Illustrating the appeal of such stories, books from series, such as J. K. Rowling's Harry Potter, R. L. Stine's Goosebumps, and Alvin Schwartz's Scary Stories, were most frequently cited in a survey of 266 low-income fourth- and fifth-grade students who were asked: "Was there one book or experience that first interested you in reading?" (Ujiie & Krashen, 2002). Ujiie and Krashen's findings are consistent with the research on young people's general reading preferences for horror, adventure, and comedy. Moreover, Scholastic (2008) also found that as a result of reading Harry Potter, three in four Scholastic survey participants said their experience "made them more interested in reading other books," as well (p. 50). In addition, it is noteworthy that the aforementioned stories are all part of book series, another overall reading preference of children. Yet, what is it about reading stories in a series that is of such interest to kids; wouldn't they shy away from book series because more reading is required?

Series

In a market research survey of book purchasing habits, Ferguson (1998) reports that 75% of teens like to buy books in a series or by the same author. Publishers and researchers alike recognize that series have a broad appeal to young readers (Cho & Krashen, 1995; Coles & Hall, 2002; Ferguson, 1998; Hechinger, 2008; Maughan, 2002; Scholastic, 2008; Sturm, 2003; Worthy et al., 1999). In a 1995 study regarding the Sweet Valley High series and English learners, Cho and Krashen established that when a reader chooses a series, he or she has the benefit of staying "with material that he or she finds interesting," and taking advantage "of background information to make the text more comprehensible" (p. 19). Krashen (1993) suggests that "light reading," like the Sweet Valley High series, can lead to more serious, heavier reading.

While the Harry Potter series is not "light" like the Sweet Valley High books, it has certainly led to more reading. Reading books by the same author about the same topic is also known as "narrow reading." This narrow reading of book series can be of some concern to teachers and parents who may worry that students' reading isn't broad enough. Krashen (2009) addresses this by saying: "Narrow readers, we should be assured, do not typically stay narrow ... . [These] readers gradually broaden their reading interests as they read more and their interests evolve" (p. 25). Supportive of Krashen's argument, the 2008 Scholastic Kids and Family Reading Report, as noted earlier, indicated that 75% of Harry Potter readers claimed reading the series led them to also take interest in other books. More interesting yet, Harry Potter readers, especially those that read all seven books in the series, were more passionate about reading than non-Potter readers in the study (Scholastic, 2008). Thus, "light" or "narrow" reading of book series provides a foundation on which children can expand their reading preferences to include a heavier or broader range of reading materials.

Magazines

Like series, which offer consistent, familiar content, magazines are also a strong preference of young audiences. In analyzing the 1994 reading preference data of nearly 8,000 primary and secondary students in England, Coles and Hall (2002) noted that periodicals were increasing in popularity. Ten years later, Clark and Foster (2005) surveyed a new generation of 8,206 students. Overall, more than 75% of the students rated magazines among their most preferred reading material. By gender, boys showed an overall preference of 71%, while girls showed an even higher preference at approximately 83% (see Figures 3.2.1 and 3.2.2). By age, over 71% of primary grade students (grades K–5) and 77% of secondary students (grades 6–12) prefer magazines. Consistently, Nippold, Duthie, & Larsen (2005) found a 73% preference rating for magazines with the teens in their study.

To accommodate the popularity of magazines among their 426 sixth-grade study participants, Worthy et al. (1999) actually adjusted the reading preference categories of their data analysis. Their student questionnaire offered a reading preference category entitled "magazines about people," but this wasn't enough. In addition to this category, many of the students listed the specific names of different types of magazines in the section of the questionnaire for "other" preferred reading materials. Most frequently listed were teen, music, video game, and ethnically

GIRLS: Percentage of approximately 3,865 girls in the Clark and Foster (2005) study that prefer selected reading materials. *(Percentages are rounded to the nearest whole number.)**

Percentage	Select Reading Material or Genre
83%	Magazines
70%	Text messages
64%	Television-related books and magazines
63%	Websites
55%	Catalogues
55%	Song lyrics
55%	Jokes
54%	Fiction

	62%	*Adventure*
	57%	*Comedy*
	53%	*Horror/ghost*
	49%	*Realistic teen fiction*
	39%	*Romance/relationships*
	35%	*Crime/detective*
	35%	*Animal-related*
	28%	*Science fiction (fantasy)*
	20%	*Sports-related*
	19%	*War/spy-related*

Percentage	Select Reading Material or Genre
44%	Newspapers
43%	Comics
42%	Poetry
34%	Plays
28%	Cookbooks
26%	Informational (factual) books
24%	Manuals
21%	Travel books
18%	Annuals
15%	Graphic novels

*The information in this figure has been adapted from the Clark and Foster (2005) study of students enrolled in schools that were participating in the Reading Connects initiative of the National Literacy Trust, funded by the Department for Education and Skills in the United Kingdom. This research can be accessed online at http://www.literacytrust.org.uk/research/readsurvey.html.

FIGURE 3.2.1   Girls' Reading Preferences.

focused magazines. A preference for magazines about cars was also indicated in the "other" section of the questionnaire. Subsequently, it appears that both boys and girls have a robust preference for a range of magazines.

Television- and Film-Related Magazines and Books

In contrast to the generalized survey category of "magazines about people" that Worthy et al. (1999) employed in their research instrument, Clark and Foster (2005) took an alternate approach. They included "television/fan magazines and books" as an entirely independent reading preference category in their student questionnaire. The category for television- and fan-related texts demonstrated a preference rating of over 60% for primary students and 55% for secondary students, garnering fifth place out of 24 different categories on which children were surveyed.

In concert with Clark and Foster's (2005) findings, Ferguson (1998) observed that more than half of the youth in her survey of book buyers were inclined to purchase a book that corresponded with a movie they had recently seen. Sturm (2003) also noted a connection between movie releases and children's library book selections. As his study coincided with the release of the teen surf film *Blue Crush*, which features female surfers, Sturm observed that girls correspondingly borrowed books about surfing from the library. All of these findings are congruent with Krashen's (1993) argument that television and film can stimulate or influence what children choose to read. Beers (1996a, 1996b) suggests that in viewing all or parts of a film version of a book, students gain a context for a story, which could support their engagement as they initiate reading. Thus, like series, reading materials associated with television and film enable children to both engage with subject matter that they already find intriguing and capitalize on background information, which helps to make text more comprehensible to readers.

It is interesting to note that like blockbuster movie trailers, some publishers have started to create video book trailers and "webisodes" as a means to introduce prospective audiences to new reading materials. For example, author Jay Asher anonymously posted a video on the website You-Tube that related to and coincided with the recent release of his teen book, *Thirteen Reasons Why*. Other new teen series, such as Evermore by Alyson Noel and Luxe by Anna Godbersen, also have videos on YouTube. While existing research demonstrates that many children prefer to read books and magazines related to television and film,

BOYS: Percentage of approximately 4,341 boys in the Clark and Foster (2005) study that prefer selected reading materials. *(Percentages are rounded to the nearest whole number.)**

Percentage	Select Reading Material or Genre	
71%	Magazines	
65%	Websites	
62%	Jokes	
59%	Comics	
55%	Text messages	
52%	Television-related books and magazines	
51%	Fiction	
	65%	*Adventure*
	58%	*Comedy*
	54%	*Horror/ghost*
	48%	*War/spy-related*
	44%	*Crime/detective*
	40%	*Sports-related*
	37%	*Science fiction (fantasy)*
	22%	*Realistic teen fiction*
	19%	*Animal-related*
	9%	*Romance/relationships*
50%	Newspapers	
39%	Catalogues	
34%	Song lyrics	
32%	Manuals	
30%	Informational (factual) books	
24%	Annuals	
23%	Graphic novels	
22%	Poetry	
21%	Plays	
18%	Travel books	
16%	Cookbooks	

*The information in this figure has been adapted from the Clark and Foster (2005) study of students enrolled in schools that were participating in the Reading Connects initiative of the National Literacy Trust, funded by the Department for Education and Skills in the United Kingdom. This research can be accessed online at http://www.literacytrust.org.uk/research/readsurvey.html.

FIGURE 3.2.2 Boys' Reading Preferences.

more research will be needed to examine the budding relationship between online video book trailers and children's reading preferences.

Comics

Like magazines, comics (exclusive of Manga and graphic novels) consistently rank high among young readers. For example, Nippold et al. (2004) and Worthy et al. (1999) found comics to be a preference of students in their studies, with a higher representation among boys. Even with graphic novels as an independent category, Clark and Foster (2005) similarly noted an overall preference for comics by more than 50% of the youth in their study, with a higher preference by boys. By gender (grades K–12), boys demonstrated a preference rating of 58%, while girls showed a preference rating of 43%. By grade level, nearly 69% of primary students and approximately 44% of secondary students indicated a preference for reading comics.

Notably, Clark and Foster (2005) also found that lower income students receiving free school meals (FSMs) showed a slightly elevated preference for comics than non-FSM students (+2.6%). This slight elevation is significant, considering that in comparison to middle income students, FSMs demonstrate an overall reduced preference for reading materials such as fiction (–13.6%), factual books (–7%), magazines (–7.4%) and websites (–12.4%). Research suggests that while access to books and other reading materials may be limited in lower-income communities, which tend to have smaller and fewer libraries and retailers, comics sometimes remain accessible in grocery and drugstores (Neuman & Celano, 2001; Worthy et al., 1999).

Congruent with the abovementioned research, in a comparative study between 302 California seventh graders from a school in which 82% of the student body was eligible for reduced cost or free school meals and 269 seventh graders from a middle class suburban school, Ujiie and Krashen (1996) observed that, with greater frequency among boys, children from the FSM school reported just as much comic book reading as the children from the middle class school. In both the FSM and middle class schools, comic book readers tended to read more books. Moreover, the students' frequency of comic book reading was associated with their level of reading pleasure and satisfaction.

Significant, too, is the finding that the comic book readers at the FSM school not only read more than their peers, but also read more than their counterparts at the middle class school, including those who were interested in other reading materials. These results indicate that comic book reading does not hinder students from taking up other kinds of reading, but rather provides evidence that as "light reading," comic book reading paves a way toward students' interest and proficiency in "heavier reading" (Krashen, 1993).

Like book series and other reading materials that correspond with television and film, comics can also lay the groundwork for young readers to augment their reading experiences with other genres and materials. While existing research shows a heightened preference for reading comics among boys and girls, more research is needed to explore the relationship between children's reading preferences and Manga/graphic novels, which have become more abundant in recent years.

Gender Differences

Although different reading preferences have been shown to exist for girls and boys, it is important to note that among avid readers, there may be fewer differences between genders. In one study, Strommen and Mates (2004) report that sixth- and ninth-grade students who are "readers" read a wide variety of materials and believe reading helps to stimulate the imagination and deepen one's understanding of the world. In looking at young library patrons, Sturm (2003) found that overall, the children in his study "showed little gender differences in their preferences" (p. 6). In evaluating the habits of teens that purchase books, Ferguson (1998) found that generally both boys and girls in this group bought fiction more often than factual books. This group's gender-neutral preference for fiction is inconsistent with the literature, which suggests that there is a significant difference between boys' and girls' preferences for fiction and factual reading materials.

Hegemony

The research demonstrates that girls generally choose fiction more frequently than boys, and boys choose nonfiction more frequently than girls (Boltz, 2007; Boraks et al., 1997; Childress, 1985; Clark & Foster, 2005; Davis, 2007; Nippold et al., 2005; Sturm, 2003). Davis offers an explanation for this phenomenon in her evaluation of 88 case studies about seven- and eight-year-old children from various cultural and socioeconomic backgrounds in England. She found that "hegemonic cultural norms may operate at a macro level to position certain kinds of reading as feminine" (p. 232), such as fiction books and magazine reading. Nonfiction texts and newspaper reading is positioned as masculine. She posits that this ideology is congruent with research, "which, typically, has found that gendered models of reading hold for most older children" (p. 232). Clark and Foster reported complementary overall findings: greater percentages of girls prefer magazine and fiction-based texts while boys prefer news and information-based texts. In analyzing kindergarten and first-grade students' library book selections, Childress also observed that the girls and boys in her study exhibited divergent reading preferences even before they developed the skills of proficient independent readers. By first grade, girls most frequently selected fiction stories, while boys usually selected factual books, although they entertained other genres more often than girls.

Girls

As indicated above, hegemonic norms may underpin girls' heightened preferences for certain reading materials. For example, girls more frequently prefer to read catalogues, song lyrics, poetry, and cookbooks (Clark & Foster, 2005; Sturm, 2003), each of which could be perceived as stereotypical "feminine" material. In addition, research shows that girls like to read sequenced fiction-based stories—in other words, series books (Coles & Hall, 2002; Worthy, et al., 1999). Hence, if girls could add a category to one of the student questionnaires that have been employed by researchers to measure children's reading preferences (Clark & Foster, 2005; Coles & Hall,

2002; Nippold et al., 2005; Worthy et al., 1999), it's possible they might dedicate a whole section to "Book Series."

With respect to fiction as a multifaceted genre, studies also indicate that girls have a much greater preference for realistic teen fiction, as well as romance and/or relationship stories, plays, and animal stories (Clark & Foster, 2005; Coles & Hall, 2002; Sturm, 2003). Publishers hold the opinion that because young readers live in a real world, they want to know what to expect by "reading up"—reading stories about characters older than themselves (Maughan, 2002; Reno, 2008). While more research is needed to confirm this opinion, Ferguson's (1998) observations that female book buyers more frequently select books from the young adult section of bookstores might suggest that girls choose young adult materials as a means to reading up. In short, girls show a higher preference for magazines, poetry, and other materials associated with stereo-typical feminine reading materials. When it comes to fiction, however, they like funny, scary, adventure-based fiction as much as boys, and also prefer genres such as romance and realistic fiction. Moreover, girls may be more apt than boys to engage in book series.

Boys

If boys could add a category to a future questionnaire intended to survey children's reading preferences, there's a good chance they might call it "Gory & Gross." Hetchinger (2008), writer for the *Wall Street Journal*, reports that "[p]ublishers are hawking more gory and gross books to appeal to an elusive market: boys" (p. 1). While more research is needed to confirm that there is a direct relationship between boys' reading preferences and heightened sales of particular book titles, Hetchinger presents intriguing data about the book publishing industry. For example, he writes that Scholastic's 1997 launch of the *Captain Underpants* series by Dav Pilkey was seen as a "major victory" in capturing the boy audience (p. 2). With 37 million copies in print, the *Captain Underpants* book series spawned *The Day My Butt Went Psycho!* trilogy by Andy Griffiths, which boasts 1.2 million copies. Newcomer *Sir Fartsalot Hunts the Booger*, by third-grade teacher Kevin Bolger, went into a second printing with over 50,000 copies in just two months of its debut. Hetchinger also offers a quote from the president of Penguin Razorbill imprint, Ben Schrank, who posits: "[T]he industry must publish fiction that will pull a boy away from a videogame" (p. 2).

Consistent with hegemonic norms, studies show that boys are more likely to read informational materials about videogames and other topics, such as sports and cars and trucks (Sturm, 2003; Worthy et al., 1999). In terms of fiction genres, boys are more likely to read fantasy (inclusive of science fiction), crime/detective stories, and war/spy-related fiction (Clark & Foster, 2005; Sturm, 2003). They also have a stronger preference for comics, graphic novels, and joke books (Clark & Foster, 2005). Sullivan (2004) notes that boys also like to read baseball cards and cereal boxes.

Adding to the discussion, Boltz (2007) suggests that boys' reading preferences are influenced by their hegemonic stance as efferent readers. Efferent readers read for specific information, as in looking for an answer to a question (Rosenblatt, 1978). For example, readers take an efferent stance in the reading of technical papers, newspapers, and nonfiction computer books. The boys in Davis's (2007) study talked about their observations of men engaged with these materials. In addition, more boys than girls in Clark and Foster's (2005) study viewed reading as a tool for getting a job. Consequently, if boys read what they read because they identify with men (Sullivan, 2004), it makes sense that boys would interact more frequently with information-based books and texts, including newspapers, annuals, and manuals. In short, boys show a higher preference for comics, joke books, news, informational texts, and other stereotypically masculine reading materials. When it comes to fiction, they like funny, scary, adventure-based fiction as much as girls, and also prefer genres such as fantasy, crime/detective stories, and war/spy fiction. Moreover, boys may be more apt than girls to engage in materials about gross and gory topics.

Potential Trends in Reading Preferences

How might reading preferences shift in future years? In 1994, survey data indicated an increased preference for magazine reading among British children (Coles & Hall, 2002). By 2004, magazines represented children's most preferred reading material overall (Clark & Foster, 2005), with a preference rating of 75.5%. Second only to magazines, was children's preference for reading Internet websites (63.6%), followed by cell phone text messages (61%), materials that were not as developed or accessible in the previous decade. Also significant is Clark and Foster's findings that 51% of primary and secondary students would prefer to engage in reading response activities such as "designing websites." This is perhaps an indication that children may be attracted to interacting with digital media. In light of these findings, it will be fascinating to follow how the evolution of new media technologies may influence children's reading preferences over the next decade.

Given the explosion of technological advances, there will be numerous opportunities for researching shifts in children's reading preferences. While there is not a documented correlation between children's reading preferences and trends in publishing, publishers are nonetheless utilizing new media technologies to create interactive reading experiences that have never before existed. With regard to new digital media, Semuels (2008), reporter for the *Seattle Times* newspaper, writes about the rapidly growing e-book market for kids. Her story features an eight-year-old boy who can curl up in bed and engage with a digital version of Dr. Seuss's *Horton Hears a Who*, which is read to him from the computer. According to Semuels, children's publishers are not only releasing and marketing e-books to children via websites and virtual world games, but also sponsoring book clubs, chat rooms, and reading games. The latter is supported by Clark and Foster's (2005) finding that overall, 62% of elementary school children (grades K–5) would prefer to engage in reading games as a way to help them read more. Semuels closes her article with a telling quote from Mark Shatz of Random House Digital. He says: "[T]he revenue opportunity for publishers who make the effort [to adapt print books to digital] is at a point where you can pretty easily justify the cost to convert the files" (p. 2). His comment may foreshadow an increase in digital books in the near future. As current research regarding digital book media is limited, it will be interesting to see what scholars observe about children's book preferences and digital book media in upcoming years.

WHAT CAN TEACHERS DO TO SUPPORT CHILDREN'S READING PREFERENCES?

- Learn about students' interests.
- Help ensure that students have access to a wide range of reading materials, including information-based as well as fiction-based texts.
- Encourage students to choose their own reading materials.
- Establish a classroom routine for daily reading of materials selected by children.
- Authorize the reading of magazines, comics, graphic novels, and other nontraditional materials in the classroom.
- Validate students' "narrow reading" of series and books by the same authors.
- Select a variety of materials for language arts lessons that reflect a balance of gendered reading preferences.
- Model personal reading engagement with a diverse collection of reading materials.

—Denise Davila and Lisa Patrick

In the realm of multimodal text formats, children's book publishers are also producing new compositions for storytelling. For example, Patrick Carman's new book series Skeleton Creek is presented in two different media, print and digital video. In the print book, readers encounter the story from the point of view of the male lead character, Ryan. Online, the female lead character, Sarah, reveals her story through videos on a special website. The book provides readers website addresses and passwords to access the videos via the Internet. In addition, Scholastic has an elaborate author and fan website to accompany the series. Here, too, research will also be needed to explore the impact of multimodal storytelling on children's reading preferences.

Conclusion

Now, let us return for a moment to the book lists at the beginning of the article. We posed the question, "Which list reflects the kinds of texts that young audiences most prefer?" The first list includes recent Newbery Award winners. The second list reflects some of the bestselling books children mentioned in the various reading preferences studies that were reviewed in this article. On this note, Krashen (2006), in his analysis of public library circulation of award-winning children's books, found that libraries carry fewer award winners than bestsellers because bestselling children's books, which usually include series, are borrowed more frequently. He suggests possible implications of his findings: "children don't know what is best for them … [or] that Newbery and Caldecott judges have different standards than the real audience of children's and adolescent literature" (p. 35). We think it is noteworthy that bestselling books closely match what real audiences of both boys and girls prefer as demonstrated by the research.

To recapitulate, boys and girls equally like fiction, which includes adventure, horror, and humor. Harry Potter and Goosebumps are examples of bestselling book series that have scared children to the bone, yet have left them in stitches with laughter. Beyond these similarities, "boys and girls generally opt for stereotypical preferences for fiction" (Clark & Foster, 2005, p. 37). Girls prefer stories about romance, realistic fiction, and animals, while boys prefer stories about science fiction (fantasy), sports, crime investigation, and war or spy topics. Boys demonstrate a greater preference for comics, news, and informational materials, while girls demonstrate a greater preference for catalogues, song lyrics, and poetry. With regard to other types of materials, boys and girls alike demonstrate strong preferences for reading magazines, websites, jokes, and television- and film-related subject matter.

Finally, there's no single answer to the question, "What do young audiences prefer to read?" Rather, there are myriad possibilities. As noted earlier in this article, research suggests that among avid readers, differences in genre and format preferences are inconsequential because such readers tend to take up a diverse range of reading material. Just as children currently have strong preferences for reading subject matter that they access on websites or interactively construct via text messaging, it is inevitable that children's reading preferences will continue to shift with the evolution of new media and technologies.

Perhaps recent trends will influence the design of survey instruments that will be employed to measure children's future reading preferences. Maybe we will see questionnaire checkboxes for categories such as "digital books" and "multimodal stories." If we're lucky, we might even see a survey with different sections dedicated to "book series" and "gross and gory topics."

Children's Literature Cited in the Article

Asher, J. (2007). *Thirteen reasons why.* New York: Razorbill.

Bolger, K. (2008). *Sir Fartsalot hunts the booger.* New York: Razorbill.

Carman, P. (2009). *Skeleton creek.* New York: Scholastic.

Godbersen, A. (2007). *Luxe.* New York: HarperCollins.

Griffiths, A. (2003). *The day my butt went psycho*! Logan, IA: Perfection Learning.

Kadohata, C. (2004). *Kira-Kira.* New York: Atheneum.

Noel, A. (2009). *Evermore.* New York: Macmillan Children's Books.

Pascal, F. (1983–1999). Sweet Valley High series. New York: Random House Children's Books.

Patron, S. (2006). *The higher power of Lucky.* New York: Atheneum.

Perkins, L. R. (2005). *Criss cross.* New York: Greenwillow.

Pilkey, D. (1997–2006). Captain Underpants series. New York: Blue Sky.

Rowling, J. K. (1998–2007). Harry Potter series. New York: Arthur A. Levine.

Schlitz, L. A. (2007). *Good masters! Sweet ladies! Voices from a medieval village.* Somerville, MA: Candlewick.

Schwartz, A. (1981–1991). Scary Stories series. New York: HarperCollins.

Seuss, Dr. (1954). *Horton hears a who.* New York: Random House Books for Young Readers.

Stine, R. L. (1992–1997). Goosebumps series. New York: Scholastic.

Stine, R. L. (2006–2007). Goosebumps Graphix series. New York: Scholastic.

Stine, R. L. (2008–2009). Goosebumps Horrorland series. New York: Scholastic.

References

Beers, K. (1996a). Part I. "No time! No interest! No way!" The three voices of aliteracy. *School Library Journal, 42*(2), 30–33.

Beers, K. (1996b). Part II. "No time! No interest! No way!" The three voices of aliteracy. *School Library Journal, 42*(3), 110–133.

Boltz, R. (2007). What we want: Boys and girls talk about reading. *School Library Media Research, 10,* 1–19.

Boraks, N., Hoffman, A., & Bauer, D. (1997). Children's book preferences: Patterns, particulars, and possible implications. *Reading Psychology, 18,* 309–341.

Childress, G. (1985). Gender gap in the library: Different choices for girls and boys. *Top of the News, 42*(1), 69–73.

Cho, K. S., & Krashen, S. (1995). From Sweet Valley Kids to Harlequins in one year. *California English, 1*(1), 18–19.

Clark, C., & Foster, A. (2005). Children's and young people's reading habits and references: The who, what, why, where, and when. London: National Literacy Trust.

Coles, M., & Hall, C. (2002). Gendered readings: Learning from children's choices. *Journal of Research in Reading, 25,* 96–108.

Davis, P. (2007). Discourses about reading among seven- and eight-year-old children in classroom pedagogic cultures. *Journal of Early Childhood Literacy, 7,* 219–252.

Ferguson, A. (1998, October 12). Reading is cool. *Publisher's Weekly, 245*(41), 28–31.

Hechinger, J. (2008, August 8). Problem: Boys don't like to read. Solution: Books that are really gross. *The Wall Street Journal.* Retrieved July 30, 2009, from http://online.wsj.com.

Iyengar, S., & Ball, D. (2007). *To read or not to read* (Research Report #47). Washington, DC: National Endowment for the Arts.

Kiefer, B. (2010). *Charlotte Huck's children's literature.* New York: McGraw Hill.

Kim, J., & Krashen, S. (2000). Another home run. *California English, 6*(2), 25.

Krashen, S. (1993). *The power of reading.* Englewood, CO: Libraries Unlimited.

Krashen, S. (Spring, 2006). Stephen Krashen: Pleasure reading. *Young Learners* [Special issue]. Retrieved from http://www.iatefl.hu/docs/Stephen_Krashen.pdf.

Krashen, S. (2009). Anything but reading. *Knowledge Quest, 37*(5), 18–25.

Maughan, S. (2002, November 11). Betwixt and be 'tween.' *Publishers Weekly.* Retrieved July 24, 2009, from http://www.publishersweekly.com/

McKenna, M. C., Kear, D. J., & Ellsworth, R. A. (1995). Children's attitudes toward reading: A national survey. *Reading Research Quarterly, 30,* 934–956.

Neuman, S., & Celano, D. (2001). Access to print in low-income and middle-income communities: An ecological study of four neighborhoods. *Reading Research Quarterly, 36,* 8–26.

Nippold, M., Duthie, J., & Larsen, J. (2005). Literacy as a leisure activity: Free-time preferences of older children and young adolescents. *Language, Speech, and Hearing Services in School, 36,* 93–102.

Reno, J. (2008, May 14). Generation R (R is for reader). *Newsweek Web.* Retrieved July 25, 2009, from http://www.newsweek.com/id/136961.

Rosenblatt, L. M. (1978). *The reader, the text, the poem: Transactional theory of the literacy work.* Carbondale: Southern Illinois University Press.

Schatz, A., Pierce, K., Ghalambor, K., & Krashen, S. (2008). More on the "literacy crisis": Do children like to read? *Knowledge Quest, 37,* 70–71.

Scholastic. (2008). 2008 Scholastic kids and family reading report. Retrieved September 16, 2009, from http://www.scholastic.com/aboutscholastic/news/readingreport.htm.

Semuels, A. (2008, December 29). Children's book market ready to embrace a digital world. *The Seattle Times.* Retrieved July 29, 2009, from http://seattletimes.nwsource.com.

Strommen, L., & Mates, B. (2004). Learning to love reading: Interviews with older children and teens. *Journal of Adolescent and Adult Literacy, 48,* 188–200.

Sturm, B. (2003). *The information and reading preferences of North Carolina children.* Chicago: American Association of School Librarians/ALA. Retrieved September 16, 2009, from http://www.ala.org/ala.

Sullivan, M. (2004, August 1). Why Johnny won't read. *School Library Journal, 50*(8), 36–39.

Ujiie, J., & Krashen, S. (1996). Comic book reading, reading enjoyment, and pleasure book reading among middle class and Chapter 1 middle school students. *Reading Improvement, 33,* 51–54.

Ujiie, J., & Krashen, S. (2002). Homerun books and reading enjoyment. *Knowledge Quest, 31*(3), 36–37.

Ujiie, J., & Krashen, S. (2006). Are prize winning books popular among children? An analysis of public library circulation. *Knowledge Quest, 34*(3), 33–35.

Worthy, J., Moorman, M., & Turner, M. (1999). What Johnny likes to read is hard to find in school. *Reading Research Quarterly, 34,* 12–27.

APPENDIX A

Researcher	Main Objectives & Instrument	Population	Key Findings of Study Related to Children's Reading Preferences
Boraks, N., Hoffman, A., and Bauer, D. (1997).	**Objective.** Examine the patterns of children's reading preferences by literature genre, grade level, gender, and geographic location. **Instrument.** Questionnaire ("complete the sentence" format).	Students: 315. Boys: 154; Girls: 161. Grades: 3–5. Location: Urban and suburban public school in Ohio & Virginia. Ohio: 4 classes; mid-upper income. Virginia: 2 classes; lower income.	**A.** "Enormous diversity" (p. 319) among favorite books. **B.** Authors Roald Dahl and R. L. Stine mentioned most often. **C.** Boy preferences across geographic locations were more alike. **D.** Girl preferences were more varied. **E.** Boys generally prefer fantasy-based fiction. **F.** Girls, especially as they get older, prefer realistic fiction. **G.** Most books preferred by boys had a male protagonist. **H.** Girls tended more toward female protagonists, but also read books with male leads. **I.** Geographic differences in preferences were evident. [Ohio: more award winners. Virginia: more "fantasy" such as T.V. cartoon "spin-offs" (p. 325).] **J.** Teachers, classrooms, and peers impact genre preferences. **K.** "Major reasons" (p. 332) for preferences are related to the plot and emotional impact of a book.
Childress, G. (1984).	**Objective.** Identify the age at which children begin to exhibit gender-related preferences in their choices of recreational library reading. **Method.** Observation and Library circulation data analysis. Phase 1: four weeks. Phase 2: eighteen weeks.	Grades K–1. Location: Elementary school in Maryville, Tennessee.	**Phase 1 (4wks):** **1A.** Approx. 70% of boys chose nonfiction. **1B.** Approx. 70% of girls chose fiction more often. **Phase 2 (18wks.):** **2A.** Kinder boys chose nonfiction and fiction with nearly equal frequency at approx. 50% ea. **2B.** Kinder girls chose fiction 81% of the time. **2C.** First-grade boys chose nonfiction 60% of the time. **2D.** First-grade girls chose fiction approx. 80% of the time. **Other findings:** Kinder and first-grade boys were more flexible in reading choices than girls.

| Clark, C. and Foster, A. (2005). | **Objective.** Investigate: a) why some children choose to read and some do not; and b) what could be done to engage reluctant readers. **Instrument.** Questionnaire (multiple-choice format). | Students: 8,152. Grades K–12. Location: England. | **A. Overall. A1.** Students generally held positive attitudes toward reading. **A2.** Outside of school, students read a diverse range of texts other than books, such as magazines, websites, and comics. **A3.** With regard to fiction, students most preferred adventure, comedy, and horror/ghost stories. **A4.** Activities such as engaging with websites, meeting authors, and playing games would encourage students to read more. **B. Gender. B1.** Girls enjoyed reading more than boys. **B2.** Girls and boys preferred different reading materials. **B3.** More boys than girls said they read because it would help them get a job. **B4.** While magazine reading was highly preferred overall, a greater percentage of girls preferred magazines. **B5.** A greater percentage of girls also preferred TV program periodicals, fiction, poetry, plays, and catalogues. **B6.** A greater percentage of boys preferred comics, factual books, newspapers, and joke books. **B7.** In terms of fiction, more girls preferred realistic fiction, and romance/relationship stories. More boys preferred science fiction/fantasy, sports stories, war/spy stories, and crime stories. **C. Age. C1.** Secondary students were more likely to read websites and newspapers. **C2.** Primary students were more likely to read joke books, comics, factual books, and fiction. **D. Socioeconomic. D1.** Students' access to materials influenced their reading preferences. **D2.** Students in free school meal programs were more likely to read joke books and comics and less likely to read websites, fiction, and factual books. |

(Continued)

Researcher	Main Objectives & Instrument	Population	Key Findings of Study Related to Children's Reading Preferences
Coles, M. and Hall, C. (2002).	**Objective.** Examine the relationship between achievement in English and students' reading habits. **Phase 1 Instrument.** National Questionnaire (constructed to mirror 1971 Whitehead investigation.) **Phase 2 Method.** Semi-structured interviews with a 1% sample pool throughout the country. Data collected in 1994.	Students: 7,976. Grades: K–12. Primary Schools: 110; Secondary Schools: 59. Location: England.	A. **Amount of Reading: A1.** Over the last 20 years, reading has increased for boys and girls age 10 and for girls age 12. It has remained the same for boys age 12 and girls age 14. It has declined for boys age 14. **A2.** Boys read less than girls due to factors such as soccer, peer culture, and inclination toward physical activities. B. **Book Choices: B1.** In proportion to their total reading diets, girls read more adventure, horror/ghost, animal, and school-related stories. **B2.** The most significant difference is in girls' choice of romance/relationship books. **B3.** Boys read more science fiction, fantasy, sports, war, and spy stories. **B4.** Boys also read more comics, joke books, and humorous fiction. C. **Reader Types: C1.** Boys are more likely to be "hybrid" readers, choosing books from different categories. They are also likely to read more "adult fiction." **C2.** Girls are more likely to choose series books and children or teen fiction. **C3.** Girls read periodicals like boys. D. **Attitudes: D1.** Girls more than boys express positive attitudes toward reading. **D2.** Girls are more likely to see educational benefits of reading than boys. **D3.** Boys are more likely to think of reading as a leisure pursuit.

Citation	Objective / Instrument	Sample	Findings
Nippold, M., Duthie, J., and Larsen, J. (2004).	**Objective.** Investigate the views of young people toward reading as a leisure activity in relation to other options for their free time. **Instrument.** Written surveys completed by participants.	Students: 100 in grade 6; 100 in grade 9. Location: Western Oregon public schools from lower middle-income neighborhoods.	**A.** For all students combined, the most popular reading materials were magazines, novels, and comics. **B.** The least popular materials were plays, technical books and newspapers. **C.** Older students showed a stronger preference for magazines than younger students. **D.** Girls showed a stronger preference for poetry than boys. **E.** Boys were more likely to report than girls that they spent no time reading for pleasure. **F.** Interest in pleasure reading declined in sixth and ninth graders.
Sturm, B. (2003).	**Objective.** Explores the questions: a) what are children interested in when they enter the library?; and b) do children's interests vary by gender? **Instrument.** Written surveys completed by young library patrons during National Library Week. **Analysis.** 2,000 of the 150,000 survey cards were selected at random for analysis.	Young Library Patrons. Boys: 943; Girls: 1,057. Grades: pre-K–12. (Focus grades 1–8.) State library system of North Carolina. Young library patrons, who completed a library survey card for a contest prize from the Start Me Up! program were selected at random for the study.	Results are most pertinent to library patrons ages 7–13. For the top 4 categories: **A.** Most popular topic was Animals (approx. 34% of total). This preference peaked at age 7. **B.** Interest in science was evenly distributed between genders. This preference peaked at age 9. **C.** Sports were predominantly a male preference. **D.** Literature was predominantly a female preference. This preference remained fairly constant. **Overall**, youth showed little gender difference in preference. **E.** Most children requested literature by a specific author or series.
Ujiie, J. and Krashen, S. (1996).	**Objective.** Examine the extent to which comic book reading varies with social class, especially with consideration of differences in literacy development. **Instrument.** Written questionnaire: 1. How often do you read comics? 2. How often do you read for pleasure? 3. Do you like to read? 4. Do you read books?	Students: 571. **Sample I:** 302 Students. Chapter 1 school. 82% School Meal program. 28% Limited English Proficiency. **Sample II:** 269 Students. Middle class suburb school. 30% School Meal program. Approx. 4% Limited English Proficiency. Approx. 58% GATE. Location: 2 Middle Schools near Los Angeles, CA.	**A. Overall (both schools). A1.** About half of girls never before read comic books. **A2.** Boys were more involved in comic books. **A3.** For boys, higher frequency of comic book reading correlated with reading for pleasure, book reading, and liking to read. **B. Sample 1 (Chapter 1 school). B1.** Boys did not read as much in general nor did they enjoy reading as much as the middle class boys (Sample 2). **B2.** Chapter 1 comic book readers: a) read more than their peers; and b) read more than non-comic book readers from the middle class.

(Continued)

Researcher	Main Objectives & Instrument	Population	Key Findings of Study Related to Children's Reading Preferences
Worthy, J., Moorman, M., and Turner, M. (1999).	**Objective.** Study the reading preferences of middle school students and the reading materials available to them in their schools. **Instruments.** A. Reading Preferences and Access Survey with multiple-choice and open-ended questions. **B.** Reading Attitudes Survey. **C.** State Reading Competency tests. **D.** Interviews of teachers and librarians. **Analysis.** Top reading preferences were compared by gender, achievement, income level, and attitude.	Students: 356. Boys: 127. Girls: 229. Grade 6. Location: Three schools in an economically and ethnically diverse district in Texas. [12 Language Arts teachers' classes; 3 school librarians.]	**A. Overall. A1.** Students most preferred scary materials. **A2.** Students sought text by particular authors. **A3.** Students also highly preferred comics and cartoons, as well as magazines. **A4.** The following materials were also preferred: drawing books, books and magazines about cars and trucks, series books, funny books, and books about animals. **B. Gender. B1.** Boys ranked almanacs and books about cars and trucks higher than girls. **B2.** Girls ranked funny novels and series higher. **C. Achievement. C1.** The highest-achieving students ranked books for adults and funny novels higher. **C2.** The lowest achieving students ranked drawing books and books about cars and trucks higher than their counterparts. **D. Attitude. D1.** Students with the highest scores for recreational reading ranked picture books and books and magazines about cars and trucks higher. **D2.** Students with the lowest scores ranked funny books and series higher. **E. Socioeconomic. E1.** Students from low-income families ranked books about animals higher on their list of preferences. **F. Access. F1.** 56% of the students said they purchased their reading materials. **F2.** 44% reported that they borrowed materials from the school, classroom or public library. **F3.** The availability of the most popular reading materials at school is limited.

Discussion Questions

1. Summarize the research presented in the article related to students' reading interests and how they change over time.
2. If you were teaching eighth grade students in a social studies class, what are some books you could use that would be likely to match their interests? Identify at least five books and give a rationale for your choices, using information from the article as support.

Conclusion

Chapter Activities

Activity 3.1
Using the directions in this chapter, develop a systematic deletion cloze using a passage from a middle or secondary school textbook.

Activity 3.2
Use a textbook readability checklist to assess a textbook identified as being appropriate for students in one or more middle- or secondary-level grades.

Activity 3.3
Select one of the interest inventories listed in the "online resources" section of the chapter. Administer the inventory to a student in either middle or secondary school. Analyze the results. Write several paragraphs outlining the information you learned from the interest inventory and what implications it would have for the student's teacher. Identify at least three books that you would give to this student if he was in your class. Explain your choices using data from the interest inventory for support.

Online Resources

Interest Inventories

ALA Teen Reading Interest Survey
www.ala.org/yalsa/sites/ala.org.yalsa/.../Teen%20Reading%20Interest%20Survey.docx

Getting to Know My Students as Readers
https://www.scholastic.com/teachers/blog-posts/alycia-zimmerman/getting-know-my-students-readers/

Using Interest Inventories with Struggling or Unmotivated Readers
http://cw.routledge.com/textbooks/9780415802093/news-updates/Interest-Inventories.pdf

Interests and Reading Survey
https://readingapprenticeship.org/wp-content/uploads/2014/01/RFU-append-interests-survey2.pdf

Read–Write–Think Reading Survey
http://www.readwritethink.org/files/resources/lesson_images/lesson11/ReadingSurveyHandout.pdf

Close Reading and Study Skills

In middle and secondary schools, the majority of reading is done from an efferent stance, which means for the purpose of learning new information. This is in contrast to reading for an aesthetic stance, which is reading for enjoyment. Because of this focus, it is important to utilize instructional approaches that require students to use strategies for effectively learning new information from text.

Chapter Focus Questions

By the time you finish this chapter, you should be able to answer these questions:

1. What are some effective instructional strategies that model effective interaction with text?
2. How can these instructional strategies be used to help middle and secondary readers develop skills that will help them become independent readers?

Close Reading

Close reading is an instructional approach that has become increasingly popular due to its inclusion in the Common Core State Standards. It is a process through which students are guided through reading and rereading complex texts by the teacher, who focuses students' attention on particular aspects of the text. Some teachers refer to it as teaching the students to be "text detectives." The overall goal of close reading is to develop students who are independent readers who can effectively interact with texts on their own.

Close reading is just one type of classroom reading instruction and should be used along with guided reading, independent reading activities, and other literacy-related instruction for a well-balanced curriculum.

Process of Close Reading

The general outline of close reading usually involves four stages—pre-reading and three readings for different purposes. Not all texts will require all four stages; the teacher should decide how many readings are needed for the selected text.

During pre-reading activities, students are briefly introduced to the text, with the teacher giving only enough information to get the students into the text. It is important that the teacher not "give away" any information that the student should be able to figure out on his own while reading. These pre-reading activities are quite different from the usual pre-reading activities used by teachers to introduce text-based lessons. The introduction to the text should be very brief.

The first reading of the text focuses on what the text says—in other words, basic comprehension and understanding of the text.

The second reading of the text focuses on how the text works. At this point, the students will examine the choices made by the author, in terms of author's craft and text structure, and how those choices impact the message and the reader.

The third reading of the text focuses on what the text means. Students are encouraged to make text connections, including text-to-text, text-to-self, and text-to-world connections. "Text-to-text" connections are considered in the broadest sense of the word "text" to include paintings, movies, dances, photographs, multimedia, etc., not just "text" in the conventional sense of words on a page.

Planning for close reading requires advance preparation on the part of the teacher, who must read the text closely to identify any aspects of the text that might be unfamiliar to the students and to identify unfamiliar vocabulary or concepts.

Many close reading activities involve the students in *annotating* the text; in other words, they are asked to write on the text (or to use sticky notes if they cannot write directly on the copy of the text they are provided.) Some annotations students make may be related to keywords and phrases, confusing concepts, inferences, main ideas, text structure, etc. Students work cooperatively in pairs or small groups while making annotations.

Close Reading and Text Sets

As defined by Serafini (2013, p. 300), "Close reading entails the formulation of arguments and the presentation of evidence to support one's claims." One approach to encouraging close reading activities that require students to provide evidence of their conclusions is to use text *sets*. Text sets are simply collections of texts on the same topic. Students read closely each text, or segments of each text, and can then compare the facts and opinions presented in each one. Text sets can include both fiction and non-fiction works related to the topic of study. This approach encourages students to think critically and to realize that all information printed in a book is not necessarily a "fact."

Text Mapping

Text mapping, which was developed by David Middlebrook, is a process very similar to the annotation process used in close reading. In text mapping, the text is photocopied and made into a scroll so that the pages can be laid out next to each other. Because all the pages can be seen at one time, this allows students to see how the pages of the text relate to each other.

Literacy-Related Study Skills

There are a number of established *study skill routines* that should be taught to students in middle and secondary classrooms. These routines support students' reading by providing them with a framework that can be used to structure the students' interaction with information text. Some of the most well-known study skill routines include SQ34, SQ4R, PQRST, and Read Around the Text.

Each of the study skill routines should be explicitly taught to students, modeled and practiced with guidance before students are expected to utilize the routines independently. *Anchor charts* providing reminders to the students about the routines can be developed and displayed in the classroom, or teachers may create bookmarks with the same information that students can use while reading to remind them of the steps of the routine.

SQ3R

SQ3R is a study routine first introduced by Francis P. Robinson in 1946. During SQ3R, students are encouraged to interact with the text to be read in a specific manner. Each step in the process is named to help the students remember what should be done. The steps in the SQ3R routine are **S**urvey, **Q**uestion, **R**ead, **R**ecite, and **R**eview.

SQ4R

SQ4R is an adaptation of SQ3R. The steps for SQ4R are **S**urvey, **Q**uestion, **R**ead, **R**ecite, **R**eview, **R**eflect. Note that the fourth "R" is "reflect." This step was added to encourage students to relate the information learned in the text with their prior knowledge, and to try to make connections between the text and themselves, the world, and other texts.

PQRST

PQRST is a study routine that is very similar to SQ3R and SQ4R. The steps of PQRST are **P**review, **Q**uestion, **R**ead, **S**ummarize, **T**est.

Read Around the Text

Read Around the Text is a study routine that can be taught to students to help them learn to interact effectively with texts. As described by Goodman (2005), the strategy has six steps:

1. Look at the pictures. What ideas are being presented?
2. Look at the captions and read them.
3. Look at the maps, charts, and graphs. Discuss what information they presented.
4. Look at the titles and headings. What is the big idea?
5. Read the first and last lines of each paragraph for more information.
6. Ask questions. Give yourself a reason to read.

Fostering Authentic Inquiry and Investigation through Middle Grade Mystery and Suspense Novels

Yolanda Hood and Vicky Zygouris-Coe

In this article, Hood and Zygouris-Coe outline an approach using mystery and thriller trade books to teach students the inquiry cycle. They also use these books to provide motivation and to support the development of rich discourse based on open-ended questions.

LEARNING OBJECTIVES

1. Asking good questions is critical for establishing an interesting and rich discussion about text. How do open-ended questions assist in supporting these deep discussions?
2. What is "inquiry" and how does it relate to literacy?

Fostering Authentic Inquiry and Investigation through Middle Grade Mystery and Suspense Novels

Yolanda Hood and Vicky Zygouris-Coe

Introduction

According to the Common Core State Standards (Council of Chief State School Officers & National Governors' Association [CCSSO & NGA], 2010), college and career readiness also requires research and media skills that should be embedded throughout the standards.

Middle level students are expected to learn and be able to locate, read, comprehend, evaluate, synthesize, and report on information, conduct research to answer a variety of questions and solve problems, and analyze and create print and nonprint texts in conventional and emerging media forms. Young Adult (YA) literature is the perfect way to engage middle level students while covering these standards. According to Joyce Stallworth, "Today's young adult literature is sophisticated, complex, and powerful. It deserves to be part of the literary tradition in middle and high schools" (2006, p. 59). Teachers can easily meet learning goals because every literary element that is found in the literary canon is witnessed in quality young adult literature. Furthermore, teachers who use YA literature can meet their learning goals while providing "middle level students with opportunities to see their potential through characters that speak to them as teenagers" (Perry & Stallworth, 2013, p. 17).

Our Situated Context

In this article, we, a department head of curriculum materials center libraries and a reading education professor at a Southeastern university, wish to encourage the use of the mystery and suspense genre in YA literature as a tool for fostering authentic inquiry and investigation in grades 6 through 8. Mystery and suspense is a genre of natural inquiry. Questions have to be answered and research undertaken in order to solve the mystery. Often, the reader can engage right along with the protagonist as he or she attempts to solve the mystery.

There are numerous mystery and suspense titles available for grades 6 to 8 that engage readers in a complex mystery, raise open-ended questions, are relevant to readers' lives, are pleasurable to read, promote research and investigation about the problem, and result in rich discussions. When searching for these titles for the classroom, a school librarian is an excellent resource. Other resources, the ones that we consulted, are Booklist's recommended crime books and the Edgar Awards (for best mystery/suspense fiction) Youth and Young Adult nominees and winners.

The titles that we read are psychological thrillers, and some are genre blends of mystery/suspense with supernatural, steampunk, and science fiction elements. We intentionally chose titles that had been published within the past five years in order to offer teachers and middle level students an opportunity to try newer YA works. For the purposes of this article, we chose to present our thoughts (Lave & Wenger, 1991) on how teachers can use one of the YA books, *Under the Egg*, to develop and promote authentic inquiry and investigation. We conclude by presenting teachers with a very brief summary of the remaining YA books we examined on this topic (see Figure 4.1.1).

Under the Egg

"Sorry, Theo, it's bigger than the both of us now," perfectly sums up Laura Marx Fitzgerald's middle grade mystery, *Under the Egg* (2014, p. 198). This beautifully written book involves readers in carefully reading historical details, piecing the puzzle together, and tracking down clues from modern New York City to World War II (WWII) and back. Teachers can use the book as a class novel, as a class read-aloud, or in literature circles (and for independent reading purposes). The characters are real and engaging, and chapters are relatively short with action moving fairly quickly. But, what makes it the perfectly blended middle grade novel is the fact that the plot is full of historical and artistic curiosities that naturally generate solid questions that beg for young sleuths to dig in and further investigate.

Theodora (Theo) Tenpenny is introduced to the readers in a most tragic way. Coming home from a scavenging trip, she finds her grandfather, Jack Tenpenny, surrounded by emergency services and neighbors in the road just minutes before he dies. Theo's grandfather uses those last minutes to summon strength and encourage his granddaughter to look under the egg where she will find both a letter and a treasure. The egg refers to one of Jack's paintings that hangs over the mantel: the painting that Theo accidently spills rubbing alcohol over. But, it is a lucky accident, indeed, as the rubbing alcohol removes the top layer of paint to reveal another painting underneath. The new painting resembles the work of Renaissance artist Raphael. If it is a Raphael, the work could potentially save Theo and her mother from financial ruin. But, how is one to know this for certain? Theo and her new friend Bodhi must embark on an investigation to uncover the mystery behind the painting. From the very beginning of the novel, *Under the Egg* lends itself to authentic inquiry: Why would someone paint over another painting?

Especially important about *Under the Egg* is that the protagonists model authentic inquiry and rich research. Theo and Bodhi begin with a Google search to gain an understanding of practices and procedures for restoring and dating artwork as well as determining the value of a piece of artwork. The girls realize, however, that research and the knowledge attained from it do not happen within a vacuum. They visit the library and befriend Eddie, the newly minted hipster librarian, who finds books to provide some historical and biographical context to their mystery and also introduces them to government websites that provide veterans affairs information. The information they access through this last research effort actually provides them with an important lead in eventually finding out about the rightful owner of the painting. The girls also reach out to experts in the field, seeking help from a community minister to translate Latin when their language translation phone app fails to provide a clear understanding of text on the painting and interviewing a WWII veteran in a nursing home to garner further information about Jack and his time in the war. As the girls continue to gather information, they realize that they have to make sense of all of the information they have gathered through their research efforts. And so they embark on a process of "mining" the information, critically thinking about it, and making inferences using evidence from "data." They analyze the information to determine what is helpful and what is not. They talk through the process and listen to each other's thoughts and perspectives. They think about the clues, ask questions, and seek more information until they find pieces to the puzzle that actually fit. In this novel, all types of research are utilized, with no one type being privileged over another. The girls use Google searches and phone apps to help them in their quest for meaning, and they are also introduced to a host of survivor archives (i.e., primary documents) through the Center for Jewish History.

Under the Egg even models for readers that our research sometimes seems dead in the water. Early on, when the girls are told that their painting is not a Raphael and not of the Renaissance period, the girls question the reasons why it may not be; in doing so, they emulate researchers' habits of mind as they ask the question, "Why would you create a fake Old Master by painting over an old canvas, and then paint over it again?" (p. 72). Furthermore, this book teaches middle level students that there are multiple perspectives on phenomena, events, or evidence, that it is important to look at all perspectives as they seek answers to specific questions, and that it is important to look for the bigger picture.

This novel fits into English language arts, social studies/history, and art class curricula and can easily be paired with any number of nonfiction works about the Renaissance, the Jewish Holocaust, and World War II. Finally, *Under the Egg* also lends itself to inquiry, open-ended, and essential questions that have no single or correct answer so that middle level students have many opportunities to actively embrace the research process. Inquiry questions facilitate mining of the text and promote understanding (Fisher, Frey, & Lapp, 2015; McTighe & Wiggins, 2013). Teachers can team teach with school librarians and explore many of the kinds of research and resources that Theo and Bodhi use in the novel. Teachers can also consider (virtual or physical) field trips to museums and archives, not to mention inviting experts into the classroom to offer related information on the historical and other events and questions that arise in *Under the Egg*. (See Table 4.1.1 for further inquiry questions, resources, and suggestions.)

TABLE 4.1.1 *Under the Egg:* Teacher Suggestions and Resources for Promoting Authentic Student Inquiry and Extended Learning

Essential Question: *Does famous or recovered artwork belong to the public (in a museum) or to the private collector?*

Inquiry Questions

- What was the Renaissance and why was it so important historically and artistically?
- What is iconography and how does it apply to Renaissance art?
- Who is Raphael and why is he important?
- What other artists influenced Raphael's art?
- What do World War II and great art have to do with each other?
- Who are the Monument Men?
- What are the Geneva Conventions?
- Is there still unrecovered art from World War II?
- Is art from World War II in museums or in the hands of private collectors?
- Is there art that was inspired from the World War II period of horror and tragedy?
- Is it easy to steal a great or classic work of art? Is there evidence about great art heists?

Additional Resources

Human Resources	Online Resources	Media Resources
• Invite a historian to class to discuss art that is stolen and then recovered.	• Library of Congress http://www.loc.gov/ for primary documents on World War II, Jewish history; The Smithsonian for photos and images on the Monuments Men. http://www.smithsonianmag.com/history/true-story-monuments-men-180949569/?no-ist • Learn about the Holocaust http://www.ushmm.org/learn • Learn about World War II through images http://www.loc.gov/today/cyberlc/feature_wdesc.php?rec=4613	• The Monuments Men http://www.monuments-men.com/
• Chat via Internet with museum curators about art and to whom it belongs.	• Archives of American Art & The Monuments Men http://www.aaa.si.edu/exhibitions/monuments-men.	• *Herb & Dorothy* http:// www.pbs.org/independentlens/herb-and-dorothy/and/or http://herbanddorothy.com/
• Invite an artist to talk about art collectors, either in person or via Internet chat	• United States Holocaust Memorial Museum—see Looted Art section http://www.ushmm.org/research/research-in-collections/search-the-collections/bibliography/looted-art.	• *The Rape of Europa* http://www.pbs.org/therapeofeuropa/

General Resources

- About Laura Marx Fitzgerald, author of *Under the Egg*
- http://www.lauramarxfitzgerald.com/#!books/cnec
- Interview with the Laura Marx Fitzgerald, author of *Under the Egg* https://fearlessfifteeners. wordpress.com/2014/03/18/all-four-kids-an-interview-with-laura-marx-fitzgerald-author-of-under-the-egg/
- Learn about the Renaissance http://www.learner.org/interactives/renaissance/
- Who was Raphael? http://www.nationalgallery.org.uk/artists/raphael
- View Raphael's work at the National Academy of Art http://www.nga.gov/content/ngaweb/features/slideshows/raphael.html#slide_1
- Learn about the Geneva Conventions http://www.pbs.org/wgbh/amex/honor/filmmore/ps_geneva.html
- Famous art heists http://www.pbs.org/independentlens/stolen/famousheists.html

Other

- Current art debate: Who owns the Elgin Marbles? Greece or Great Britain? http://www.nytimes.com/2015/05/15/world/europe/greece-british-museum-elgin-marbles.html?_r=0

Gleason, Colleen. (2013). *The Clockwork Scarab: A Stoker and Holmes Novel.* **San Francisco, CA: Chronicle Books.**

Bram Stoker's sister and Sherlock Holmes's niece put aside their differences to solve the disappearance of two society girls and ponder how the young man from the future has arrived in their world.

Johnson, Maureen. (2011). *The Name of the Star.* **New York, NY: G.P. Putnam's Sons.**

American high school student, Rory, is attending her senior year of high school at a British boarding school when a Jack the Ripper copycat murderer begins unleashing his terror on London. For mature readers.

Klise, James. (2014). *The Art of Secrets.* **Chapel Hill, NC: Algonquin Books.**

Saba Khan's apartment has burned to the ground in a fire that has been ruled arson. The students at Saba's school come together to raise funds so that Saba's family can get back on their feet, and a work by outsider artist, Henry Darger, might help do that.

Sanderson, Brandon. (2013). *The Rithmatist.* **Illus. Ben McSweeney. New York, NY: Tor.**

In this alternate history Joel attends Armedius Academy, one of the most prestigious Rithmatist training sites in the United Isles. Here, Joel helps to solve the mystery of the disappearance of young Rithmatists from the school.

Watson, Jude. (2014). *Loot: How to Steal a Fortune.* **New York, NY: Scholastic Press.**

The McQuinn twins discover each other and learn of a mysterious curse that could threaten their lives all on the same night.

FIGURE 4.1.1   Other YA novels used for our study.

As Steven Wolk states, "No longer is the curriculum simply the novel or the facts to be learned but, rather, the middle level students and their teacher together using books, other authentic resources, and their own opinions and experiences. ..." (2009, p. 666). *Under the Egg* is a wonderful way to explore the ethical complexities of war and the spoils of war, how museums have built their amazing collections over the centuries, and what constitutes ownership of great works of art. There are no simple or "right" answers to these questions, but the authentic research and types and amount of critical thinking that middle level students will undertake as they discuss and formulate their answers could generate a love for, and an understanding of, inquiry and investigation. The possibilities are both tangible and endless. It is our hope that teachers will embrace the untapped potential of quality YA literature for developing middle level students' content, literacy, and research knowledge and skills.

References

Council of Chief State School Officers & National Governors' Association (CCSSO & NGA). (2010). *Common core state standards for English language arts & literacy in history/social studies, science, and technical subjects*. Washington, DC: Author.

Fisher, D., Frey, N., & Lapp, D. (2015). Learning cycles that deepen students' interaction with text. *Voices from the Middle, 22*(4), 15–19.

Lave, J., & Wenger, E. (1991). *Situated learning: Legitimate peripheral participation*. Cambridge, UK: Cambridge University Press.

McTighe, J., & Wiggins, G. (2013). *Essential questions: Opening doors to student understanding*. Alexandria, VA: ASCD.

Perry, T. B., & Stallworth, J. (2013). 21st century students demand a balanced, more inclusive canon. *Voices from the Middle, 21*(1), 15–18.

Stallworth, B. J. (2006). The relevance of young adult literature. *Educational Leadership, 63*(7), 59–63.

Wolk, S. (2009). Reading for a better world: Teaching for social responsibility with young adult literature. *Journal of Adolescent & Adult Literacy, 52*(8), 664–673.

Young Adult Literature Cited

Fitzgerald, L. M. (2013). *Under the egg*. New York, NY: Dial.

Gleason, C. (2013). *The clockwork scarab: A Stoker and Holmes novel*. San Francisco, CA: Chronicle Books.

Johnson, M. (2011). *The name of the star*. New York, NY: G.P. Putnam's Sons.

Klise, James. (2014). *The art of secrets*. Chapel Hill, NC: Algonquin Books.

Sanderson, B. (2013). *The Rithmatist*. New York, NY: Tor.

Watson, J. (2014). *Loot: How to steal a fortune*. New York, NY: Scholastic.

Discussion Questions

1. Using the steps outlined in the article, create a graphic organizer that could be used to explain the inquiry cycle to middle school students.
2. What is the role of the "essential questions" in the inquiry process?
3. How does the inquiry approach foster the development of critical thinking and critical literacy skills?

Learning Cycles That Deepen Students' Interactions with Text

Douglas Fisher, Nancy Frey, and Diane Lapp

F isher, Frey, and Lapp describe the use of a learning cycle that encourages students to interact at a deep level with text. As you read this article, think about how this approach relates to close reading.

LEARNING OBJECTIVES

1. What are text-dependent questions? What challenges do students face in responding to text-dependent questions?
2. Why is it important to encourage students to provide evidence for their responses to questions about text? How does this help prepare them to learn independently from texts?

Learning Cycles That Deepen Students' Interactions with Text

Douglas Fisher, Nancy Frey, and Diane Lapp

Adults in the school system understand the need to deepen students' interactions with text.

In fact, it's pretty obvious why they do. As individuals who are successful in their daily lives, they have developed sophisticated ways for interacting with text that ensure they understand what they've read. Those deep interactions with text occur in the workplace and in higher education.

For example, Angul, a food services manager at SeaWorld, has to read a wide variety of documents in a given day, from employment applications to invoices, as well as guest compliments and complaints and memos regarding park operations. We asked her to collect the texts she read on a given day so that we could determine their complexity. We discovered that this job, obtained soon after Angul graduated from high school, required that she regularly read texts at the postsecondary level.

But did Angul know in middle school that would be a job requirement? And would telling her in middle school that she would someday have to read diverse, complex texts at work have made a difference in terms of her interest in reading such texts before she was expected to do so? We think not. And that's a problem. In many conversations about deepening students' interactions with texts, there is a lack of relevance. Teachers know why students should read a text deeply, but students often don't. If a close analytic reading is going to work, teachers must ensure that students are inspired by the texts they read. And by inspired, we don't necessarily mean that they have a visceral reaction and want to save a whale, even though sometimes texts do elicit strong responses from readers.

Thankfully, there are things that teachers can do to inspire their readers. And part of that inspiration comes from really understanding what the text says. We have

Another **compelling question.**
Investigate ...
Read multiple complex **texts** and
discuss ideas with others in order
to
identify **evidence,**
take a **stance,**
convey an **experience,**
craft an **argument.**
Inspire us to
present, debate, write.

Present, debate, write.
Inspire us to
craft an **argument,**
convey an **experience,**
take a **stance,**
identify **evidence.**
Discuss ideas with others in order
to
Read multiple complex **texts** and
Investigate ...
another **compelling question.**

FIGURE 4.2.1   Reversible Poem about Complex Texts.

summarized our ideas for inspiring readers in a reversible poem. Take a minute to read the text in Figure 4.2.1. Reversible poems present the same words forward and backward, but the meaning changes slightly when the text is read in the reverse order. It's kind of like coming full circle to develop understanding.

Compelling questions should not give away the ideas within a text.

So what does truly understanding the text mean for teachers? We see this as a cycle that begins with a compelling question and then involves reading and writing, with a chance for students to use the information they have learned to share with others, which in turn invites them to ask more questions, once again facilitating additional reading, learning, discussing, and identifying still more new questions. But to be even more practical, we'll explore each of those phases in greater depth.

Compelling Questions

As McTighe and Wiggins (2013) note, essential questions are motivating. Students are invited into a text by the right question because they want to know the answer to the question. They learn that both literary and informational texts have answers to the big questions in life. They also learn that the answers may surprise them, and further that authors, characters, and contexts shape the answers. Although teachers can create the questions, we have found it very useful for students to brainstorm a list of questions and then to have them vote, as a class, on the questions they want to address.

For example, the following questions are among others selected by middle school students over the past few years:

- What is your superpower?
- How do the choices we make affect the world around us?
- Do we change the world or does the world change us?
- Is social media really social?

It's important to note that these compelling questions should not give away the ideas within a text, but rather the question should inspire students to read widely to determine what they think about the question.

Close Reading

The next step is to teach students to read complex texts closely. A great deal has been written of late about the procedures for close reading, such as annotating a text and rereading it to deepen understanding (e.g., Boyles, 2013). Both of those steps are appropriate habits that students must develop as they learn to read closely. But even applied in tandem, they are insufficient to ensure that students understand complex texts deeply.

One key to deepening students' understanding of texts during close reading involves the questions that teachers ask. The questions ultimately take students on a journey, from the literal level to the structural level to the inferential level. We have organized this journey as three overarching questions (Fisher, Frey, Anderson, & Thayre, 2014):

- What does the text say?
- How does the text work?
- What does the text mean?

Figure 4.2.2 is a list of sample text-dependent questions that align with each phase of deepening students' interaction (and, by extension, their understanding of the text). The questions are not simply context for checking student understanding but also serve as primary scaffolding for students in terms of understanding the text. Readers start with a literal understanding of the text. As they reread, discuss, and think about the text, they develop a richer understanding of the text's structure. Following that, they begin to make logical inferences and deepen their understanding even further. In other words, text-dependent questions play a critical role in students' understanding, as do the discussions students have with their peers.

Collaborative Conversations

Simply stated, learning is a social endeavor. To really deepen students' interactions with texts, they must talk about those texts. They must stake a claim and provide evidence for their ideas. They must follow the rules of discussion, remain on topic long enough to interrogate their ideas, and ask questions of one

Text-dependent questions play a critical role in students' understanding, as do the discussions students have with their peers.

Phase	Content components	Sample questions
1) What does the text say?	• General understanding • Key details	• Why does Anne have a diary in the first place? • What kind of "early life" did Anne have? • Describe Anne's family and social circle. • What restrictions were placed on Jews? • Explain Anne's feelings about school. What evidence supports your opinion?
2) How does the text work?	• Vocabulary • Text structure • Author's craft	• What does the saying "paper is more patient than man" mean? How is this relevant to Anne beginning her diary? • How does Anne's style in writing about the restrictions placed on Jews affect the tone of this entry? • Describe the passage of time in this entry. • Describe the tone of this entry. • How does Anne share that the situation in Holland is progressively getting worse?
3) What does the text mean?	• Inferences • Opinions and arguments • Intertextual connections	• What is the purpose of this entry from Anne? What is she attempting to get across to her diary, Kitty? • Describe whether Anne is able to connect with other people she knows. What leads you to think this? • Explain what was happening in Germany during 1933 that would motivate the Frank family to flee to Holland.

Source: Fisher, D., Frey, N., Anderson, H., & Thayre, M. (2014). *Text-dependent questions, Grades 6–12: Pathways to close and critical reading.* Thousand Oaks, CA: Corwin. Used with permission.

FIGURE 4.2.2   Sample Text-Dependent Questions.

another. Of course, each of those behaviors must be taught. Students require a lot of practice if they are to engage in the types of collaborative conversations that will guide their understanding. We have found it particularly useful to provide them with sample sentence frames that they can use to guide them as they discuss complex texts with their peers.

Unlike some implementation efforts, the sentence frames that we recommend are aligned with the cognitive moves of argumentation. There are different frames for making a claim and supporting a claim, for example. Figure 4.2.3 highlights a sample list of sentence frames that are useful in guiding students' collaborative conversations. The goal is to use those frames to move students' conversations beyond the sentence level. By modeling conversations for and with them, students realize that language exchanges grow through interactions that involve the

Making a claim	I observed_____when_____.
	I compared_____and_____.
	I noticed_____when_____.
	The effect of_____on_____is_____.
Providing evidence	The evidence I use to support_____is_____.
	I believe_____(statement) because_____ (justification).
	I know that_____is_____because_____.
	Based on_____, I think_____.
	Based upon_____, my hypothesis is_____.
Asking for evidence	I have a question about_____.
	Does_____have more_____?
	What causes_____to_____?
	Can you show me where you found the information about_____?
Offering a counterclaim	I disagree_____because_____.
	The reason I believe_____is_____.
	The facts that support my idea are_____.
	In my opinion_____.
	One difference between my idea and yours is_____.
Inviting speculation	I wonder what would happen if_____.
	I have a question about_____.
	Let's find out how we can test these samples for_____.
	We want to test_____to find out if_____.
	If I change_____(variable in experiment), then I think _____will happen, because_____.
	I wonder why_____?
	What caused_____?
	How would this be different if_____?
	What do you think will happen if_____/ next?
Reaching consensus	I agree_____because_____.
	How would this be different if_____?
	We all have the same idea about_____.

Source: Ross, D., Fisher, D., & Frey, N. (2009). The art of argumentation. *Science and Children, 47*(3), 28–31.

FIGURE 4.2.3   Language Frames for Argumentation.

creation of sentences connecting several of the sections shown in Figure 4.2.3. It's important to remind students to be as intent on listening as they are on speaking.

Being Inspired

None of us, much less our middle school students, read texts closely only so that we can say we read texts closely. We read closely and want to deepen our interactions with texts when there is something important and worthwhile to do after the reading. And that is the answer to the question: Why should students care about deepening interactions with text? Because they are inspired. They are inspired to engage in research and investigation. They are inspired to present or debate. They are inspired to continue discussing a text, perhaps even with a Socratic Seminar. And they are inspired to write about the text.

Consider an Anne Frank diary entry, since most middle schoolers read this text. What might students be inspired to do, if they really did understand the text deeply? Some might want to write in response; others might want to engage in research; and still others might want to debate or discuss the situation. In other words, the students would care about their deepened understanding of the text. They would realize that the processes we've used, from the compelling question to the close reading to the collaborative conversations, are valuable. As Jeff Wilhelm would say, reading the text would be in service of something much more important.

And, having been inspired by the texts, students would want to read more, read better, and ask new questions. Thus the cycle begins again and middle school English becomes a forum for inquiry and investigation. And that would serve students well. We end by encouraging you to select texts that both inspire and challenge your students, and of course involve them in this process. Doing so creates a cycle of entwined competency and engagement that results in students becoming more proficient readers who keep on reading.

References

Boyles, N. (2013). Closing in on close reading. *Educational Leadership, 70*(4), 36–41.

Fisher, D., Frey, N., Anderson, A., & Thayre, M. (2014). *Text-dependent questions, Grades 6–12: Pathways to close and critical reading.* Thousand Oaks, CA: Corwin.

McTighe, J., & Wiggins, G. (2013). *Essential questions: Opening doors to student understanding.* Alexandria, VA: ASCD.

Ross, D., Fisher, D., & Frey, N. (2009). The art of argumentation. *Science and Children, 47*(3), 28–31.

Discussion Questions

1. What are the three "over-arching questions" that Fisher, Frey, and Lapp have identified for close reading activities?
2. Why is collaborative conversation an important part of reading comprehension for middle and secondary readers? How can you foster these rich conversations in your classroom?

Conclusion

Chapter Activities

Activity 4.1

Select a mystery or thriller book appropriate for middle or high school students. If you have not already done so, read the book. Give the complete citation for the text.

Using Table 4.1.1 in the Hood and Zygouris-Coe article as a guide, create a chart that could be used to guide your utilization of this book to promote authentic student inquiry.

Activity 4.2

Using the text you used for Activity 4.1, write two compelling questions, like those mentioned in the Fisher, Frey, and Lapp article, that could be asked to students who are reading this text.

Activity 4.3

Explore the text-mapping website listed in the Online Resources section of this chapter. Click on "overview" in the site navigation box. Select a chapter from a middle or high school textbook and create a scroll for that chapter, following the directions on the website. Think about how you would have students mark that scroll in order to help them better comprehend the text, then mark the scroll as if you were a student.

Activity 4.4

Choose one of the study skill routines mentioned in this chapter. Locate a recent research article that provides evidence regarding the use of this routine for improving students' learning from text. Give the complete citation for the article. Write a brief summary providing an overview of the findings of the research.

Online Resources

The Textmapping Project
http://www.textmapping.org/index.html

References

Goodman, A. 2005. "The Middle School High Five: Strategies Can Triumph." *Voices from the Middle* 13(2): 12–19.

Serafini, F. 2013. "Close Readings and Children's Literature." *The Reading Teacher* 67(4): 299–301.

CHAPTER 5

Vocabulary Development

A person's *vocabulary* consists of the words they know and use in their writing, listening, speaking, and reading. Research has consistently shown that vocabulary knowledge is one of the most important factors in reading comprehension.

Chapter Focus Questions

Read through these questions before you begin reading the chapter:

1. Name the four vocabularies and suggest one way that you can support students' adding words to that vocabulary.
2. What are some criteria to consider when you are selecting vocabulary to teach students?
3. What are some instructional strategies that support students' vocabulary development?

Multiple Vocabularies

Although we often speak of a person's "vocabulary" as if it was one thing, people actually have four different vocabularies! We have two *receptive vocabularies*—listening and reading—as well as two *expressive vocabularies*—speaking and writing. One of the challenges of vocabulary instruction is that a word may be in one, two, three, or all four vocabularies.

For a person to really "know" a word—to be able to understand it when it is heard or read, and to use it when speaking or writing—a word must be present in all four vocabularies. Words knowledge must have both depth and breadth. Students need to have extensive knowledge of word meanings (depth) as well as an understanding of how words are connected to other similar words (breadth).

Background Knowledge and the Magazine Reading Students Choose

Rachael Gabriel, Richard Allington, and Monica Billen

I f middle school students are given the opportunity to select magazines of interest to them, how will their choices match with their reading levels and prior knowledge? What role does specific vocabulary play in these choices? Gabriel, Allington, and Billen answer these questions in the following article.

LEARNING OBJECTIVES

1. Think about magazines that you read when you were in middle school and high school. How did your prior knowledge play a role in assisting your comprehension of these texts?
2. How might magazines be used to increase students' vocabulary and improve their reading comprehension?

Background Knowledge and the Magazine Reading Students Choose

Rachael Gabriel, Richard Allington, and Monica Billen

Teachers and researchers have long been aware of the role of background knowledge in facilitating the meaning-making processes of comprehension. In our study of middle school students' magazine reading habits we were surprised to find that students, at least implicitly, know it, too.

The importance of background knowledge is reflected in the texts students choose to read on their own, their decisions about initiating leisure reading, and the ways in which they use what they've read in conversations and their social lives. In this article, we describe the findings of our longitudinal study of middle school students' magazine-reading habits (Gabriel & Allington, 2009, 2010) as they relate to a question we often asked ourselves as teachers: Can students read difficult but self-selected texts—and if so, how? We begin by describing what we learned about background knowledge and specific vocabulary from our interviews and observations of students reading magazines, and then discuss implications for instruction that facilitates connections between students' in- and out-of-school literacies.

The Reading They Choose

Great consensus exists in the fields of reading and magazine marketing about the primacy of magazine reading as a leisure activity among young adolescents. Magazines are among the top ten items young adolescents will purchase with their own money (Magazine Publishers of America, 2004), they are the source of text that young adolescents are most likely to read in their leisure time (Hughes-Hassell & Rodge, 2007), and even middle school students who claim not to read in their free time do report reading magazines (Gabriel & Allington, 2009, 2010; Carnell, 2005; Hall & Coles, 1999, 2001). Further, research converges on the theme that students make rather predictable magazine choices, with topic preferences falling neatly along gender lines and special interests. That is, girls tend to choose fashion and lifestyle magazines, with the occasional hobby or sport-related title; boys tend to choose sports and electronics magazines, with the occasional hobby-related title (Hughes-Hassell & Rodge, 2007). This pattern held true in our study and suggests that the choice of what to read has some embedded social implications and is centered around topics students already know and talk about.

To begin our study, we invited 200 sixth-grade students across two rural districts in the Southeastern part of the US to participate in a study of magazine reading habits over a two-year period. The districts serve a student body of approximately 7,300 students. In the first, the student population is 93% white and 53% economically disadvantaged; in the second, it is 94% white with 61% economically disadvantaged. We asked all students to fill out surveys about their magazine reading habits and motivation to read, and we administered a brief reading comprehension measure (the Test of Silent Contextual Reading Fluency), which we compared with their state test scores in reading.

We then randomly selected 100 students (half of the participants) to receive two magazines of their choice for free over the next two years. Though students had over 30 magazines to choose from, eight choices emerged as clear favorites, with more than half of the students choosing at least one of the top eight (see Table 5.1.1). We used a variety of readability and leveling systems to estimate the average difficulty of individual passages within each magazine and were surprised

TABLE 5.1.1   Eight Most Popular Magazines with Estimated Levels

Magazine title	Number of times selected	Topic	Estimated range of grade-level equivalents*	Students who chose this title but read below its range of levels
Twist	19	Lifestyle	2nd–7th grade	0/19
Tiger Beat	12	Lifestyle	2nd–7th grade	0/12
North American Whitetail	11	Hunting	5th–12th grade	8/11
GamePro	14	Video games	6th–12th grade	10/14
PC Gamer	10	Computer games	6th–12th grade	5/10
Dirt Rider	8	Outdoor sports	5th–12th grade	4/8
J-14	15	Lifestyle	2nd–11th grade	0/15
Seventeen	8	Lifestyle	3rd–11th grade	0/8

*Given that no readability or leveling system is specifically designed for use with magazine texts, levels were calculated using the lowest and highest levels generated by either of two readability formulas and one qualitative leveling rubric in order to present the widest possible range.

to find that students consistently chose magazines that, according to multiple measures of text difficulty, were above their reading level.

In order to investigate whether and how students read and understood the difficult texts they chose, we carried out in-depth interviews with 30 of the students at the six-month, one-year, and two-year anniversaries of their free subscriptions. Fifteen boys and 15 girls made up a convenience sample from the group of students who chose at least one of the eight most popular magazines. We asked students to tell us which sections they tended to read as well as when, where, and why they read their magazines. We then asked them to turn to a page of a recent issue they had not yet seen but would normally read, and then read us a section of about 100 words. While we listened, we took a modified version of a Running Record assessment by calculating fluency, recording miscues, and asking students to retell what they read at the end of the passage.

The first thing we noticed when we asked students to choose the passage they read to us was that students chose what to read by looking for passages that have to do with something they already know. On our previous paper-and-pencil surveys, students overwhelmingly responded that they had a favorite section of each magazine (e.g., advice, reviews, letters, back cover) that they routinely flipped to and read. When interviewed in person, however, most students reported and demonstrated simply browsing for whatever was "interesting," "caught my interest," or "looked good."

When we probed a bit further, we found a strong pattern in students' rationale for which passages looked good or seemed interesting: they picked something that built on or related to something they already knew. For example, out of a page of reviews for different video games, students will read the review of the game they own or have experience with—explaining that things that are familiar "catch my eye." Given a choice among several interviews with celebrities within a few pages of each other, students read the interview with the celebrity they are most familiar with. Though it may be that familiarity brings a level of comfort when reading aloud in front of adults, it also seems to be grounds for initiating reading (especially when flipping pages) and a highly reliable strategy for identifying texts students can read independently.

Specific Vocabulary and Student Success

Out of the 30 students, only 2 selected passages that our running record indicated were on their frustration levels. Other students were able to find a passage on their independent or instructional level on their first attempt. Each of the 28 students who could read their magazines with accuracy provided retells that were sufficient to convince us of their ability to recall and understand the text, despite its relative difficulty. This was surprising to us given the difficulty of many of the magazines they chose. For example, we estimated that the average level of passages in *GamePro* would be accessible to 6th–12th-grade readers with lexiles ranging from 960–1480, Fry Readability scores from 7th–12th grade, and qualitative leveling rubric estimates of 7th–10th grade (Chall, Bissex, Conrad, & Harris-Sharples, 1999). Though 14 students selected *GamePro,* only 4 read at or above a 6th-grade level when they made their selection as 6th graders. Still, during our interviews, students easily conquered words representing the technical vocabulary of computer games as well as brand and character names.

Lifestyle magazines that were popular with female students presented a wider range of text difficulty, with passages ranging from elementary to high school levels. Still, students consistently chose texts of at least 100 words that they could read quickly and with accuracy during our Running Record protocol. They similarly provided thorough retells, often adding their opinions and making connections to other things they knew about the celebrities and the fashion trends they read about. Young hunters (mostly boys) who had selected *North American Whitetail* as one of their magazine choices also explained the terms and tools of their interest area as we engaged them in discussions about the difficult passages they read and retold. Words unfamiliar to us and difficult in terms of length, spelling, multiple meanings, and levels of abstraction were easy for these students, who regularly found themselves steeped in conversations using such words.

Using the Texts They Choose

It was clear to us that students were successful with these challenging texts precisely because they had the relevant background knowledge, specific vocabulary, and motivation to engage with texts that described things they know and care about. This finding—that students will choose to conquer and enjoy texts that are challenging by any measure (sentence length, complexity, frequency of unfamiliar words, assumed background knowledge, etc.) when they have the background knowledge, vocabulary, and interest—has several implications for teachers working to address reading and writing standards, especially those included in the Common Core. Here, we give examples using Common Core anchor standards for Reading and Language in grades 6–12.

First, given that magazines provide a bank of texts in a variety of formats (advertisements, interviews, features, profiles, reviews) and on a variety of levels, magazine excerpts may effectively be used either to introduce or practice standards related to informational or literary texts. For example, a teacher may demonstrate Reading Anchor strand one ("Read closely to determine what the text says explicitly and to make logical inferences from it") using an interview from *Twist* to introduce new material in a familiar, high-success text. Students may then be asked to extend what they have learned about making inferences to a set of authentic texts, including grade-level academic texts. Or, if students struggle with Reading Anchor strand four ("Interpret words and phrases as they are used in a text, including determining technical, connotative, and figurative meanings, and analyze how specific word choices shape meaning or tone") after an initial lesson, it could be reintroduced in the context of a nonacademic text (magazine) in order to provide support for students who had struggled with text difficulty or engagement in the first lesson.

Alternatively, a teacher may demonstrate a new standard using a grade-level academic text, and then provide a variety of magazines with which to practice independently or in groups. Providing a variety of texts for practice allows students the opportunity to choose what they read—a practice that is consistently associated with higher comprehension and motivation (Guthrie & Humenick, 2004). Rather than assigning boys to a certain text and girls to another, thereby reinforcing a gender binary and assuming the interests of individuals, teachers could provide several text options and allow students to group themselves around them. Since magazines offer a bank of texts on a variety of levels, students are more likely to find something they can and want to read in a magazine they choose than in a book or basal reader.

Text options can be drawn from a combination of magazines, high-interest books, local news sources, and online magazines or related sites that represent students' out-of-school interests. Though magazines are not often found in classroom libraries, a year-long magazine subscription costs about as much as two paperbacks for a classroom library and provides monthly install-ments with timely coverage. As we found in our surveys, students are most likely to read their magazine "as soon as it comes," due to the excitement of what we have termed *the novelty factor*. This finding holds true in summer reading programs as well, where studies have shown that students read more text more frequently when the texts are delivered to students at regular intervals rather than provided all at once (Lindsay, 2010).

Drawing from traditional out-of-school texts, such as magazines, as part of regular instruction not only acknowledges students' out-of-school literacy but makes explicit connections to the skills and strategies students use to read, understand, and apply the texts they choose. This also expands the set of texts students have access to for practice beyond grade-level, academic materials—an advantage that provides differentiated material for both struggling and advanced readers. The same techniques could be used with online texts in classrooms and communities where the Internet is easily accessible. Magazines and other media outlets regularly make their content available on-line for free, which allows students, teachers, and librarians to avoid the cost of subscriptions in areas where schools and most homes have reliable Internet access.

Using the Words They Know

Another classroom strategy that builds on our observations of middle school magazine reading habits involves highlighting and increasing students' specific vocabulary knowledge. Though knowledge of academic vocabulary is often a challenge for students in middle and high school (Fisher & Frey, 2011), it is important to remember that students may have rich and varied vocab-ularies related to their out-of-school experiences and leisure reading. One of the strategies that can be used to build on this sometimes-untapped fund of knowledge is to ask students to discuss the relationships between words they know well. This increases awareness of word knowledge and builds explicit knowledge about the ways in which authors make words work together.

For example, students who are hockey players outside of school often know a variety of terms and metaphors related to the quality of the ice they skate on. Given the chance to generate some of these terms, students could "demonstrate understanding of word relationships and nuances in word meanings" (Common Core Standards: Knowledge of Language, L.11.12.5) by organizing the words along a spectrum from least to most intense or desirable (adapted from

Beck, McKeown, & Kucan, 2002). This activity would allow teachers to establish a discussion about the multidimensional, contingent nature of word meanings that could be carried into discussions of words that come up in class texts or vocabulary study.

As Beck, McKeown, and Kucan (2002) have pointed out, words that are considered low-frequency, highly specialized, or technical in a school context ("tier 3" words), may in fact be high-frequency and high-utility ("tier 2" words) to individual students when engaged in particular out-of-school pursuits. Providing a forum for using and making connections between these words allows students to build explicit knowledge about how words work. Similarly, using these words to enrich connections to academic and new vocabulary by generating associations and modeling the conceptual relationships between them allows students to use their out-of-school funds of knowledge to support and build their academic vocabularies. Indeed, the complex task of finding a relationship between words that are not automatically related (a hunter's instinct and an author's virtuosity; an athlete's agility and a character's animosity) is not only robust vocabulary instruction (Beck, McKeown, & Kucan 2002), it is also a way to bridge students' in- and out-of-school literacies.

Our study of middle school students' magazine reading habits not only underscored the importance of background and specific vocabulary knowledge, but also highlighted students' potential to build and use such knowledge in and outside of school. We were encouraged to observe students reading challenging texts in their leisure time for enjoyment, information, and even, at times, to fit in with their peers. We are even more encouraged when we imagine the ways in which teachers might use magazines as instructional supports for engagement, differentiation, and practice, as well as the ways in which teachers might tap into students' out-of-school word knowledge in order to help students use known words to learn new words.

CONNECTIONS FROM READWRITETHINK

Magazines in the Classroom
ReadWriteThink.org has several resources on using magazines in the classroom

Magazine Redux: An Exercise in Critical Literacy
Paper and pixels get compared in this lesson in which students compare both printed and online versions of a magazine.

http://www.readwritethink.org/classroom-resources/lesson-plans/magazine-redux-exercise-critical-214.html

I've Got It Covered! Creating Magazine Covers to Summarize Texts
Start the presses! Catchy titles, eye-popping graphics, and attractive fonts are all on students' agendas in this lesson as they create magazine covers to summarize a topic.

http://www.readwritethink.org/classroom-resources/lesson-plans/covered-creating-magazine-covers-1092.html

Zines for Kids: Multigenre Texts about Media Icons
Students use ReadWriteThink tools to create magazines about prominent figures using a variety of writing genres and styles.

http://www.readwritethink.org/classroom-resources/lesson-plans/zines-kids-multigenre-texts-1013.html

Profile Publisher
Students use the Profile Publisher to draft online social networking profiles, yearbook profiles, and newspaper or magazineprofiles for themselves, or other real or fictional characters.

http://www.readwritethink.org/classroom-resources/student-interactives/profile-publisher-30067.html

Lisa Fink
www.readwritethink.org

References

Beck, I., McKeown, M., & Kucan, L. (2002). *Bringing words to life: Robust vocabulary instruction.* New York, NY: Guilford Press.

Carnell, E. (2005). Boys and their reading: Conceptions of young people about the success of *Full On* magazine. *The Curriculum Journal, 16,* 363–389.

Chall, J., Bissex, G., Conrad, S., & Harris-Sharples, S. (1999). *Qualitative assessment of text difficulty: A practical guide for teachers and writers.* Brookline, MA: Brookline Books.

Fisher, D., & Frey, N. (2011). Academic language in the secondary classroom. *Principal Leadership, 11*(6), 64–66.

Gabriel, R., & Allington, R. (2009, December). *Middle schoolers and magazines: Can they read difficult but self-selected texts?* Paper presented at the National Reading Conference, Albuquerque, NM.

Gabriel, R., & Allington, R. (2010, December). *Leveling magazines: Considerations for selecting and using magazines in classroom and school libraries.* Paper presented at the National Reading Conference/Literacy Research Association, Fort Worth, TX.

Guthrie, J. T., & Humenick, N. M. (2004). Motivating students to read: Evidence for classroom practices that increase motivation and achievement. In P. McCardle & V. Chhabra (Eds.), *The voice of evidence in reading research* (pp. 329–354). Baltimore: Paul Brookes.

Hall, C., & Coles, M. (1999). *Children's reading choices.* London, UK: Routledge.

Hall, C., & Coles, M. (2001). Boys, books, and breaking boundaries: Developing literacy in and out of school. In W. Martino & B. Meyenn (Eds.), *What about the boys? Issues of masculinity in schools* (pp. 211–234). Philadelphia, PA: Open University Press.

Hughes-Hassell, S., & Rodge, P. (2007). The leisure reading habits of urban adolescents. *Journal of Adolescent and Adult Literacy, 51,* 22–33.

Lindsay, J. (2010). *Children's access to print material and education-related outcomes: Findings from a meta-analytic review.* Napier, IL: Learning Point Associates. Retrieved from: http://www.learningpt.org/pdfs/RIFandLearningPointMeta-FullReport.pdf.

Magazine Publishers of America. (2004). *Teen market profile.* New York, NY: Author.

Discussion Questions

1. Explain the connection between specific vocabulary and the students' ability to read and comprehend texts that appeared to be at a frustrational reading level for them.
2. What are two strategies mentioned by the authors that can be used to incorporate the use of magazines in improving students' vocabulary and comprehension?
3. Isabel Beck's work with vocabulary 'tiers' is well-known and is mentioned on page 170 in this reading. Do some additional reading about her vocabulary-related research. Write a brief summary describing each vocabulary tier.

How Can Teachers Increase Classroom Use of Academic Vocabulary?

Lisa Larson, Temoca Dixon, and Dianna Townsend

In the article, "How Can Teachers Increase Classroom Use of Academic Vocabulary," Larson, Dixon, and Townsend define "academic vocabulary" and explain why it must be a focus of instruction in the content areas.

LEARNING OBJECTIVES

1. Think about vocabulary instruction you experienced as a middle or secondary school student. How were words "taught" in the content areas and do you think this instruction was effective? Why or why not?
2. The article discusses the use of "word walls" and tiers of vocabulary instruction. What do you know about each topic? How could word walls be used along with the three vocabulary tiers to support students' learning of academic vocabulary?

How Can Teachers Increase Classroom Use of Academic Vocabulary?

Lisa Larson, Temoca Dixon, and Dianna Townsend

My seventh-grade students are in their seats, shifting their gazes between the large poster paper hanging on the white board, the colored markers in my hand, and the timer. The prefix *re-* is written on top of the page. As soon as I give my class the signal, hands shoot into the air, calling out words such as "*rewrite, repost, redraw, reform*" during a collective 10-minute brainstorm.

Students suggest words and I add them to the growing list, *if* they properly use the prefix. At the end of 10 minutes, we count our words; it is a great list.

At this point, I explain, "Once you learned the prefix *re-*, you packed your word bank." (See Fig. 5.2.1.) Then I flip through the posters from other classes and point out, "Yet, you still did not think of all the words other classes found. Once you understand word parts, you have access to an incredible number of words." My students argued, "Ms. Dixon, why are we learning vocabulary in social studies?" I watched as my students looked at each of the lists, the class word wall, and back at me. I saw them realize what I had been trying to explain: active vocabulary practice is invaluable to their academic success. Why? Because active vocabulary practice helps young adolescent learners develop academic language and access academic texts.

As social studies teachers, one teaching in a rural middle school and one teaching in an urban middle school, we value "rich vocabulary instruction" (Beck, McKeown, & Kucan, 2002, p. 108). Given that our students are encountering increasingly academic texts in our classrooms, this type of instruction is exactly what they need in order to access those texts. Our students represent typical rural and urban populations from low socioeconomic backgrounds, and we see national achievement trends for these groups playing out in our classrooms. Since the National Assessment for Educational Progress (NAEP) began measuring reading achievement in 1992, the nation's fourth and

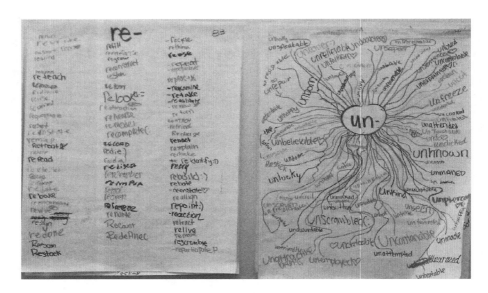

FIGURE 5.2.1   Example of a Morphology Brainstorming Activity.

eighth graders have shown little to no growth (U.S. Department of Education, 2007). Recently, our state adopted the Common Core State Standards (CCSS), developed by the National Governors Association Center for Best Practices, Council of Chief State School Officers. CCSS promises to increase the rigors of reading. With the evidence that students have difficulty with academic language, the new standards have the potential to further amplify the literacy gap.

A critical component to academic reading comprehension is understanding the vocabulary, and gaps in vocabulary knowledge are a factor for low reading achievement (Harmon, Hedrick, & Wood, 2006; Kelley, Lesaux, Kieffer, & Faller, 2010; Lesaux, Kieffer, Faller, & Kelley, 2010). In order to make sense of increasingly dense academic texts, middle-level students must possess strategies to understand and use words, which will, with other types of text-based support, increase comprehension. For these reasons, academic vocabulary has received a great deal of attention in both the research and practitioner literature (see Baumann & Graves, 2010, for an overview). However, for our purposes, it is the definition provided by Flynt and Brozo (2008) that is most applicable to the classroom; academic vocabulary is "word knowledge that makes it possible for students to engage with, produce, and talk about texts that are valued in school" (p. 500).

What is Effective Academic Vocabulary Instruction?

As part of an action research project, we examined and supplemented our practice for helping our students build academic vocabulary knowledge. Our research question for the project was based on Blachowicz and Fisher's (2000) assertion that students should be responsible for taking an active role in learning new vocabulary words. Active engagement means "learning the meaning of specific words (where it is important to make connections between and among words and concepts), and learning strategies to become independent word learners" (p. 505). Therefore, our purpose for this project was to answer the question: How can we enhance young adolescents' active engagement with academic vocabulary while engaging with texts in our social studies classes?

To start, we built a common understanding of academic vocabulary words, considering both general academic words and content-specific words. For general academic word knowledge, we relied on Coxhead's (2000) work. She created a list of 560 academic vocabulary word families consisting of thousands of terms students would most likely see across content areas. However, this list was never intended as a prescriptive list of words to teach, and we did not use it that way. Rather, we used the list as a guide for the type of word we wanted to attend to as we encountered them in the texts we were reading. For example, *proceed,* a word from the list, can mean to move forward, and *proceeds* can indicate the money received from an economic venture. Different forms of this word can be found in many other content areas, often with varying meanings. In science, students must follow lab *procedures*, and in math, solving equations requires a specific *process*. In social studies, students can read about a funeral *procession*. The discussion of words at this basic but interconnected level is important to the deeper learning of words and supports the principle of active engagement. As we encountered general academic words in our instructional texts with our students, we would stop to run short pair-shares or whole-class discussions on how these words are used in various contexts.

Active Academic Vocabulary Practice in Social Studies Classrooms

The following are strategies from our action research project that we found to be the most effective in engaging middle-level students in building academic vocabulary knowledge and increasing access to academic texts.

Word Walls

Word walls provide visual support for all learners in their acquisition of academic vocabulary. Corson (1997) tells us that "words are only fully learned when they are available for active use" (p. 699). We learned that it is important when creating a word wall that the words are terms students have created and manipulated, not simply words up for display (Fisher & Frey, 2008). The organization of word walls varies; some walls arrange terms in alphabetical order, some use common themes or units of study (Fisher & Frey, 2008; Yates, Cuthrell, & Rose, 2011).

In creating our word walls, we engaged students in decisions about the placement of the words according to Beck, McKeown, and Kucan's (2002) tiers (see Fig. 5.2.2). Our students were already comfortable with these categories from our previous work together. Tier 1 words are basic, everyday vocabulary; Tier 2 words are similar to general academic words; and Tier 3 words equate with content-specific words. The discussions about where words belonged provided students with the opportunity to deepen their ownership of the words. We also found that

FIGURE 5.2.2   Example of a Student-Designed Word Wall in a Social Studies Classroom.

simple prompts for entry and exit slips were time-efficient ways to help students pay attention to and use word wall words. Examples of entry slip prompts are:

- Write down the words____,____, and ____ from our word wall and, with a partner, write down everything you think you know about them.
- Here are two questions we'll be answering today: Which word wall words do you think will be most important in today's lesson? Why?

Examples of exit slip prompts are:

- Write down one new thing you learned today and use at least two of our word wall words in your response.
- Look around at our word walls. Which words were the most important from today's lesson? What makes those words important today?

Morphology Practice with Matching Activities

Morphology, the study of word structure, including roots, bases, and affixes, is an extremely powerful tool for building academic language proficiency. The majority of the words on Coxhead's (2000) list are complex in nature, as are many social studies content area words. Consider, for example, the terms *civil disobedience, jurisdiction, communism,* and *revolution*. The activity illustrated at the beginning of our article is one way we engaged our young adolescent learners in building word structure knowledge (see Fig. 5.2.1). Another activity we found particularly engaging for students is a matching activity (Townsend, 2009).

Each student received a slip of paper that had something in common, morphologically, with two other students' slips of paper. For example, the words may have had the same Latin root or the same prefix. Students circulated around the room, with a time limit, to find their group members. Once groups were assembled, each group used textbooks and dictionaries to determine the meanings of their common word parts. Each group then generated additional words using their word parts and taught another group about the new terms. Building students' word awareness in this manner broadened their vocabulary knowledge without explicit instruction of each individual word. Such awareness-building plays "an important role in vocabulary growth which in turn impacts reading comprehension" (Nagy, Berninger, & Abbott, 2006, p. 134). And, as with all activities, the target words and word parts for the morphological activities were instructionally meaningful for the texts we were engaging with at the time.

Word Sorts

Word sorts can engage middle-level students in finding similarities and differences in word structures and word meanings (Templeton, Bear, Invernizzi, & Johnston, 2010). One example of a word sort involved students receiving (or making!) a set of slips of paper, each with a term related to the Civil War. Students then sorted their terms into "people," "places," "events" or other self-selected categories. This particular sort included the category "military words." We were then able to assess a student's understanding of an individual word, such as *Copperheads* (see Fig. 5.2.3), by asking him to justify his category choices, thus uncovering misconceptions to be explored.

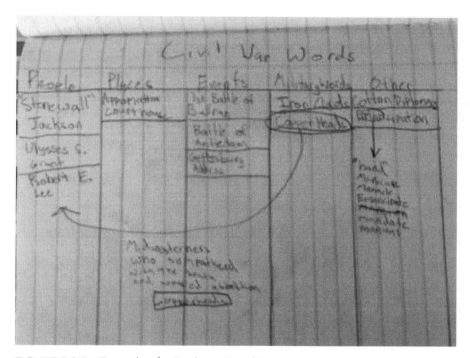

FIGURE 5.2.3   Example of a Student's Word Sort.

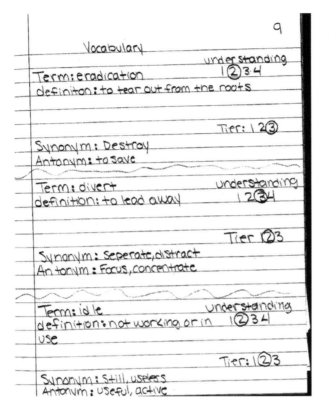

FIGURE 5.2.4   Example of a Student's Vocabulary Journal.

Word sorts can also be used to further awareness of morphology (Templeton, et al., 2010). For example, in the same unit, *emancipation* was analyzed for its root "man," and students made connections to words like *manacle* and *mandate*. Students then practiced with word sorts comprised of Civil War terms that shared common roots or affixes.

Vocabulary Journals

Vocabulary journals in content areas allow adolescent students to work with vocabulary terms using an "introduce, define, discuss, and apply" sequence (Fisher & Frey, 2008, p. 67). The variations in the set-up of the journal reflect the needs of individual content areas. Interactive notebooks in a social studies classroom may include a vocabulary section for each unit. Students record word sorts, vocabulary, student-friendly definitions, and visual representations for each term. In our classes, students reviewed, referenced, and revised their vocabulary records as they continued to construct more knowledge (see Fig. 5.2.4). Word learning is incremental in nature, and depth of word knowledge is built as students encounter words across various texts and contexts. Therein lays the power of vocabulary journals; students can revisit words, adding information about those words as they learn new nuances of and contexts for those words. Every page or section of a vocabulary journal then authentically grows as students' word knowledge grows.

Conclusion

Active academic vocabulary practice helps middle-level students actively engage with and use the challenging academic language of the content areas. The strategies we have included are only a few of the ones used successfully in word study. Other successful strategies may include student discussions, role plays, jeopardy-esque games, flash cards, comic strips, acrostic poems, and a plethora of other writing assignments.

After working with the prefix *re-*, the social studies class mentioned above studied Reconstruction. Drawing the students' attention to the word *reconstruction* was built into the introduction to this unit. Based on the students' prior understanding of the prefix *re-*, they were able to infer what we would learn while studying America's reconstruction of the South. This was not a separate vocabulary lesson, but rather a quick review and application check for understanding that we slipped right into our daily instruction. Focused vocabulary instruction is not about cutting curriculum or extending teachers' instructional day; rather, we learned from this action research project that it is about embedding a strategic, focused vocabulary curriculum, centered on meaningful words and word parts from our texts, into our lessons.

References

Baumann, J. F., & Graves, M. F. (2010). What is academic vocabulary? *Journal of Adolescent & Adult Literacy, 54,* 4–12.

Beck, I. L., McKeown, M. G., & Kucan, L. (2002). *Bringing words to life: Robust vocabulary instruction.* New York, NY: Guilford Press.

Blachowicz, C. L. Z., & Fisher, P. (2000). Vocabulary instruction. In M. L. Kamil, P. B. Mosenthal, P. D. Pearson, & R. Barr (Eds.), *Handbook of reading research* (Vol. 3). Mahwah, NJ: Lawrence Erlbaum.

Corson, D. (1997). The learning and use of academic English words. *Language Learning, 47,* 671–718.

Coxhead, A. (2000). A new academic word list. *TESOL Quarterly, 34,* 213–238.

Fisher, D., & Frey, N. (2008). *Improving adolescent literacy: Content area strategies at work.* Upper Saddle River, NJ: Pearson Education.

Flynt, E. S., & Brozo, W. G. (2008). Developing academic language: Got words? *The Reading Teacher, 61,* 500–502.

Harmon, J. M., Hedrick, W. B., & Wood, K. D. (2006). Research on vocabulary instruction in the content areas: Implications for struggling readers. *Reading & Writing Quarterly, 21,* 261–280.

Kelley, J. G., Lesaux, N. K., Kieffer, M. J., & Faller, S. E. (2010). Effective academic vocabulary instruction in the urban middle school. *The Reading Teacher, 64,* 5–14.

Lesaux, N., Kieffer, M., Faller, S. E., & Kelley, J. G. (2010). The effectiveness and ease of implementation of an academic vocabulary intervention for linguistically diverse students in urban middle schools. *Reading Research Quarterly, 45,* 196–228.

Nagy, W., Berninger, V., & Abbott, R. (2006). Contributions of morphology beyond phonology to literacy outcomes of upper elementary and middle school students. *Journal of Educational Psychology, 98,* 134–147.

National Governors Association Center for Best Practices, Council of Chief State School Officers. (2010). *Common Core State Standards.* Washington, DC: Author.

Templeton, S., Bear, D. R., Invernizzi, M., & Johnston, F. (2010). *Vocabulary their way: Word study with middle and secondary students.* Boston, MA: Pearson Education.

Townsend, D. (2009). Building academic vocabulary in after-school settings: Games for growth with middle school English-language learners. *Journal of Adolescent & Adult Literacy, 53*, 242–251.

U.S. Department of Education. (2007). *NAEP data explorer.* Washington, DC: Institute of Education Sciences, National Center for Educational Statistics.

Yates, P. H., Cuthrell, K., Rose, M. (2011). Out of the room and into the hall: Making content word walls work. *The Clearing House: A Journal of Educational Strategies, 84*(1), 31–36.

Discussion Questions

1. Define "academic vocabulary" and explain its importance in both reading comprehension and in content-area literacy.
2. List the instructional strategies described by the authors. Briefly explain how each one helps support vocabulary instruction.

Vocabulary Assessment as a Predictor of Literacy Skills

Beverly A. DeVries

I n this article, Beverly DeVries explores the impact of vocabulary development on reading comprehension and discusses several formal and informal ways to assess vocabulary learning.

LEARNING OBJECTIVES

1. What are some factors that impact students' vocabulary development?
2. How does vocabulary impact reading comprehension?

Vocabulary Assessment as a Predictor of Literacy Skills

Beverly A. DeVries

These laments from fifth-grade teachers are common comments of many classroom teachers. I have found often times students do not comprehend text because they lack the vocabulary to understand the passage. They may be able to give a "dictionary" definition of words, but they do not fully understand the words and the relationship between words as they read informational texts.

> My students are fluent readers, but they do not understand what they read.

> I have the same problem; they really sound good when they read aloud, but they cannot answer any of my questions.

Importance of Vocabulary in Reading Comprehension

Students' knowledge of words is the single greatest predictor of their reading comprehension (Baumann, Kame'enui, & Ash, 2003); and for bilingual students, vocabulary knowledge is an important precursor for literacy skills (August & Shanahan, 2006; August, Carlo, Dressler, & Snow, 2005). Because students' vocabulary is such an important component of reading comprehension, it is imperative we teachers understand factors that affect students' vocabulary, methods of assessing vocabulary, and strategies that engage students as they learn new words.

Factors That Affect Students' Vocabulary

What are some factors that affect students' vocabulary? Environment is one of the greatest factors (Blachowicz & Fisher, 2005). Children in families with parents with postsecondary degrees know approximately 20,000 words when they enter the first grade, while children from families with parents with less education know approximately only 5,000 words (Hart & Risley, 2003). These children hear a robust vocabulary as they carry on conversation with adults during mealtime, outings, and while doing chores or playing together in the home. For example, consider the children who hear their mothers complaining about the sweltering heat or the frigid winter versus children who hear their mothers talking about the hot day or the cold day. Learning words in a natural context is one way children add new words to their lexicon.

Parents and caregivers who read and discuss quality literature with children also facilitate children's vocabulary growth (Hart & Risley, 2003). Researchers have found that reading quality literature develops children's vocabulary (Yopp & Yopp, 2007; Beauchat, Blamey, & Walpole, 2009; Rasinski & Padak, 2004) because authors use a rich vocabulary to paint vivid pictures in readers' minds. Consider the following rich vocabulary from Coleen Salley's *Epossumondas Saves the Day* (2006): *puny, cypress, ornery, lumbered, humongous, scrawny, dawdling;* and the rich vocabulary found in Ruth Heller's books on the parts of speech. In *A Cache of Jewels* (1987), children learn about a cache of jewels, a gam of whales, a bevy of girls, a muster of peacocks, a kindle of kittens, and many other nouns used to describe a group of the same type of creatures. When adults share these books with children, we should stop, explain the word, have the child repeat the word, and later use it in daily conversation so the word becomes a part of the children's vocabulary. This type of engagement also encourages children to become curious about words.

Another vicarious experience in which children increase their vocabulary is by watching educational television programs and videos with an adult. Educational television programs take children to places they have never seen. When viewing a video about an animal not found in their region of the country, they learn not only about the animal, but also learn about the animal's natural habitat, their predators, and animals to which they are prey. From an educational program the children hear the words repeated often throughout the program and learn the meaning of the word in that context.

Children's environment and vicarious experiences during their pre-school years depend on children's home life. However, once children get to school, teachers are responsible for facilitating children's vocabulary growth. Teachers must intentionally use a rich vocabulary in order to raise the curiosity of students. Consider two teachers: Mr. Johnson tells his students not to procrastinate, but get on task; while Mr. Olson tells his students to get busy. Mr. Johnson is introducing his students to *procrastinate* in a natural context. If he also uses *procrastinator* during the conversation, students learn the relationship between these two words.

As we observe students in small groups, we become aware that our students come to our classes with a wide range of vocabulary skills. Observation is one informal way to assess students' vocabulary in a natural setting; however, since it is our responsibility to facilitate the vocabulary growth of all students, we need to assess students formally and informally so we can facilitate the vocabulary growth of all students. There are a number of assessment instruments we can use.

Formal Assessments

Formal assessments are standardized; they have been tested to make sure they are valid and reliable. Formal assessments are often used to see if students in any given grade are performing at the grade level and/or to measure yearly growth. Many formal vocabulary assessment group instruments are multiple-choice tests. For example, Iowa Test of Basic Skills (Grades K–8), Metropolitan Achievement Tests (Grades K–12), and California Achievement Test (Grades K–9) have multiple choice vocabulary subtests. Students read a sentence or short phrase with the target word and must choose the best synonym from a list of four or five words. For example, in the following sentence, students are asked to choose the best synonym for *little:* Mary had a *little* glove for her baby doll. The list consists of *exotic, minute, ordinary, colorful, mammoth.* As all of us educators realize, with multiple choice tests there is the possibility that students guess at the answer, which makes the test scores not an accurate indication of students' vocabulary development.

The Peabody Picture Vocabulary Test-Revised (Dunn & Dunn, 1997) is not a group test, but is given individually to assess a student's receptive vocabulary. The student is shown four pictures on one page. The test administrator pronounces a word that corresponds to one of the pictures, and the student points to the correct picture. The test begins with simple objects such as a *bed, flower,* or *car* and progresses to more advanced words such as *attire, incisor, convergence.* Of course, even with this test, it is possible that students guess; however, it is more obvious to us because we are administrating it and observing the student as s/he gives his/her response.

Informal Assessment

Informal assessments are not norm referenced and are not given under standardized conditions. Some informal assessments that we can use to assess students' vocabulary are observation, pretest writing exercise, cloze, maze, and checklists based on state standards. The most informal, yet a very helpful assessment is your *observations* of student during small group work and conversations with the students. When we observe young children saying *ball* for footballs, basketballs, tennis balls, ping pong balls; or saying *flower* for sunflower, tulip, roses and daisies; we can conclude that the child has a limited vocabulary. When we who work with older students and hear them calling all bodies of water a *lake* even though it is a river or an ocean, we can conclude that the student has a limited vocabulary. Observation is the first indication that the student has a limited vocabulary.

Pretest writing exercise is another informal method to assess if students know words associated with particular units. For example, if the unit is on the various types of clouds, students can be given approximately five words from the unit that we are sure they know such as *clouds, rain, weather,* and *thunder,* and give them some words that are introduced in the unit and may be unfamiliar to them—*cumulus, stratus, cirrus,* and *nimbostratus.* Students are given the task to write a short paragraph using the words. We teachers can assess from the paragraphs which words the children know. If we are concerned about how our teaching impacts student learning, we can give the same exercise as a posttest to calculate student learning gains for each student and for the class.

The modified *cloze test* is an informal assessment to assess students' knowledge of technical terms associated with a particular subject. To modify the cloze test, we can alter the cloze test and delete only the words that are the technical terms for that topic so we can assess which words students can use in context.

The *maze test* is similar to the cloze test. A passage is still given to the students, but instead of blanks, students are given three words from which to choose. For example, the students in the following sentence must choose the best word. The (mammoth, ravenous, zealous) mountain was a challenge to the mountain climbers. As with any multiple-choice test, there is the possibility that students guess on the maze test.

A *checklist* based on state standards or the Common Core State Standards (CCSS) is another tool to informally assess students' vocabulary. Checklists are not based on particular terms, but rather on competencies that are taken from state standards or the CCSS. We can create a checklist with the standards listed on left-hand column with students' names across the top. Each quarter we take time to assess which students have mastered the standard, which students are still developing the standard, and which students have not even begun to develop the standard. We can use these checklists as one way to determine what skills we must still teach to the entire class or to a small group.

Once we determine students' vocabulary level, we must use that information provided by the assessments to drive our class, small group, and individual instruction.

Which Words to Teach?

It is estimated that students learn about 2,700 to 3,000 new words a year, or seven words a day (Snow, Burns, & Griffin, 1998). I attempted to do an Internet search on how many new words enter the English vocabulary each year. The answers varied from 800 to 20,000. Even if I accept the low number of 800, it means that approximately 21 to 22 words are added to the English lexicon each day. How do we get students excited and curious about new words? The primary answer to that question is: we teachers need to be excited and curious about learning new words! We also need to understand that knowing a word is more than looking it up in a dictionary, writing its definition, and using it in a sentence.

Learning new words results in students "owning" the words. "Owning" a word implies that the word is part of their receptive (reading and listening) and expressive (writing and speaking) vocabulary. They know how to pronounce it, know its multiple meanings, know its relationship to other words, know its connotation in different contexts, and know how its morphology.

What words should teachers consider teaching? In the following section, I will offer some suggestions for us to consider for all grade levels.

Words With Multiple Meanings and Used as Multiple Parts of Speech

We must get students to understand that words have multiple meanings. Many common words that young readers know and recognize have multiple meanings. For example, take the word *duck*. Many students know it as a noun—the barnyard duck, or as a verb—to duck under the umbrella. But what if they encountered the following sentence: We enjoyed the tour as the guide drove us through the forest and into the lake on an old World War II duck. To teach students that words have multiple meanings, when familiar words are encountered in an unfamiliar way, we must explicitly teach how that word and other words have multiple meanings and can be used as multiple parts of speech.

To pique students' interest in homographs, write some on the board and ask students to pronounce them, A few homographs I like to give my college students are *consent, wind, minute, progress, console, bow,* and *compact.* Even my college students enjoy this little activity. Working with homographs help students become aware of multiple meanings of words.

Words: Their Origins and Forms

Teaching students that English words have origins from the Latin, Greek, and other languages helps them understand that words with similar roots or affixes will help them comprehend the meaning of many words with similar roots (Kieffer & Lesaux, 2007; Staudt, 2009). Even young students can readily learn the meaning of the suffix *-ful* when they add *-ful* to words they already know such as *playful, joyful,* and *powerful.* It is also helpful for students to learn common root words. For example, if students know that *auto* means "self"; they will understand words such as *autobiography, autograph,* and other words with the *auto* root. Teaching students how *employ, employer, employee, employment,* are forms of the same word, can help them learn relationships among words and more readily learn meanings of words.

Synonyms and Antonyms

Teaching synonyms and antonyms of words helps students in all grades learn relationships among words and helps them in their writing as they make vivid word choices. For example, teaching that *exuberant* is a synonym of *happy* and that *fulgent* is a synonym of *dull* can help students comprehend quality literature that uses rich vocabulary and can also impact students' writing.

Teaching How Authors Give Definitions in Passage

Many authors who write for children and young adult literature use an appositive phrase, definition, synonym, antonym, or examples within a sentence to clarify the meaning of a word. For example, an author who is introducing the concept of oxidation in a science text may use an appositive phrase to define oxidation: "Oxidation, the union of a substance with oxygen, is a common chemical reaction that occurs daily." Other authors may include the definition and examples in the sentence: "My grandmother likes to plant perennials such as lilies and roses because they come up every spring and she does not need to replant them." Both of these sentences will give the readers some indication of the meaning of the words. It is prudent for us to show how authors use these techniques so students understand that often the definition of new words is given within the passage.

Teaching Key Words Used in All Subjects

It is important to teach students words that become a task they must perform in multiple subjects such as social studies, literature, science and math. *Summarize, analyze, synthesize, compare, contrast, explain, describe, define,* and *elaborate* are tasks students are required to do in every subject. Even first graders are familiar with comparing and contrasting two objects or two versions of a fairy tale. With young students, we need to teach the difference between *compare* and *contrast,* and the difference between *summarizing* and *elaborating.* Using a short informational passage, we can tell students we are going to summarize the information. We can then give a short summary. Then, using the same passage, we tell students we are going to elaborate on the details of the passage. After elaborating on the details, we can ask student to discuss the difference between summarizing and elaborating, based on your examples. Many students need explicit instruction in understanding the difference between these tasks. Of course, after we teach the difference between any of these words, we need to have them practice the tasks.

Figurative Language

I enjoy reading passages in which authors create colorful images in my mind through the use of figurative language. Teaching students the many figurative forms of language such as onomatopoeia, metaphors, similes, personification, puns, idioms, and oxymorons helps them understand why some writing is intriguing while other writing is "flat or tasteless." Even very young children encounter figurative language when authors use onomatopoeia: Cows moo, ducks quack, pigs oink, fire truck zoom, twigs snap, and trucks vroom. To teach any figurative language technique, we can search for them during our shared reading and then invite students to write them down when they encounter them in their daily readings and to display them on a bulletin board so they can share them with their classmates. Encouraging students to illustrate their findings, helps others understand the meaning. Idioms can be humorous when students illustrate them in a literate sense. Imagine illustrating the idiom: "I'm in a pickle."

In the following section, I will share some strategies that I have found to make vocabulary building enjoyable for both me and my students.

Strategies to Build Vocabulary

All learning should be fun and engaging! We need to model the enjoyment of pronouncing polysyllabic words, listening to the wonderful sounds in words, and using them in our daily conversation.

Large Group Instruction

Students learn new words through explicit instruction (Manyak & Bouchereau-Bauer, 2009; Townsend, 2009; Flynt & Brozo, 2008). However, we must build on what students already know, and teach them relationship between words.

Total Physical Response (TPR)

James Asher (1982) understood the importance of focusing on kinesthetic learning when he developed the Total Physical Response (TPR) strategy. The TPR strategy emphasizes the use of the entire body to act out the word. This strategy is especially helpful to English learners as they learn new verbs such as *sink, float* or *search*. However, all students learn the difference among such words as *saunter, meander, shuffle,* and *march* as they saunter, shuffle, or march around the room.

Neologisms

Learning new words should be interesting for students of all ages. Upper elementary students through high school enjoy using coin words. One way to interest students in new words is to introduce the word *neologisms* and with the aid of the Internet, direct students to Merriam-Webster's website that has the fist of most recent neologisms. For example, *ginormous,* a word known to many teens, finally entered the Merriam-Webster dictionary in 2007. Other words that made the entry that year are *Bollywood, agnolotti, crunk, smackdown, snowboardcross, sudoku,* and others.

We can invite students to choose a word, look it up on Merriam-Webster's website and teach it to a small group of three or four classmates. Each student in the small group has a different word. They learn each of the group's words and decide how they will explain each word to the entire class. Groups can be encouraged to state the word, to pantomime the word, or use the Total Physical Response strategy. Creating a Neologisms bulletin board encourages students to continue to search for new neologisms. One requirement for bulletin board words is to have students write out the word, give a good synonym and draw an illustration that depicts the word.

Action Jeopardy

This Action Jeopardy is a modified form of Townsend's (2009) Action Jeopardy. The game is based on vocabulary lists from any content area. You can create a paper form of jeopardy by dividing a large piece of poster board into four columns and four or five rows. The columns are labeled: *Definition, Synonym, Antonym, Sentence*. In the definition column, you write the definitions of the targeted words. In the synonym column, you write a synonym for each word. In the antonym column, goes an antonym for each of the target words. In the sentence column, you write a sentence with a blank for the target word. Dividing the class into small groups of three or four, follow the rules of TV Jeopardy game. The following websites offer free game boards so the game can be played on an electronic board: http://quizboxes.com, http://jc-schools.met/tutorial/PPT-games, and http://warp.bytu.edu/jeopardy.

Frayer Model Graphic Organizer

The Frayer Model, designed by Dorothy Frayer and her colleagues at the University of Wisconsin, encourages students to focus on finding a synonym and antonym for the key term and giving an example of what the term is and what the term is not. Each word is written on a separate card as shown in the example.

SYNONYM Huge		ANTONYM Tiny
	ginormous	
EXAMPLE Hippo		NON-EXAMPLE Ant

Small Group Strategies
Synonym/Definition/Concentration

This particular strategy is based on the commercial format of Memory and can be used to reinforce the understanding of vocabulary words associated with any topic in any subject. To make the cards, you select the 10 to 15 words that students must know from a particular unit. Cut a 4 × 6 index card in half to create a 2 × 3 card (the size of a playing card). Write one word on each card and one definition on a card. If you select 10 words, you will have 20 cards for the game. To play, the cards are turned upside down, shuffled and put into neat rows and columns so students can remember where particular cards are on the table. Students take turns turning over two cards. If the student matches a vocabulary word with its definition and can use the word correctly in a sentence, the student gets to keep both cards. If the student does not have a match, he again turns each card upside down in the place in which he picked them up. When all the cards are gone, the student with the most cards "wins" the game.

Word Sorts

Word sorts can be used with any subject matter. After students have studied a unit, you give a list of major terms from the unit and invite them to sort the word in a manner that shows relationships. You can give them some guidelines by telling them there are two major categories and each main category has three sub-points. For example, after studying World War II, you may give a list of countries that were allies with the United States and other countries that were fighting against the allies. You can also give a list of major battles that the allies won and a list of those that they lost, along with major generals from the Allies and from our enemies.

Summary

Building students' vocabulary aids their comprehension. We are responsible to pique students' interests in words so they will enjoy learning new words and using them to comprehend texts and to use in their writing and conversation. Using a variety of strategies keeps vocabulary building interesting because students become bored when they do the same activity over and over again.

References

Asher, J. (1982). *Learning another language through actions.* Los Gatos, CA: Sky Oaks Productions.

August, D., Carlo, M., Dressier, C., & Snow, C. (2005). The critical role of vocabulary development for English language learners. *Learning Disabilities Research and Practice, 20*(1), 50–57.

August, D., & Shanahan, T. (2006). Developing literacy in second-language learners. Report of the National Panel on Language Minority Children and Youth. Mahwah, NJ: Erlbaum.

Baumann, J.F., Kame'enui, E.J., & Ash, G.E. (2003). Research on vocabulary instruction: Voltaire redux. In J. Flood, D. Lapp, J.R. Squire, & J.M. Jensen (Eds.), *Handbook on teaching the English language arts,* (2nd ed.), pp. 752–785. Mahwah, NJ: Erlbaum.

Beauchat, K.A., Blarney, K., & Walpole, S. (2009). Building preschool children's language and literature one storybook at a time. *The Reading Teacher, 63*(1), 26–29.

Blachowicz, C., & Fisher, P. (2005). Vocabulary lessons. *Educational Leadership, 61*(6), 66–69.

Dunn, L.M., & Dunn, L.M (1997). *Peabody Picture Vocabulary Test.* (3rd ed.). AGS Publishing.

Flynt, E., & Brozo, W. (2008). Developing academic language: Got words? *The Reading Teacher 61*(6), 500–502.

Hart, B., & Risley, T. (2003). The early catastrophe: The 300 million word gap. *American Education, 27*(1), 4–9.

Kieffer, M.J., & Clausen-Grace, N. (2009). Facilitating engagement by differentiating independent reading. *The Reading Teacher, 61*(2), 134–144.

Kieffer, M.J., & Lesaux, N. (2007). Breaking down words to build meaning: Morphology, vocabulary, and reading comprehension in the urban classroom. *The Reading Teacher, 67*(2), 134–144.

Manyak, P.C., & Bouchereau-Bauer, E. (2009). English vocabulary instruction for English learners. *The Reading Teacher, 63*(2), 174–176.

Rasinski, T.V., Padak, N.D. (2004). Beyond consensus-beyond balance: Toward a comprehensive literacy curriculum. *Reading and Writing Quarterly, 20,* 91–102.

Risko, V.J., & Walker-Dalhouse, D. (2010). Making the most of assessments to inform instruction. *The Reading Teacher, 63*(5), 420–422.

Snow, C., Burns, M., & Griffin, P. (Eds.). (1998). *Preventing reading difficulties in young children.* Washington, DC: National Academy Press.

Staudt, D.H. (2009). Intensive word study and repeated reading improves reading skills for two students with learning disabilities. *The Reading Teacher, 63*(2), 142–151.

Townsend, D. (2009). Building academic vocabulary in after-school settings: Games for growth with middle school English-language learners. *Journal of Adolescent and Adult Literacy, 53*(3), 242–251.

Yopp, R.H., & Yopp, H.K. (2007). Ten important words plus: A strategy for building word knowledge. *The Reading Teacher, 61*(2), 157–160.

Children's Book Cited

Gwynne, F. (1998). Illus. F. Gwynne. *A little pigeon toad.* New York: Alladdin.

Gwynne, F. (1988). Illus. F. Gwynne. *A chocolate moose for dinner.* New York: Alladdin.

Gwynne, F. (1988). Illus. F. Gwynne. *The king who rained.* New York: Alladdin.

Heller, R. (1998). *A cache of jewels.* Ulus. Ruth Heller. New York: Puffin.

Salley, C. (2006). *Epossumondas saves the day.* Illus. J. Stevens. Orlando, FL: Harcourt, Inc.

Discussion Questions

1. Name some ways in which vocabulary learning can be informally assessed in the classroom.
2. What are some instructional strategies that effectively support students' vocabulary development?

Conclusion

Chapter Activities

Activity 5.1

Select one of the Read-Write-Think activities listed on page 170 in the Gabriel, Allington, and Billen article. Go to the website and read through the activity. Complete one of the activities as if you were a student. Submit your completed activity and answer these questions:

1. What did you like/dislike about the activity?
2. How would this activity support the development of students' vocabulary?

Activity 5.2

Select a chapter from a science or social studies text written for middle or secondary students. Step into the shoes of the classroom teacher and develop a word wall like the one described in the Larson, Dixon, and Townsend article for that chapter. Include words in each vocabulary tier.

Select one word from each tier in your word wall and explain why you selected that word and how it fits into that particular tier.

Activity 5.3

Using the directions located at the "Vocabulary Strategies" link in the Online Resources section of this chapter, create a semantic feature analysis that compares the following types of governments: oligarchy, monarchy, democracy, federal republic, and dictatorship. Be sure that you have enough features listed so that each of the items to be compared have a different pattern of + and − markings. If not, you need to add additional features until they do, so that it is possible to distinguish among the different types of government.

Activity 5.4

Select a chapter from a science or social studies textbook designed for use in middle or secondary school. Create a cloze assessment, a modified cloze assessment, and a maze assessment based on the vocabulary in this chapter.

Online Resources

Doing It Differently: Tips for Teaching Vocabulary
http://www.edutopia.org/blog/vocabulary-instruction-teaching-tips-rebecca-alber

Vocabulary Strategies
http://www.readingeducator.com/strategies/vocabulary.htm

11 Tips on Teaching Common Core Critical Vocabulary
https://www.edutopia.org/blog/teaching-ccss-critical-vocabulary-marilee-sprenger

Vocabulary and the Common Core
http://achievethecore.org/page/974/vocabulary-and-the-common-core

References

Beck, I., McKeown, M., and Kucan, L. 2002. *Bringing Words to Life: Robust Vocabulary Instruction*. New York: Guilford.

Brabham, E., et al. 2012. "Flooding Vocabulary Gaps to Accelerate Word Learning." *The Reading Teacher* 65(8): 523–33.

Frayer, D., Frederick, W. C., and Klausmeier, H. J. 1969. *A Schema for Testing the Level of Cognitive Mastery*. Madison, WI: Wisconsin Center for Educational Research.

Marzano, R. 1984. "A Cluster Approach to Vocabulary Instruction: A New Direction from the Research Literature." *The Reading Teacher* 37(3): 168–73.

Comprehension and Text Structure

During reading, expert readers utilize a number of effective strategies to support their comprehension. Active reading of the text is critical for understanding. Students need to monitor their comprehension and know when to use strategies to support their understanding if they are struggling to make sense of a text. In this chapter, you'll learn about these comprehension strategies and text structures commonly found in informational texts at the middle and secondary level.

Chapter Focus Questions

1. What are some research-based comprehension strategies that are used by active readers and how do they support understanding of the text?
2. What types of text structures are commonly found in informational text written at the middle and secondary level?
3. How can you support the development of students' metacognition and why is this important for reading success?

Research-Based Comprehension Strategies

Educational researchers have identified these comprehension strategies as being effective for enhancing reading comprehension:

Monitoring Comprehension

Helping students learn to monitor their comprehension can be accomplished by supporting the development of metacognitive knowledge. In addition, instructional activities that make students aware of their monitoring are necessary.

Related Instructional Strategies

- VIP/insert/think notes
- Text coding
- Think aloud
- Selective reading guide
- Response sheet/double entry journal

Using Graphic and Semantic Organizers

Graphic organizers are visual representations of text. Semantic organizers are visual representations that are related to word meanings. Both types of organizers support students' comprehension by assisting them in organizing information and in seeing relationships among information. Instructional activities in which students complete provided graphic organizers or create their own organizers support students' comprehension.

Related Instructional Strategies

- Plot structure maps (narrative text)
- Frayer Model
- Graphic representations of expository (informational) text
- Concept maps
- Semantic feature analysis

Recognizing Text Structure

Good readers are able to use what they know about the structure of texts to assist them in selecting and remembering important information and relationships among that information. Students must know about the different text structures that are found in narrative and expository text.

Related Instructional Strategies

- Text pattern guide
- Plot structure maps
- Graphic representations of expository text
- Close reading
- Selective reading guide

- Text mapping
- Teach internal text structure
- Teach external text structure

Summarizing

Learning to summarize what has been read helps students focus on the important aspects of a text. Summarizing is not the same as retelling. Retelling implies that the student can restate or repeat what was read; summarizing requires that the student sift out just the most important aspects of what was read so that she can restate it in her own words.

Related Instructional Strategies

- Somebody wanted but so
- Story pyramid (narrative)
- Whip around
- Sum it up
- 3-2-1
- GIST

Using Prior Knowledge

Good readers use their prior knowledge and experiences to help them understand a text, and are able to relate new information in the text to their existing cognitive structure.

Related Instructional Strategies

- Brainstorming/list-group-label
- ABC brainstorming
- Carousel brainstorming
- Picture walk/Text walk
- SQ3R or SQ4R
- PQRST
- Read around the text
- Knowledge ratings
- Anticipation guide, anticipation/reaction guide
- Word splash
- Possible sentences
- Probable passages
- Prop predictions
- Character quotes
- Invented dialogues
- Jackdaws

Using Mental Imagery

Many good readers visualize as they read; in other words, they can "make a movie" of the events in the story or text as they read. This visualization helps students to see interrelationships among concepts in the text.

Related Instructional Strategies

- Talking pictures
- Guided imagery

Generating and Answering Questions

Good readers are able to ask their own questions about the information in the text they are reading and to answer questions posed by others.

Related Instructional Strategies

- Three-Level Reading Guide
- Question Answer Relationships (QARs)
- Anticipation/Reaction Guide
- Response sheet/double entry journal
- Inquiry chart

Collaborative Read-Alouds

Engaging Middle School Students in Thoughtful Reading

Susan E. Elliot-Johns and Enrique A. Puig

In "Collaborative Read-Alouds: Engaging Middle School Students in Thoughtful Reading," authors Elliott-Johns and Puig describe an approach to encourage students' engagement with text. Collaborative read-alouds are described and related to close reading and the support of student discourse to enhance comprehension and learning.

LEARNING OBJECTIVES

1. Collaboration is especially important for middle and secondary school learners. What do you remember about educational psychology or human development that supports this view?
2. What are some familiar instructional approaches or strategies that support students' meaningful discourse about text?

Collaborative Read-Alouds

Engaging Middle School Students in Thoughtful Reading

Susan E. Elliot-Johns and Enrique A. Puig

"If we expect meaningful participation and high-level thinking from each student in a small group, we must first plan group tasks carefully and teach discussion skills explicitly."

(Chiaravalloti, 2010, p. 20)

Renewed conversations about close reading in relation to implementation of the Common Core State Standards (CCSS) offer the opportunity to hone both traditional and innovative instructional practices for promoting and supporting middle level students' literacy learning.

Wozniak (2011) makes a strong case for "reading and talking about books" as integral to effective interventions that promote positive attitudes toward reading, encourage students to become more engaged readers, and work to improve test scores. Wilhelm (2013) reminds us that we sometimes focus "too much on the *what* and not enough on the *why* and *how* of reading" (p. 56).

Close reading from a learner's perspective is a self-regulatory behavior intended to enhance and expand understanding. It is an in-the-head call-to-action proficient readers employ when they reread with critical purpose. Close reading as strategic activity requires students to slow down their reading process, pay close attention to the text, and systematically return to the text to enhance and expand understanding (Bass & Linkon, 2008; Paul & Elder, 2003). Determining what the text says explicitly and implicitly, questioning, making inferences, and using textual evidence to support hypertextual, textual, and subtextual interpretations are all key components of close reading; all can be effectively and efficiently demonstrated through a collaborative read-aloud. We define hypertextual interpretations as the questions generated by the reader that are grounded in the text at hand and subtextual interpretations as the implied meaning prompted by the text. Both hypertextual and subtextual interpretations are dependent on the reader's purpose and background knowledge.

Collaborative read-aloud is an instructional practice involving a shared responsibility for an oral reading of a text by a teacher and students to promote interest and engagement across content areas. Consistent with the theme of deepening students' interaction with texts, we propose this instructional practice as a component of intentional and coherent literacy instruction—and as instruction that also supports the development of "close reading" behaviors through "close listening" (Brown & Kappes, 2012). Collaborative read-alouds can increase engagement and understanding as well as enjoyment of the text. In an era of core standards, we share and discuss both the features and benefits of collaborative read-alouds and the importance of including student voices in guiding instructional decisions. We also emphasize how the routine inclusion of collaborative read-alouds, over time, can enhance both instructional practice and student engagement with learning.

During a collaborative read-aloud, both the teacher and selected student, or students, are responsible for the reading. In some cases, it may be a student alone who does the reading. The collaboration comes to fruition when an observant teacher collaborates with a student, or students, to read a selection aloud. Only one text is needed. Ideally, the teacher and/or student(s) have read the selection previously before reading it aloud; that said, opportunities for a "cold read" may occur over time, and those may also be perfectly appropriate. A list of recommended titles for collaborative read-alouds with young adolescents is included (Figure 6.1.1) to help teacher colleagues begin integrating this instructional practice into middle school classrooms.

What Are the Features and Benefits of Collaborative Read-Alouds?

Collaborative read-alouds evolved from the traditional read-alouds employed in many learning environments. Read-alouds are generally accepted by classroom practitioner-scholars and university research-scholars as an instructional practice used in most classrooms. The benefits of traditional read-alouds as an instructional practice to support students' literacy acquisition and development is well documented (Albright & Ariail, 2005; Elliott-Johns, 2013; Press, Heneberg, & Getman, 2009; Roser, Martinez, & Fowler-Amato, 2011). While traditional read-alouds still have potential as a powerful instructional practice when conducted effectively, practitioner-scholars may be missing its full potential when sharing this practice with adolescent students.

A hebegogical perspective supports literacy acquisition by incorporating many voices with a focus on generating a critical view of the text at hand (Elliott-Johns, Booth, Rowsell, Puig, & Paterson, 2012). We make the distinction as follows: A pedagogical perspective accounts for student behavior in the primary grades, while a hebegogical perspective pertains more

- *Daddy's Roommate*, by Michael Willhoite (gay parenting)
- *Encounter* by Jane Yolen, illustrated by David Shannon (discovery of the New World)
- *Frida* by Jonah Winter, illustrated by Ana Juan (artist biography)
- *I Never Knew Your Name* by Sherry Garland, illustrated by Sheldon Greenberg (teenage suicide)
- *Lincoln and Douglass: An American Friendship* by Nikki Giovanni, illustrated by Bryan Collier (Civil War)
- *Madama Butterfly—Giacomo Puccini* by Monica E. Lapenta, illustrated by Stefania Pravato (female suicide)
- *Michelangelo* by Diane Stanley (biography)
- *Nelson Mandela: Long Walk to Freedom* abridged by Chris Van Wyk (apartheid), illustrated by Paddy Bourma
- *Pink and Say* by Patricia Polacco (Civil War)
- *Rose Blanche* by Roberto Innocenti (Holocaust)
- *Smoky Night* by Eve Bunting, illustrated by David Diaz (Los Angeles riots)
- *Fly Away Home* by Eve Bunting, illustrated by Ronald Himler (homelessness)
- *The Lotus Seed* by Sherry Garland, illustrated by Tatsuro Kiuchi (Vietnam War)
- *The Yellow Star: The Legend of Christian X of Denmark* by Carmen Agra Deedy, illustrated by Henri Sorensen (Nazi invasion)
- *Wilfrid Gordon McDonald Partridge* by Mem Fox, illustrated by Julie Vivas (Alzheimer's)
- *Winters Gift* by Jane Monroe Donovan (death and hope)
- *Freedom Like Sunlight* by J. Patrick Lewis (poetry about famous African Americans)
- *Shipwrecked: The True Adventures of a Japanese Boy* by Rhoda Blumberg (Japanese immigration in the 1800s)
- *To Hell With Dying* by Alice Walker, illustrated by Catherine Deeter (death and dying)
- *We Are the Ship: The Story of Negro League Baseball* by Kadir Nelson (African-American baseball league)

FIGURE 6.1.1 Recommended Read-Alouds. Twenty Recommended Crossover Picture Books for Collaborative Read-Alouds.

to adolescent behavior (Elliott-Johns et al., 2012; Puig & Froelich, 2011). We have frequently observed well-intended and experienced practitioner-scholars immerse middle level students in an instructional practice better suited for younger students only to then be dismayed by the lack of engagement among the students.

We emphasize that collaborative read-alouds are not round-robin reading. Rather, a collaborative read-aloud is an instructional practice involving a shared oral reading of a text by a teacher and students to promote interest and engagement, factoring in the strengths and needs of adolescents. As with a traditional read-aloud, only one text is needed, but unlike with a traditional read-aloud, more than one voice may be employed in the reading. In essence, collaborative read-aloud represents a hybrid practice that strives to use the best instructional techniques associated with interactive read-aloud and Readers' Theater to develop innovative classroom practice that mobilizes student engagement.

Guidelines for Implementing Collaborative Read-Alouds

- Keep the introduction brief and conversational and avoid prescribed story review or series of questions.
- Share predictions and anticipation.
- Use new and important words in conversation.
- Ask questions that make intertextual connections (personal, textual, and global).
- When possible, share personal connections to other texts or events.
- Include explorations of text-dependent questions and connections to promote conversation.
- Discuss characters in the text.
- Discuss illustrations as necessary.
- Discuss central themes.

When introducing a collaborative read-aloud, begin by exploring the main idea or central theme in the text, share predictions and anticipations, and introduce new and important vocabulary in conversation with students. Be sure to enable students to share intertextual connections to other texts or world events and to ask questions that also encourage all learners to make those connections. Continue to model and encourage listeners to make their own text-to-self, text-to-text, and text-to-world connections as outlined in the Four Resources Model (Luke & Freebody, 1999). Attention to text-to-text and text-to-world connections will also enable meaningful explorations of text-dependent questions and connections that promote conversation and, in turn, provide the teacher opportunity to assess students' voices.

During collaborative read-aloud and ongoing conversation, teachers and students may explore and discuss different characters in the text and the ways the narrative evolves; include discussion of illustrations to enhance (a) the conversation and (b) listeners' understanding of, and engagement with, the text. Although any text can be used for a collaborative read-aloud, we have found crossover picture books often have the strongest appeal.

Crossover picture books are usually narrative text with characters and issues that pertain to young adolescents. They generally contain more sophisticated themes than traditional children's picture books, and the illustrations are usually more complex, thus prompting deeper thinking and discussion. Similar to young adult novels, crossover picture books attract young adolescents through content, vocabulary, relevance, perspective, genre, and illustrations.

Understanding the Importance of Student Voice in Guiding Instruction

A growing body of research clearly identifies student voice as essential to authentic education (Alexander, 2008; Barnes, 2008; Booth, 2013; Gilles, 2010; Mercer & Hodgkinson, 2008). In our current research and practice, we continue to advocate for increased awareness and understanding of why student voice matters; we're also intent on exploring how teachers can integrate opportunities to promote student voice in literacy learning across the curriculum (Elliott-Johns, et al., 2012).

Understanding the importance of using student voice to guide instructional decisions also relates directly to the implementation of collaborative read-alouds with young adolescents in contemporary learning environments (e.g., developing text-dependent conversations focused on meaning). In addition, teachers must be asking three critical questions linked to instruction. Using "pause ... ponder ... partner" as a strategy, consider:

- What is occurring with these adolescent learners during reading?
- How do I interact with what is occurring?
- Am I intentionally and coherently assisting or assessing performance?

Before we consider interacting with what is occurring, and reflecting on whether we're assisting or assessing performance, we must identify what is occurring with learners during reading. Using student voices, an observant practitioner can then determine how to interact with what is occurring and reflect on whether he or she is assisting or assessing student performance. Think of it as a genuine conversation during which you listen intently so you can respond effectively to promote forward shifts in thinking.

Conclusions

As close reading makes a romantic resurgence into an expanding repertoire of strategic activities, collaborative read-alouds (in which the teacher is not the only voice) is a viable instructional practice with potential to support student learning beyond core standards and across content areas. Like Readers' Theater and interactive read-alouds, collaborative read-alouds entice middle level students to engage with text and to revisit personal interpretations on sound criteria. It sets the stage for student voice (e.g., the collaborative selection of texts by teachers *and* students and shared voices in the reading), thus also fostering active participation from a variety of readers and listeners. In our experience, it can be a highly useful (and adaptable) instructional practice when employed by practitioner-scholars across all content areas to promote transdisciplinary literacy acquisition. Furthermore, it can be used to promote close listening and close reading as a strategic activity for deeper comprehension—and, thereby, more meaningful interactions with text.

Encouraging practitioner-scholars' conversations around collaborative read-aloud provides numerous professional learning opportunities to amplify student voices in contemporary learning environments. Doing so also further supports the development of intentional and coherent instructional practice informed by research.

References

Albright, L. K., & Ariail, M. (2005). Tapping the potential of teacher read-alouds in middle school. *Journal of Adolescent & Adult Literacy, 48*, 582–591.

Alexander, R. (2008). Culture, dialogue, and learning: Notes on an emerging pedagogy. In N. Mercer & S. Hodgkinson (Eds.), *Exploring talk in schools: Inspired by the work of Douglas Barnes* (pp. 91–114). Thousand Oaks, CA: SAGE.

Barnes, D. (2008). Exploratory talk for learning. In N. Mercer & S. Hodgkinson (Eds.), *Exploring talk in schools: Inspired by the work of Douglas Barnes* (pp. 1–16). Thousand Oaks, CA: SAGE.

Bass, R., & Linkon, S. L. (2008). On the evidence of theory: Close reading as a disciplinary model for writing about teaching and learning. *Arts and Humanities in Higher Education, 7*(3), 245–261.

Booth, D. (2013). *I've got something to say: How student voices inform our teaching*. Portland, ME: Stenhouse.

Brown, S., & Kappes, L. (2012). *Implementing the Common Core State Standards: A primer on "close reading of text."* Washington, DC: The Aspen Institute. Retrieved from http://www.aspendrl.org/portal/browse/DocumentDetail?documentId=1396&download

Chiaravalloti, L.A. (2010). "Wouldn't she notice he had mud on his shirt?": Scaffolding meaningful discussions. *Voices from the Middle, 18*(2), 16–25.

Elliott-Johns, S.E. (2013). What are the merits and challenges of reading aloud in class? In K. James, T. Dobson, & C. Leggo (Eds.), *English in middle and secondary school classrooms: Creative and critical advice from Canada's teacher educators* (pp. 168–171). Toronto, ON: Pearson Education.

Elliott-Johns, S. E., Booth, D., Rowsell, J., Puig, E. A., & Paterson, J. (2012). Using student voices to guide instruction. *Voices from the Middle, 19*(3), 25–31.

Gilles, C. (2010). Making the most of talk. *Voices from the Middle, 18*(2), 16–25.

Luke, A., & Freebody, P. (1999). A map of possible practices: Further notes on the four resources model. *Practically Primary, 4*(2), 5–8.

Mercer, N., & Hodgkinson, S. (Eds.). (2008). *Exploring talk in schools: Inspired by the work of Douglas Barnes*. Thousand Oaks, CA: SAGE.

Paul, R., & Elder, L. (2003). *The thinker's guide to how to read a paragraph: The art of close reading*. Dillon Beach, CA: The Foundation for Critical Thinking.

Press, M., Henenberg, E., & Getman, D. (2009). Read-alouds move to the middle level. *Educator's Voice, 2*, 36–42.

Puig, E. A., & Froelich, K. S. (2011). *The literacy coach: Guiding in the right direction* (2nd ed.). Boston, MA: Allyn & Bacon/Pearson.

Roser, N., Martinez, M., & Fowler-Amato, M. (2011). The power of picturebooks: Resources that support language and learning in middle grade classrooms. *Voices from the Middle, 19*(1), 24–31.

Wilhelm, J. (2013). CODA: The power of pleasure: What about helping students forge their own reading lives? *Voices from the Middle, 21*(1), 56–58.

Wozniak, C. L. (2011). Reading and talking about books: A critical foundation for intervention. *Voices from the Middle, 19*(2), 17–21.

Discussion Questions

1. What is the "hebegogical" perspective outlined in the article and how does it relate to the collaborative read-aloud?
2. In the article, Elliott-Johns and Puig mention the "Four Resources Model." What is this model? If you're unsure, do some research and summarize what you learn.
3. Why is student voice critical in middle and secondary literacy instruction?

Thinking While Reading

The Beautiful Mess of Helping Adolescents Discover and Celebrate How Their Minds Work

Maggie Beattie Roberts and Kritin Robbins Warren

In this article, Roberts and Warren explore their idea of an "independent reading journey," a process that supports students as they become active and critical readers of text.

LEARNING OBJECTIVES

1. Why is it important for students to learn to read actively?
2. What are some instructional strategies or approaches that you know which can be used for this purpose?

Thinking While Reading

The Beautiful Mess of Helping Adolescents Discover and Celebrate How Their Minds Work

Maggie Beattie Roberts and Kritin Robbins Warren

Middle school is beautiful—and sometimes a bit messy. Young adolescents are in the throes of discovering themselves and how they relate to the world. They are in the midst of deep analytical thinking, busy analyzing friends' actions, making meaning of their families, synthesizing their place within their peer groups. In any given moment, they're interpreting texts from friends, song lyrics from favorite artists, passing looks from other students. Our middle level students are doing the beautifully messy work of understanding themselves, creating ideas about how the world works, and figuring out how to fit into it all.

It's surprising, then, that when we ask them to do similar thinking as readers of texts, it falls flat or doesn't translate. The same thinking skills vibrant in their social-emotional lives can, at times, lay dormant when asked to analyze, interpret, or synthesize ideas from a text. When this happens, responses to reading feel phoned in, thrown together, or not given much care. They feel more like responses to assignments and less like personal discoveries.

We began craving a way to help our students' reading lives mirror more closely their layered social lives and deep discovery of themselves. We knew, chances were good that this recalibration of their reading lives wasn't going to happen in one assignment or one unit. We found ourselves seeking "a long game," a way students could discover themselves as readers and thinkers of texts that stretched across the year. Growth and discovery takes time. We knew we couldn't rush the process. We also knew this long game had to stem from the students—the books they were reading, the ways their minds worked, their own pacing. Agency, independence, and choice are crucial for any personal discovery, and they would be for this kind of reading discovery too.

So we began a year of teaching with an inquiry, "How can we help our students discover and celebrate how their minds work to think deeply about a text?" Our answer became the *Independent Reading Journey*.

What Are Independent Reading Journeys?

An independent reading journey is a month-long process during which each student selects a book of her choice to read, analyze, and critique. Students begin their journeys by capturing their initial thoughts and musings while they read. Then, after a week or so of this work, students annotate their initial thinking and explore their thoughts in a variety of ways. Independent reading journeys culminate at the end of the month in a formal piece of writing, showing the analysis or critique of a text. (Each stage is described in detail and paired with examples of student work below.)

Students complete one reading journey a month across the school year during students' independent reading time. In Kristen's eighth-grade reading workshop, students have time each day to read books of their own choosing independently. Our goal is for these journeys to empower students' own self-exploration and thinking process, so choice over book selection is key. Students are empowered when they choose books that inspire them, whether fiction, nonfiction, or poetry. If book choice is the fuel for each reading journey, then each book is the vehicle for the student to explore his own thinking pathways.

We arrived at the creation of these independent reading journeys because reading and thinking about texts felt mechanical for many of our students. We wished for reading response experiences to feel organic, curious, and natural, rather than rushed or forced. We knew we were fighting against old systems of schooling, as Ken Robinson, author of *Creative Schools*, states in his TED talk (2006). "We have to go from what is essentially an industrial model of education ... which is based on linearity and conformity ... We have to recognize that human flourishing is not a mechanical process; it's an organic process" (15:45). Lingering for a month in an independent reading journey is important for students to have authentic, unharried reading experiences that are balanced with reading time and response time.

Most students read more than one book a month, while focusing on one book for their independent reading journey. It's important for students to have plenty of reading time where they don't "produce" anything. As Donalyn Miller and Penny Kittle remind us, it is absolutely necessary for students to have time where they can simply read. The work of each stage is subtle enough that students can dip in and dip out of their journeys while preserving their independent reading.

Let's take a look at the process.

Stage One: Gathering Annotations
The first stage of an independent reading journey begins with students tapping into what catches their attention as they read a text. This stage guides readers to notice where and when

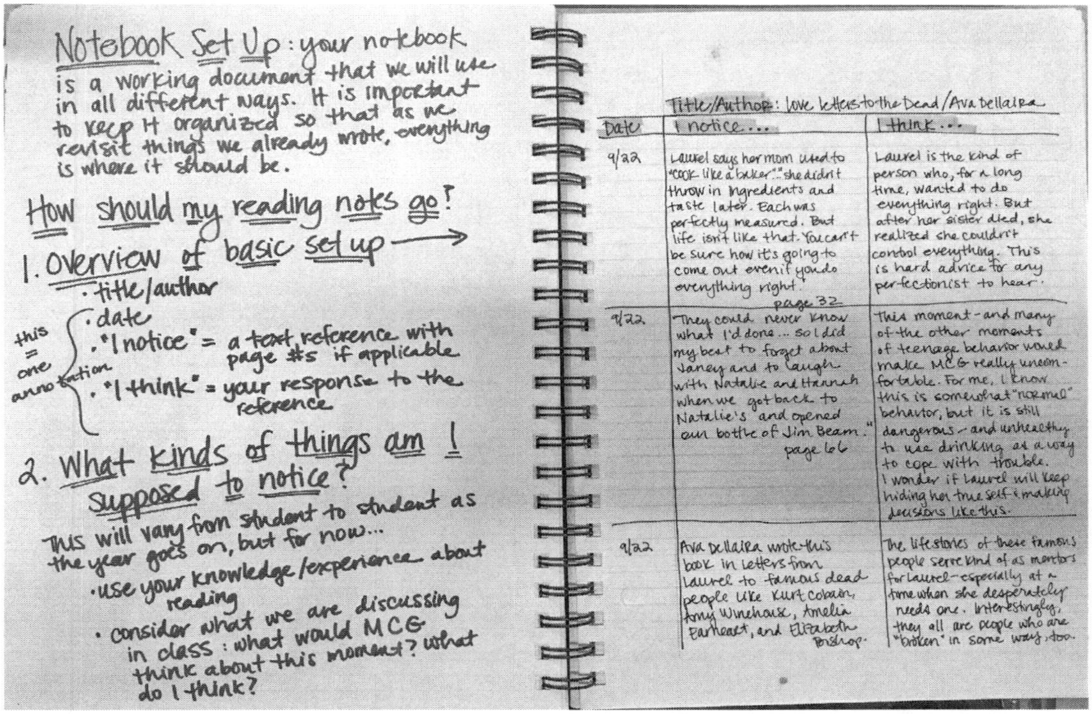

FIGURE 6.2.1 Kristen Models Her Reading Response Notebook During the First Stage.

they instinctively stop and pause to think, even if only for a split second. We ask students to jot down those moments and their thoughts in their reading notebooks periodically while reading.

As you can see in Figure 6.2.1, we use a simple, effective note-taking framework: a two-column chart with one side labeled *I Notice* ... and the second labeled *I Think* ... We help students find their best method to interrupt their reading momentarily to think: Do they need to mark the spot in the story and revisit it when they aren't "lost in the book"? Is it an urgent thought they should try to capture in their notebooks before it leaves? It's important to help students find their rhythms as readers—their natural timing—of stopping to notice and reflect.

The work of this first stage helps readers do three things: notice *when* to stop, *what* to notice, and *what* to think. First, many readers will need more help noticing when to stop in a text to notice and think. In their recent *Notice and Note* series, Kylene Beers and Robert Probst offer concrete signposts, noticeable points in a text that stand out as significant, as places to pause and think (2012). They help young adolescents learn *when* to stop in a text to notice and note by clarifying exactly when in a text one might stop and think. For instance, they describe Contrasts and Contradictions, when a character does something unexpected, as helpful places to pause and think. This explicit naming of when to stop, notice, and take note crystallizes the universal moments in texts when something is worth noticing and thinking about.

In addition to figuring out when to stop and think, students tend to need help with *what* to notice. Teach them that as readers, we often underline, flag, or mentally file parts of a text we're called to linger on. Perhaps the main character has a major realization, you notice a theme beginning to develop, or you're struck by a metaphor. In Figure 6.2.1, Kristen models what she notices as she reads and offers explicit coaching of what kinds of things to notice. For instance, she coaches her students to notice things being taught in the current unit or discussed in class. It's important to let them know that they'll notice different things and that's okay. After all, this practice has its roots in Louise Rosenblatt's transactional reading theory, where each student may notice different aspects of the same text (1978). Responding to reading isn't formulaic or one-size-fits-all. Even when students read the same text, they each notice what their eyes are drawn to see.

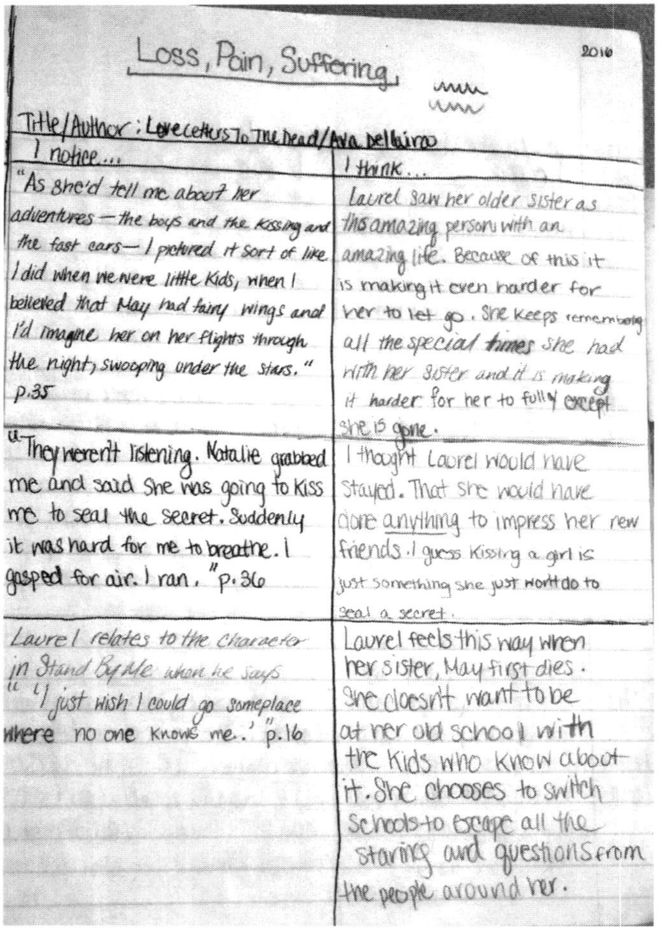
Loss, Pain, Suffering 2016

Title/Author: Love Letters To The Dead/Ava Dellaira

I notice...	I think...
"As she'd tell me about her adventures — the boys and the kissing and the fast cars — I pictured it sort of like I did when we were little kids, when I believed that May had fairy wings and I'd imagine her on her flights through the night, swooping under the stars." p.35	Laurel saw her older sister as this amazing person with an amazing life. Because of this it is making it even harder for her to let go. She keeps remembering all the special times she had with her sister and it is making it harder for her to fully except she is gone.
"They weren't listening. Natalie grabbed me and said she was going to kiss me to seal the secret. Suddenly it was hard for me to breathe. I gasped for air. I ran." p.36	I thought Laurel would have stayed. That she would have done anything to impress her new friends. I guess kissing a girl is just something she just won't do to seal a secret.
Laurel relates to the character in Stand By Me when he says "'I just wish I could go someplace where no one knows me.'" p.16	Laurel feels this way when her sister, May first dies. She doesn't want to be at her old school with the kids who know about it. She chooses to switch schools to escape all the staring and questions from the people around her.

FIGURE 6.2.2 Zaria's Annotations During Stage One.

Lastly, during this first stage, some students will need support figure out exactly *what* to think. Kristen routinely provides guiding questions or sentence starters that encourage the development of their thinking:

- *Why is this moment important?*
- *What do you find surprising about this moment?*
- *This makes me wonder …*
- *This makes me think …*

Students can staple these supports into their notebooks or use them as a bookmark for support as they discover their thinking.

Stage Two: Annotating Initial Annotations

In the midst of middle school beautiful messiness, while students are often in a rush when it comes to schoolwork, their initial ideas are generally the start of something great. So during stage two, we encourage students to revisit, reflect, and revise their initial thoughts. Students have typically made serious progress in a book by this stage, as they are in the second week of their month-long journey. They'll be poised to have deeper insights on earlier ideas because they have more text under their belts, and, when given the opportunity to reflect, realize how much more they have to say!

When students annotate their initial annotations, they return to their notes and look for "the good stuff." Lucy Calkins (Calkins, Ehrenworth, & Lehman, 2012) calls a similar process "reading them as if they are gold" meaning to reread a text or notes, mining for "gold" (p. 8). In addition, Chris Lehman (2012) encourages students to "return to their notes to develop larger concepts" when reflecting on their notes (p. 33). Specifically, we have students re-read what they've written with a different color pen in hand, ready to underline or circle their most thought-provoking ideas. Students read with a sense of curiosity, ready to find places they have more to say in their notes or want to explore. Students tend to add on to what they've initially written using sticky notes or the space in the margins.

Students can struggle in the best of ways during this stage, as we are asking them to wrestle with extending their thoughts: How *does* one say more about an idea? Thought-provoking ideas tend to be ideas we want to work through or feel in our gut like we're onto something. When students are saying more about their initial notes, questions and sentence starters like these can help:

- *In this moment, what complex emotions does the character feel?*
- *This makes me wonder …*
- *Now I understand that …*
- *This connects to …*
- *What I'm really trying to say is …*
- *What might this book actually be about?*

This gives students the nudge into deeper analysis and offers different layers of support for a variety of learners. In Kristen's class, some students linger with one support for a few series of

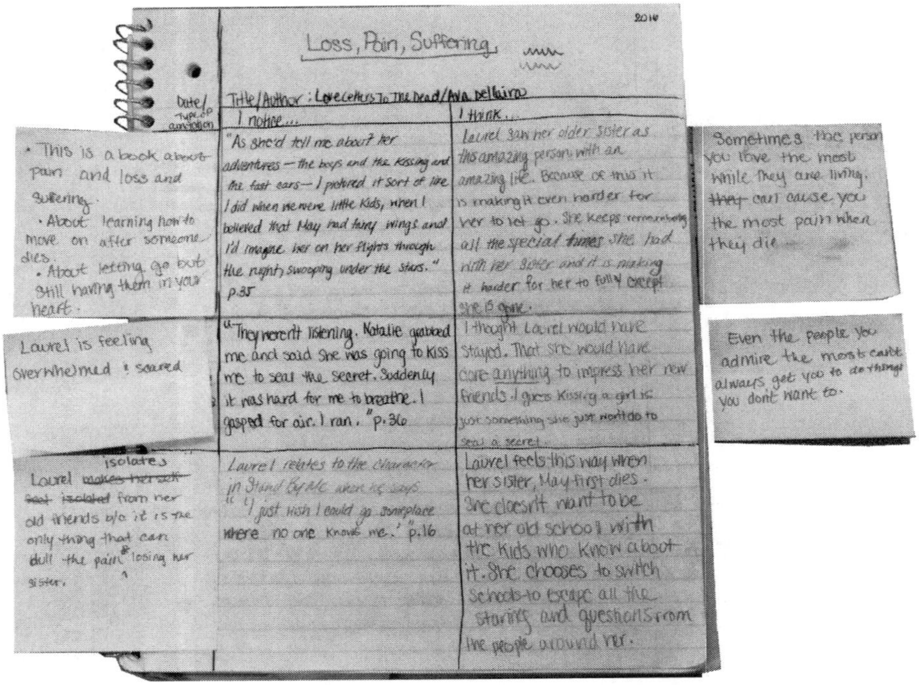

FIGURE 6.2.3   Zaria Annotates Her Initial Annotations Using Sticky Notes.

reading journeys, for instance, naming complex emotions. While other students move through these sentence starters, trying out different ones all year. Some internalize these supports quite quickly or annotate their thinking without scaffolding at all.

Kristen models the hefty work on thinking about her own thinking explicitly and energetically. This is reflective, metacognitive work, and it is the catalyst for deeper thinking and analysis. For instance, after reading through her initial annotations, Kristen might say, "Ok, while reading *Love Letters to the Dead,* I jotted about the devastation the main character felt after losing her family." After naming the complex emotions the character feels, she continues by saying, "I'm realizing that it's important to remember the intangible gifts in life. They can help us move forward in times of deep struggle." Then she jots that thinking on sticky note, laying it over her initial jots. Lucy Calkins often says that reading work is life work, and when students watch their teacher read meaningfully, they'll be more motivated to go on such thinking journeys themselves (Calkins, Ehrenworth, & Lehman, 2012).

After students begin annotating their initial annotations, remind them of the opportunities to explore life through a text. During this stage, encourage students to make connections within their larger annotations. Making connections deepens the bond to the text and draws a reader inward. It's also common during this stage for students to notice patterns of thinking across their jots. Perhaps they have a lot of annotations surrounding a particular character or they realize their ideas are often connected to a certain topic or theme. Celebrate these patterns, as they are a way for students to see how things connect or why they might circle back to one idea.

A highlight of this stage is watching students discover all the ideas they have about a text and discover their voices as readers and thinkers. While the work of this stage is happening during independent reading or outside of school, make sure to invite students to share some of their developments. This opportunity of collaboration celebrates growth from initiation thinking to more revised thinking and inspires students to learn from each other's unique thinking. It's beautiful to watch students be impressed with each other from listening to the insights into their reading.

Stage Three: Thinking Guides

In this third stage, when students have finished their books and have finished their annotations, we offer students a canvas—a blank sheet of paper—to illustrate the journey of thinking they've traveled over the past two or three weeks and to develop new lines of thinking. This stage is punctuated by questions that drive inquiry: What thoughts do you have about this text? How are your ideas connected? Is there one big idea you want to think about more? What have you realized? This stage gives students the freedom to explore their thinking and find ways to bring it all together visually.

While students begin with the same materials—blank paper, colored pencils, markers—each child illustrates the development of his or her own thinking process across a chosen text. Students visually organize their thinking in a way that makes sense to them, with some similarities to Tony Buzan's Mind Maps. We highly encourage the expression of development, ramblings and musings where students track smaller realizations across the page that lead to larger thoughts. Students vary in their representations of thinking; some students are more linear where others are more abstract. We encourage students to illustrate and use color symbolically, as this is the stage to explore all the ways their individual minds work best.

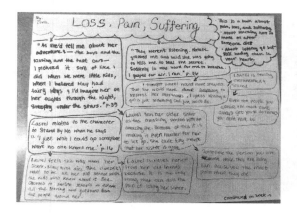

FIGURE 6.2.4   Zaria's Thinking Guide.

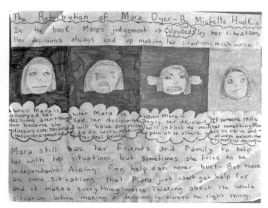

FIGURE 6.2.5   Kyndal's Thinking Guide.

We lean on the power of modeling to help students navigate this process. We show students our Thinking Guides to explicitly teach different ways to express the development of thinking, from flow charts to webs to timelines (see Figure 6.2.6 for examples). For example, after reading *I'll Give You the Sun*, Kristen might say,

> When I read over my annotations, what I noticed is that I basically can't stop thinking about the role of art in this book, and I want to think about it some more. I'm going to create a web and simply put "ART" in the middle of my page. Then I'm going to create some branches for Noah, Jude, their mom … I'm going to use arrows to show how my ideas grow. I may draw some connecting lines and then write how they connect. And, since this is about art, maybe I'll create some of my own that will symbolize each of the characters."

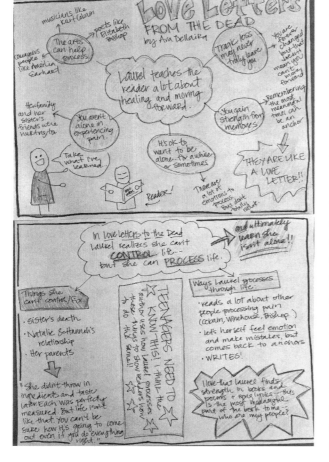

FIGURE 6.2.6   Two of Kristen's Thinking Guides to Model Stage 3 for Students.

Narrating your thought process helps students get acquainted with how *their* minds work and helps them better articulate their processes. Later, students can narrate their processes for each other and for you. As students are working and you move around the room, a lot of explicit teaching comes into play. You can visibly see the thinking that is usually invisible, and this allows you lots of possibilities for feedback.

The next day, students display their Thinking Guides around the room and take a walking tour, noticing the different ways their peers have represented their thinking. These walking tours allow room for peer-led teaching. This creates a real audience for their work, which increases engagement and pride students have in their work, as well as encourages risk-taking for trying new structures of thinking.

This third stage gives students a canvas to push their thinking and create material to draw upon during the final stage of their reading journeys. Students are set up more successfully because they've had room to develop complex, independent thinking prior to a formal piece of writing.

Stage Four: A Destination

As journeys have a destination, we help students culminate their independent reading journeys into a final piece of writing. The platform of this final stage is up to you and could be a variety of forms: a published essay, a notebook entry, or a speech. In Kristen's class, this looks like a blog post, where students turn their thinking guides into organized pieces of writing for a digital audience. We found particular success with publishing online, due to its interactive nature. Publishing online creates an expansive audience of readers, as well as facilitates a culture of response through peer-led comments. This authentic audience boosts engagement and work quality and amplifies student voices in a way that's broader than handing in a paper to one reader—the teacher. Blogging platforms like *Wordpress* and *Kidblog* are known for their ease of use, safety, and simplicity.

We confer with writers often during this stage and help them set sail into their own thinking discoveries. For the first few reading journeys, students sit in the computer lab with their Thinking Guides close by, using them as an unconventional outline of sorts. Although these guides tend to be organized in nonlinear ways, they provide an authentic jumping off point for students to dive into their writing headfirst, leading with their big ideas. While it might feel risky at first, as students don't have a bulleted list of points, we've found most students have a built-in navigational system for composing a piece of writing and transfer their ideas into purposeful paragraphs quite seamlessly (see Figure 6.2.7 for Zaria's final piece of writing).

This last stage celebrates the destination of the journey—students have propelled themselves to their own original thinking, following the natural ways their minds work when thinking about

Love Letters To The Dead by Ava Dellaira is a book about loss, pain, suffering, and learning to heal. In the book the main character, Laurel begins writing to dead people as a school assignment. It soon grows into a way she copes with the death of her sister, May and begins moving on. This is a book about learning how to move on after someone dies. It is about letting go but still knowing that they will always be in your heart.

Losing someone can change you. Most of the time you can't do anything about that, but you're the one who can decide whether it will make you better or worse. It may feel like you have lost all hope after someone dies and that you now have no one else, but you must remember that they will always be in your heart. Even if it's hard for you to accept you should know it's true. Don't shut everyone out when you're going through a hard time because if you continue to do it they might not be there to help you when you feel like you can't go on and realize you need them. The pain and ache you feel will get better as the days, then weeks, then months, then years go by. You will start to heal. Your wounds will close and begin to fade away. They will be gone, but never forgotten in your heart.

FIGURE 6.2.7   An Excerpt of the Beginning and Ending of Zaria's Final Blog Post. For the Full Post, Visit: Http://Ow.ly/Yp7bb.

a text. Students have had the time to investigate the corners of their thinking, following leads or hunches about a text, character, theme, conflict.

Implications for Teaching and Learning across the Year

We began a year of teaching with an inquiry: "How can we help our students discover and celebrate how their minds work to think deeply about a text?" Throughout this year of inquiry, we had ahas, disappointments, and questions. We share a few of our questions and discoveries here, as they may help you with this work:

When do I teach into this process? At first, it felt like we were teaching into this process a lot! In fact, September became a unit on launching strong independent reading, and a majority of our whole-class lessons were on the four stages. We walked through the first journey together, leaning on a lot of modeling and coaching. And while launching these journeys took a bit of time at the beginning of the year, students needed less whole-class teaching as they began their second, third, and fourth journeys. By the year's end, students were moving through the process independently with ease and confidence—one of our biggest hopes for them.

When do students do this work? On a practical level, we discovered most of first stage of annotations happened during independent reading periods or outside of class. We tended to give students class time for the work of stage two—annotating annotations—often less than 15 minutes. We found students needed a bit of extra support during this stage, so we dedicated small bits of class time for that work. By the time students got to stage three, they generally had an idea for what they wanted to explore in their thinking guides. We tended to give them one period in class for that work. This way, they had access to their peers to discuss and compare as well as our coaching.

How does this fit with whole-class teaching and units of study? We knew we wanted this to complement our whole-class teaching and units of study and **not** become our entire reading curriculum. We were a little nervous at first because we dedicated a lot of class time to it. However, we found that with each reading journey under their belts, students had greater and greater independence with their processes.

How does this work impact daily teaching and learning? One discovery we made was recognizing how transferrable this process became. For instance, we noticed how students independently made thinking guides while in a unit on analyzing poetry. Or students "annotated their annotations" while researching for their argument essays. This transference was exciting: It showed how students internalized their own thinking and analysis process.

We opened a window into each child's mind and the way each worked. Studying each student's independent process revealed different needs that otherwise we could have missed. We saw who struggled making inferences and who struggled to connect smaller ideas to larger ones. We saw the child who lingered in books that were too easy for her and the one who struggled to find time to read. These observations helped personalize daily instruction and identify which students needed more help.

The Journey of the Long Game

We knew this would be a long-game approach to reading—setting up a process that students would move through again and again across the year, independently. And where students didn't unlock the inner workings of their minds after the first or second reading journey, they ended the year having a more confident grasp on how they make meaning, analyze, and critique a text—on their own.

Since students move through this month-long process repeatedly, they have the opportunity to "see learning as recursive," as Donna Santman says in *Shades of Meaning* (2005). Learning doesn't move forward in a steady line but loops back over itself and accumulates. And strong learners build space into their learning opportunities to step back and think about how they have grown and what goals they might create for the future. (p. 18) Because independent reading journeys are cyclical across the year, students have multiple opportunities to practice and outgrow their prior work.

In *The Book Whisperer*, Donalyn Miller (2009) shares she "realized that every lesson, conference, response, and assignment I taught must lead students away from me and toward their autonomy as literate people" (p. 16). We found that with each reading journey, students moved further away from us and more toward themselves. This was our hope for our students' independent reading journeys.

We want this confidence and independence for our readers as they go into high school. We want students to know what to do and how to think *independently* when handed a book in English class. This work allows students to recognize and take pride in their unique thinking processes and how their ideas resonate with a larger community of readers and thinkers.

References

Beers, G. K., & Probst, R. E. (2012). *Notice & note: Strategies for close reading.* Portsmouth, NH: Heinemann.

Calkins, L., Ehrenworth, M., & Lehman, C. (2012). *Pathways to the Common Core: Accelerating achievement.* Portsmouth, NH: Heinemann.

Lehman, C. (2012). *Energize research reading and writing: Fresh strategies to spark interest, develop independence, and meet key Common Core standards, grades 4–8.* Portsmouth, NH: Heinemann.

Kittle, P. (2012). *Book love: Developing depth, stamina, and passion in adolescent readers.* Portsmouth, NH: Heinemann.

Miller, D., & Anderson, J. (2009). *The book whisperer: Awakening the inner reader in every child.* San Francisco, CA: Jossey-Bass.

Robinson, K. (2006, Feb.) *Ken Robinson: Do schools kill creativity?* [Video file]. Retrieved from https://www.ted.com/talks/ken_robinson_says_schools_kill_creativity

Rosenblatt, L. M. (1978). *The reader, the text, the poem: The transactional theory of the literary work.* Carbondale, IL: Southern Illinois University Press.

Santman, D. (2005). *Shades of meaning: Comprehension and interpretation in middle school.* Portsmouth, NH: Heinemann.

Discussion Questions

1. The authors state, "... it is absolutely necessary for students to have time where they can simply read." Do you agree or disagree with this statement? Why?
2. Create a graphic organizer that outlines the stages of the independent reading journey. Include the purpose, activities, and benefits of each stage in your organizer.

CHAPTER 6

Conclusion

Chapter Activities

Activity 6.1
Select one of the reading comprehension strategies identified in this chapter. Research the strategy. Create an anchor chart or a strategy bookmark that could be given to middle or secondary school students to remind them what the strategy is, when to use it, why to use it, and how to use it.

Activity 6.2
Read the additional information about collaborative read-alouds available at the link in the Online Resources section of this chapter.

   Identify a text appropriate to share with a middle-level class. Following the directions on the website (Part 1), plan a collaborative read-aloud for that text.

Activity 6.3
Conduct research on the benefits of student choice and independent free reading time. Locate at least three recent research articles that provide support for these approaches. Use the information from the articles to develop a brochure that could be shared with other teachers to encourage them to incorporate choice and independent reading into their literacy curriculum.

Activity 6.4

Read the information about typical text structures found in informational text, which is available in the text structure link in the Online Resources section of this chapter. Using a middle- or secondary-level science or social studies text, identify one text example of each type. Then, locate an appropriate graphic organizer for each of the text types using the text structure graphic organizers link. Complete one graphic organizer for each of your text-type examples.

Online Resources

Collaborative Read-Alouds: Engaging Middle School Students in Thoughtful Reading

http://www.readwritethink.org/professional-development/strategy-guides/teacher-read-aloud-that-30799.html

Text Structure

http://www.adlit.org/strategies/23336/

Text Structure Graphic Organizers

https://education.illinoisstate.edu/downloads/casei/3-01-04-handout%20TextStructureRe-sources%201.pdf

Academic Literacy

Academic literacy is the ability to make meaning of academic content presented in a variety of "texts," including texts in both traditional and digital formats. People who are academically literate can read, write about, and critically discuss texts, as well as create their own.

Chapter Focus Questions

1. Academic literacy is based on students' ability to think critically and to express their own ideas and opinions. Is this consistent with the current school "system" experienced by today's students?
2. How teachers use digital technologies to capture students' attention and to enhance their learning in middle- and secondary-level classrooms?

Using Literature to Teach Inference across the Curriculum

William P. Bintz, Petra Pienkosky Moran, and Rochelle Berndt

William Bintz explores various meanings of the term "inference" in his article, "Using Literature to Teach Inference across the Curriculum," and presents a variety of ways to support students' inferencing abilities.

LEARNING OBJECTIVES

1. Define "inference" in your own words.
2. Explain why the ability to make inferences is critical for academic literacy.

Using Literature to Teach Inference across the Curriculum

William P. Bintz, Petra Pienkosky Moran, and Rochelle Berndt

> *"Inference is a statement about the unknown made on the basis of the known."*
>
> —Hayakawa, 1939

More than 70 years ago, S. I. Hayakawa, noted linguist, teacher, and statesman, recognized the power and potential of inference. Today, increasing numbers of teachers at all grade levels are doing the same.

They are recognizing that inference is a powerful way of thinking and an important 21st century skill for all students to use and develop across the curriculum. One sixth-grade teacher and her students experienced it for themselves. She stated:

> At the beginning of the year, I taught *Tiger Rising* (2002) by Kate DiCamillo. It is a wonderful book to teach inference. There is a symbol of a suitcase in that book. Students totally grasped the idea of a suitcase and its relationship to inference. Every character in the book has a suitcase and that is how you learn about the character—through that character's suitcase. And all people have a suitcase in real life. It was a very powerful symbol for my sixth-graders and an overarching theme for the year. I didn't plan it. My students just took the symbol and made it their own.

In addition to inference, increasing numbers of teachers are also recognizing that developing and implementing integrative curriculum is important at all grade levels, especially in middle grades education. It is one of seven design elements found in *Turning Points 2000* (Jackson & Davis, 2000) and a core characteristic of successful middle schools in *This We Believe* (National Middle School Association, 2003) and

Research & Resources in Support of This We Believe (Anfara et al., 2003). Using literature to teach inference across the curriculum is an effective way to implement this design element.

This article shares literature and strategies to teach inference across the curriculum in middle grades education (grades 5–8). We begin with background on inference and then share literature and strategies to teach inference in science, social studies, mathematics, and language arts.

Background on Inference

Inference is a popular but nebulous term. This is due in large part to the fact that inference has been defined in many different ways. Among others, it has been defined as making predictions, drawing conclusions, using context clues, activating background knowledge, filling gaps, creating interpretations, visualizing meaning, and dealing with ambiguity. These definitions share two important understandings about inference—namely, that it is "the heart of meaning construction for learners of all ages" (Anderson & Pearson, 1984, p. 107), and it involves the ability to read between the lines (Harvey & Goudvis, 2007).

Inference can be understood on multiple levels. At one level, it can be viewed as an inherent, natural thinking process that individuals use to pose and solve problems. Specifically, it is a constructive thinking process by which individuals continually create and evaluate competing hypotheses in an attempt to progressively refine their thinking and understanding in order to ultimately solve a problem (Phillips, 1988). This process occurs as meaning is continually created and reconstructed, and is based on the notion that "confirming and disconfirming leads to new inferences and new predictions" (Goodman, 1996, p. 114). From birth, humans constantly, routinely, and almost effortlessly make inferences.

At another level, inference can be viewed as an integral part of the reading process. It posits that readers must do more than just read words in a text. They must lift up the words and go beneath them (Keene & Zimmerman, 2007). In addition, readers must be active, curious, use background knowledge, and recognize text clues to make sense of text. Simply stated, readers must understand seen and unseen text (Tovani, 2000) or, as Gallagher (2004) stated, "[R]eaders must see and consider things that are literally not on the printed page" (p. 80).

Inference is not uninformed guessing. The distinction is important. Guessing does not necessarily require supporting textual evidence, but inference does. It requires that "readers merge their background knowledge with clues in the text to come up with an idea that isn't written down in the text. ... readers base their inferences on text evidence—that's what makes inferring different from guessing" (Harvey & Goudvis, 2005, p. 1). Moreover, "inferences are not random. While they may surface mysteriously with a sudden jump of recognition (a sense of 'Ah ha!'), inferences are very orderly. In short, inferences are informed guesses based on supporting evidence" (Kurland, 2000, p. 1).

Literature and Strategies

Literature is a powerful way to teach inference across the curriculum. Here, we provide picture-books (see Appendix A), young adult literature (see Appendix B) and instructional strategies to teach inference in science, social studies, mathematics, and language arts.

Inference in Science

"An inference is a hypothesis drawn from both previous knowledge and current cues, such as spoken words and sounds; written words and pictures; graphs and information; physical, emotional, and environmental prompts; and reactions of others. The person making the inference continues to gather information to test the correctness of the hypothesis. In short, it is thinking." (7th/8th-grade teacher)

Inference means readers go beyond surface understandings and delve deeper into meanings of text. In other words, they must know what text says and what text means. "What It Says, What It Means" is a strategy we used with *Uno's Garden* (Base, 2006) to integrate literacy and science (see Table 7.1.1).

Uno's Garden is an ecological account of what happens when humans occupy a natural area. Uno lives in a forest. More people join him. Uno's forest becomes a village, then a city. As the number of people increases, the number of plants and animals decreases. People leave. Uno tends his garden. A snortlepig appears. In the end, Uno and the snortlepig die. Plants grow again

TABLE 7.1.1   What It Says, What It Means (using *Uno's Garden*, Base, 2006)

What It Says	What It Means
1. Uno decides to live in the forest because it is beautiful.	1. The forest is in ecological balance with the appropriate numbers of plants and animals.
2. When the town becomes a city, scientists begin studying the animals.	2. As the city grows, fewer and fewer animals exist until there are none; scientists are compelled to study these organisms before they disappear.
3. Uno remains in the city and continues to tend his garden with a few plants and one animal (snortlepig).	3. Uno's garden is the only source of living plants and a single animal in the decaying city.
4. Uno's children and grandchildren document the gradual return of plants and animals to the deserted city.	4. If left to its own, nature will regenerate itself over time and ecological succession occurs.
5. The forest and the city are in perfect balance again.	5. Plants, animals, and humans can all thrive together with appropriate planning and consideration for all (sustainable ecosystem).
6. The snortlepig is never seen again.	6. The snortlepig died, the species is now extinct, and extinction is forever.

and animals return. People again populate the area, but this time they build sustainable homes. The snortlepig is never seen again.

The story illustrates *ecological succession*—the sequence of changes in community development. The inference is that humans need to be aware of the impact they have on their environment and make efforts to live in sustainable ways.

"What It Says, What It Means" helps teach inference. As shown in the left column of Table 7.1.1, readers record ideas explicitly stated in the text. In the right column, they make inferences from these ideas. An inference from "The snortlepig is never seen again" is that the snortlepig died, the species is extinct, and extinction is forever. An inference from "Uno's children and grand-children document the gradual return of plants and animals to the deserted city" is that nature regenerates itself over time and ecological succession occurs.

Inference in Social Studies

"Inference is the ability to draw a conclusion based on direct or indirect information discerned through conversation or text." (6th-grade teacher)

Readers make inferences based on text evidence and actual outcomes. "Inference Sheet" (Adams & Pierce, 2006) is a strategy used with *Fly Away Home* (Bunting, 1993) to integrate literacy and social studies (see Table 7.1.2).

In *Fly Away Home,* a little boy and his father live in an airport. They are homeless. To avoid notice, they sleep sitting up and move from terminal to terminal. The boy resents others who do have homes and wants him and his dad to have their own home. One day the boy sees a bird that has accidentally flown into the airport and is trying to escape. The bird finds a way out and flies to free-dom. The story ends on a hopeful note. Like the bird, the boy hopes one day to also fly away home.

TABLE 7.1.2   Inference Sheet for Fly Away Home (Bunting, 1993)

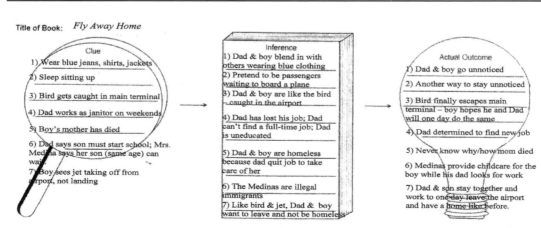

The "Inference Sheet" strategy illustrates the relationship between context clues, inferences, and actual outcomes. One relationship in the story involves the father, his son, and the Medina family (another homeless family living in the airport). The little boy's father says he must go to school. The Medina family, who has a son the same age, say their son has to wait before he goes to school. A plausible inference is that the Medina family is here illegally and must remain unnoticed.

Another relationship involves the little boy, a trapped bird, and a jet plane. At the end of the story, the boy looks out an airport terminal window and sees a jet plane taking off. He also sees a trapped bird trying to escape to freedom. A plausible inference is that, like the plane and bird, the boy wants to leave the airport and be free.

Inference in Mathematics

"Readers use their own schema, connections with the text, and prior life experiences, and combine this thinking with the text evidence (both pictures and words) and clues that the author leaves for the reader to form [original] thinking about the text." (7th-grade teacher)

Inference is often taught as a language-based, cognitive process, but illustrations and picture clues are also important to teaching inference. Text clues help students develop linguistic skills while picture clues (illustrations) help them develop non-linguistic skills. Together, they provide powerful tools for teaching and learning inference.

"Collaborating with the Author" is a strategy that supports inferential thinking before, during, and after reading (Tovani, 2000). It highlights the importance of textual and picture clues, as well as the processes of inference, prediction, confirmation, and disconfirmation (Goodman, 1996). Table 7.1.3 illustrates this strategy, used with *One Riddle, One Answer* (Thompson, 2001) to integrate literacy and mathematics.

One Riddle, One Answer is a story about Aziza, a sultan's daughter who loves numbers and riddles. When the sultan sought a suitable husband for Aziza, she posed a riddle and agreed to marry whomever could answer it. Many suitors answered but all were wrong. Finally, a farmer named Ahmed provided the correct answer. Aziza and Ahmed were married.

The "Collaborating with the Author" strategy is particularly suited for a teacher read-aloud. Before reading aloud, teachers distribute the strategy sheet. Then they place numbered sticky notes at strategic places in the text—episodic changes, for example—and number the rows on the strategy sheet to correspond with the numbered sticky notes. Teachers read up to the first sticky note, stop, then invite students to record text and picture clues as well as inferences and predictions based on these clues. Teachers then read to the second sticky note and follow the same procedure, inviting students to check whether their predictions are confirmed or dis-confirmed. Teachers follow the same procedure until the reading is completed. After reading, teachers invite students to write a brief summary representing their most important understandings of the text.

TABLE 7.1.3 Collaborating with the Author (Tovani, 2000; using *One Riddle, One Answer* [Thompson, 2001])

Text Clues	Picture Clues	Inferences	Predictions	Confirmed	Disconfirmed
1) Her favorite subject was numbers.	Palace is decorated with circles, rectangles, squares.	Riddles are difficult to solve. The riddle deals with mathematics.	Aziza will make riddle very difficult; it will be difficult to solve.		
2) Let any number try to solve the riddle; only one will win. A scholar said the sun; a soldier said a sword.	Numbers are displayed on the flag. Each looks like the number 7.	Neither sun nor sword satisfies all 4 statements in the riddle. The number 7 doesn't, either.	The answer deals with an important number or math concept or both.		
3) A merchant said money, saying that in all matters that count, money always comes first.	Aziza looks dejected. The answers aren't close to solving the riddle.	Answers so far are clues: sun rhymes with the word one; sword looks like the number 1; people count money; much counting starts at the number 1.	The answer to the riddle is something involving a number, probably the number 1.		
4) Ahmed said the riddle speaks of numbers and the answer is the number one.	Design on Persian rugs looks like the number 1; the horse's blanket looks like 1/100; the sand dunes look like 1, 2, 3; the clouds look like $1 \times 10 = 10$.	The number 1 means different things depending upon how it is used and where it is placed with other numbers.	The answer to the riddle is the number 1.		

The answer to the riddle is the number 1. The riddle illustrates how the number 1 is used as the starting point in counting (1, 2, 3 …), as well as how it can be used, depending upon where it is placed, with another number to make fractions (1/100), to make large numbers smaller (19), and to make smaller numbers larger (91).

This story provides an engaging and informative context for seeing relationships between numbers involving the number one. It also highlights implications of these relationships for understanding concepts such as counting, smaller and greater numbers, fractions, and multiplication. From a literacy perspective, the story promotes and supports inferential thinking throughout the text. The following sentences are illustrative:

"He (sultan) had many sons, but only one daughter."

"The riddle has only one true answer."

"Whoever can answer the riddle will be the one I would be happiest to marry."

"Perhaps there will be one," Aziza said. "And one is all that is needed."

"Only one will win the hand of the sultan's daughter."

"Will you hear one more answer?" Ahmed said. (Thompson, 2001)

Each sentence illustrates the importance for readers to infer multiple meanings of the word "one." In this story, the word "one" refers to the number one (the answer to the riddle) and also to one person (one suitor can offer only one answer). In addition to these linguistic clues, the story includes beautiful illustrations that provide visual clues for answering the riddle. The combination of linguistic and visual clues provides readers with a holistic view of making inferences from text.

Inference in Language Arts

"When teaching inference, I say look for evidence in the novel or story to back up any information and draw a conclusion about a character or situation." (7th/8th-grade teacher)

Readers use background knowledge with text clues to make inferences. "BK + TC = I" (Harvey & Goudvis, 2007) is a strategy used with *The Watertower* (Crew, 1994) to teach inference in language arts (see Table 7.1.4).

The Watertower is a mystery in which a rusted watertower stands on the outskirts of a town. It has a logo printed on the side. One day Bubba and Spike climb the watertower for a swim in the tank. Afterwards, Bubba loses his swimming trunks. Spike runs to get another pair. Bubba swims in the tank again and emerges a changed boy. He now possesses the same crazed expression people in town wear whenever they look at the watertower. Bubba shuts the hatch and heads home. The townspeople wait for him and for the next person who swims in the watertower.

One way for teachers to use the "BK + TC = I" strategy is to first do a book chat focused on mystery stories. Next, have students record background knowledge about mystery stories and share favorite mystery writers. During reading, students can record text clues and inferences based on these clues. In literature circles after reading, students should note and discuss inferences similar to or different from their own.

TABLE 7.1.4 "BK + TC = I" ("Background Knowledge + Text Clues = Inference" using *The Watertower* [Crew, 1999])

Background Knowledge	Text Clues	Inference
Mystery stories are fun and exciting to read. My favorite mystery writers include Edgar Allen Poe, Agatha Christie, Arthur Conan Doyle (Sherlock Holmes stories), and Nathaniel Hawthorne. Gary Crew is a famous writer from Australia. He writes creepy mysteries. Some aren't solved. He leaves that up to the reader. The settings are rural towns and involve mysterious objects. Characters find more than they hoped for.	1) The watertower stood on Shooters Hill casting a long, dark shadow across the valley .... 2) Bubba climbed into the tank. "I'll be all right," he muttered. "I'll be all right." 3) Then something moved. Something Bubba couldn't quite make out. 4) "My mother will be worried. You know what a worrier she is. She'll be scared something happened to me, won't she?" 5) Bubba shut the hatch with a thud. Deep in the tank, the water eddied and swirled.	1) The watertower is ominous and affects everybody in the valley. 2) Bubba is frightened of swimming in the tank and thinks something is lurking in the water. 3) There was something evil on top of the tower waiting for Bubba to come back to the top. 4) Something bad has happened to him. Maybe something, or somebody, has taken control over him and is now making him believe things that aren't true. 5) Bubba has been changed. Although the hatch is closed, the watertower is waiting for the next victim.

Final Thoughts

"I would say [inference] is embedded in everything that I do because the basis of inference is thinking about text on your own." (Middle School Reading Specialist)

It is important that teachers across all grade levels and content areas teach inference. One reason is that inference is an important academic and life skill. In fact, it has been identified as a 21st century skill that is required for success in a complex, changing world. It is also a tested skill, appearing more and more on national and state standardized tests. Moreover, it is being tested across content areas and in a variety of ways, such as inferring meaning from charts and graphs (math and science), inferring meaning from cultural and social change over time (social studies), and inferring themes, character actions and motives, and author's purpose (language arts). Still another reason is that teaching inference, like the teaching of reading and writing, is not the sole responsibility of the English/Language Arts teacher. Inference is an interdisciplinary concept involving thinking and learning skills that extend throughout the curriculum. Thus, all content area teachers need to teach students how to make inferences, to "read between the lines," and, even more important, to think between the ears.

References

Adams, C. M., & Pierce, R. L. (2006). *Differentiating instruction: A practical guide to tiered lessons in the elementary grades*. Waco, TX: Prufrock Press.

Anderson, R. C., & Pearson, P. D. (1984). *A schema-theoretic view of basic processes in reading comprehension* (Technical Report No. 306). Urbana, IL: Center for the Study of Reading.

Anfara, V. A., Jr., Andrews, P. G., Hough, D. L., Mertens, S. B., Mizelle, N. B., & White, G. P. (2003). *Research and resources in support of this we believe*. Westerville, OH: National Middle School Association.

DiCamillo, K. (2002). *Tiger rising*. Somerville, MA: Candlewick.

Gallagher, K. (2004). *Deeper reading*. Portland, MA: Stenhouse.

Goodman, K. (1996). *On reading*. Portsmouth, NH: Heinemann.

Harvey, S., & Goudvis, A. (2005). *The comprehension toolkit: Infer meaning*. Portsmouth, NH: Heinemann.

Harvey, S., & Goudvis, A. (2007). *Strategies that work: Teaching comprehension for understanding and engagement* (2nd ed.). Portland, ME: Stenhouse.

Hayakawa, S. I. (1939). *Language and thought in action*. New York, NY: Harcourt Brace Jovanovich.

Jackson, A. W., & Davis, G. A. (2000). *Turning points 2000: Educating adolescents in the 21st century*. New York, NY & Westerville, OH: Teachers College Press & National Middle School Association.

Keene, E. O., & Zimmerman, S. (2007). *Mosaic of thought: The power of comprehension strategy instruction* (2nd ed.). Portsmouth, NH: Heinemann.

Kurland, D. (2000). *Inference: The process*. Retrieved from http://www.criticalreading.com.

National Middle School Association. (2003). *This we believe: Successful schools for young adolescents*. Westerville, OH: Author.

Phillips, L. M. (1988). Young readers' inference strategies in reading comprehension. *Cognition and Instruction, 5*, 193–222.

Tovani, C. (2000). *I read it, but I don't get it: Comprehension strategies for adolescent readers*. Portland, ME: Stenhouse.

Appendix A: Picturebooks

English/Language Arts

Base, G. (2008). *Enigma*. New York, NY: Abrams Books for Young Readers.

Buchholz, Q. (1999). *The collector of moments*. New York, NY: Farrar, Strauss and Giroux.

Crew, G. (1999). *The watertower*. New York, NY: Crocodile Books.

Jennings, P. (1992). *Grandad's gift*. New York, NY: Viking Press.

Johnson, A. (1996). *The aunt in our house*. New York, NY: Orchard Books.

Joy, N. (2007). *The secret Olivia told me*. East Orange, NJ: Just Us Books.

Macauley, D. (1990). *Black and white*. New York, NY: Houghton Mifflin.

Muth, J. (2008). *Zen ties*. New York, NY: Scholastic.

Tan, S. (2004). *The lost thing*. Vancouver, BC: Simply Read Books.

Van Allsburg, C. (1986). *The stranger*. New York, NY: Houghton Mifflin.

Whitman, W., & Long, L. (2004). *When I heard the learned astronomer*. New York, NY: Simon & Schuster.

Yamaka, S. (1995). *The gift of Driscoll Lipscomb*. New York, NY: Simon & Schuster.

Social Studies

Browne, A. (1998). *Voices in the park*. New York, NY: DK Publishing.

Bunting, E. (1993). *Fly away home*. San Anselmo, CA: Sandpiper Press.

Bunting, E. (2001). *Riding the tiger*. New York, NY: Clarion Books.

Crew, G. (2003). *The viewer*. Vancouver: Simply Read Books.

Decker, T. (2005). *The letter home*. Asheville, NC: Front Street.

Fox, M. (2000). *Feathers and fools*. San Diego, CA: Harcourt.

Garland S. (1994). *I never knew your name*. New York, NY: Ticknor & Fields.

Hazen, B. S. (1979). *Tight times*. New York, NY: Puffin Books.

Innocenti, R. (1985). *Rose Blanche*. Mankato, MN: Creative Education.

Levine, E., & Nelson, K. (2007). *Henry's freedom box*. New York, NY: Scholastic Press.

Sakai, K. (1990). *Sachiko means happiness*. San Francisco: Children's Book Press.

Yolen, J. (1992). *Encounter*. San Diego: Harcourt Brace Jovanovich.

Science

Bardoe, C. (2006). *Gregor Mendel: The friar who grew peas*. New York, NY: Abrams Books for Young Readers.

Base, G. (2006). *Uno's garden*. New York, NY: Abrams Books for Young Readers.

Dyer, S. (2002). *Five little fiends*. New York, NY: Bloomsbury Children's Books.

Eversole, R. (1995). *Flood fish*. New York, NY: Knopf Books for Young Readers.

Hooper, M. (1998). *The drop in my drink*. New York, NY: Viking.

Kramer, S. (1995). *Theodoric's rainbow*. New York, NY: Scientific American Books for Young Readers.

Lavin, C. (2003). *Amoeba hop*. Congers, NY: Puddle Jump Press.

Locker, T. (1995). *Sky tree: Seeing science through art*. New York, NY: HarperCollins.

Parker, S. (1995). *Isaac Newton and gravity*. New York, NY: Chelsea House.

Swope, S. (2004). *Gotta go, gotta go*. New York, NY: Farrar, Straus and Giroux.

Weisner, D. (1992). *June 29, 1999*. New York, NY: Clarion Books.

Wick, W. (1997). *A drop of water*. New York, NY: Scholastic.

Mathematics

Anno, M. (1995). *Anno's magic seeds*. New York, NY: Philomel Books.

Anno, M., & Anno, M. (1983). *Anno's mysterious multiplying jar*. New York, NY: Philomel Books.

Friedman, A. (1994). *A cloak for the dreamer*. New York, NY: Scholastic.

Friedman, A. (1994). *The king's commissioners*. New York, NY: Scholastic.

Lasky, K. (1994). *The librarian who measured the Earth*. Boston: Joy Street Books.

Leedy, L. (2007). *It's probably Penny*. New York, NY: Henry Holt.

LoPresti, A. S. (2003). *A place for zero: A math adventure*. Watertown, MA: Charlesbridge.

Neuschwander, C. (1997). *Sir Cumference and the first round table*. Watertown, MA: Charlesbridge.

Pilegard, V. W. (2003). *The warlord's puppeteers*. Gretna, LA: Pelican.

Schwartz, D. M. (1999). *If you hopped like a frog*. New York, NY: Scholastic Press.

Schwartz, D. M. (2005). *If dogs were dinosaurs*. New York, NY: Scholastic Press.

Thompson, L. (2001). *One riddle, one answer*. New York, NY: Scholastic.

Appendix B: Young Adult Literature

English/Language Arts

Choldenko, G. (2004). *Al Capone does my shirts*. New York, NY: Puffin Books.

Jennings, P. (2005). *Funniest stories*. New York, NY: Viking.

Selznick, B. (2007). *The invention of Hugo Cabret*. New York, NY: Scholastic.

Tan, S. (2009). *Tales from outer suburbia*. New York, NY: Arthur A. Levine Books.

Social Studies

Feelings, T. (1995). *The middle passage: White ships/black cargo*. New York, NY: Dial Books.

Levine, K. (2002). *Hana's suitcase*. Morton Grove, IL: Albert Whitman.

Tan, S. (2007). *The arrival*. New York, NY: Arthur A. Levine Books.

Walker, S. M. (2005). *Secrets of a civil war submarine*. Minneapolis, MN: Carolrhoda Books.

Science

Morgan, J. (2002). *Born with a bang*. Nevada City, CA: Dawn Publications.

Morgan, J. (2003). *From lava to life*. Nevada City, CA: Dawn Publications.

Sis, P. (2003). *The tree of life*. New York, NY: Frances Foster Books.

Wick, W. (1997). *A drop of water*. New York, NY: Scholastic.

Mathematics

Huff, D. (1982). *How to lie with statistics*. New York, NY: W. W. Norton & Company.

Isdell, W. (1993). *A gebra named Al*. Minneapolis, MN: Free Spirit Publishing.

Morgan, R. (1997). *In the next three seconds*. New York, NY: Lodestar Books.

Smith, D. J. (2002). *If the world were a village*. Tonawanda, NY: Kids Can Press.

Discussion Questions

1. Write a definition of an "inference" that you could share with a middle-level student.
2. Why is the ability to make inferences especially important in 21st-century classrooms?

Developing Disciplinary Literacy through Classroom Blogging

Corrine M. Wickens, Michael Manderino, and Elsa Andreasen Glover

I n the following article, Wickens, Manderino, and Glover explore an instructional approach that engages middle-level students in writing blogs to enhance their academic literacy development.

LEARNING OBJECTIVES

1. Brainstorm some ways that you can think of to use a blog to support students' literacy development.
2. What are some drawbacks or issues you can see with the use of blogs in the classroom? How could these be overcome?

Developing Disciplinary Literacy through Classroom Blogging

Corrine M. Wickens, Michael Manderino, and Elsa Andreasen Glover

As students enter middle grades, they are faced with navigating multiple sub-ject-specific courses that require attention to the texts, tasks, habits of thinking, and language practices unique to each discipline. Likewise, the expected range, complexity, and genres of texts have significantly increased with the Common Core State Standards (National Governors Association Center for Best Practices & Council of Chief State School Officers, 2010).

Similarly, new technologies have amplified the types of texts (e.g., video, info-graphics, flash animation) and ways to communicate subject-area knowledge, making learning in the disciplines all the more complex. These recent shifts have created new challenges to content instruction. As such, it has become increasingly necessary to integrate digital literacy and disciplinary literacy instruction so that students can develop the reasoning skills required of the varied disciplines. Moreover, to develop as critical readers and writers in the disciplines, students must be able to effectively navigate the multiple ways disciplinary knowledge is created, communicated, and critiqued in the 21st century.

In this article, we describe Elsa Glover's efforts to bridge digital literacies with disciplinary literacy. We demonstrate how classroom blogging activities can facili-tate the development of disciplinary thinking and reasoning: literature served as the foundation in a seventh-grade English language arts (ELA) class, while historical texts were used in four social studies classes. To this end, we illustrate how Elsa engages her students in teacher-framed inquiry, supports their reading of disciplinary texts, and encourages student interpretation and writing through their classroom blog.

Disciplinary Literacy

Noting longstanding resistance from teachers to integrating literacy into the content areas (Alvermann, O'Brien, & Dillon, 1990; O'Brien, Stewart, & Moje, 1995; Pressley, 2004), adolescent literacy researchers have called for a different framing of literacy integration in secondary grades, that of "disciplinary literacy." Whereas content area literacy treats reading comprehension as a generalized set of skills that can be used regardless of discipline, disciplinary literacy recognizes the specialized nature of learning in varied disciplines and the differentiated literacy needs that support that learning (Moje, 2008; Shanahan & Shanahan, 2008, 2012). In other words, disciplinary literacy foregrounds the discipline itself—the nature of the questions that are asked, the problems intrinsic to those different disciplines, and the approaches to solving those problems.

The "intellectual problems" inherent in different disciplines then give rise to particular literacy practices unique to each discipline (Bain & Harris, 2009). In this way, disciplinary literacy is generally understood as the ways of reading, writing, and thinking in the disciplines through the use of discipline-specific strategies (Lee & Spratley, 2010; Moje, 2008; Shanahan & Shanahan, 2008). To develop such discipline-specific strategies, the language and literacy practices that govern a discipline need to be considered when planning instruction (Fang, 2012; Shanahan & Shanahan, 2008).

Classroom Blogging to Promote Disciplinary Literacy

The recent increase in the use and popularity of blogging has given rise to a tool that can enhance the reading and writing of disciplinary texts. Originally described as a "Web log," now condensed to "blog," blogging is a form of immediate and global self-publishing available via the Internet (Sullivan, 2008). This sense of immediacy facilitates a more personal and interactive textual form, as well as a relationship between author, text, and reader, in which the reader can comment directly back to the writer.

Classroom blogs can be a powerful platform to develop disciplinary habits of thinking, including reading and writing about a range of disciplinary texts (Colwell, 2012). Blog tasks can be integrated with and into disciplinary units of study around "essential" questions (big ideas/big questions) to investigate an intellectual problem, granting students voice and space to engage in disciplinary inquiry (Buehl, 2011). Blogging can also provide opportunities for teachers and students to engage in collaborative meaning making around disciplinary texts and allow for increased opportunities for participation. In addition, blogging can foster writing development when situated with authentic purposes and authentic audiences (Lapp, Wolsey, & Shea, 2012). Finally, blogging can serve as a powerful tool to apprentice students' reading, writing, thinking, and talking in the disciplines because the teacher can model the writing process along with them.

Background and Context

Elsa Glover has been a middle school teacher for 16 years. She began blogging with her students three years ago after becoming a member of a technology initiative in her district. She created a classroom blog using kidblog.org, a free and K–12-friendly blogging platform, to experiment with ways to communicate with students outside of the classroom. She quickly realized that many of her students embraced writing on the blog, providing more detail and longer posts than with traditional writing tasks.

Subsequently, she structured the blog to be integrated into her English language arts and social studies curriculum. In order to do that, she felt her students needed an audience other than herself. She reached out to Corrine and Michael, asking them to co-design curricular units that focused on disciplinary literacy instruction. Through this partnership, she began incorporating more disciplinary reading, writing, and reasoning into her classes, especially through the blog entries.

Through this author partnership, Elsa has used blogging as a tool to support the literary analysis of two novels (*The Outsiders* [Hinton, 1967] and *The Giver* [Lowry, 1998]) in her ELA class and to cultivate historical reasoning in two units of study in social studies (Industrial Revolution and World War I). Two separate blog spaces were created—one for the ELA class and one for the social studies classes. Elsa framed each unit of study around an overarching essential question (e.g., in history, "How did the Industrial Revolution play a role in making the US the superpower that it is today?"). She then introduced a sub-question each week (e.g., "How did the Labor Movement impact the Industrial Revolution?"). Students would respond on the blog to the question. After students' initial posts, the students' blogging partner would respond and comment back to them.

Depending upon the circumstances, Elsa's seventh graders have blogged with her, with each other, and even with some university students in local secondary teacher education programs. Because of these varied contexts, we focus not upon the blogging interactions, but upon the framing of the tasks as illustrative of disciplinary literacy instruction.

Blogging in ELA and Social Studies Classrooms

Teacher-Framed Inquiry

First and foremost, inquiry is at the heart of disciplinary practice (Buehl, 2011; Manderino & Wickens, 2014; Wilhelm, 2007). The quest to address and find answers to problems drives the knowledge that is produced, communicated, and critiqued in the disciplines (Shanahan, 2009): *Why does this happen the way it does? What is going on? Why do people act as they do?* These questions often take the form of "essential questions" that help provide a significant organizing framework for instruction (Wiggins & McTighe, 2005). More importantly, when effectively integrated into the curriculum, these questions demonstrate real intellectual problems in the discipline.

FIGURE 7.2.1   English Language Arts Blog Post from *The Outsiders*.

To effectively incorporate disciplinary literacy into the classroom, teachers need to model an inquiry-oriented stance that is reflective and thoughtful. Example questions in English language arts, for instance, might include: *How is the author using symbolism to communicate her message? Why is this character acting this way?* Example prompts in social studies might include: *How might we corroborate this evidence? What other evidence might we use?* Through classroom blogging, teachers can demonstrate an inquiry stance through the framing of the question(s) to which students respond. In units anchored by a novel in ELA, for example, Elsa uses language that demonstrates this text-based inquiry. In Figure 7.2.1, note how she uses the text to demonstrate her own text-to-self and text-to-world connections that lead to her question about who could be considered a hero in *The Outsiders* (Hinton, 1967).

Even beyond the textual connections, however, Elsa demonstrates powerful use of teacher-framed inquiry through her questions. First, she asks different kinds of questions of her students that at times bridge students' own personal connections to the text and at other

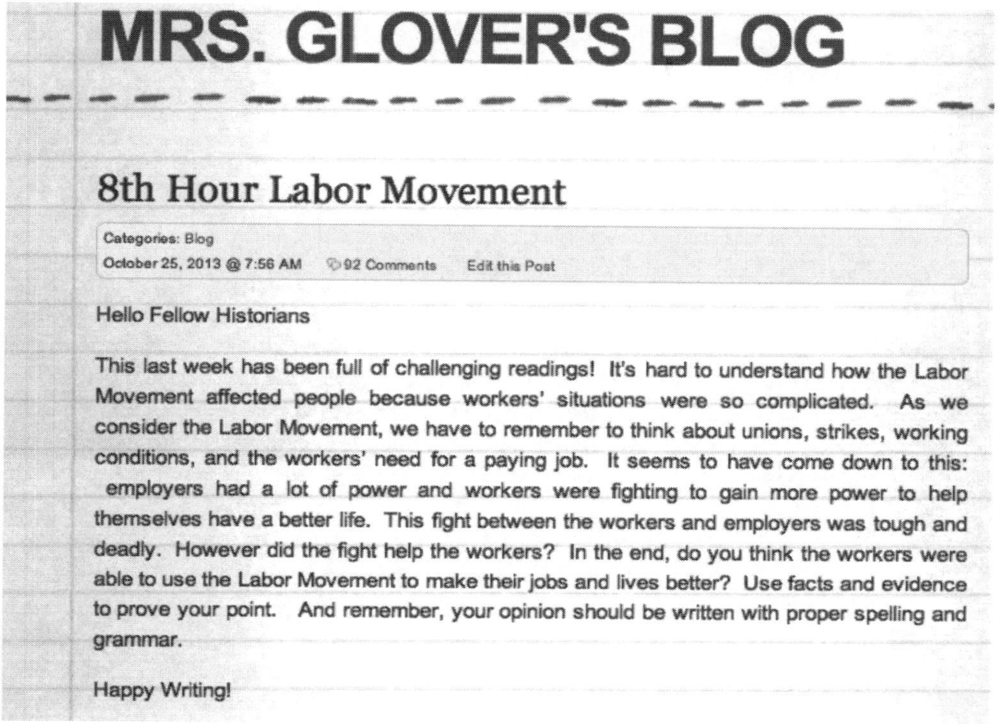

MRS. GLOVER'S BLOG

8th Hour Labor Movement

Categories: Blog
October 25, 2013 @ 7:56 AM   💬 92 Comments   Edit this Post

Hello Fellow Historians

This last week has been full of challenging readings! It's hard to understand how the Labor Movement affected people because workers' situations were so complicated. As we consider the Labor Movement, we have to remember to think about unions, strikes, working conditions, and the workers' need for a paying job. It seems to have come down to this: employers had a lot of power and workers were fighting to gain more power to help themselves have a better life. This fight between the workers and employers was tough and deadly. However did the fight help the workers? In the end, do you think the workers were able to use the Labor Movement to make their jobs and lives better? Use facts and evidence to prove your point. And remember, your opinion should be written with proper spelling and grammar.

Happy Writing!

FIGURE 7.2.2   Social Studies Blog Post from Industrial Revolution Unit.

times require text-dependent responses. Currently, helping students to meaningfully engage with texts and to critically evaluate texts for their literary devices is a huge challenge. Second, Elsa uses open-ended questions to accomplish this. By asking open-ended questions, she encourages and validates students' voices, opinions, and ability to construct arguments in ELA contexts.

Inviting Students into the Disciplines

A central premise of disciplinary literacy is the notion of apprenticing students into the disciplines (McConachie & Petrosky, 2010; Schoenbach, Greenleaf, & Murphy, 2012). Within this classroom relationship, the expert models given tasks, talks through a process, and slowly releases responsibility to the students. In doing so, students gain insider knowledge about the processes, skills, and language of that field. This accomplishes the goal of disciplinary literacy—to provide students access to the ways disciplinary specialists read, write, and talk in their respective disciplines; in other words, help students think and act like disciplinary insiders.

In order for students to engage as disciplinary insiders, they need this expert modeling about how to think in specific discursive contexts; that is, they need to understand how experts in ELA talk and think differently from those in social studies, art, chemistry, or computer science. Elsa regularly models her own thinking and writing in each post, as she does in her post discussing the Labor Movement as part of the Industrial Revolution unit in social studies (see Fig. 7.2.2).

utopia

February 7, 2014 @ 11:13 AM   **89 COMMENTS**   Edit this Post

Hello Fellow Anthropologists:

Sometimes our perception of our own lives and worlds is very different from how others may perceive us. Kim Kardashian says, "<u>I play into the perception of me, but it's not really me.</u>" I think she understands that the world has one idea of who she is and she'll play along with that perception when she is out in public. However, Kim knows that she really isn't that person. In private, I bet Kim is a different person. She understands that her perception and the public's perception of herself do not need to match. Understanding different perceptions of ourselves and our communities is one thing anthropologists do. They notice unique characteristics of a community and then try to determine how these characteristics are perceived within the community.

We've read a few things in the book now and have begun working in our Field Notebooks. I'm curious about all the unique characteristics we've seen in the first few chapters of The Giver. Would those unique qualities fit our ideas of utopia or dystopia? Does Jonas think he lives in a utopia? In this blog entry, choose 1 unique characteristic about the Community. Be sure you describe this characteristics and explain why it is unique. It would be really helpful to quote the text when doing this. Then decide if you think this characteristic provides us with a utopian or dsytopian view of the Community. Last, do you think Jonas thinks these characteristics are utopian? Why or why not?

Best of luck and happy writing!

FIGURE 7.2.3   English Language Arts Blog Post from *The Giver.*

Likewise, through her blogging tasks, Elsa invites students into the disciplines by modeling her own connections and questions. She positions herself as one who interrogates texts to construct her own evidence-based responses, rather than as one who possesses the single right answer. Thus, while she shares her own expertise, she encourages students to join her in investigating these questions and to create their own interpretations.

Elsa also works to invite students to become disciplinary insiders by creating parallels to students' everyday lives through the use of popular culture references and visual images. Doing so serves as a bridge to the more discipline-specific way of thinking she wants from her students. For example, in Figure 7.2.3, Elsa references a quote from pop culture icon Kim Kardashian to help students think about similarities and differences in their own lives from the Community in *The Giver.* What is important to note is Elsa's overarching support of students as they attempt to access this complex text: having them take on the stance of anthropologist. She has her students create "field notebooks," as anthropologists might when studying a new culture. For this specific text, Elsa uses multiple supports that her students need, because many are novices in reading and deeply analyzing dystopian literature. The pop culture reference allows students to reflect upon their relationship to their own culture, thereby becoming better able to analyze the unique cultural contexts created by Lowry in this novel.

Student Interpretation and Argumentation

In the midst of modeling that is continuous and ongoing, the novice should begin to take on the practices and behaviors of experts in that field. In the disciplines, this means that students begin to "think like" historians, scientists, mathematicians, literary critics—people engaging in inquiry-oriented tasks based in true "intellectual problems" of the field. In ELA, these intellectual problems are driven by the desire to understand the human condition as expressed through the written word and through powerful images and metaphors used to communicate those experiences. In social studies, intellectual problems arise because the study of the past is approximated and contested.

The study of primary and secondary sources in social studies affords students opportunities to interrogate the past for themselves and connect those issues and conflicts to the present. For instance, during the study of World War I, Elsa has students read several primary and secondary source accounts written from a variety of perspectives. Figure 7.2.4 demonstrates how Elsa frames and scaffolds the final argumentation task at the culmination of the WWI unit. In this example, students are prompted to construct a causal response to US involvement in World War I. In so doing, Elsa provides opportunities for students to grapple with texts they are reading in order to construct their own interpretations. As a result, these students are encouraged to approximate the reading and writing behaviors of disciplinary specialists in history.

Discussion and Implications

Blogging has been a powerful tool to facilitate students' disciplinary thinking and reasoning in both Elsa's ELA and social studies classrooms. Elsa has encouraged student engagement in teacher-initiated inquiry. Through her language, her modeling, and her framing of tasks, Elsa has invited students into the disciplines, helping them learn to act like disciplinary "insiders." Likewise, the tasks themselves ultimately work to build upon each other, as students grapple with particular textual and historical questions that Elsa used to connect back to larger questions of the unit and of the discipline. The reading and writing connections of the disciplines of ELA and social studies become stronger because students have the opportunities to use these tools and processes to construct their own interpretations and arguments around literary texts and historical events.

While some of the disciplinary reasoning among students could be accomplished with handwritten responses, Elsa has observed how blogging increases the quantity and depth of students' writing. First, the assignments create authentic audiences (someone other than the teacher), and since students know that they are writing so that others see their thoughts, many are more

MRS. GLOVER'S BLOG

2nd Hour Outcomes

Categories: Blog
March 6, 2014 @ 8:17 AM   42 Comments   Edit this Post

Hello Fellow Historians:

We've spent long time learning about World War I. Our president Woodrow Wilson said, "The world must be made safe for democracy." His goal for the war was that democracy would be sustained. At the end of the war, Wilson's goal was achieved.

This past week, we pinpointed several other large effects of the Great War. To begin with, the amount of death and destruction was overwhelming. The collapse of four empires also brought some change. And the effects on Americans made us look at the world differently. These long term effects changed how things worked in the world dramatically.

One result of World War I was that many people felt that the USA had finally become a world power. That makes the historian in me ask questions -- how did the US do it? But more so, how did this war launch the US further onto the world stage?

So now that you have looked at the outcomes of the war, it's time to consider how did World War I help the United States become the super-power we are today. Think this through by considering the outcomes and their long term effects on our country. Choose the effects that you think best show how the war helped us grow. Use at least 3 facts to support your opinion.

Happy Writing!

FIGURE 7.2.4   Social Studies Blog Post from WWI Unit.

thoughtful in their writing. Second, blogging allows for different kinds of interactions, one of which involves peer-to-peer blogging. These interactions have helped students elaborate and clarify their thinking without Elsa having to be the authority and "telling them what is right and wrong." Last, Elsa notes a shift in her own instruction. With the blog, she has become more conscious and intentional around the use of disciplinary language and discourse with her students. Through the classroom blogs, Elsa has incorporated essential components of disciplinary literacy in both her ELA and social studies classrooms by creating a shared inquiry space, modeling disciplinary habits of thinking, and engendering argumentation structures in response to the inquiry.

Many secondary teachers may be confused by the language around "disciplinary literacy," thinking it might be just a new name for content area literacy. However, it is clear that the primary areas of emphasis are significantly different: content area literacy focuses on general reading comprehension skills; disciplinary literacy teaches the language and literacy tasks intrinsic to the disciplines themselves. Though literacy tools are embedded in and throughout Elsa's curriculum to bolster students' acquisition of content knowledge and interpretation of disciplinary texts, the reading and literacy tools are not the ends unto themselves. (For more detailed discussion of the differences between content area literacy and disciplinary literacy, see Shanahan & Shanahan, 2012.)

Finally, we want to note that discussion of Elsa's classroom blogging is not about highlighting another "cool technology tool," but to demonstrate how blogging has facilitated the incorporation of central components of disciplinary literacy in her ELA and social studies classrooms. Likewise, blogging does not represent a discrete task, but is connected to all the other reading, talking, writing, and thinking going on in the classroom. Moreover, her inquiry questions, the "intellectual problems," ground the instruction, and students learn to cycle back to the big questions to get to the all-important "so what?" questions. It is these questions, after all, that are at the heart of disciplinary literacy and disciplinary inquiry.

References

Alvermann, D. E., O'Brien, D. G., & Dillon, D. R. (1990). What teachers do when they say they're having discussions of content area reading assignments: A qualitative analysis. *Reading Research Quarterly, 25*, 296–322.

Bain, R., & Harris, L. M. (2009). A most pressing challenge: Preparing teachers of world history. *Perspectives, 47*(7), 33–36.

Buehl, D. (2011). *Developing readers in the academic disciplines*. Newark, DE: International Reading Association.

Colwell, J. (2012). Using a collaborative blog project to introduce disciplinary literacy strategies in social studies pre-service teacher education. *Journal of School Connections, 4*(1), 25–52.

Fang, Z. (2012). Language correlates of disciplinary literacy. *Topics in Language Disorders, 32*, 19–34.

Hinton, S. E. (1967). *The outsiders*. New York, NY: Viking Press.

Lapp, D., Wolsey, T. D., & Shea, A. (2012). "Blogging helps your ideas come out." *California Reader, 46*(1), 14–20.

Lee, C. D., & Spratley, A. (2010). Reading in the disciplines: The challenges of adolescent literacy. New York, NY: Carnegie Corporation of New York.

Lowry, L. (1998). *The giver*. Boston, MA: Houghton Mifflin.

Manderino, M., & Wickens, C. M. (2014). Addressing disciplinary literacy in the common core state standards. *Illinois Reading Council Journal, 42*(2), 28–39.

McConachie, S. M., & Petrosky, A. R. (2010). *Content matters: A disciplinary literacy approach to improving student learning.* San Francisco, CA: Jossey Bass.

Moje, E. (2008). Foregrounding the disciplines in secondary literacy teaching and learning: A call for change. *Journal of Adolescent & Adult Literacy, 52*, 96–107.

National Governors Association Center for Best Practices & Council of Chief State School Officers. (2010). Common core state standards for English language arts and literacy in history/social studies, science, and technical subjects. Washington, DC: Author. Retrieved from http://www.corestandards.org/ela-literacy.

O'Brien, D. G., Stewart, R. A., & Moje, E. B. (1995). Why content literacy is difficult to infuse into the secondary school: Complexities of curriculum, pedagogy, and school culture. *Reading Research Quarterly, 30*, 442–463.

Pressley, M. (2004). The need for research on secondary literacy instruction. In T. L. Jetton & J. A. Dole (Eds.), *Adolescent literacy research and practice* (pp. 415–432). New York, NY: Guilford.

Schoenbach, R., Greenleaf, C., & Murphy, L. (2012). *Reading for understanding: How reading apprenticeship improves disciplinary learning in secondary and college classrooms.* Hoboken, NJ: Wiley.

Shanahan, C. (2009). Disciplinary comprehension. In S. E. Israel & G. G. Duffy (Eds.), *Handbook of research on reading comprehension* (pp. 240–260). New York, NY: Routledge.

Shanahan, T., & Shanahan, C. (2008). Teaching disciplinary literacy to adolescents: Rethinking content-area literacy. *Harvard Education Review, 78*(1), 40–61.

Shanahan, T., & Shanahan, C. (2012). What is disciplinary literacy and why does it matter? *Topics in Language Disorders, 32*, 7–18.

Sullivan, A. (2008, Nov. 1). Why I blog. *The Atlantic.* Retrieved from http://www.theatlantic.com/magazine/archive/2008/11/why-i-blog/307060/.

Wiggins, G. P., & McTighe, J. (2005). *Understanding by design.* Alexandria, VA: Association for Supervision and Curriculum Development.

Wilhelm, J. D. (2007). *Engaging readers and writers with inquiry: Promoting deep understanding in language arts and the content areas with guiding questions.* New York, NY: Scholastic Books.

Discussion Questions

1. How do the authors differentiate between "content area literacy"' and "disciplinary literacy"?
2. What are ways that blogging enhances middle-level students' academic literacy development?

CHAPTER 7

Conclusion

Chapter Activities

Activity 7.1
Select one of these instructional strategies explored in the Bintz article: What it Says, What it Means; Inference Sheet or Collaborating with the Author. Using one of the picture books listed in the article's appendix, create an example of the selected strategy based on that children's book.

Activity 7.2
In the Wickens, Manderino, and Glover article, the use of blogging with students was explored. A related, technology-based approach is to have students create a wiki. Read about wikis at the link in the Online Resources section of this chapter.

Select a chapter from a middle- or secondary-level science or social studies textbook. Select one of the "Twelve Top Wiki Activities for the Classroom" from the website. Create a wiki that you could use in the classroom to support student learning of the selected textbook chapter.

Online Resources

Academic Literacy
https://albertweideman.com/what-is-academic-literacy/

How to Use Wiki in the Classroom
https://elearningindustry.com/how-to-use-wiki-in-the-classroom

Aesthetic Reading

The word "aesthetic" is an adjective that is used to describe something that is related to beauty. It may seem odd to describe reading as "aesthetic," but in this sense, it refers to reading for enjoyment or for the pure love of the experience.

Chapter Focus Questions

1. Think about your experiences in the middle and secondary grades in school. How much emphasis was given on reading for enjoyment? Why do you think this is the case?
2. Vygotsky and other researchers showed that learning is social. What are some ways you can think of that reading and literacy instruction can capitalize on the knowledge that adolescents desire to be part of a social group?

Self-Selected Reading

As indicated repeatedly in research, the volume, or amount, or reading completed by a student dramatically impacts that student's reading development. In the upper elementary grades, middle grades, and in high school, students should be reading at least 30 minutes per day—uninterrupted reading time—in addition to reading that is completed during literacy or content area instruction. Ideally, students should be reading materials that they have self-selected. Allowing students to choose the books they are reading increases motivation and interest.

SSR and DEAR

Sustained Silent Reading (SSR) or DEAR (Drop Everything and Read) are common names for dedicated time slots that are set-aside in schools for reading. For these time periods to be effective, everyone in the school, including teachers, staff, custodians, administrators, students, parents, aides, etc.—anyone who is in the building at that designated time slot—should literally "drop everything and read." Not only does this provide an uninterrupted time for students to read self-selected texts, the fact that the adults in the school are also reading provides the students with reading role models, and builds a schoolwide attitude that reading is important.

Students should always have a book available to read at any time. This alleviates the need for them to select a book during the actual reading time. Many students who do not want to read will dawdle at the bookshelf for the entire reading time, pretending to be choosing a book. If required to have a book available to read at all times, there is no opportunity to select a book during the dedicated SSR time slot. Students can select books before school, after school, when they are finished with assigned work, etc., but should not be allowed to select books during the SSR reading time slot. As an additional benefit, since students have books to read right at hand, reading becomes the "thing to do" when they have finished their assigned work, are waiting a few minutes until it is time for lunch, etc. Reading becomes the culture of the classroom and the school.

Literature Circles

The original idea of "literature circles" is said to have been developed in the early 1980s by a fifth grade teacher in Arizona. Research on literature circles has been conducted extensively by Harvey Daniels, who has also published numerous books and articles about using literature circles for both narrative and expository text.

In general, a literature circle is a way of structuring students' interaction with texts. Students work in small groups of four or five. They read the same book—ideally one which they have chosen themselves—and then meet on a regular basis to discuss different aspects of the reading. Each member of the group has a specific role to fulfill during the group discussion. Daniels identified these roles as:

Discussion Directors

Role: Develop four to five questions about the reading to discuss with the group.

Literary Luminaries

Role: Identify examples of author's craft that can be examined by the group.

Illustrators

Role: Create and share artwork to give an impression of setting or characters in the book.

Word Wizards

Role: Select important or interesting words from the text to teach to the members of the group.

Creative Connectors

Role: Share text-to-self, text-to-text, and text-to-world connections with the book and encourage others in the group to do the same.

In the years since the introduction of literature circles, these roles have been renamed numerous times, and many teachers have created and added their own roles to those identified by Daniels. This is an excellent way to meet specific goals that you might have for your students; create a specific role that addresses that goal and incorporate it into the literature circle structure. For example, you may add the role of "media master," whose task it is to share images or videos related to the text that was read or the "summarizer," whose job it is to provide the group with a summary of what was read. To enhance students' writing development through the literature circle, some teachers have added the "author's craft detective" role, which fosters the examination of choices made by the author in regard to the elements of effective writing, such as word choice, presentation, or organization of ideas.

Because of the extensive focus on discussion of books, reading, writing, and vocabulary, literature circles are an excellent way to meet many of the Common Core standards for literacy. Due to the incorporation of self-selection and cooperative learning, they also tend to be highly motivating for middle-level and high school students.

Book Clubs

Book clubs are an informal version of literature circles. Students may select the club they wish to join, based on the book that will be read. Some teachers identify a list of books to be read and allow the students to select one book from the list; all the students who select the same book are then part of the same book club.

Book clubs generally meet on a regular basis, at least two to three times each week, to discuss the reading they have completed. Unlike literature circles, there are no specific roles for each student to complete, so the teacher must be careful that the discussion focuses on the book and the students do not get off-topic. For this reason, it is often best to do book clubs with students who are experienced with literature circles—the literature circles have already provided them with the structure they need to know how to productively discuss a text.

Book clubs are often less formal than literature circles. They can be held before or after school, or even during the summer, to encourage students to read outside of the classroom. Many schools have multiage book groups, and some middle- and secondary-level book clubs include both students and teachers. As long as the teachers are careful not to "control" the discussion or to monopolize the conversation, belonging to a book club with adolescent readers can be a very eye-opening experience for the teachers!

When One Size Does Not Fit All

Making Newbery Literature Accessible for All Students

Amy Broemmel, Jeannete Wysmierski, and Ines Gibson

In this article, Broemmel, Wysmierski, and Gibson provide an analysis of the Newbery Award and Honor books in terms of their genre, difficulty, diversity, and appeal for students.

LEARNING OBJECTIVES

1. How familiar are you with the Newbery Award? Can you name several books that have received this prestigious award?

2. One criticism of the Newbery Award is that the books are for children and adolescents but the award is given by adults. How do you think the award lists might change if it were students selecting the books? What criteria would students find more important than adults? Why?

When One Size Does Not Fit All

Making Newbery Literature Accessible for All Students

Amy Broemmel, Jeannete Wysmierski, and Ines Gibson

Raymond, a fourth grade student, is required to read four Newbery Medal or Honor books independently during the school year, as are all fourth graders in his school. His teacher is experienced and well meaning: her research-based teaching methods demonstrate an understanding of the value of independent reading, and she appreciates the proven quality of Newbery books. Nevertheless, as a reluctant reader, Raymond is attracted to a narrow range of books and he has a specific mental checklist when selecting a book to read. Is the length of the book less than 200 pages? Are there illustrations? Are the chapters short? Is the story about a boy?

An unenthusiastic reader like Raymond is just one example of the students we nurture in our diverse classrooms today, students who bring their individual characteristics and backgrounds to the texts they read. We know that our students are changing. Birth rates and immigration trends are affecting the demographic makeup of the United States overall and our classrooms in particular. In 1970, students in K–12 classrooms in the U.S. were 79% non-Hispanic White, 14% Black, 6% Hispanic, and 1% Asian or other races (Crouch & Zakariya, 2007); however, by 2010, the pre-K–12 student population was 59% non-Hispanic White (Frey, 2011). Some estimates suggest that non-Hispanic Whites may make up less than 53% of the U.S. population by the year 2050 (Day, 2001).

Not only are the faces of our students changing, our classroom expectations for them are changing. The demand for students who are prepared to succeed in college and in careers that reflect our global community is increasing, and the Common Core State Standards (CCSS) have been touted as a response to these increased expectations. As full implementation of these standards nears in 46 states that adopted the associated English Language Arts (ELA) portion of the CCSS, many teachers are critically examining the kinds of texts their students are reading. Reading Anchor

Standard 10 specifically indicates that students should be able to "[r]ead and comprehend complex literary and informational texts independently and proficiently" (Common Core State Standards Initiative, "Anchor Standards for Reading"), suggesting that students need to be pushed to read more nonfiction alongside more challenging fiction texts. The Common Core ELA standards emphasize that readers need to extend their thinking about texts and demonstrate thoughtful literacy, which occurs when readers connect ideas in text to themselves, to other literary pieces, and to their environment and life experiences (Allington, 2006). However, as specifically stated in Reading Anchor Standard 10, matching reader to text and task requires considering "reader variables (such as *motivation, knowledge, and experience*) [emphasis added]" (Common Core State Standards Initiative, "Anchor Standards for Reading," 2010), alluding to the need for teachers to find texts that suit diverse students.

Few teachers question the need to provide students with more time to read, but in an instructional environment where program fidelity and standardized testing reign, it can be a challenge to dedicate precious minutes of instructional time to providing students with opportunities for meaningful interactions with books. In that vein, teachers understand that book choices, including those for their classroom libraries, warrant thoughtful consideration. Indeed, it is generally accepted that students need to have access not only to books they can read, but also to books in which they are interested (Stead, 2009). With this objective—to provide students with variety in an effort to spark interest, match ability, create engagement, encourage perseverance, and find joy in literacy—teachers are tasked with finding great books. Limited by time and resources, they often turn to readily available lists of books that have been vetted in some manner, whether by content experts or via national awards.

The Newbery Award and Honor books are among the most prestigious of these, becoming almost instant classics upon being named as award recipients. Since the Newbery medal and honor books are widely recognized and marketed as high quality children's literature, teachers and parents often encourage students to read these selections (Silvey, 2008). Although we do not doubt the excellent quality of the Newbery selections, we did wonder if they remain varied enough to meet the interests and needs of the diverse learners who are filling our classrooms. The purpose of this inquiry was to determine patterns in the literary elements and general characteristics of Newbery books in relation to the students and expectations associated with today's elementary and middle-school classrooms.

Considering the Newbery

Beginning in 1922 and every year since, the American Library Association has awarded the Newbery Medal, named for John Newbery, an eighteenth century British bookseller, to the author whose book published in the previous year was the most significant contribution to American literature for children up to age 14. The committee members determine if a book is a "significant contribution" by evaluating the story's theme, plot, characters, setting, and the overall clarity and organization of the book (American Library Association, 2011). Overall, the awarding process as defined is inclusive of many types of literature, protagonists and subjects, though the conclusions drawn from past analyses of winners have been varied. An early examination of the books appearing on the list found stereotypical and derogatory portrayals of female characters (Feminists on Children's Literature, 1971), but Kinman and Henderson (1985) found little to support that notion in the decade following, suggesting, "Any seemingly biased or stereotypical behavior was dictated by the mores of the time, locale, and culture of the story and necessary for an accurate account of the times" (p. 888). An additional 1994 review of the Newbery Award winners through a multicultural lens indicated a slightly more complex assessment of the books, suggesting that some Newbery books "... portray the characters in a stereotypical light" (Gillespie, Powell, Clements, & Swearingen, p. 48), while others are very useful for helping students "understand, accept, appreciate, and respect diverse cultures" (p. 49). More recent analyses continue to address this kind of complexity. Miller (1998) endorses the Newbery selections on an individual basis, but argues that collectively they lack the minority representation present in American society. Ujiie and Krashen (2006) conclude that award winning books (not exclusive to, but including Newbery winners) rarely appear on bestseller lists, and question whether that is a result of children, "not knowing what is best for them" (p. 35) or whether the judges employ different standards than the "real audience of children's and adolescent literature" (p. 35). Finally, a 2013 study emphasizes the utility of recent (2002–2011) Newbery books for teaching character education, while acknowledging that they are not perfect due to "limited representation of racial diversity and disability" (p. 60). Clearly, the question addressed by Silvey's (2008) *School Library Journal* article, "Has the Newbery Lost Its Way?" is open for debate.

Analyzing the Newbery Books

From 1991 until 2012, there were 22 Newbery medals awarded, one for each year. In addition, 66 books were recognized as Newbery Honor books, resulting in a total of 88 Newbery titles from 1991–2012 considered in this study. Because both medal and honor books bear the prestigious Newbery insignia on their covers and therefore receive noted publicity and draw student attention, both were included in this study. In analyzing books from two decades only—the 1950s and the 1990s—Lathey (2005) concludes that Newbery protagonists reflect the societal challenges in which the books were written, making the protagonist potentially more relatable to contemporary readers. In order to minimize the effects of changes in social attitudes over time often reflected in literature, our research included only the last two full decades and the first two years of the current decade of award history. The information for this study was gathered from reviews of the books, author websites, Internet databases (including the Accelerated Reader Book Finder) and interviews with elementary school library specialists. For each title, data were collected for the following elements:

- Reading level
- Word count

- Genre
- Gender of the protagonist
- Age of the protagonist
- Ethnicity of the protagonist
- Presence of multicultural elements in the plot or theme

Results

Reading Level

Most states are now being guided by the Common Core ELA standards, which value increased complexity in text based on qualitative and quantitative measures. Given that quantitative evaluation is a feature in text complexity, we investigated factors related to the readability of these books. Following the common practice of many school libraries, we considered the Accelerated Reader (AR) level of each book. Renaissance Learning (2010), the program's publisher, uses the Advantage-TASA Open Standard (ATOS) readability formula, which includes word length as a measure of semantic difficulty, sentence length as a measure of syntactic difficulty, word frequency, and book length to calculate text difficulty. Like many readability measures, the ATOS formula has limitations. Within a text, readability results are affected by the passage characteristics and text structure; thus they provide only a guideline for practitioners. In fact, the titles with the highest Accelerated Reader level were nonfiction pieces like Susan Campbell Bartoletti's *Hitler Youth: Growing Up in Hitlers Shadow* and Russell Freedman's books *The Voice that Challenged a Nation: Marian Anderson and the Struggle for Equal Rights* and *Eleanor Roosevelt: A Life of Discovery*. In our study, excluding outlying points, the average AR level for Newbery books was fifth grade, third month, while the median level was fifth grade, first month. The range was from third grade, fifth month to seventh grade, eighth month. Complete details are included in Table 8.1.1. As the data indicate, the range of the suggested reading levels does not include all elementary grades while many books could be considered too "easy" for middle school readers. Leal and Chamberlain-Solecki (1998) came to a similar conclusion in their analysis of Newbery books from 1922 to 1977. Using the Fry readability formula, which centers on the number of syllables in words and the number of sentences in the passage, they found the average grade level for Newbery books to be sixth grade, eighth month and there were no awarded books with a readability measure below fourth grade. Considering students of typical ability, only learners in approximately fourth grade or higher could independently read a Newbery book fluently. Put another way, elementary students who read below grade level and many reluctant readers would most likely strain to read a Newbery book independently.

Word Count

Readers, both capable and struggling, often consider a book's length when selecting books to read (Ross, 2010). Some readers are intimidated by long books or lack the perseverance or tenacity to complete them while others are attracted to the challenge of reading longer selections. Knowing that Common Core ELA standards advocate thoughtful consideration of reader

TABLE 8.1.1   Newbery Medal and Honor Books 1991–2012, by Level and Word Count

Reading Level	Number of Newbery Books n=88	Average Word Count
3.5–3.9	7	28,568
4.0–4.4	8	36,351
4.5–4.9	23	39,496
5.0–5.4	21	56,879
5.5–5.9	14	44,111
6.0–6.4	7	34,351
6.5–6.9	2	33,154
7.0–7.4	0	0
7.5 and up	6	25,644

variables, including motivation to read longer books, we also considered word count in our analysis. Average word counts for the Newbery books in this study are included, according to reading level, in Table 8.1.1. When considered as a single group, these books have, on average, 41,205 words, with the median falling at 40,035 words. The number of words in each book ranges from 1,060 to 100,214, indicating that the length of Newbery books, as defined by word count, is quite diverse, suggesting even less tenacious readers might find a Newbery book that they interpret as being of manageable length.

Genre

The Common Core ELA standards also emphasize the importance of text variety and expect that students will be reading informational text in addition to the literature so commonly found in elementary classrooms. Thus, we categorized each book in the study according to genre in order to see the variety available to teachers selecting books from this renowned list. Figure 8.1.1 shows that 36% of the awarded books are historical fiction, 32% depict modern realism, 15% are fantasies, 10% are nonfiction pieces, 5% are books of poetry, and 2% of the stories are science fiction.

The Newbery Award Selection Committee has chosen more than twice as many historical fiction and modern realism pieces as all other genre categories combined. These popular titles include medal winners like Christopher Paul Curtis's *Bud, Not Buddy,* and Karen Hesse's *Out of the Dust,* and honor books like Carl Hiaasen's *Hoot,* and Kate DiCamillo's *Because of Winn-Dixie.* It is possible that American writers produce more historical fiction and modern realism than other genres; however, the implications are still important. Nonfiction, poetry, and science fiction are underrepresented in Newbery books. Interestingly, over 50% of the award and honor-winning nonfiction books are biographies, which have similar literary qualities as historical fiction. While this is not a fault of the award process, teachers should be aware of

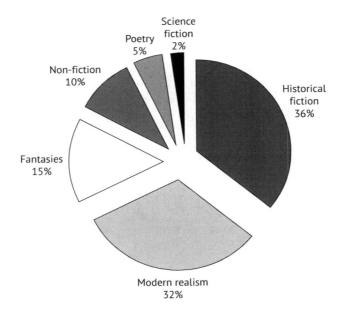

FIGURE 8.1.1   Newbery Books 1991–2012, by Genre.

the preponderance of award-winning historical and realistic fiction when selecting materials for their classroom libraries.

Gender, Diversity, and Other Cultural Considerations

Because students engage with a story's characters, the characteristics of the protagonist including gender, age, and ethnicity were considered essential elements to be analyzed in this study. As concluded by Harper and Brand (2010), in order to truly relate to the story, the reader must develop a feeling, often relatedness or empathy, toward the main character, seeing the characters or the situation they experience as a reflection of who the reader is. In some cases, the character provides insight into someone unfamiliar to the readers, but in whom they still have interest (Harper & Brand, 2010). Children differ on many dimensions and, as such, connect to text and the characters portrayed in it using different sets of background knowledge. They visualize situations presented in text and make judgments based on what they know (Cunningham & Allington, 2011). In classrooms of diverse students, it is not unexpected that readers will relate to and find interest in different characters. Though children are multifaceted and vary on many attributes, characters that are of a student's gender and similar age are often more relatable. As established by Silvey (2008) after interviewing a national pool of teachers and librarians, the most popular Newbery winners have characters and situations that resonate with a wide range of readers in diverse settings.

The issue of gender is complex, involving both a gender's presence and role depiction in literature. Some researchers suggest that authors and educators need to increase their efforts to provide students with literature modeling the roles males and females play in modern society

(Kortenhaus & Demarest, 1993). There is concern that even when gender representation is equitable, gender stereotypes are still reflected in children's literature (Gooden & Gooden, 2001). This study considered only the physical gender of the protagonists of Newbery books, rather than the roles or stereotypes that may have been communicated in the storyline. We used the 2010 United States census, which determined there are 155.6 million (51%) females and 151.4 million (49%) males as a basis for comparison of the Newbery protagonists. In the analysis for this study, 54% of the protagonists are female and 46% are male, suggesting that at least, in terms of percentages, both females and males are fairly represented in Newbery books.

The age of the protagonist in each book in the study's population was also identified. The average age of the main character is thirteen, the median age is twelve, and the ages range from nine to adult. Conceivably, a reader who is ten years old or older could relate to the protagonist in most of the books in the study's population. Technically, this does match the readability levels nicely, since fourth grade students generally turn ten at some point during the school year.

There are cultural and social viewpoints and specific beliefs reflected in every children's book (Jipson & Paley, 1991). Because it seems natural and normal, it may be difficult for a teacher to recognize a particular perspective or value system presented in a story if it matches the teacher's own perspective (Wollman-Bonilla, 1998). Instead of recognizing a specific cultural or social viewpoint, the teacher sees simply life portrayed. Understanding the essence of diversity requires recognizing that what is familiar is one socio-cultural experience in a spectrum of experiences. As we have discussed, it is advised in Common Core standards that teachers be cognizant of student experiences when matching text to reader. The plots and themes across the selection of Newbery books in this study are creative and diverse. Additionally, several ethnicities are represented in the main characters of the sample studied. The representation is unequal, however, with certain ethnicities disproportionate to their existence in America's population constellation. In 74% of the Newbery books in the study's population, the protagonist is White, while 16% of the books have a Black protagonist and 8% present an Asian protagonist. Hispanic and Native American protagonists represent the final 2%, with each appearing in only one book.

The ethnicities represented in these books, in terms of White and Black, are actually representative of our particular state, the ethnicities of the protagonists do not align with the national census, which reports that in 2010 the U.S. population included 72.4% White persons, 16.3% Hispanics, 12.6% Black persons, 0.9% Asians, and 0.9% Native Americans (U.S. Census Bureau). Furthermore, comparing the ethnicities of school-aged children to that of the protagonists results in an even more disparate picture since young people are a more diverse group than the overall population (see Figure 8.1.2).

The Hispanic population is the fastest growing population segment across the United States; between 2000 and 2010, the Hispanic population increased 43%, while America's population grew 9.7% overall. Yet out of the 85-book sample population of Newbery Medal and Honor recipients, only one, Margarita Engle's book, *The Surrender Tree,* a collection of poetry about Cuba's war for independence, has a Hispanic protagonist. Interestingly, Rosa, the protagonist in the story, could be classified as Black rather than Hispanic because she is a freed slave. If this

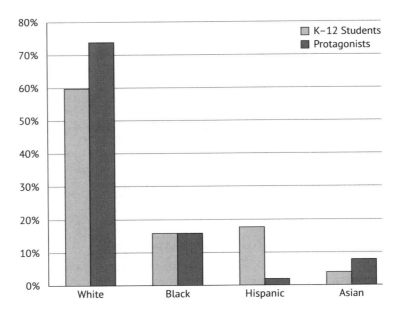

FIGURE 8.1.2   Ethnicities of K–12 Students in the U.S. in 2003 (Crouch & Zakariya, 2007) and the Protagonists in Newbery Books from 1991 to 2012.

reclassification is made, none of the books in our sample has a Hispanic protagonist. Regardless of the classification of this particular book, it is clear that the Hispanic culture's social viewpoints, especially in a modern society, are underrepresented in Newbery books.

In this study, each book, regardless of the protagonist's ethnicity, was also examined for the presence of multicultural elements and perspectives, significant elements in setting, plot, or theme related to several cultural or ethnic groups. For example, although the main character in *Maniac Magee* is white, the culture of a predominantly black neighborhood is described in the storyline and a main theme is acceptance of diversity. Thus, this book was considered multi-cultural in this study. Another Newbery book identified as multicultural was one of the newest honor winners, Thanhha Lai's *Inside Out and Back Again*, a historical fiction piece about a girl from Saigon who moves to Alabama and struggles to find comfort when faced with so many cultural differences. Even with the definition of diversity expanded to include elements other than simply the protagonist's ethnicity, less than 30% of the books in this study were considered culturally diverse.

Implications for Practice

The Newbery Award Selection Committee has specific standards to consider in their evaluation of the story's theme, plot, characters, setting, and the overall clarity and organization of the book (American Library Association, 2011), and neither student demographics nor Common Core ELA requirements are, understandably, among the criteria for this award. Our goal, however, was to consider the literary characteristics of Newbery books and their usefulness in meeting the needs of a diverse student population including students with different backgrounds, socioeconomic conditions, and varying attitudes towards reading. Considering this, our analysis suggests that the Newbery books are generally targeted, both in terms of readability and interest, to fourth and fifth grade readers of typical ability, though it could be argued that the content of many is more applicable to middle school students. Gender and ethnicity representations are generally comparable to that of the U.S. population, except when it comes to the representation of Hispanic protagonists. The vast majority of the books on this list are fiction, predominantly of the historical and modern realistic genres. If used in elementary schools, the books fit the expectations set forth by the Common Core ELA standards in terms of challenging and complex texts. We believe the Newbery Medal and Honor books provide a worthwhile starting point for both novice teachers and experienced practitioners who are looking to refresh their classroom libraries. Specifically, we must acknowledge that the Newbery Award generally indicates that the book contains particular characteristics that align the winners with the kinds of classic literature students will be expected to read throughout their school careers. As such, we believe Newberys can be an important teaching tool for teachers striving to develop readers (and writers) capable of reading and understanding these kinds of books, and we briefly discuss three ways to capitalize on their use in the classroom.

Independent and Instructional Reading

We stand by the idea that teachers who have spent time getting to know their students' interests, strengths, and weaknesses are best equipped to judge the appropriateness of Newbery books for their particular situations. Certainly, if a student has the motivation and experience to independently follow the intricacies of a complex plot line or possesses the reading tenacity to tackle such a task, these kinds of books should be readily available for independent reading. However, simply providing access to these books is not enough for most students. Many students entering the intermediate grades lack the necessary vocabulary or domain knowledge to take on such a challenge independently (Hirsch, 2003), and must understandably rely on guided instruction in order to make strides toward the expectations identified by the CCSS. Opportunities to read these challenging texts must be accompanied by teacher instruction in the forms of guided discussion, meaningful vocabulary use, and scaffolded employment of higher-order literacy skills like interpreting figurative language, analyzing complex text structures, and assessing character development over time. With these kinds of teacher-guided instructional supports in place, such students may be willing to explore texts that they might otherwise avoid, and develop both critical literacy skills and the kinds of book knowledge necessary for future academic success along the way.

Small Parts in Writing Instruction

There is little doubt that Newbery books, and all books really, are best enjoyed in their entirety. However, we can also see great benefit in selectively using pieces of the beautifully crafted language so prevalent in the award winners as a means of teaching concepts related to writing. Often, writing instruction in the upper elementary grades focuses on the kinds of writing valued on tests, but even a simple perusal of the CCSS for writing suggests that is not enough, as students are expected to use techniques like dialogue and description to develop their narrative writing, in particular. Hansen (2010) suggests that by using mentor texts, teachers can, "... invite their students into the worlds of professional writers who know a great deal about ... how to relay content in a captivating manner" (p. 96). Gilrane (2010) echoes those sentiments, suggesting that we must capitalize on the idea that "children who are writers come to depend on the books they read for models of good writing" (p.136), and passages from Newbery books can serve well as this model. Consider the craft lessons that could be developed during either a study of Karen Hesse's rich free verse in *Out of the Dust,* or an investigation of the way Kate DiCamillo uses her narrator to seamlessly weave definitions of interesting words into the text of *The Tale of Despereaux.* Teachers can capitalize on the very characteristics that give Newbery books their distinctiveness by selectively including them as mentor texts in writing instruction.

Exploration of Diversity

Finally, while our research found that ethnicities portrayed in the Newbery Award and Honor books are not representative of the students filling our classrooms, they do appear to be doing a better job than children's literature overall. Over the past 50 years, great strides have been made in this area of children's literature (Galda, Cullinan, & Sipe, 2010), but Hansen-Krening, Aoki, and Mizokawa (2003) still found that people of color were the focus of only about 3% of books published after 1999. If we are to prepare students to be productive members of contemporary society, an understanding of its citizens is required; if we are truly preparing them for the global society in which we live, it is imperative. Though children should be taught that humans are more similar than different, they must also recognize that culture provides not only a sense of belonging but also a system of values and beliefs (Gillespie et al., 1994). Thus, it makes sense that, "we can no longer afford to merely look inward, reading and learning only from literature that reflects who we are and our own corner of the world" (Yokota, 2009, p. 66). Considering the results of this study, we echo the almost 20-year-old conclusion that teachers should be both careful and deliberate when selecting books for the classroom library so that diversity is represented in their selections (Gillespie et al., 1994).

It is clear that Newbery Medal and Honor winning authors produce literature that is distinct, high quality, and challenging and that these books should be available in classroom or school libraries. We do caution that these books neither reflect the population of students found in our nation's schools nor do they, as a group, represent a wide enough range of genres. Thus, if our goal goes beyond the idea that students *can* read, and embraces the larger aim that all of our students *choose* to engage in literacy as they read and respond to increasingly complex texts, then we believe that as teachers, we have a responsibility to provide a greater variety of texts in our classroom libraries.

What About Raymond?

After careful searching, Raymond, our unenthusiastic reader, finally chose four Newbery books to complete his reading requirement. He read *Joey Pigza Loses Control, The Tale of Despereaux,* and *Because of Winn Dixie* on his own, but he needed help to make it through *Holes*. In the end, his Newbery requirement exposed him to excellent and enjoyable literature. However, he may need a wider range of choices in order to develop into an avid, rather than reluctant, reader. We hope his teachers use their knowledge about his needs, interests and experiences as a basis for continuing to expose him to high quality books, even if the titles may not have made it onto the Newbery list.

References

Allington, R. (2006). *What really matters for struggling readers.* Boston, MA: Pearson.

American Library Association. (2011). Retrieved from http://www.ala.org

Barry, A.L., Rice, S., & McDuffie-Dipman, M. (2013). Books with potential for character education and aliteracy-rich social studies classroom: A research study. *The Journal of Social Studies Research, 37,* 47–61.

Common Core State Standards Initiative. (2011). College and Career Readiness Anchor Standards for reading. Retrieved from http://www.corestandards.org/the-standards/english-language-arts-standards/anchor-standards/college-and-career-readiness-anchor-standards-for-reading/

Crouch, R., & Zakariya, S.B. (2007). The United States of education: The changing demographics of the United States and their schools. Retrieved from Center for Public Education website: http://www.centerforpubliceducation.org/You-May-Also-Be-Interested-In-landing-page-level/Organizing-a-School-YMABI/The-United-States-of-education-The-changing-demographics-of-the-United-States-and-their-schools.html

Cunningham, P.M., & Allington, R.L. (2011). *Classrooms that work: They can all read and write* (5th ed.). Boston, MA: Pearson.

Day, J.C. (2001). National population projections. *U.S. Bureau of Census.* Retrieved from http://www.census.gov/population/www/pop-profile/natproj.html

Feminists on Children's Literature. (1971). A feminist look at children's books. *School Library Journal, 17,* 19–24.

Frey, W.H. (2011). A demographic tipping point among America's three-year-olds. Retrieved from Brookings website: http://www.brookings.edu/research/opinions/2011/02/07-population-frey

Galda. L., Cullinan, B.E., & Sipe, L. (2010). *Literature and the child* (7th ed.). Belmont, CA: Wadsworth.

Gillespie, C.S., Powell, J.L., Clements, N.E., & Swearingen, R.A. (1994). A look at the Newbery Medal books from a multicultural perspective. *The Reading Teacher, 48*(1), 40–50.

Gilrane, C. (2010). So many books—how do I choose? In D. Wooten & B. Cullinan (Eds.), *Children's literature in the reading program: An invitation to read* (pp. 130–140). Newark, DE. International Reading Association.

Gooden, A.M., & Gooden, M.A. (2001). Gender representation in notable children's picture books: 1995–1999. *Sex Roles, 45*(1), 89–101.

Hansen, J. (2010). Young writers use mentor texts. In D. Wooten & B. Cullinan (Eds.), *Children's literature in the reading program: An invitation to read* (pp. 88–98). Newark, DE. International Reading Association.

Harper, L. J., & Brand, S.T. (2010). More alike than different: Promoting respect through multicultural books and literacy strategies. *Childhood Education, 86*(4), 224–233.

Hirsch, E. (2003). Reading comprehension requires knowledge of words and the world. *American Educator, 27*(1), 10–13, 16–22, 28–29, 48.

Jipson, J., & Paley, N. (1991). The selective tradition in teachers' choice of children's literature: Does it exist in the elementary classroom? *English Education, 23*(3), 148–159.

Kinman, J.R., & Henderson, D.L. (1985). An analysis of sexism in Newbery Medal award books from 1977 to 1984. *The Reading Teacher, 38*(9), 885–889.

Kortenhaus, C.M., & Demarest, J. (1993). Gender role stereotyping in children's literature: An update. *Sex Roles, 28*(3), 219–232.

Lathey, J. (2005). Challenges then and now: A survey of protagonists in Newbery awards books, 1950s and 1990s. *Children and Libraries 3*(3): 20–24.

Leal, D.J., & Chamberlain-Solecki, J. (1998). A Newbery medal-winning combination: High student interest plus appropriate readability levels. *The Reading Teacher, 51*(8), 712–715.

Miller, B.J.F. (1998). What color is gold? Twenty-one years of same-race authors and protagonists in the Newbery medal. *Journal of Youth Services in Libraries, 12*(1), 34–39.

Renaissance Learning. (2010). Retrieved from http://www.renlearn.com/ar/overview/atos

Ross, C.S. (2001). Making choices: What readers say about choosing books to read for pleasure. *The Acquisitions Librarian, 25,* 5–21.

Silvey, A. (2008). Has Newbery lost its way?; Snubbed by kids, disappointing to librarians, the recent winners have few fans. *School Library Journal, 10,* 38.

Stead, T. (2009) *Good choice! Supporting independent reading and response in K–6.* Portland, ME: Stenhouse.

Ujiie, J., & Krashen, S. (2006). Are prize-winning books popular among children? An analysis of public library circulation. *Knowledge Quest, 34*(3), 33–35.

U.S. Census Bureau. (2011). Multiple data retrieved from http://factfinder.census.gov

Wollman-Bonilla, J.E. (1998). Outrageous viewpoints: Teachers' criteria for rejecting works of children's literature. *Language Arts, 75*(4), 287–295.

Yokota, J. (2009). Learning through literature that offers diverse perspectives: Multicultural and international literature. In D. Wooten & B. Cullinan (Eds.), *Children's literature in the reading program: An invitation to read (3rd ed.)* (pp. 66–73). Newark, DE. International Reading Association.

Children's Literature Cited

Bartoletti, S.C. (2005). *Hitler youth: Growing up in Hitler's shadow*. New York, NY: Scholastic Inc.

Curtis, C.P. (1999). *Bud, not Buddy*. New York. NY: Yearling.

DiCamillo, K. (2003). *The tale of Despereaux*. New York, NY: Scholastic.

DiCamillo, K. (2000). *Because of Winn Dixie*. Somerville, MA: Candlewick Press.

Engle, M. (2008). *The surrender tree*. New York, NY: Henry Holt and Company, LLC.

Freedman, R. (1993). *Eleanor Roosevelt: A life of discovery*. New York, NY: Clarion Books.

Freedman, R. (2004). *The voice that challenged a nation: Marian Anderson and the struggle for equal rights*. New York, NY: Clarion Books.

Hiaasen, C. (2002). *Hoot*. New York, NY: Alfred A. Knopf.

Hesse, K. (1997). *Out of the dust*. New York, NY: Scholastic Inc.

Lais, T. (2011). *Inside out and back again*. New York, NY: Harper Collins.

Spinelli, J. (1990). *Maniac Magee*. Boston, MA: Little, Brown and Company.

Discussion Questions

1. What were some issues about Newbery Award books raised in the analysis described in the article? Which of these did you find the most surprising?
2. What are some ways that Newbery Award books can be used to meet the requirements of the Common Core Standards?

Motivating and Engaging Students in Reading

Jenna Cambria and John T. Guthrie

H ave you ever wondered why some students seem very motivated to participate in literacy activities and others cannot be budged? In this article, Cambria and Guthrie explore ways to motivate students to read.

LEARNING OBJECTIVES

1. Do you like to read? Why or why not?
2. What role do teachers play in motivating students to read and write?

Motivating and Engaging Students in Reading

Jenna Cambria and John T. Guthrie

You can certainly ignore motivation if you choose. But if you do, you may be neglecting the most important part of reading. There are two sides to reading. On one side are the skills which include phonemic awareness, phonics, word recognition, vocabulary, and simple comprehension. On the other side is the will to read. A good reader has both skill and will. In the "will" part, we are talking about motivation to read. This describes children's enjoyments, their wants, and their behaviors surrounding reading. A student with skill may be capable, but without will, she cannot become a reader. It is her will power that determines whether she reads widely and frequently and grows into a student who enjoys and benefits from literacy. So we think you should care about motivation because it is the other half of reading. Sadly, it is the neglected half.

What Is Motivation?

Many teachers think of a motivated reader as a student who is having fun while reading. This may be true, but there are many forms of motivation that might not be related to fun and excitement. What we mean by motivation are the values, beliefs, and behaviors surrounding reading for an individual. Some productive values and beliefs may lead to excitement, yet other values may lead to determined hard work.

We talk about three powerful motivations that drive students' reading. They operate in school and out of school, and they touch nearly every child. Some students may have all of these motivations and some may have only one. For some students, these motivations appear in the positive form driving students toward reading. For other students, the motivations are negative and push students away from books. When we

Jenna Cambria and John T. Guthrie, "Motivating and Engaging Students in Reading," *New England Reading Association Journal*, vol. 46, no. 1, pp. 16–29. Copyright © 2010 by New England Reading Association. Reprinted with permission. Provided by ProQuest LLC. All rights reserved.

talk about reading motivations we refer to (1) interest, (2) dedication, and (3) confidence. An interested student reads because he enjoys it; a dedicated student reads because he believes it is important, and a confident student reads because he can do it. We discuss each of these in this essay with an emphasis on dedication.

Research says that skill and will (motivation) go together. Usually, students who are gaining in skill are gaining in motivation as well; a student whose motivation increases because she is inspired by a terrific teacher will grow in reading skills. Research also says that these three motivations are independent. A student may be interested and read for enjoyment, but not dedicated and not seeing the importance of hard work in reading. A student may also be interested and want to read but not be confident in her ability. So confidence can be a problem when other motivations are not a problem for a student. Research also says that motivation comes from the teacher in the classroom. Of course, motivation may be stimulated by home and may be influenced by peers, but the teacher is the main actor influencing a student's development of reading motivation.

What Can a Teacher Do?

We offer six motivation practices that teachers can implement daily in the classroom. These practices can be brought into every lesson and directed to every student. Teachers do not have to wait for motivation to come from the outside. They can make it happen any time they want to implement one of these six practices. Research undergirds the impact of these practices on students becoming avid readers and on students becoming achieving readers. We provide examples of these practices from the literature and from our own experiences in our research and teaching.

Motivations to Read—Interest, Confidence, Dedication

Interest
When we think of motivation our mind first turns to interest. Motivation is enjoying a book, being excited about an author, or being delighted by new information. Researchers refer to interest as intrinsic motivation, meaning something we do for its own sake. On a rainy day, we might rather read our favorite mystery than do anything else. We are not trying to get a reward when falling into a novel.

Motivation also brings to mind the reward for success. Who doesn't like to win a trinket for hitting the target with a dart at the State Fair? Who doesn't want to earn serious money for working hard in a career? These are extrinsic rewards because someone gives them to us. We do not give them to ourselves, and these rewards do propel us to put out effort, focus energy, and get up in the morning.

Yet, extrinsic rewards do not motivate reading achievement in the long term. Students who read only for the reward of money, a grade, or a future job are not the best readers. The reason is that if you read for the reward of a good quiz score, what happens after the quiz is that you stop reading. If the test score is the only thing that matters, it is OK to take shortcuts, not really understand, or cheat. It encourages students to become more interested in the reward than the learning. None of these generate long-term achievement. Sometimes a reward, such as candy or early recess, will jump-start a group of students to read in this moment for this purpose. But if the motivation is not intrinsic, it will not increase achievement in the long term.

For some individuals, grades represent their quality as a student and a reader. Being a high achiever is a symbol of how they are doing. A high grade is an icon of success and these students strive to feel successful. One student told us that he read as practice to improve as a reader and get better grades. He said, "Reading a lot helps you read better 'cuz at first I wasn't a very good reader but now I'm doing real good." This point came up again and again. Another boy said, "If I keep reading then like you can do better in high school and then you'll get good, better grades." Readers who identify with school see grades as an emblem of their success and a reason to have confidence.

Interest comes in two forms—situational and enduring. Situational interest is fascination with a detail in the here and now: a picture in a book, a link in a Website, a funny comment by a character, or an amazing fact about animals will all excite situational interest. This does not last until tomorrow or next week. Situational interest does not generate achievement because it is locked into the local event. Situational interest can become enduring if it recurs with teacher (or other) continuing support. If a student finds one type of novel he likes, such as realistic fiction, and is helped to find more and to understand them fully, he may, over time, grow an enduring motivation for reading fiction. But the situational motivation is not sufficient to assure the full maturation of intrinsic motivation. One of our goals in schools is to foster intrinsic motivation, the enjoyment and fulfillment in reading.

Confidence as a Reader

Belief in yourself is more closely linked to achievement than any other motivation throughout school. The reason is that confidence, which refers to belief in your capacity, is tied intimately to success. This link occurs for simple, daily reading tasks. A student who reads one page fluently thinks he can read the next page in the same book proficiently. The link is also forged for reading in general. A student who reads fluently and understands well is also sure of himself as a reader. In and out of school, people like the things they do well.

Conversely, students who struggle begin to doubt their abilities. They expect to do poorly in reading, writing, and talking about text. The real dilemma is that lower-achieving students often exaggerate their limitations. Believing they are worse than they really are, they stop trying completely. Retreating from all text interactions, they reduce their own opportunity to do what they want to do more than anything—to be a good reader. Their low confidence undermines them even further in a cycle of doubt and failure. By middle school, breaking this cycle is a formidable challenge for teachers.

Partly due to their long history of difficulty, middle school students need a safe environment. As Nicole Connolly, a middle school teacher, said about her struggling readers:

> I know from a teacher's perspective, the first thing that you do in the classroom
> is that you have to create a safe environment, an environment where they feel

comfortable, they feel safe, they feel respected and they feel heard. Absolutely under no circumstances is any child ever going to be laughed at for saying anything wrong or that seems off the mark. Especially teaching Reading/Language arts, sometimes the poetry can be a little deep and for example, today the poem was about suicide and you know there are raw feelings that start to come out so you have to set that environment. By this point, I am a quarter of the way through the school year so that environment is set in my room. It's very trusting right now, but that's the first thing you have to do is just make it a safe environment. When the relationships start to build, you are really giving each child a voice that only comes from confident relationships. It's not easy.

For many students, a trusting relationship with their teacher makes all the difference in building confidence.

Dedication

Although intrinsic motivation is desirable because it is gratifying for the student, and because it energizes students to achieve, this type of motivation is not always possible in school. There are assignments that are not desirable to a student, yet are part of the curriculum. There are books that do not appeal to some individuals, yet at a given moment in a given school, it is necessary to read them. What motivation enables students to read in this situation? The reason to read in this case is the students' belief that reading is important, the students' persistence in reading whatever the assignment, and the students' organization that enables them to put forth effort effectively. We call this dedication.

Every student has the potential to be dedicated. Skill may be hard for some students to develop, but dedication is related to will. It is up to a student to decide whether to be dedicated or not. Students are either avoidant, dedicated, or somewhere in between the two. In this section, we will describe avoidant and dedicated behaviors in the words of middle school students. These signs are showing their value of reading, being well organized, and making efforts to be successful in reading. Essentially, dedicated students *persist, plan,* and *place a priority* on their reading. These are the three key signs of dedication in students.

Signs of Dedication

The primary signs of dedication are persisting, valuing and planning.

Persisting

One of the most important distinctions between dedicated and avoidant students is that avoidant students do not make the connection between their efforts and the outcomes. A seventh grade teacher, Taysha Gateau-Barrera, told us that "Dedicated students know that they don't improve by mistake. They make continued efforts to try hard and be well-organized because they want to be successful in school."

Avoidant students make up excuses, avoid eye contact, or lack organizational skills. In our interviews we asked students to give an example of a time when they avoided a reading assignment:

Interviewer:	Can you give an example of a school reading assignment you and your friends avoided?
Student:	I didn't want to do it because it was kind of hard. And so, I kept on walking around the classroom trying to avoid it. I didn't want to do this because it was fifteen minutes of class and I didn't have time to finish it so I didn't do it.
Interviewer:	Can you think of another example of a reading assignment that you and your friends tried to avoid?
Student:	Uh-uh. Because after that we failed.

For these students, avoidance had unfortunate consequences. Avoidance is a particularly powerful sign because it stops all learning abruptly. If a student wants to read and tries to read well she may learn. If another student refuses to interact with text, all hope for gaining skill, knowledge, or experience from text is dashed.

Valuing the Practical and Personal

The centerpiece of dedication to reading is believing in its importance. In our interviews with students, many talked about the practical importance for reading. But they also talked about the role of reading in helping them form an identity. One struggling reader said:

> Reading is important 'cause basically you need it for everything really. You need it like if you're going shopping, in a restaurant, obviously in education, when you're reading the newspaper, or reading a book or in everyday life you will need it. I guess that's why I love acting now because to get by as a youngster, I played the part of a reader and in that way I developed a coping strategy. In secondary school, everything changed because it was more competitive. I got bullied because I had to get the teacher to come and read to me. Recently I had the experience of being Mary Warren in the play The Crucible. I was honored I had been chosen to read the part, but petrified I couldn't come up with goods. I allowed myself to embrace the character, even using my fear of reading to empathize with the character's fear of being in the courtroom. I love reading and the feeling it gives me and I hope I will always feel like this, willing to accept bigger reading challenges (Barden, 2009, p. 298).

Valuing Knowledge—From Reading

Dedicated students read to attain information that expands their knowledge of their perceived world. Reading is a vehicle to take them to the knowledge they want. Unlike the kids who are reading for practice, these students seek information for its own sake.

One middle school student said:

Interviewer:	Does reading information books help you?
Student:	Well, it informs us because we read about the Titanic, and it happened on April 12. It's not boring, it's more like fun because they give you information and stuff about the past.

This high-achieving, dedicated student valued the knowledge learned from many different information books over an extended period of time:

Interviewer: Do you learn anything from information books in school?

Student: It actually teaches you things and makes you really think about life that's going on on this earth.

Interviewer: Can you think of some reading assignments that you had to do where you actually learned something new? Something you didn't know before?

Student: In science [we read about] this bacteria that I didn't know about and it's called hiking disease. When you're hiking and you get some water from the pond and it's this little bug that if it hits you too long it can make you very sick.

Interviewer: Okay. How about another class where you learned something new?

Student: In social studies because we had to talk about South Africa and countries.

Interviewer: How long have you felt that you can learn something new from reading assignments?

Student: Before middle school.

Values for The Future

Dedicated high school students think about their future. Here is one example:

Interviewer: Why do you think it's important for you to be a good reader?

Student: Well I guess if you are a good student and get a good education then you can go somewhere in life.

Interviewer: Can you tell me why—why do you say it's very important for you to read?

Student: Because by being a good student you get in good colleges, and that's what I'm trying to do.

Another dedicated, high-achieving student reported:

Interviewer: Can you tell me more about why you said being a good reader will help you in the future at school?

Student: Being a good reader will help you in the future because like if you got a job, you read a lot, like, even if you didn't like it. If you didn't read in school, you wouldn't know the meaning of it.

Some students have career goals that they link to school subjects. Here is a dedicated female:

Interviewer: Can you think of some examples of reading assignments that you had to do and you believed those will help you in the future?

Student: I sort of want to be a vet when I get older, so readings in science and learning about chemicals help me. Learning how to write things and all that stuff will help me later on.

Interviewer: And how long have you felt that reading things like that will help you in the future?

Student: For a while cuz my parents said they will.

We can all learn from a page out of the book written about Whitney High School in Cerritos, California. After languishing for years in poverty and low achievement, this school was transformed by a charismatic principal into the highest achieving school (highest SAT scores) in California. Every student graduated into college. Celia, a veteran of three years in the school, expressed the motivations of students at Whitney High. Asked to comment on the "best about life and learning at Whitney" she replied:

> Basically, all the academic courses themselves? Unimportant. While they do play [some] part in academics in college I suppose, they won't stick with you the rest of your life. What is the most important, I think, is the discipline you have to learn when your teachers force you to do this assignment or read that book; it's the fact that you've had to do it that will be most important in college because when mom and dad aren't there strangling you and chaining you to your text, you will get the lock and chain out and force yourself to work (Humes, 2003, p. 139).

Celia went on to talk about the sources of her self-discipline when she was asked about what she thought influenced her:

> I guess it comes out of knowing what your parents want and striving to please them, yet also knowing what you want and trying to stay true to yourself ... In Whitney it was possible to find people who were like me, and liked me, rather than merely tolerated me. People who were interested in who I was ... They were there when home life was rough, and held my hand walking forward in my life (Humes, 2003, p. 141).

Planning for Literacy

The two main signs of dedication, *persistence* and *valuing,* often become visible in students' planning and organization. Dedicated students plan for success. They are organized with their assignments and their time. They schedule their work and do not forget their assignments. Dedicated students prioritize because being a good reader is part of who they are and getting good grades in reading is an icon of their success. Within their agenda of social, electronic, extracurricular, and out-of-school pursuits, dedicated students prioritize reading as a necessity of life.

Connections of Interest, Confidence, and Dedication

The motivations are synergistic. They work together to propel students forward. Interest and confidence feed into dedication which is the factor that directly improves achievement. For example, some students enjoy reading. Their enjoyment leads them to commit time, effort, and concentration, which produces good grades and high test scores. But this effort and valuing are the dedication part of motivation. So, interest leads to dedication and the dedication impacts achievement.

A similar pattern works for confidence. Students who believe in themselves are willing to tackle challenges. Their confidence leads them to work hard when they have to. Confident students commit time and energy to tasks because they expect to succeed. But again, the time and effort are part of their dedication, and it is the dedication which generates a high standing in the class. In conclusion, interest and confidence do not empower students to achieve highly unless the students are also dedicated. But when interest and confidence are harnessed to dedication, students will score highly on tests, get good grades, and be worthy citizens of the literate classroom (Cambria, Coddington, Guthrie, & Wigfield, 2010). This leads to a focus on dedication in the classroom.

Research Base on Dedication in Reading

When we refer to dedication in reading we mean doing the reading because it is important. This meaning has two halves. On one side it is an action or a behavior. It is something students do. On the other side it is not a blind behavior, but is a deliberate decision to read because of values the student may hold deeply.

In doing the reading, a dedicated student does not work simply for a moment. He spends a long time when it is needed and puts forth supreme effort if there are obstacles or challenges in the reading. The dedicated reader finishes the work he begins. He is conscientious about simple but key school behaviors, such as handing in homework on time. In a survey of secondary students, Lens, Simons, and Siegfried (2002) reported that persistent students gave more effort to be a good student, invested long periods of time with close concentration, studied frequently during the week, and did homework on the weekends, as well as filling all their course requirements daily. Such persistence is positively correlated with achievement and with feelings of being capable of completing the work successfully (Wigfield, Klauda, & Cambria, in press).

Valuing

The main reason that the dedicated reader persists in working hard is because he believes that reading is important. For secondary students, this valuing is central to students' identity. Researchers show that dedicated students strongly agree that "My performance is important for becoming the person I want to be" (Greene, Miller, Crowson, Duke, & Akey, 2004). In other words, for the dedicated student reading is useful because it will help accomplish a future goal (Wigfield & Eccles, 2000).

Dedicated readers are likely to have a lot of self-discipline in general. They agree with statements such as:

- "I am reliable."
- "People can count on me to keep on schedule."

- "I am good at resisting temptation."
- "I am not easily discouraged" (Tangney, Baumeister, & Boone, 2004).

Studies show that middle school students who strongly agree with statements like these are exceptionally high achievers and students who strongly disagree with them are low achievers (Duckworth & Seligman, 2006). Students who avoid work are likely to believe they can succeed by just behaving nicely, impressing the right people, showing that they like the teacher, being lucky, or getting other people to help them (Nicholls, Patachnick, & Nolen, 1985). In fact, self-discipline is even stronger than IQ in predicting grades in reading and other subjects (Duckworth & Seligman, 2005). In other words, dedication to reading is actually the same as self-discipline applied to reading in school.

Distinctions Between Dedication and Intrinsic Motivation

It is important not to confuse dedication and enjoyment in reading. A person who reads all the time for pleasure and enjoyment is intrinsically motivated. Such a person may put in high amounts of time and effort in reading, but it is for the benefit of enjoyment such as solving the mystery, following the character, or gaining information about a favorite topic. In contrast, the dedicated student reads whether it is interesting or not. She does the reading because she values the benefit it provides her. These benefits may include growing into the kind of person she wants to become, attaining high achievement to show success as a student, or satisfying family expectations that she has incorporated into her own value system. Therefore, reading for enjoyment and reading for dedication are two different things. Students can be one but not the other. One student could be dedicated but not interested, whereas another could be interested but not dedicated. A few students may be both dedicated and interested. Researchers have found that in the elementary grades, students who are both dedicated and interested, achieve far higher, and read more proficiently than students who do not have both of these motivations working for them (Guthrie, Coddington, & Wigfield, 2009).

Dedication Impacts Achievement in Grades K to 12

When children enter school some are more interested in reading than others. Whether their parents read to them daily, they acquired a curiosity by being exposed to attractive books, or reading came easily to them. Motivated first graders gain rapidly in reading achievement. In this case, motivation is usually interest and enjoyment in reading. It is not a one-way street. Children who grow rapidly in learning to read during the primary grades also grow in motivation. So skill in reading and motivation to reading are hand in glove and operate reciprocally in the primary grades (Morgan & Fuchs, 2007).

As students enter the intermediate grades of three to five, some students become dedicated as well as interested. They see reading as a contributor to who they will become. It has been shown that interest alone does not assure that a student will be a high achiever in the intermediate elementary grades; however, dedication alone does not assure high achievement either. When outstanding students can integrate their interest (reading what they like) and dedication (reading what they must), their test scores and grades show positive effects (Guthrie, Coddington, &

Wigfield, 2009). As students enter middle school, their dedication to reading takes the form of identity as a student. During grades six to nine, students who believe that being a good student is part of who they are and those who embrace the goals of learning through text are the highest achievers. Dedication takes over as the most reliable motivation to fuel achievement. Some of these students may also be intrinsically motivated and enjoy reading (Otis, Grouzet, & Pelletier, 2005), but that is not the primary driver of their achievement across subject matters and through time.

At the high school level, dedication to reading may take the form of attempting to understand texts as deeply as possible. This aspiration to comprehend fully is termed *mastery goals* by Pintrich and his colleagues (Pintrich, 2000). These students want to piece together the different sections of a text and integrate them fully with what they already know about the topic in the information or the character in literature. Not only do these students read conscientiously, but they seek deeper meanings and relish the challenge of complexity in books. Students who retreat from mastery goals and seek only to avoid getting low grades will obviously be the lower achievers.

Across the grade levels, confidence in one's ability to read is a key attribute of success. Overwhelmingly, at all grade levels, the lowest achievers believe that it is futile to hope that they can read like many of their classmates. They feel helpless. In their overwhelming sense of incompetence, these students cannot put forth effort even when it is possible to succeed. Thus, resilience is pervasive for achievers, and discouragement is the hallmark of low achievers across the grade span of K to 12.

Motivational Practices in the Elementary Classroom—CORI

There are five motivation practices that are well supported in research. These practices foster all of the motivations we mentioned including interest, dedication, and confidence. Found in the classrooms of many outstanding teachers in primary and intermediate classrooms, these practices are not revolutionary, yet they are all too rare. To investigate how to generate and sustain motivation, we developed Concept-Oriented Reading Instruction focused on grades three to five. Over 10 years, we performed 11 experiments with 75 statistical comparisons of experimental and control groups (Guthrie, McRae, & Klauda, 2007), and other researchers have also documented their effectiveness (Guthrie & Humenick, 2004). Currently, we are documenting the impacts of CORI in middle school. These practices are not restricted to special events or grand occasions in which students have rare opportunities, such as a field trip to a museum. These are daily actions that motivate long-term achievement including the following: success, thematic units, choice, relevance, and collaboration or teacher-student interaction. We next address each of these.

Success
In some schools with some curricula, some administrators claim that they support struggling readers by giving them special instruction or collaboration with peers to help them decipher the texts. But this is not sufficient. Texts have to be user friendly to the student. By user friendly,

we mean that students can read a text aloud with 90% accuracy. Another standard for readable text is summarizing. Students should be able to write a coherent summary of a paragraph or a page in the text used for instruction. Selecting readable texts is a challenge and often means that multiple texts are needed in the classroom. In CORI, we provide a class book for whole class instruction in a reading strategy; however, for guided reading, text-based writing, and other independent reading activities we provide trade books of multiple levels. A reasonable rule of thumb is that the range of reading skill is the same number as the grade level. For example, in Grade 5, there are five or more years of reading level difference between the lowest and highest students. It is unthinkable that students in Grade 5, who read at the third-grade level, can make sense of a text that is appropriate for a fifth grader reading at the eighth-grade level.

Much more differentiation of text, books, Internet sites, and materials within the classroom instructional framework is necessary to insure the success of all students. Without success, the students never gain confidence or they lose the resilience they had when they came to the classroom. Though the benefit of a readable text is enjoyable to imagine, the disaster of an overly difficult text is a measurable consequence for deepening the dilemmas of struggling readers.

Students' confidence or self-efficacy is increased by their experiences of success in reading. When teachers locate texts at students' levels, and enable students to realize that they are reading them fluently with understanding, students gain confidence. Although it may sound utopian, success is the royal road to confidence. There is no alternative. Having a football star come to school and say that the kids are all stars in reading is entertaining. But it does not fool students into actually believing in their capacities. The football star may increase students' energy to read for a day. But students' success in specific reading tasks with praise from the teacher will fuel their reading for the long term. As Schunk (2003) and other researchers have reported, helping students perforin competently, set their own goals, use teacher feedback, and gauge their own skills are the key ingredients in nurturing self-confident readers.

Thematic Unit

Alongside success, the practice of providing a thematic unit is a powerful tool for developing students' confidence. Thematic units may be literary, topical, or discipline based. For example, in CORI in elementary school, we provide thematic units on survival in plant and animal communities. We bring in information books on ecology and how animals live together. We also integrate stories, legends, and novels such as *Julie of the Wolves* by George, *Hatchet* by Paulsen, or Caduto and Bruchac's *Keeper of the Animals: Native American Stories and Wildlife Activities for Children*. In teaching the theme we emphasize the broad conceptual topic with individual questions for the week and individual questions for each day. We emphasize how answering today's question relates to the general topic and how answering it relates to yesterday's question. We help the students identify which portions of text are answering the questions for each day and how the readings across time are expanding their knowledge of survival.

A thematic unit across time has the benefit of nurturing students' confidence in reading. When the students see the topics, key questions, and essential portions of text linked together, they gain a sense that they can read. They expand their belief that they can answer the questions and perform the reading activities that enable them to be functioning members of a class discussion or a team project.

Choice

A favorite motivator of many teachers is choice. There is nothing more gratifying than seeing a student who has found the perfect book or has discovered an author she can call her own. Beyond selecting books for reading, we promote many forms of mini-choices that can be applied in every lesson. For example, students can choose which piece of a text to read. In a novel, a student may select one character about whom to specialize. She becomes expert on what this character does, thinks, and feels. It is her character. While she may know all the characters, the plot, and the theme, she nevertheless claims ownership of a significant slice of the novel. In an information book reading activity, students can select a significant concept in which to specialize. In a lesson on non-fiction, a teacher may assign which page to read in a short section of a book. Students can read to explain their section to the team or the class. To show their understanding, students can choose three of five questions posted on the overhead projector to answer in a discussion or in writing. On another occasion, students may show their learning by choosing whether to answer three teacher questions or to write a summary of a small section of text.

As one teacher reflected:

> I have been in education for 15 years and I have always known that choice was huge. But after going through CORI and giving some of those reluctant readers those opportunities for choice about books and partnerships, it was so empowering for them. I've actually done some things to transfer that to what I continue to do in my classroom.

Relevance

Teachers practicing the art of relevance enable students to connect the books of instruction to their lives. In CORI for elementary school, we provide a simple, hands-on activity to generate interest in reading. For example, one hands-on activity we used was dissecting an owl pellet. As many teachers have experienced, the students scream with delight when they discover a skull of a mouse in the pellet from an owl. When they piece together the bones with the skull and decide that this owl had eaten a mouse, they see animal survival in a totally vivid way. After this 20-minute experience, students read avidly for 5 to 10 days about how animals live, find food, and defend themselves from predators. Providing the owl pellet experience is providing relevance for reading. Not only do books about owls and mice come to life, but the broader issues of predation, competition, and food webs are suddenly interesting. A student has looked at his own owl pellet, has had a personal experience of excitement. This excitement transfers to a text with photographs of plants, animals, and predation. In middle school CORI, we are providing similar relevance through videos of hunting in the Serengeti or symbiosis on a coral reef. For these middle school students, the video experience generates intense interest in reading.

Practices of relevance in the classroom can take many forms. For example, providing historical narratives about Central American Indians for Hispanic students from Central America is generating relevance for text reading. Some forms of culturally relevant teaching may generate relevance, but not all of them do. Having African American students read biographies of Booker T. Washington and Harriet Tubman does not automatically generate relevance simply because the texts are about African Americans. If the students do not feel connected to those African Americans in the biographies, relevance will not be generated. Cultural relevance can be an especially powerful motivational practice for minority students if they frequently feel little kinship and possess little background experience with traditional texts peopled with European American populations (Tatum, 2005).

Beyond locating books that students can connect to, teachers can create tasks that enable students to build relevance for text. For example, in the "bubble project" for fourth graders, teachers encouraged students to provide a social critique of advertisements (Gainer, Valdez-Gainer, & Kinard, 2009). After locating ads for clothing to perfume to sports events, students studied the texts. They questioned the meanings, authors' intentions, and gender biases in the text. They wrote replies to the ads in the form of a bubble spoken by a character. The students experienced humor, social critique, and sheer enjoyment in this literacy event. Students saw that the text was relevant not only to their material interest, but to their thoughts and attitudes about popular culture. Such activities enable students to see that reading is important to their interests and their interactions with others.

Collaboration and Relationship-Building

At the elementary school level, social relationships are paramount for students' development as readers. In CORI, we provide partner reading, team summarizing, group posters, and peer conferencing. Each is carefully orchestrated to assure full participation and accountability, for individual work as well as for group products.

In both primary and intermediate levels, research supports the power of motivational and emotional support for building motivation. A nationwide observational study of primary classrooms showed that when teachers were sensitive to student interests, invited student input into classroom decisions, and avoided harsh criticism, students gained in reading achievement. The effect was strongest for at-risk students and low income populations (Hamre & Pianta, 2006). For example, Mrs. Warren has morning meetings in her elementary classroom. She allows students to have friendly interactions and she greets each one by name daily. They share recent experiences and build a repertoire of songs, games, and poems that encourage a sense of belonging (McTigue, Washburn, & Liew, 2009).

This collaborative emphasis may be especially valuable for African American students. In a study of 10- to 11-year old African American students, Dill and Boykin (2000) showed that collaborative learning environments had advantages over individual learning environments. A collaborative (or communal) learning setting increased the recall of stories that were read during collaborative interactions compared to individual reading. More centrally, enjoyment of the learning activity, and the desire to participate in similar activities in the future, were accelerated by the collaborative learning structures for the African American students. One source of such a benefit may be elaborated discussion.

Evidence suggests that African American students respond to collaborative learning opportunities by discussing text in relatively elaborate ways. In an experimental study, Webb and Farivar (1994) showed that African American students who were taught communication and helping skills in small group work during the reading of story problems had more elaborative and rich discussions than comparison groups. On the other hand, European American students did not benefit from the training in communication skills. Thus, African Americans were more cognitively responsive in social interactions around text, and thus, gained cognitive competencies in these settings.

Further evidence that teacher-student relationships in the classroom may be important to engagement and achievement in literacy was presented by Decker, Dona, and Christenson (2007). They examined the associations between the teacher-student relationship and outcomes for African American students who were behaviorally at-risk for referral to special education. Students were identified by their teachers as having behavior problems. Participants were 44 students and 25 teachers from two suburban and three urban elementary schools in a mid-western state. A multi-rater, multi-method approach was used. As both teacher and student reports of teacher-student relationship quality increased, there were also increases in positive social, behavioral, and engagement outcomes. Additional analyses of teacher-student relationship patterns showed that as the relationship pattern improved, there were increases in positive social, behavioral, and engagement outcomes for students. Especially intriguing was the finding that as kindergarteners increased in their reporting of wanting to be closer to their teachers, their letter naming fluency increased. Thus, cognitive effort in reading and social interactions with teachers and classmates are intricately connected.

Teaching Practices for Middle School Classrooms

How do middle school teachers foster the motivation of struggling students? Outstanding teachers who motivate all their students offer a wide platform in the classroom. They nurture confidence, dedication, and interest through many avenues. We next tap into the experiences of other educators who recommend the following: (1) creating relationships, (2) building success, (3) assuring relevance, (4) fostering awareness, (5) affording choices, and (6) arranging social goals.

Teaching Practices for Motivation	Aspects of Motivation
Creating relationships	Confidence
Building success	Confidence
Assuring relevance	Dedication
Fostering awareness	Dedication
Affording choices	Interest
Arranging social goals	Interest

Creating Relationships

As Nicole Connolly, a middle school teacher, said:

> I think the number one influence for student motivation is relationships. Relation-
> ships, especially at the middle school level, are key. It's not so much what it is that you
> teach the students, but what counts is the students knowing that you care about them
> and that you are willing to show that you care about them. Then they are willing to do
> what they need to do for you. So for me, definitely number one is relationship building
> with the students.

This is accentuated for lower achievers. Students who struggle need to connect with their teachers before they will put forth the effort necessary for school success. According to Santa (2006), the principal of an academy for "students who don't do school," the content and teaching techniques play second fiddle to human relationships. She says:

> Students tend to work harder for teachers they like and put little effort into classes where
> they feel disconnected and misunderstood. Strategic instruction within classroom contexts
> where students feel they belong plays an integral role in learning. Students put more effort
> into learning when they have a relationship with their teachers; they don't want to let their
> teachers down (Santa, 2006, p. 472).

The research literature on the roles of teacher-student relationships and students' social motivations in achievement is abundant. For example, students who seek to cooperate with the teacher and help other students academically, consistently get better grades than students who are less socially adept. Obviously, a classroom with many students who are antisocial, disruptive, and abusive to other students will be much less productive academically than other classrooms. As a result, teacher time invested in creating an atmosphere of trust, respect for others, compliance with rules, and personal responsibility toward social norms will be handsomely repaid in student comfort and learning (see Wentzel & Wigfield, 2009).

Building Success

The first step in ensuring success is making certain that students can read the book in the curriculum with relative case. It is crucial to have books be like Goldilocks' porridge: not too hard, not too easy, but just right. One middle school teacher said:

> I had a little guy, Anthony, who was struggling in choosing books. I took the time to let that
> student know that I cared about how he was going to choose and helped him find a good
> readability level for him. It was a good match; it was a good fit and he finished a 220-page
> novel, which was huge for him. It was really cool. The father came in and wanted to meet
> me because his son in seventh grade had never read a novel.

Difficulty of books is the largest, single barrier to middle school students' confidence in reading. When students encounter a story that is beyond their comprehension, or an information text with vocabulary that is utterly impossible for them, they not only reject the book but turn off from all reading. Our interviews with discouraged struggling readers reveal one overwhelming theme:

- "The books are too hard."
- "They are really confusing."
- "I can't read the words."

Teachers often believe that challenging books are good prods for student learning and the students need to be working hard to gain skill. That may be true for high-achieving, confident readers. However, students with a history of not being able to read the texts in the classroom have lost their confidence, have little resilience, and may have developed many strategies of avoidance, like procrastination.

The single largest factor contributing to low reading achievement is avoidance of books, especially information texts, in all subject matters of literature, science, social studies, math, and others. Students who initially find reading a little tough tend to avoid the book whenever possible and put in minimum effort. Obviously, this prevents them from gaining skill and they enter a cycle of failure to read and avoidance. The most powerful way to break this cycle is to locate books that are within the readability level of the learner.

Before students will try and try again to tackle new challenges, they need to believe in themselves. This belief in oneself propels students toward higher achievement because they expect to succeed. Putting forth effort in reading depends mainly on whether you have succeeded in reading tasks in the past. A volume of research shows that teachers who enable students to succeed grow the confidence of their readers (Schunk, 2003). Teachers can promote this confidence building by providing small steps for success. First, teachers can set goals for reading words, sentences, or paragraphs, and then students take the role of setting their own goals. But many students do not quite know whether they achieved a goal, such as understanding a paragraph, or not. Accurate feedback from the teacher is crucial. The feedback should be specific to the students' task achievement rather than a general "good job." A teacher might say, "Wow! You put yourself in the character's situation and figured out how he may feel," which is more effective than simply saying "nice reading." As students learn to set goals and recognize their achievements, their resilience expands. They bounce back from failure. They sustain their concentration for longer times. Becoming actively persistent is the essence of becoming dedicated in reading. However, this persistence cannot come from a void. It is grounded in the belief that reading is important.

Assuring Relevance

Students do not become dedicated to reading unless it is important to them. Obviously it is not the sounding out of words or the piecing together of paragraphs that creates relevance. It is the content and substance of books that they must value to grow in dedication. Students' first reason for being a dedicated reader is that the texts are relevant to them.

In one survey, teachers found that African American students overwhelmingly selected literary texts in which they could connect to the characters. For example, one student stated that he liked the book *Getting' Through Thursday* by Cooper because "They go through almost the same thing we go through. That's why I chose this story instead of the other one. It's a good book to me because they had to pretend they were having a party because the mom didn't have any money" (Gray, 2009, p. 477). It was not the genre nor having African American characters in the book nor having a particular theme that mattered. It was connecting to the character that was the most important criterion used by students to select books.

Making reading relevant for your students can be a challenging task. As Cheryl Nuhfer, a middle school teacher, said:

> It's hard to take a child whose parent has been a farmer all his life and that's what they are going to do. Why do they have to know Shakespeare? Why do they have to know Chaucer? Why do they have to know literature? There isn't a real strong connection there. They have to know how to read a bill of sale and more functional types of reading. I think there is a disconnect between 'the curriculum with the classics' and the need to know.

As this teacher continued, "The irrelevance is probably the biggest factor in students' avoidance of reading."

One poignant way to make books relevant in the classroom is through videos. For example, a brief video of 2 to 10 minutes can set the historical scene for a novel set at the turn of the 19th century in Europe. If the topic of global warming is the subject of an information text that students will be reading, a brief video of icebergs melting in the Arctic or glaciers disappearing from high mountains will galvanize students' attention. As a resource for relevance, The Discovery Channel has more than 50,000 1 to 30 minute videos that can be viewed in any classroom in which the district has an "inexpensive" subscription. When students observe a video, they have had a vivid, personal encounter which they can take to text, bringing the print to life. When students candidly say that the text connects to them, they recognize the benefit of literacy and value its role in their lives.

Fostering Awareness

For many students, the benefits of reading to their reading today or in the future are simply not obvious. As one teacher said, "It's difficult for a middle school child to think too much past Friday's next dance." However, teachers can help students create an awareness of the contribution of reading to their lives through a range of activities. In middle school, students are seeking freedom and are keen to read about people's experiences of freedom. In secondary school, students can explore freedom by reading a book such as *The Breadwinner* by Deborah Ellis about Parvana, a 12-year old girl living in Afghanistan under Taliban rule. The novel depicts Parvana when she poses as a boy in order to earn money for her family by serving as a reader to illiterate soldiers in the local marketplace. She enjoys a measure of freedom by making her femininity invisible. Through open discussion of multiple perspectives on such a novel, students gain insights not only to their personal dynamics, but to the roles of reading in expanding their horizons (Bean & Harper, 2006).

When some students encounter information text in elementary school they quickly awaken to the benefits of reading. In classroom surveys in an elementary school in a low income neighborhood, students who read information books were primarily motivated by the knowledge gained from reading. As kids said:

- "I like dolphins. I think they are cool because they live in the ocean and I like oceans."
- "It was important because I like different cultures."
- "I liked it because it was about an Indian and I am interested in Indians."

In choosing expository text with guidance from teachers, students came to the realization that they were able to pick up cool information about their favorite topics (Edmunds, 2006). Although it was not measured in this survey, it was highly likely that such an activity will spur students to realize that reading and books are valuable to them, which will fuel their longer-term dedication to reading.

Teachers have used a range of simple activities to foster awareness of reading's benefits. For example, one teacher provided a simple t-chart with observations in a column on the left and inferences in a column on the right. As students read a narrative or an information book, they mark observations (which are literal meanings from the book) in the left-hand side under the observation column. On the right-hand side, under the inference column, students write information from their own knowledge and experience that enables them to connect parts of the texts to each other, or portions of the passages to their background experiences. As the students draw the observation-inference chart, they can easily be led to the realization that the book is bringing information to them and they are bringing information to the text. With the twin recognitions that they are an active learner and the book is an agent of knowledge growth, children see reading as important and value the literacy experience (Nokes, 2008). In these concrete situations, a particular book has helped a student on a specific day with a concrete task of mind expansion.

As students grow in awareness of how reading connects to them, their valuing of reading expands in breadth and depth. With awareness-expanding discussions with the teacher, students can expand their recognition that reading impacts their school success, their prospects for further education, their career potentials, and their prospects in the world of gainful employment. Such awareness gives a rationale for their persistence in reading challenging texts for long periods of time. It enables them to sustain their energy in reading when their interest is not stimulated. Although reading for interest is desirable and enjoyable, it is not always possible. The complementary motivation of being dedicated can bridge the individual into achievement when the luxury of interesting text is not within reach. Thus, dedication which merges persistence and planning with the value system of the reader is an enduring motivation that can be fostered daily in classrooms from K to 12.

Fostering students' dedication cannot be accomplished only by encouraging effort. A lot of effort doing the wrong thing will not improve students' achievement. Expert teachers also enable students to become aware of how they work as learners. Teachers have to help students work smart as well as work hard. Carol Santa, a remarkable teacher and past president of the International Reading Association reports from her school for unmotivated students saying:

> We help our students understand what active engagement and learning effort look and feel like. We might say, 'Read this page, then stop and respond in your journal.' During a lecture we stop and ask students to summarize what they have heard to a partner. They read and respond by drawing, making a concept map, taking notes, or asking questions. Throughout this activity we engage students in conversations: 'How are you going to persist actively in learning this information? What active strategies did you use to grapple with meaning? Why does learning take work?' (Santa, 2006, p. 472).

Santa expects students to combine planning with their persistence to be effective. As she continues:

> Teachers who help students to work smart help them learn active strategies. When students rely too much on strategies, students may get turned off and disengaged from reading. But if students do not learn reading strategies, they lack the tools to read effectively and their persistence cannot be as valuable to them (Santa, 2006).

Massey and Heafner (2004) recommend well known tools for reading as follows: To persist effectively, students should use these strategies: (1) establish purpose for reading, (2) make connections to background knowledge, (3) understand the arrangement of texts, (4) make connections between texts, (5) monitor comprehension through questioning, and (6) synthesize information across texts. With these tools, students will read for understanding and their effort at comprehension will pay off for them.

Too many teachers think of motivation for reading and strategies for reading as opposites. Either we are teaching hard, academic strategies or we are having a motivational day. Students benefit most when motivations and strategies are fused together. If students become excited about a book or a topic, they need strategies for learning from the book or enjoying it fully. Conversely, if students have a few effective strategies they will never use them if they are bored, avoidant, or otherwise unmotivated for reading. Therefore, teaching students to be dedicated readers requires helping them to work smart as they put forth high effort.

Affording Choices

More popular than any motivational support is affording choices, which is widely supported in the professional literature (O'Brien & Dillon, 2008). However, misconceptions abound. For example, many teachers provide "sustained silent reading" time to give students a chance at self-selection. Yet, this technique is often misunderstood as the only way to give choice. Myriad little choices can be given during any lesson, which enable students to express small preferences that spur their reading. In a middle school classroom, one of us asked a small group of struggling readers, "What choices did your teacher give you today?" Students replied:

- "We could read with a partner or not."
- "We could take notes or not."
- "We got to choose which color card to write our question on."
- "We could choose the word we thought was the key word in the paragraph."

Then we asked the $64 million dollar question: "How did having a choice help you read?" Students erupted with sublime self-reflections, such as:

- "Having a choice whether to partner read made me feel better."
- "I could read alone, which helps me concentrate."
- "I could read by myself, which is faster for me.
- "I liked finding my own key word on the page."

Remarkably, these struggling readers were aware of how choice helped them think during reading. These mini-choices lent students a bit more investment into the hard work of learning to write good summaries. The total time for the choices was 2 minutes out of a 45-minute period, which was not excessive. Content of the lesson was not compromised. Teacher planning time was minimal. In other words, the benefits were palpable in the classroom. The costs were minimal to the teacher. Our nagging quandary is this: Why don't more teachers make more use of mini-choices in teaching reading?

Arranging Social Goals

Just as a student will work hard to maintain a good relationship with a teacher, students seek to win the respect of their friends and classmates. In this light, students will be dedicated to their reading when reading has a role in their social interactions with classmates. One way to set up social goals among students is to create a project that will call for a student's organization and persistence in reading. For example, one of the teachers we interviewed told us that she "will try to buddy them up so they will share the novels they are reading in a literature circle sort of thing, or even a book sharing recommendation." For example, in CORI, students work cooperatively to build a group poster. The group selects a theme related to survival in nature, such as mutualism or predation. Each student reads and writes to create a contribution to the poster. They organize their work, create a timeline, and share their work with each other building toward the culminating point of explaining their poster to another team or to the class. This gives each student a social framework in which their dedication to reading will bring positive social interactions with their teammate.

When students see that teachers are supporting their active collaboration, they become more cooperative and dedicate themselves to reading more conscientiously than if they are continually required to toil in isolation. Many partnerships, team efforts, group projects, and peer cooperatives have been shown to motivate students, and some have been shown to increase reading comprehension directly (Murphy, Wilkenson, Soter, Hennessey, & Alexander, 2009).

Professional Development

Teaching to the second side of reading, the will to read, like teaching to the first side, is a matter of teacher expertise. There is no formula or off-the-shelf program for motivating students. The good news is that teachers can rapidly learn to be more effective at encouraging engagement. With a short amount of professional development, teachers can learn to give choices that lend students a sense of empowerment (Reeve, 1996). In a slightly longer, but realistic amount of time, teachers can gain a grip on implementing all the CORI teaching practices for elementary school mentioned here. For secondary level, a book and guide for self-reflection about engagement is available (Guthrie, 2008). Our message for teachers and administrators is that a manageable amount of reading, thinking, and sharing among teachers, followed by trial in the classroom, will cultivate the culture of engagement in classrooms and schools.

References

Barden, O. (2009). From "acting reading" to reading for acting: A case study of the transformational power of reading. *Journal of Adolescent and Adult Literacy, 53,* 293–302.

Bean, T.W., & Harper, H.J. (2006). Exploring notions of freedom in and through young adult literature. *Journal of Adolescent and Adult Literacy, 50,* 96–104.

Cambria, J., Coddington, C.S., Guthrie, J.T., & Wigfield, A. (2010, March). Dedication as a mediator of motivation and achievement. Poster presented at the annual meeting of the Society for Research on Adolescence, Philadelphia.

Decker, D.M., Dona, D.P., & Christenson, S.L. (2007). Behaviorally at-risk African American students: The importance of student-teacher relationships for student outcomes. *Journal of School Psychology, 45,* 83–109.

Dill, E.M., & Boykin, A.W. (2000). The comparative influence of individual, peer tutoring, and communal learning contexts on the text recall of African American children. *Journal of Black Psychology,* Special issue: African American culture and identity: Research directions for the new millennium, *26,* 65–78.

Duckworth, A.L., & Seligman, M.E.P. (2005). Self-discipline outdoes IQ in predicting academic performance of adolescents. *Psychological Science, 16,* 939–944.

Duckworth, A.L., & Seligman, M.E.P. (2006). Self-discipline gives girls the edge: Gender in self-discipline, grades, and achievement test *scores. Journal of Educational Psychology, 98,* 198–208.

Edmunds, K.M. (2006). *What teachers can learn about reading motivation through conversations with children,* (pp. 414–424). Newark, DE: International Reading Association.

Gainer, J.S., Valdez-Gainer, N., & Kinard, T. (2009). The elementary bubble project: Exploring critical media literacy in a fourth-grade classroom, *The Reading Teacher, 62,* 674–683.

Gray, E.S. (2009). The importance of visibility: Students' and teachers' criteria for selecting African American literature. *The Reading Teacher, 62,* 472–481.

Greene, B.A., Miller, R.B., Crowson, H.M., Duke, B.L., & Akey, K.L. (2004). Predicting high school students' cognitive engagement and achievement: Contributions of classroom perceptions and motivation. *Contemporary Educational Psychology 29,* 462–482.

Guthrie, J.T. (Ed.). (2008). *Engaging adolescents in reading.* Thousand Oaks, CA: Corwin Press.

Guthrie, J.T. & Humenick, N.M. (2004) Motivating students to read: Evidence for classroom practices that increase reading motivation and achievement. In. P. McCardle & V. Chhabra. (Eds.) *The voice of evidence in reading research* (pp. 329–354). Baltimore: Brookes Publishing.

Guthrie, J.T., Coddington, C.S., & Wigfield, A. (2009). Profiles of motivation for reading among African American and Caucasian students. *Journal of Literacy Research, 41,* 317–353.

Guthrie, J.T., McRae, A., & Klauda, S.L. (2007). Contributions of Concept-Oriented Reading Instruction to knowledge about interventions for motivations in reading. *Educational Psychologist, 42,* 237–250.

Hamre, B.K., & Pianta, R.C. (2005). Can instructional and emotional support in the first-grade classroom make a difference for children at risk of school failure? *Child Development, 76,* 949–967.

Humes, E. (2003). *School of dreams: Making the grade at a top American high school.* New York: Harcourt, Inc.

Lens, W., Simons, J., & Siegfried. (2002). From duty to desire. In F. Pajares, & T. Urdan (Eds.) *Academic motivation of adolescents* (221–241). Greenwich, CN: IAP Press.

Massey, D.D., & Heafner, T.L. (2004). Promoting reading comprehension in social studies. *Journal of Adolescent & Adult Literacy, 48,* 26–40.

McTigue, E.M., Washburn, E.K., & Liew, J. (2009). Academic resilience and reading: Building successful readers. *The Reading Teacher, 62,* 422–432.

Morgan, P.L., & Fuchs, D. (2007). Is there a bidirectional relationship between children's reading skills and reading motivation? *Exceptional Children, 73,* 165–183.

Murphy, P.K., Wilkinson, I.A.G., Soter, A.O., Hennessey, M.N., & Alexander, J.F. (2009). Examining the effects of classroom discussion on students' comprehension of text: A meta-analysis. *Journal of Educational Psychology, 101,* 740–764.

Nicholls, J.G., Patashnick, M., & Nolen S.B. (1985). Adolescents' theories of education. *Journal of Educational Psychology, 77,* 683–692.

Nokes, J.D. (2008). The observation/inference chart: Improving students' abilities to make inferences while reading nontraditional texts. *Journal of Adolescent and Adult Literacy, 51,* 538–546.

O'Brien, D.G., & Dillon, D.R. (2008). The role of motivation in engaged reading of adolescents. In K.A. Hinchman & H.K. Sheridan-Thomas (Eds.), *Best practices in adolescent literacy instruction* (pp. 78–98). New York: Guilford Press.

Otis, N., Grouzet, F.M.E., & Pelletier, L.G. (2005). Latent motivational change in an academic setting: A 3-year longitudinal study. *Journal of Educational Psychology, 97,* 170–183.

Pintrich, PR. (2000). Multiple goals, multiple pathways: The role of goal orientation in learning and achievement. *Journal of Educational Psychology, 92,* 544–555.

Reeve, J. (1996). *Motivating others: Nurturing inner motivational resources.* Boston, MA: Allyn and Bacon.

Santa, C.M. (2006). A vision for adolescent literacy: Ours or theirs? *Journal of Adolescent and Adult Literacy, 49,* 466–476.

Schunk, D.H. (2003). Self-efficacy for reading and writing: Influence of modeling, goal setting, and self-evaluation. *Reading & Writing Quarterly: Overcoming Learning Difficulties, 19,* 159–172.

Tatum, A. (2005). *Teaching reading to black adolescent males: Closing the achievement gap.* Stenhouse publishers. Portland, ME.

Tangney, J.P., Baumeister, R.F., & Boone, A.L. (2004). High self-control predicts good adjustment, less pathology, better grades, and interpersonal success. *Journal of Personality, 72,* 271–322.

Webb, N.M., & Farivar, S. (1994). Promoting helping behavior in cooperative small groups in middle school mathematics. *American Educational Research Journal, 31,* 369–395.

Wentzel, K.R., & Wigfield, A. (Eds.). (2009). *Handbook of motivation at school.* New York: Routledge.

Wigfield, A., & Eccles, J.S. (2000). Expectancy-value theory of achievement motivation. *Contemporary Educational Psychology, Special Issue: Motivation and the Educational Process, 25,* 68–81.

Wigfield, A., Klauda. S.L., & Cambria, J. (in press). Development of self-regulatory processes. In D.H. Schunk & B.J. Zimmerman (Eds.), *Handbook of self-regulation of learning and performance.* New York: Routledge.

Children's Book References

Caduto, M.J., & Bruchac, J. (1997). *Keeper of the animals: Native American stories and wildlife activities for children.* Golden, CO: Fulcrum Publishing.

Cooper, M. (1998). *Getting' through Thursday.* New York: Lee and Low Books.

Ellis, D. (2000). *The breadwinner.* Berkeley, CA: Publisher Group West.

George, J.C. (1972). *Julie of the wolves.* New York: Harper Collins.

Paulsen, G. (1987). *Hatchet.* New York: Scholastic, Inc.

Discussion Questions

1. How does confidence play a role in reading motivation? What can you do as a teacher to help students develop confidence about their reading ability?
2. List the six "teaching practices for motivation" recommended by the authors. Suggest one way that you could integrate each of these practices in a middle- or secondary-level classroom.

Conclusion

Chapter Activities

Activity 8.1
Read one of the Newbery Award or Newbery Honor books for the current year. Using the Broemmel, Wysmierski, and Gibson article as a guide, analyze the book. Then suggest at least two ways this book could be used to meet Common Core Standards.

Activity 8.2
Administer a reading interest survey to a student in a middle- or secondary-level grade. Write a brief analysis of the results and suggest five texts that would be appropriate for this student, based on his/her reading level and interests.

Online Resources

Literature Circle Resources
litcircles.org
www.litcircles.org

Getting Started with Literature Circles
http://www.readwritethink.org/classroom-resources/lesson-plans/literature-circles-getting-started-19.html

iPad Literature Circles
http://www.ipadlitcircles.com/

Book Club Resources

How to Launch Your Own Student Book Club
http://www.scholastic.com/teachers/asset/teaching-tips-inspire-independent-reading-form-book-club

It's Not Just for Oprah: Book Clubs for Kids
http://www.greatschools.org/students/books/255-book-clubs-for-kids.gs

Newbery Award Resources
Newbery Award Home Page (American Library Association)
http://www.ala.org/alsc/awardsgrants/bookmedia/newberymedal/newberymedal

Text-Based Lessons

I t is not enough to simply assign text readings to a class; in order for students to learn from the assigned text, teachers need to make sure that the students actively engage with the content. In addition, to build motivation and interest, activities that involve collaboration with peers are also recommended.

In order to ensure that students learn effectively from texts, teachers need to develop text-based lessons that include pre-reading activities, during reading activities, and post-reading activities. By following this outline for text-based lessons, student comprehension and learning will be maximized; in addition, students will learn strategies that they can use independently to become better readers when interacting with all texts.

Chapter Focus Questions

1. Think about the three phases of a text-based lesson (pre-reading, during reading, and post-reading). Brainstorm some goals that should be the focus of instruction during each phase.
2. What are some instructional strategies that can be used to meet the goals you iden-tified in question 1?

Text-Based Lessons

Pre-Reading Goals

Researchers have clearly documented that the reader, the reader's prior knowledge, and the reader's motivation for reading all strongly impact the reader's comprehension of a given text. In other words, WHO we are, WHAT we already know, and what we WANT to know will strongly impact our learning in all situations, including text-based lessons.

Pre-reading instructional strategies support students' reading comprehension for the given lesson, as well as supporting their development of metacognitive knowledge—specifically task knowledge—which will help them become more independent learners and readers in the future. There are four main goals for pre-reading instructional strategies:

- Build interest and motivation to read
- Activate, assess, and build background knowledge and encourage connections
- Generate predictions about the text
- Support students' self-questioning and setting a purpose for reading

Common pre-reading instructional strategies include knowledge ratings, anticipation guides, word splashes (also called wordless), probable sentences, possible passages, semantic impressions, prop predictions, character quotes, text mapping, and a plethora of brainstorming and predicting activities.

During Reading Goals

The main goal for instruction during students' reading of a text is to help them develop as active readers by encouraging the use of self-monitoring, self-questioning, and fix-up strategies.

Common during reading instructional strategies include text coding, think notes, annotating text, think alouds, concept maps, and graphic organizers.

Post-Reading Goals

Following the pre-reading and during reading phases of instruction for text-based lessons, students should participate in instructional strategies designed to:

- support students' connections with the text,
- deepen their understanding of the content,
- extend their knowledge of the content by relating it to other topics and subject areas, and
- require students to use higher-order thinking skills (analysis, synthesis, evaluation, and appreciation).

Frequently used post-reading instructional strategies include GIST, Whip Around, Somebody Wanted But So, 3-2-1, and many creative and written responses to text.

Designing Curriculum That Matters

Awakening Middle School Minds

Steven Wolk

In the article, "Designing Curriculum That Matters: Awakening Middle School Minds," Wolk presents ideas for personalizing curriculum for 21st-century students by differentiating the products, processes, and content of lessons and activities.

LEARNING OBJECTIVES

1. What is project-based learning and how can it be incorporated into a middle- or secondary-level classroom?
2. What are some ways that curriculum can be personalized to better meet the needs of today's learners?

Designing Curriculum That Matters

Awakening Middle School Minds

Steven Wolk

Here are three vignettes that show the special minds of middle schoolers:

Vignette one:

Some years back I was out shopping and I bumped into a former sixth grade student. She was in college at the time. After a bit of chitchat she asked me a question: "Do you know what I really remember from our class?"

When a former student who is in college asks you that question, your mind immediately floats between panic and cautious optimism. "What?" I asked.

"One day you pointed to a desk and you asked us if we could prove that the desk existed. For like an hour we talked about that, if the desk really existed and if we could prove it existed. I never forgot that."

Vignette two:

I was doing research in a sixth-grade classroom coteaching inquiry-based literature units with a focus on teaching social responsibility (Wolk, 2013). In this classroom of mainly Latinx students in Chicago, the teacher and I were in the middle of our unit on environmental literacy. The class was gathered around the large rug, and we had just read a short essay by the world-renowned biologist Edward O. Wilson titled, "The Little Things That Run the World" (1987). In the essay, Wilson writes about how vital insects are to human survival. He writes, "If invertebrates were to disappear, it is unlikely that the human species could last more than a few months" (p. 144).

After we finished the reading, George, with his big mop of hair, said to the class, "Who would have ever thought that an ant could be so important?"

Vignette three:

I was observing an eighth-grade class that was reading the young adult novel *Red Glass* (Resau, 2007). The kids were packed haphazardly around a corner of the classroom and their teacher (Karen) was stretched out on the rug reading aloud as they followed along. After the reading, Karen facilitated a conversation. The topics of their dynamic talk ricocheted like a pinball in typical middle school style: self-confidence, self-esteem, wondering if celebrities like Brad Pitt have self-doubt, our fears, the murder of Emmett Till, wondering if it's okay for boys to cry, and appreciating the "little things" in life more.

These stories show the powerful transition middle grade students are making in their abilities to engage with complex and sophisticated ideas, what Nancie Atwell refers to as "the awakening of new intellectual powers" (1998, p. 60). Anyone who spends time in a classroom with young adolescents knows that while they are stuck on a social-emotional rollercoaster, they are also hungry to explore the world and study ideas that really matter. Their minds are emerging into an infinitely more complicated and fascinating and unjust world. As Daniels and Ahmed (2015) point out, middle schoolers get a bad rap; instead of seeing those bundles of independence and hormones and attitudes as a hindrance to serious learning, we need to see it—we need to *use it*—as a path to greatness.

Designing Curriculum That Matters

Going to school is far too much about memorizing trivia for a test and far too little about what really matters in life. We need to transform a passive, disconnected curriculum usually centered on textbooks and facts into an active curriculum about life and issues that matter: to young adolescents, to the seven billion people on Earth, to the planet.

Examples of middle school students tackling important, controversial, and complex topics abound, from critical media literacy (Gainer, 2010) to violence and masculinity (Brozo, 2002); from global warming (Spires, Hervey, Morris, & Stelpflug, 2012) to self-identity (Daniels & Ahmed, 2015); from what makes someone an American (Maples & Groenke, 2009) to modern day slavery (Rojas, 2009). The way we show our respect for middle grade students is by trusting them to engage with these topics with the intellect and *heart* we know they possess. Sometimes these qualities lay dormant in their minds, fooling adults into thinking they are lazy and apathetic. But offer them a challenging and relevant curriculum that matters, and those qualities will blossom.

Literature as Inquiry

One of the best ways teachers can make learning matter is by teaching through *inquiry*. At the heart of an inquiry-based curriculum are questions: questions about the world, about life, about the human condition, about ourselves. Many of these would be questions with no single correct answer. Teaching through inquiry redefines the purpose of school for cultivating thinkers, problem-solvers, decision-makers, active citizens, and empathic people. This teaching has the vital aims of the caretaking of our democracy; solving social problems; the shaping of our moral and political "self"; cultivating intellectual curiosity; and teaching for cultural understanding and against all forms of prejudice.

For teachers to make this content and habits of mind important parts of their curriculum, they can simply walk to their closest bookshelf. We can teach just about anything from a good book.

Teaching through inquiry has become a powerful force in literacy (Harvey & Daniels, 2009; Wilhelm & Smith, 2007; Wilhelm & Wilhelm, 2010). As Wilhelm and Smith write, "Inquiry is not simply thematic study, but the exploration of a question or issue that drives debate in the disciplines and the world" (p. 233). For example, after coteaching the inquiry unit based on the young adult novel *Red Glass*, the eighth-grade teacher Karen, told me that no longer would her literature units be strictly about the book. She said:

> The novel became one component of the unit that was driven by inquiry. It has completely changed the way that I approach designing my curriculum. For example, I used to teach a unit on *To Kill a Mockingbird*. Now I teach a unit on civil rights that encompasses a variety of primary sources, articles from the past and present, documentaries, non-print texts, and the novel. We begin by inquiring whether or not Martin Luther King would be proud of our advancements in civil rights if he were alive today. Our essential question drives our unit and results in a debate that includes evidence from all the materials we've read, not just the novel. The result is a much richer experience for the students and for me. (Wolk, 2013, p. 182)

By teaching literature as inquiry, young adolescents can see that while reading and books should give us pleasure, they can also be a powerful force to explore issues and ideas that matter.

Choose Specific Books

As the "We Need Diverse Books" campaign shows, we certainly have a long way to go to bring a wider diversity to literature. Still, the world of middle grade and young adult books has never been better. By choosing books that resonate with important topics, teachers shape a unit around a question or issue or real-world problem. This way the novel *Mexican Whiteboy* (de la Pena, 2008) becomes a study of self-identity and the complexity of culture; the dystopian novel *Rash* (Hautman, 2007) explores the question, Where is the line between freedom and security?; the book *Paperboy* (Vawter, 2012) investigates living with a disability; and, to borrow a unit one of my graduate students taught to her eighth graders, the novel *Endangered* (Schrefer, 2012) becomes an inquiry into the responsibilities of global citizenship.

We can go beyond using fiction and even typical prose books and choose graphic non-fiction books, such as *Drowned City* (Brown, 2015) about the appalling aftermath of Hurricane Katrina, to explore the responsibilities of government or race and economic class in America; or Nathan Hale's (2015) graphic history of Harriet Tubman and the Underground Railroad, *The Underground Abductor*, for a study of slavery or to explore bravery exemplified in Tubman's fearless courage.

Seek Out Interesting Real-World Resources

The world is full of remarkable resources for teachers to bring into their classrooms to use with their students. While the book is the "anchor text" of the unit, we can expand far beyond it by using endless resources, just like Karen mentioned with teaching *To Kill a Mockingbird*. I divide these into two categories, short texts and non-textual resources. Examples of short texts include newspaper articles, editorials, and commentary pieces; magazine and Internet articles; poetry; essays; short stories; music lyrics; speeches; letters; picture books; and oral histories. Non-textual resources include photographs, videos, data, editorial cartoons, music, infographics, artwork, radio reports, and podcasts.

Some examples of dynamic resources I have used to connect literature to inquiry are

- When reading *La Linea* (Jaramillo, 2008), we looked at the amazing photojournalism of people from Central America hopping freight trains to get to America (Nazario, 2007).
- When reading *Black and White* (Volponi, 2006) we read and debated the *New York Times* op-ed, "Why is the NYPD After Me?" about the New York City police "stop and frisk" policy that targets African Americans and Latinos (Peart, 2011).
- When reading the science fiction novel, *The Adoration of Jenna Fox* (Pearson, 2007), seventh graders looked at the art of environmental artist Andy Goldsworthy.
- When reading *Esperanza Rising* (Ryan, 2000) to explore global and American poverty, students studied statistics of American poverty by race and geography.

Design a Project

Young adolescents today like to *make stuff*. They produce music, write blogs, edit videos, build websites, create art, and just *tinker*. At the heart of making original things in school is project-based learning, engaging kids in in-depth inquiry that results in real products, such as websites, publications, iMovies, comics, and artwork. Ideally an inquiry-based literature unit would end with a project, a way for students to take significant time to create something with intellectual and creative rigor about the unit issue or question. Some examples of projects I have had middle school students complete are

- When reading *The Adoration of Jenna Fox* students logged all of their media and technology usage for a week and graphed and analyzed their data.
- After reading *The City of Ember* (DuPrau, 2003) for an inquiry unit on environmental literacy, sixth graders researched an insect to understand its role in nature and published an information page.
- After the unit with *Esperanza Rising* students wrote a survey on poverty, gave it to over 250 community members, and graphed and analyzed the results.

Awakening to the World

Young adolescents want to *engage* the world. When I was in middle school in the suburbs of Chicago, I saw the "big city"—just fifteen minutes away—as a daunting and foreign land. But adolescents today practically carry the planet in their pockets through their phones.

Middle level students are also becoming more empathetic to the injustices in life. In another unit I cotaught in a class of sixth graders, we designed a unit about empathy with the novel *The Tiger Rising* (DiCamillo, 2001) and *Leon's Story* (Tillage, 1997), a very brief oral history of Leon Walter Tillage growing up African American in the Jim Crow South. In the middle of the book, immersed in our shared reading, after having read of the horrific injustices of the time, Alex raised his hand and said to the class in disbelief, "How could people *do that*?" I do not believe Alex was merely announcing his anger at the ugliness of racism; he was asking a genuine and difficult question about life and human nature.

Maxine Greene challenges us to help students develop a "wide-awakeness" to the world (1995, p. 4). We cultivate that awakeness by allowing them to engage with the real world, in all of its confusing mix of joy and intolerance and messiness and wonder. Middle school teachers are in a unique and exciting place to guide their students along that new and perplexing path with good books. Years ago when was I student teaching in a middle grade classroom, my outstanding cooperating teacher believed that one of her most important jobs was to make her students struggle with moral dilemmas. Middle level students *relish* that struggle; it connects to their heightened awareness of life, their fierce energy to let their voices be heard, and their passion to fix a deeply broken world. To borrow the wonderful words of Maxine Greene, "It would mean fresh and sometimes startling winds blowing through the classrooms of the nation" (1998, p. 126).

References

Atwell, N. (1998). *In the middle: New understandings about writing, reading, and learning.* Portsmouth, NH: Heinemann.

Brown, D. (2015). *Drowned city: Hurricane Katrina & New Orleans.* Boston, MA: Houghton Mifflin.

Brozo, W. (2002). "I know the difference between a real man and a TV man": A critical exploration of violence and masculinity through literary in a junior high school in the 'hood. *Journal of Adolescent and Adult Literacy, 45,* 530–538.

Daniels, H., & Ahmed, S. (2015). *Upstanders: How to engage middle school hearts and minds with inquiry.* Portsmouth, NH: Heinemann.

de la Pena, M. (2008). *Mexican whiteboy.* New York, NY: Delacourt Press/Random House Children's Books.

DiCamillo, K. (2001). *The tiger rising.* New York, NY: Candlewick.

DuPrau, J. (2003). *The city of Ember.* New York, NY: Random House Books for Young Readers.

Gainer, J. (2010). Critical media literacy in middle school: Exploring the politics of representation. *Journal of Adolescent and Adult Literacy, 53,* 364–373.

Greene, M. (1995). *Releasing the imagination: Essays on education, the arts, and social change.* San Francisco, CA: Jossey-Bass.

Greene, M. (1998). *The dialectic of freedom.* New York, NY: Teachers College Press.

Hale, N. (2015). *The Underground Abductor.* NY: Harry N. Abrams Press.

Harvey, S., & Daniels, H. (2009). *Comprehension & collaboration: Inquiry circles in action.* Portsmouth, NH: Heinemann.

Hautman, P. (2007). *Rash.* New York, NY: Simon Pulse.

Jaramillo, A. (2007). *La linea.* New York, NY: Square Fish.

Maples, J., & Groenke, S. (2009). Who is an American?: Challenging middle school students' assumptions through critical literacy. *Voices from the Middle,* 17, 28–35.

Nazario, S. (2007). *Enrique's journey.* New York, NY: Random House.

Pearson, M. (2007). *The adoration of Jenna Fox.* New York, NY: Square Fish.

Peart, N. (2011, December 17). Why is the NYPD after me? *The New York Times,* p. SR6. Retrieved from http://www.nytimes.com/2011/12/18/opinion/sunday/young-black-and-frisked-by-the-nypd.html?_r=0

Resau, L. (2007). *Red glass.* New York, NY: Delacorte Press.

Rojas, J. (2009). I am the change: Modern day slavery project. In *Learn by design: Projects and practices at High Tech Middle* (pp. 56–59). San Diego, CA: High Tech High.

Ryan, P. M. (2000). *Esperanza rising.* New York, NY: Scholastic.

Schrefer, E. (2012). *Endangered.* New York, NY: Scholastic.

Spires, H. A., Hervey, L. G., Morris, G., & Stelpflug, C. (2012). Energizing project-based inquiry: Middle-grade students read, write, and create videos. *Journal of Adolescent and Adult Literacy,* 55, 483–493.

Tillage, L. W. (1997). *Leon's story.* New York, NY: Farrar, Straus, and Giroux.

Vawter, V. (2012). *Paperboy.* New York, NY: Delacorte Press.

Volponi, P. (2006). *Black and white.* New York, NY: Speak.

Wilhelm, J. D., & Smith, M. W. (2007). Making it matter through the power of inquiry. In K. Beers, R. Probst, & L. Rief (Eds.), *Adolescent literacy: Turning promise into practice* (pp. 231–242). Portsmouth, NH: Heinemann.

Wilhelm, J. D., & Wilhelm, P. J. (2010). Inquiring minds learn to read, write, and think: Reaching "all" learners through inquiry. *Middle School Journal,* 41, 39–46.

Wilson, E. O. (1987). *In search of nature.* Washington, DC: Island Press.

Wolk, S. (2013). *Caring hearts & critical minds: Literature, inquiry, and social responsibility.* Portland, ME: Stenhouse.

Discussion Questions

1. In the article, what is the definition of "wide-awakeness" and how can this be encouraged in middle- and secondary-level students?
2. Why is teaching through inquiry critical for today's students?

Reading, Learning, and Even Arguing across Multiple Texts

Diane Barone

Diane Barone presents a multiple text approach to the text-based lesson in the following article. As you read, mentally compare and contrast her approach with the one presented in the previous article by Steven Wolk.

LEARNING OBJECTIVES

1. Teachers frequently complain that there isn't enough time to "cover" the curriculum. How could you justify, then, having students read multiple texts relating to the same topic?
2. How might the reading of multiple texts on the same topic relate to the Common Core Standards?

Reading, Learning, and Even Arguing across Multiple Texts

Diane Barone

As teachers bring Common Core State Standards to their practice, they frequently focus on one aspect of the ELA expectations. For instance, they have students participate in close reading as an individual event—an important one, but one that can be stronger by linking it to similar reading across texts (Shanahan, Fisher, & Frey, 2012; Valencia & Wixson, 2013).

While this expectation requires teachers to find multiple texts (print and electronic) on a similar topic, it is more typical of the reading we experience daily. For example, as teachers we read professional materials and ideas from the Internet to enrich our teaching practice.

Reading of multiple texts is directly tied to Reading Standard 9 of the Common Core that states: "Analyze how two or more texts address similar themes or topics in order to build knowledge or to compare the approaches the authors take." As a university professor in reading, I find that it is most beneficial if I learn about the reading of multiple texts from the experts—teachers. I visited a fifth-grade teacher to learn how she engaged students in finding meaning across multiple texts. As I observed her literacy instruction over several weeks, I discovered how one teacher built multiple text opportunities for students in which they read and wrote about the content they discovered.

Before moving to the interpretation of multiple texts, I need to describe the routines that students engaged in and how they seamlessly moved from one to another learning event. These routines were important as they kept students focused and provided the necessary time to engage with multiple texts. For instance, as students entered the room, they immediately took out a whiteboard to respond to an entry task. The entry task changed daily but often focused on nonfiction text structures.

On this day, students were to identify the text's structure and supply reasons behind their thinking. The short text had a problem–solution structure. Not all students agreed about the nature of this structure, however, as one student thought it was descriptive. The teacher allowed students to respond to each other after they had shared their thoughts with a partner. Students kindly disagreed with the dissenting student and noted that one sentence was descriptive, but the whole paragraph was problem–solution because it talked about the issue of too much trash and what to do about it. What is important about this simple teaching event is that students made decisions and supported them in writing and conversation. Students were willing to listen to the thinking of others as they pondered their own responses.

Students then read an article about symbiotic relationships, section-by-section, and discussed what they learned. For example, one section shared information about sea anemones and hermit crabs. One student said, "Really, the sea anemone just rides on the back of the hermit crab. How smart. Now I wondered why would the crab let it do that. The author knew I would ask that question and I learned that the anemone protects the crab from predators like octopuses." As students read each section, they recorded notes about each symbiotic relationship. After reading the article and discussing as they moved through it, the teacher convened the class. She only asked one question, "What do we know about symbiotic relationships after reading this article?" One student responded, "Two animals support each other in strange ways." Other students added to this response or provided examples from the text. I noted that students always went back to the text when offering a comment. I knew that this teacher had to have worked with students to ground their responses in the text.

Following the text reading, the teacher provided a list of websites that she explored with students. Students conversed with classmates at their table as they viewed the sites. For example, they explored photos about symbiosis on the Huffington Post site (http://www.huffingtonpost.com/2010/01/04/mutually-beneficial-anima_n_391888.html). Then they watched a video about ants and butterfly symbiosis (http://video.nationalgeographic.com/video/animals/bugs-animals/ants-and-termites/ant_caterpillarsymbiosis). Following these multimodal experiences, students returned to their notes and added new information.

Students created a bulletin board in their class where they identified text features, continually adding those they observed during reading (see Fig. 9.2.1). They used this board as reference material for developing their own posters to share information they had learned about symbiotic relationships. For the content purposes of their poster, the teacher had magazines, copies of articles, websites, and a multitude of books available for students. Students also brought information from home explorations and read recursively across these materials as they created their posters, making sure they included appropriate text features. From some material, they took content and featured vocabulary words. From other support materials, they viewed format and assessed which text features would be best to share certain information. They understood they had two major responsibilities: share authentic details about symbiotic relationships and make this information visually appealing.

FIGURE 9.2.1   Students Continually Added to a Bulletin Board
That Would Serve as a Reference for Additional Projects.

Figure 9.2.2 showcases the way students took on this challenge. This student featured a definition of symbiotic relationships right in the middle to show its importance. He knew the middle gathers the most attention. He noted that the critical essence of these relationships is that "animals work together." Moving to the left in this poster, we see a text box in which he shared information about sea anemones and how they find food and offer protection. He used additional text boxes to share information about pollination and animals in New Zealand. He

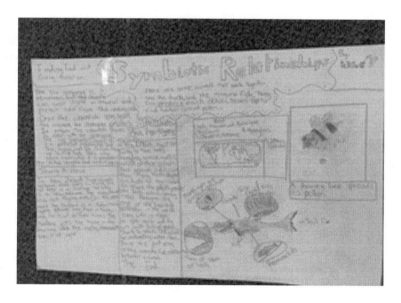

FIGURE 9.2.2   Students Developed Posters to Reflect What They Had
Learned About Text Features in General and Symbiosis in Particular.

shifted from text boxes to include a map with a key to show the locations of specific animals. He finally created visual displays for the shark and remora fish as well as the bee and pollination.

The connections between reading a variety of texts and then sharing information discovered through these explorations were obvious in this classroom, and students were clearly comfortable moving from text to text (both print and electronic). While it all looked effortless to me, I asked the teacher how this all happened; I knew that students don't just behave this way when they walk into a classroom. The teacher explained the importance of building routines first. Students knew what to expect as far as routine; each day there was an entry task followed by nonfiction exploration. Other expectations, like conversation, took more time and experience. The teacher said, "It took longer to get students to discuss, especially when they did not all agree. At first a kid would just say, 'You are wrong.' Now they say, 'I disagree because …' or 'I see your point, but did you think about … ?' This kind of thinking carried over into their reading. At first they were frustrated when different authors said things in different ways or didn't agree. I can't say they are happy about those differences, but they understand different perspectives and ways to share information."

The next big challenge was finding appropriate materials to use with students. Although the teacher still used textbooks, she shifted to featuring articles and websites. She wanted to simulate real-world experiences with common information resources. This teacher was fortunate as she had extensive materials in her school library, access to a laptop cart for website exploration, and ongoing magazine support that featured paired texts (fiction, nonfiction, poetry, plays, and persuasive pieces). She said, "It takes time to plan but I am getting better. Students love to learn about things and to share what they learn. They are also more critical about informational text; they want it to be visually appealing and accurate."

Looking back on these experiences, was it worth it to have students read across texts, discuss with classmates, and create a textual and visual interpretation of the content they explored? Could the answer be anything but yes? Students demonstrated the following learning outcomes:

- They understood the structures of nonfiction.
- They understood the importance and purpose of text features.
- They understood that they could gain different and sometimes conflicting information from multiple sources, including those that were sophisticated and complex.
- They seamlessly moved between electronic and print resources.
- They read and reread to locate information.
- They discovered the vocabulary pertinent to their topic.
- They discussed, concurred, and sometimes disagreed, but used text support for their understandings.
- They increased their background knowledge about scientific content.
- They read critically and often chastised authors for not being clearer in the way they shared information.
- They independently discovered information to add to what they learned within their classroom walls.

- They displayed motivation and persistence as they read and reread during the process of creating their posters.
- They produced informational text through the use of text features, valuing both text and visual information.

What I discovered is that students enjoyed reading across texts and sharing their discoveries, they were comfortable in learning and dealing with ambiguity as they engaged in their research endeavors, and they knew how to learn from multiple texts.

References

Shanahan, T., Fisher, D., & Frey, N. (2012). The challenge of challenging text. *Educational Leadership, 69*(6), 58–62.

Valencia, S., & Wixson, K. (2013). CCSS—ELA: Suggestions and cautions for implementing the reading standards. *The Reading Teacher, 67,* 181–185.

Discussion Questions

1. Use a Venn diagram to compare the instructional approaches outlined in the Wolk article and the Barone article.
2. How does the multiple text approach described by Barone meet the challenges posed by the Common Core Standards?

Conclusion

Chapter Activities

Activity 9.1

Select one instructional strategy listed for the pre-reading, during reading, and post-reading phases of a text-based lesson. Research each strategy and prepare a one-page handout for each one that you could share with other teachers to teach them to use that strategy with their own students.

Activity 9.2

Identify a book suitable for students in middle school. Based on the "interesting real-world resources" described in the Wolk article, identify at least five resources you could introduce to students to extend their reading of the identified book. List the citations of the resources, including links to videos or online resources, and a short description of how each resource will complement and extend the text.

Writing in the Content Areas

Content Area Writing

In addition to English/language arts teachers teaching writing as a process through the writing workshop approach, middle and secondary school content area teachers also need to incorporate writing into these subject areas. Writing workshop focuses on learning to write; content area writing places the focus on writing to learn.

Goals for Content Area Writing

Incorporating writing into the content areas (math, science, social studies, health, physical education, etc.) can help achieve many learning goals in middle and secondary classrooms.
 Content writing activities:

- help students engage deeply with the content,
- support their creation of personal connections to new content, which also aids in supporting comprehension and retention,
- create a record of students' thoughts and ideas in response to what they are reading and learning in content classrooms,
- create a record of students' struggles with understanding content (which can be examined by the teacher for insight into students' misconceptions),
- support student engagement in classroom discussion of content topics,
- enhance students' writing abilities through additional practice, and

- enhance motivation and interest in content,
- provide a social forum for the discussion of content-related topics and issues.

Some specific writing instructional strategies that can be used in content classrooms to enhance content learning and students' writing skills include RAFT (Role, Audience, Format, Topic) papers, learning journals, biopoems, invented dialogues, list articles, catalog poems, wikis, blogs, and multimedia projects.

Their Own Voices

Empowering Students with Choice in Writing Tasks

Jaime Norris

Incorporating choice into students' writing assignments can have a positive impact on their engagement, motivation, and the final product, according to this article by Jaime Norris.

LEARNING OBJECTIVES

1. When you are given a writing assignment, do you prefer to choose the content and format or do you prefer to have it assigned? Why?
2. What is a "mentor"? What role do you think a "mentor text" might have in writing instruction?

Their Own Voices

Empowering Students with Choice in Writing Tasks

Jaime Norris

Ask any young adolescent the kind of movies or books they like, and they'll instantly spring into action. They will launch into an impromptu review of one of their favorites that they watch or read over and over, or they will rehash the movie they saw the previous weekend. They'll retell their favorite parts, even offer a critique of the actors in the movie.

If you inquire, they will also tell you the movies that they were dragged to the theater to watch or about books they were forced to read. Young adolescents know the kinds of movies and literature they like. Many of them could talk about them for hours.

Why wouldn't we take advantage of that passion in our own classrooms? When students are genuinely interested in a topic, they are more likely to take pride in any work associated with it. Giving reasonable choices within the curriculum can engage the students more because they are able to choose a topic or a prompt that suits them. Writing assignments, which can create anxiety for many students, can easily utilize choice. If students are able to choose the topic or even the writing prompt, they would be more likely to put their best effort into the assignment. The students are also more likely to be engaged in learning.

Student engagement is now more important than ever. With the implementation of the new Common Core Standards comes an explicit call for more writing to be done. Starting from grade 3, the tenth writing standard for each grade level calls for students to "write routinely over extended time frames and shorter time frames" (CCSS; National Governors Association Center for Best Practices & Council of Chief State School Officers, 2010). There are three types of writing that students should be producing based on these Common Core State Standards:

CCSS.ELA-Literacy.CCRA.W.1: Write arguments to support claims in an analysis of substantive topics or texts using valid reasoning and relevant and sufficient evidence.

CCSS.ELA-Literacy.CCRA.W.2: Write informative/explanatory texts to examine and convey complex ideas and information clearly and accurately through the effective selection, organization, and analysis of content.

CCSS.ELA-Literacy.CCRA.W.3: Write narratives to develop real or imagined experiences or events using effective technique, well-chosen details and well-structured event sequences (Common Core State Standards Initiative, 2014).

The standard explicitly states that writing should become routine and specifies that this writing should be done over longer periods of time including planning, reflection and revision and in shorter periods of time, such as a single class sitting. Stated bluntly, students should be writing several times per week, if not every day. In addition, students must put forth a significant effort on writing assignments that require a complex writing process. This requires spending a significant length of time on a particular writing assignment. Thus, not only are we dealing with a high volume of student writing, we must allocate great spaces of time to working with a single piece of student-produced writing. There should be tremendous attention given to detail and careful scrutiny of selected information to use. This requires time and effort over several sittings with a text. If a student is going to spend a significant amount of time to shape and polish his writing, it is important that he has a vested interest in the writing. One way of doing this is to give students choices in the writing assignments they complete.

The positive benefits of incorporating choice in school curriculum are well documented. According to the National Research Council, (as cited in Quate & McDermott, 2009), students tend to be more engaged in school work when they have some choices in the material they study and the strategies they utilize in completing tasks. In a 2012 study of college students and their recollections of school experiences, the subjects offered suggestions of ways to improve English instruction. One assertion is that the students need more opportunities for creative writing and that teachers tend to be too rigid on reading and writing topics (Yu, 2012). Clearly, there was a lack of choice and opportunities for students to develop a sense of ownership and creativity. A focus study of teenagers echoed that encouragement to choose their own topics made their required writing assignment more interesting and engaging (Lenhart, Arafeh, Smith, & Macgill, 2008). Based on the research, we can see that student engagement can be increased by offering choices in writing assignments. Further, with just a little more thought and effort, teachers can easily provide a variety of topic choices for any mode of writing.

Careful examination of the grade level standards can guide a teacher in designing lessons and tasks for students. Infusing choice into writing assignments doesn't have to be hard or time consuming. It just takes a little thought and planning. Giving students choices can even be as simple as giving a list of four or five prompts from which they can choose. Choice on a larger scale could involve students' interests and experiences. I give my students an interest inventory sheet at the beginning of the year (see Appendix A). For quick reference, the graphic organizer is divided into four sections. The students compile lists of their beliefs, aspects of their background, hobbies, interests, and favorite things. This teaches me a little about my students in

August and then serves as their possible topics list for the rest of the year. Writing assignments can be tailored around their interests, their beliefs and family traditions, their favorite foods, and the list continues. My students are engaged in a topic that interests them, which they chose. I don't have to read 200 papers about why students shouldn't be required to wear uniforms. It's a win-win situation.

Argumentative: For This They Believe

Students have no trouble telling you their opinion if you ask them. They are quick to defend their position. Our job in teaching argumentative writing is to teach them how to do so in an effective manner. Students need to be able to assert a claim and support it with plenty of strong evidence (Calkins, Ehrenworth, & Lehman, 2012). Since students can feel as apathetic about some topics as they feel passionately about others, choice is a critical element. This can take several forms. Newspapers and other periodicals are excellent sources for editorials that focus on current events and other topics. There are many editorials that focus on topics that affect students. An editorial proposing a ban on the sale of energy drinks to minors got my students fired up. Other students found the proposed ban on plastic bags to be interesting. One possibility is to give students a choice of two or three editorials to study. Students can be grouped according to the article for which they expressed interest. They can then work collaboratively to evaluate the claim and evidence from the editorial, even develop a rebuttal argument. Alternatively, students can search independently for their own editorials based on their interests. This requires a short lesson on how to do a search on Google. For example, inputting "editorials and skateboards" into the search engine usually gives a number of choices. Students can choose an editorial and can work with a partner with that common interest or they can work alone.

Expository and Informational: The Knowledge They Seek

Expository and informational texts and tasks cover a vast array of topics from literary analysis to how-to papers to research projects. Although literary analysis is limited in the specific grade level standards and the skills they emphasize, choice can still be used effectively. In units involving multiple texts, perhaps we could give students a choice of which text to analyze. Usually by the end of the unit, students have a preference for one or the other and feel more confident to write about their preferred text. Alternatively, a choice of four different prompts may be offered, and students can decide on the one about which they feel most confident. Undoubtedly, some people will shake their heads at this, saying students would be avoiding necessary skills that they may not have mastered and that addressing these skills in their writing would help them improve. Maybe. However, if the goal is to teach effective and powerful writing, it is important that students be confident in their knowledge of the content they are writing about and be interested in the topic. Both are especially important if students will be spending a significant amount of time revising and editing their pieces.

For other expository and informational writing, the students' interest inventory can be utilized. Students' interests can be the basis for many different kinds of writing assignments. With a little help, students can formulate their own prompts. For example, an avid skateboarder may write a piece on how to do a certain skateboarding trick or discuss the pros and cons of different terrains for skateboarding.

Research papers are also an important part of informational writing. Just as students formulated a list of their interests, they can also generate a list of wonderings. *I wonder how crop circles are made. I wonder about the process of constructing a video game from the first idea to the finished product.* Students can take these wonderings and conduct research to change them from *I wonder* to *I know and I can show you*. We can utilize research projects that encourage students to discover what they've always wanted to know. In my own classes, my students conduct research projects on a chosen career. Most of them already have an idea of a career they might want to have. Some of them know they want to be a veterinarian because they love animals. Others may bounce from doctor to lawyer to teacher, depending on their mood that day. Before beginning the project, students choose a career to research. They do prewriting on why they are interested in that career and what they believe the career entails as far as the day-to-day responsibilities. Then they conduct the research and can even work collaboratively with other students with similar career interests. In their report, they would discuss their findings, which include the educational requirements, average salaries, day-to-day responsibilities, and other career aspects. While some students find that their initial anticipations were accurate, others realize that they need higher degrees in education than they had previously thought or that their salary estimations were slightly off. This is a good project for students because it is something they should be thinking about as they progress through school and start thinking about college and careers.

Narrative: The Story They Want to Tell

Students' lives are full of stories. There are stories of the exciting activities they engaged in over weekends and breaks. There are stories of triumph in their favorite sport, the story of their first dates, first loves, and more. Students can write narratives from these stories that are smoldering in their own memories. However, choice can and should still be utilized in students' personal narratives. It is tempting for teachers to keep the assignment limited to one prompt; reliving a memory is a common one. Remember, there are students for whom pleasant memories are a scarcity. Some students may not feel comfortable writing about memories, particularly if they will be participating in peer review. It is important to give a variety of prompts so students can choose the prompts they feel most comfortable writing about.

Imagined narratives are often overlooked. In my narrative unit, students write imagined narratives, and many have said that it is their favorite assignment of the year. They fondly remember the mentor texts we read and examine, but most of all, they remember the culminating task. The prompt that I give my students is simple—write the story you would want to read. There are necessary restrictions, of course. Their stories must be age appropriate, meaning no alcohol, drug, or tobacco use. They cannot use characters from other stories or movies, not even an imitation. Over the years I have added the restriction that they cannot use other students in their narratives, although they are perfectly welcome to write about themselves. These restrictions don't seem to bother them. For once, they are not limited to one prompt, and they get to choose their own story. They become truly engaged in the writing assignment.

A Few Words about Mentor Texts and Models

Obviously, we cannot simply turn students loose with a pen and a notebook. Students will not simply transform into good writers by writing notebooks full of stories and essays about their interests and curiosities. If we expect them to learn to write well, we must teach them how (Jago, 2014). One of the ways to do this is through the use of mentor texts. A writing unit cannot stand alone. If students are to become good writers, they must *examine*, not just read exemplary writing. Kelly Gallagher emphasizes that students must revisit a text repeatedly throughout the writing process (2014). Character development, vivid description, realistic dialogue, sentence structure and other elements—these are skills best taught by studying them in the literature they read and other models. In addition to guiding the students through analysis of mentor texts, the teacher should be writing along with the students. First, this shows students that writing does not have to be published in order to be considered "good." Second, this is a great way to demonstrate revision and writing techniques. Also, the teacher serves as a model, showing students that even experienced writers have to make many revisions to their writing. Plus, if teachers think aloud as they write, they serve as examples of the required thinking processes that go into writing. When I write in front of my students, they see that the writing does not have to be perfect the first time. They find great joy in contributing possible word choices and sentence structure in the teacher's writing.

The Last Word

Empowering our students to make choices in their writing tasks does require more time and effort, but in the end, it is worth the payoff. Students will be more engaged in the writing they produce and thus are more likely to invest more time into their effort than they otherwise would. True, it is easier to design one prompt. Some may argue that it is easier to instruct with one topic. Others say that it makes grading easier too. But, in the end, if students have no commitment to their writing, what will they gain from the instruction? The truth of the matter is that we teach writing for the students. It is to benefit them, certainly not ourselves. I have yet to see a teacher who was excited to go home on Friday afternoon to grade a ponderous stack of essays.

Narrowing the assignment to one prompt for all students robs them of their voice in writing. They are then writing for the teacher when they should be writing for themselves. After all, they are writing for the purpose of becoming better writers and extending their knowledge. They are writing to improve and to benefit themselves. The power to make their own choices and to be held accountable for those choices is important in ways that extend far past the classroom. As teachers, it is our responsibility to foster and encourage that process.

References

Calkins, L., Ehrenworth, M., & Lehman, C. (2012). *Pathways to the common core.* Portsmouth, NH: Heinemann.

Gallagher, K. (2014). Making the most of mentor texts. *Educational Leadership, 71*(7), 28–33.

Jago, C. (2014). Writing is taught, not caught. *Educational Leadership, 71*(7), 16–21.

Lenhart, A., Arafeh. S., Smith, A., & Macgill, A. R. (2008). What teens tell us encourages them to write. *Writing, technology and teens.* The National Commission on Writing. Pew Internet & American Life Project, 42–64. Retrieved from http://www.pewinternet.org/2008/04/24/writing-technology-and-teens/.

National Governors Association Center for Best Practices & Council of Chief State School Officers. (2010). Common core state standards for English language arts and literacy in history/social studies, science, and technical subjects. Washington, DC: Author. Retrieved from http://www.core standards.org/ela-literacy/ccra/w/.

Quate, S., & McDermott, J. (2009). *Clock watchers: Six steps to motivating and engaging disengaged students across content areas.* Portsmouth, NH: Heinemann.

Yu, E. (2012). Ready for college? What college students have to say about their high school English experiences. *English Leadership Quarterly, 35*(1), 2–6.

Appendix A: Student Interest Inventory

Student's Name

All about Me: (include information about family, pets, background, traditions, etc.)	Beliefs

Hobbies/Interests	Favorites: List other favorites here.
	Person:
	Food:
	Book:
	Music:
	Movie:
	Animal:
	Place:

Discussion Questions

1. Define "mentor text" and explain its role in enhancing students' writing.
2. What are some issues or difficulties teachers may face in implementing the approaches outlined in the Norris article? How could they overcome these issues?

Four Reasons to Write List Articles with Middle School Students

Denise M. Morgan, Leslie Benko, and Gayle Marek Hauptman

In this article, the authors discuss using "list articles" and "catalog poems" with students to encourage writing and to enhance learning in the content areas.

LEARNING OBJECTIVES

1. Do you enjoy reading "top ten" lists for topics in which you are interested? Why or why not?
2. Brainstorm a few ways that you might use "top ten" lists to enhance students' literacy learning in middle- or secondary-level classrooms.

Four Reasons to Write List Articles with Middle School Students

Denise M. Morgan, Leslie Benko, and Gayle Marek Hauptman

The siren song of the list article is unmistakable. Who isn't enticed by "10 Ways to Become More Efficient at Work," "The Best Apps You Don't Know About," or "Best Delis in NYC"? Reading list articles, in which "writers present readers with a list of possibilities inside a particular category of possibilities" (Ray, 2006, p. 230) is a mainstay of our everyday lives.

Newspapers, magazines, and websites all boost ways to do, have, know, or become through their ubiquitous publication of list articles. Yet, list article writing is often absent in schools.

Unfortunately for middle grade students, the time devoted to writing instruction and the amount of writing students have been asked to do has been minimal in classrooms (Applebee & Langer, 2009; NCTE, 2008). There is an increased emphasis on the teaching of writing with the adoption of the Common Core State Standards (CCSS). While *how* to meet these new writing standards is not being dictated, we believe that a unit of study framework can offer teachers a predictable structure that inherently addresses the CCSS and actively engages students in the process of writing (Morgan, 2012; Ray, 2006).

The seventh graders at Solon Middle School just completed a unit of study on list articles. Students of all writing abilities demonstrated higher than usual engagement with this unit, and they made deliberate writing decisions throughout the process, resulting in high-quality final drafts that reflected their individual interests. In this article, we identify how a unit of study on list articles engages students in active and purposeful writing experiences and decision making while providing much-needed differentiation within the language arts classroom. And it seems only appropriate to offer these four benefits in ... well, list format.

Four Benefits of Writing List Articles

Writing List Articles Honors Students' Interests and Choice of Topic

Choice has long been a hallmark within writing workshop (Atwell, 1998; Kittle, 2008). List articles require students to first think about topics they are interested in or knowledgeable about. Teachers model how to think through ideas using a graphic organizer and show students how they come up with their own writing ideas.

Once students select a topic, they have control over how they shape their idea. Would their topic be best suited for a "reasons why" list article, or do they have set criteria in mind that they can use to determine a "Top 5" or "10 Best"? Students must choose for themselves the direction in which they want to take their piece. For example, Caleb (student names are pseudonyms) participates in competitive Irish dancing. He identified Irish dancing as an area of interest and realized he could write list articles on the "Top 5 Irish-American Cities," "How to Excel in Irish Dancing," or the "Top 10 Irish Dance Moves." Students are encouraged to select a topic that relates to a passion, builds on background knowledge, or is an area of new interest.

Students become invested in their pieces because of their personal choice of topics. For example, writing is laborious and difficult for Matt. His IEP specifies that he is to have a scribe for all writing assignments. He identified basketball as an area of interest and narrowed his topic to the "Top 5 Jordan Basketball Shoes." He described selecting his topic as "easy." From the beginning, he worked independently, asked good questions, met deadlines, participated in writing conferences and peer reviews, and refused adult help because he *wanted* to tackle the work himself. He said, "I liked writing the list article because it was more of what I wanted to do than being told what I had to do. I had more freedom." He had a clear purpose for writing, stayed focused, and worked diligently. He was proud of his final piece.

When choice is honored, there is a rich array of topics in the classroom that reflect the students' interests and passions. From "Unveiling the Truth of *Dance Moms*: 5 Ways *Dance Moms* Is True" to "Top 5 Styles of the Season," each student is engaged and motivated to write his or her best.

Writing List Articles Requires Students to Engage in the Writing Process

Setting aside three weeks to investigate this type of writing allows time for students to get messy with their writing, planning, revising, and editing, and even allows for a change in direction of their piece early on. These are all hallmarks of addressing CCSS Writing Anchor Standard 5 (writing as a process). In addition, these experiences support students in writing over extended time frames (CCSS Writing Anchor Standard 10).

List articles begin as all writing workshops do, with studying and analyzing mentor texts. These texts help students better understand craft and structure, and give them a "big picture" understanding of what they will do with their own writing. (See Fig. 10.2.1 for examples of minilessons taught during this unit.) These texts are teacher chosen and include list articles from magazines and newspapers as well as exemplary student examples. Having a balance of professional and student examples helps students of all writing abilities see a myriad of

Mini-lessons	Focus
What Are List Articles?	Students read and identify qualities found within list articles.
Reading Like a Writer/ Mentor Texts	Students spend several days analyzing list articles. They complete a chart of writing techniques they may want to try in their own writing.
Determining Areas of Interest/Brainstorming Topics	Students complete a graphic organizer of topics they are interested in and knowledgeable about and brainstorm possible article ideas.
Establishing Criteria	Students determine the necessary criteria for their selected topic.
Researching and Citing Sources	Students determine what constitutes reliable research and then begin collecting information to support their purpose.
How to Use a Mentor Text	Students dissect how to borrow a structure or idea from a mentor text to apply to their own writing.
Writing the Introduction	Students learn to hook the reader, provide criteria for making the list, give the reader necessary background information, and consider including a range statement that helps multiple people feel the article applies to their needs (e.g., "From Maine to Florida, the east coast offers a variety of vacation destinations").
Writing Title, Subtitle, and Headings	Students determine what catchy title and/or subtitle they want for their pieces. Also, they create parallel subheadings for each section to maintain uniformity.
Organizing the List Article	Students plan where each item should go on their list.
Using Writing Techniques	Students revise their writing to include humor, sarcasm, sensory details, vivid word choices, questions, figurative language, power of three, and/or text features like bold or italics.
Writing the "About the Author"	Students experiment writing in third person about themselves and their qualifications for being an expert on the topic.

FIGURE 10.2.1   Mini-Lessons Taught During the Unit.

possibilities. Students learn to "read like a writer" with their mentor texts (Smith, 1998), and to recognize the power of this practice. Mary wrote, "The mentor texts helped me most with ideas by giving me examples of what I could do in my piece to make it better."

List writing requires students to engage in short research projects to gather the necessary information to support their purpose. Since students are creating symmetry within each section, they often need to search for information online. They learn how to cite the websites they visited, and they search for images to enhance their texts. This embedded research within writing list articles helps students work within Writing Anchor Standards 6 (use technology), 7 (engage in short research projects), and 8 (gather evidence). For example, Bob's initial idea of writing about the "10 Best Reptiles" evolved to writing about the "4 Most Deadly Reptiles," because that was what he became most interested in as he researched.

List Writing Requires Students to Make Deliberate Writing Decisions

Writing Anchor Standard 4 requires students to demonstrate that their "development, organization, and style" of a piece is appropriate to the "task, purpose, and audience." From the introduction to the conclusion, every word counts as the student creates a voice, establishes a tone, and seeks to satisfy the intended purpose.

Students identified the introduction of one mentor text as interesting and compelling. In the introduction of "The Teens Are All Right: 2011's Top 5 YA Novels," Marissa Meyer (2011) wrote: "A love story at the heart of a horror novel—why not? Mythical water horses in the modern world—sounds exciting! A theatrical fantasy populated with Shakespearean and fairy tale characters alike—oh, the possibilities!" Several students decided this effectively captured the audience's attention and wanted to try the structure themselves.

In her article about the "Top 5 *Must* Rides to Ride," Ann experimented with the opening of her article: "A 400-foot drop—why not? A rush of adrenaline followed by butterflies in your stomach—sounds exciting! A breathtaking view over the whole park or reaching speeds of 120 mph—oh, the possibilities!" Ann said she borrowed Meyer's structure because it brings the reader in more: "Marissa Meyer wrote about books, but I thought about what would go with amusement park rides and matched my description with the phrases."

When asked how he came up with subheadings for his piece, "Sports Injuries: 5 of the Most Ridiculous Ways to Get Injured," Gavin said, "When we read the examples, each author came up with something creative. So I thought of the injury for each player and an adjective that started with the same letter to describe it." His subheadings included: Sammy Sosa: Sneezing Spasm, Bill Gramatica: Celebration Catastrophe, and Kevin Johnson: Hurtful Hug.

In considering her overall structure, Irma wanted to do a recap of the "Top 5 Memorable Events from 2012," like the news channels do. After listing her top events, she recognized that Hurricane Sandy and the Sandy Hook Elementary school shooting were very different from another item she wanted to include, the viral video "Ain't Nobody Got Time for That," in which a woman describes her house catching on fire in a humorous way. Irma described her writing process:

> This section was hard to write because I had just finished writing about Hurricane Sandy and the Sandy Hook school shooting. So, I tried to transition from sad to happy. I used words that the person would do while watching the video, like giggling and laughing, to tell the reader it was OK to laugh a little. I also used a lot of exclamation points to make it lighter and more fun."

To lighten the tone, she wrote:

> All of 2012 wasn't gloomy; there were also times where we couldn't stop laughing. One of those times was when a hilarious video went viral. ... Starring in this video was a woman whose name completely described her personality—Sweet Brown. The name was a perfect fit!

Students used the writing techniques they learned from mentor texts to help them make deliberate decisions about how they wanted to craft their writing. (See Fig. 10.2.2 for one student's list article: "Top 5 YA Novels" picks.)

List Articles Provide Students with Opportunities for Deep Learning

Writing list articles motivates students to pursue a passion and take their learning deeper on their chosen topic. This kind of work supports a "thinking curriculum" (Calkins, Ehrenwroth, & Lehman, 2012, p. 9). While research is often daunting for students, they are eager to research topics they love. Randy wrote about the "Top 5 Point Guards in the NBA," and he said, "I am proud of the effort I put in. I researched a lot about the stats of each player. ... If I had time, I would write a 10-page biography on each player."

Students may start with a few ideas of what will make their list, but through the writing process, they establish the criteria to determine inclusion on the list, gather data on all the possibilities, and analyze data to determine what makes the final cut. After this extensive higher-order thinking process, during which students collect information and evaluate their options, students make their final decisions about their lists. They then conduct further research on their topics to fully explain the items included on their lists.

The students often become so knowledgeable about each item on their lists that they cannot include everything they've discovered, so they have to synthesize the information for their readers. Writing about "The NBA's Top 5," Dan described his research process: "I just thought of the leaders of every team and wrote them down. I looked at their stats. From the best statistics, I made a choice of the top five."

Jimmy created an Excel spreadsheet to sort the information he gathered so he could better rank the "Top NFL Players of 2012." He included a variety of statistics on 20 players whom he thought might make the top 10. His data gave him the support he needed to narrow his list to 10 players.

List articles not only support students in developing their writing skills, but also their research skills.

Conclusion

There is a certain freedom that list articles provide for middle level students. In part, the students enjoy being able to write with "sarcasm and humor" and to "have fun while writing." Amy mentioned, "I like this form of writing because it's a type of creative nonfiction. Usually when you think of nonfiction, you think of writing reports and facts, facts, facts. But this allowed for creativity and description." Ambika shared that this experience also allows teachers to learn about "students' interests and get to know them better." Students take ownership of their writing when writing list articles, and teachers can use that natural interest and energy to teach the students more about crafting writing and the overall writing process.

References

Applebee, A. N., & Langer, J. A. (2009). What is happening in the teaching of writing? *English Journal, 95*(8), 18–28.

Atwell, N. (1998). *In the middle: New understandings about writing, reading, and learning* (2nd ed.). Portsmouth, NH: Heinemann.

Calkins, L., Ehrenworth, M., & Lehman, C. (2012). *Pathways to the common core: Accelerating achievement.* Portsmouth, NH: Heinemann.

Kittle, P. (2008). *Write beside them: Risk, voice, and clarity in high school writing.* Portsmouth, NH: Heinemann.

Meyer, M. (2011, Dec. 19). The teens are all right: 2011's top 5 YA novels. *NPR books.* Retrieved from http://www.npr.org/2011/12/19/143589123/the-teens-are-all-right-2011s-top-5-ya-novels.

Morgan, D. N. (with Clark, B., Paris, J., & Kozel, C.) (2012). Teaching writers through a unit of study approach. *Voices from the Middle, 19*(3), 32–36.

National Council of Teachers of English. (2008). Writing now: A policy research brief produced by the National Council of Teachers of English. Retrieved from http://www.ncte.org/library/NCTEFiles/Resources/PolicyResearch/WrtgResearchBrief.pdf.

National Governors Association Center for Best Practices & Council of Chief State School Officers. (2010). *Common core state standards initiative.* Washington, D.C.: Author. Retrieved December 23, 2010 from http://www.corestandards.org/the-standards/english-language-arts-standards.

Ray, K. W. (2006). *Study driven: A framework for planning units of study in the writing workshop.* Portsmouth, NH: Heinemann.

Smith, F. (1998). *Joining the literacy club: Further essays into education.* Portsmouth, NH: Heinemann.

Discussion Questions

1. How does the use of list articles relate to adolescents' emotional and cognitive developmental levels?
2. Identify a mentor text that you could use with students to model the writing of a list or a catalog poem. It should be a book that is not listed in the article.

READING 10.3

Using Writing to Support Close Reading

Engagement and Evidence from the Text

Michelle Medlin Hasty and Kate Edwards Schrote

M any teachers use close reading as a technique to enhance students' reading comprehension. In this article, Hasty and Schrodt describe an approach through which close reading can also be used to positively impact students' writing development, as well.

LEARNING OBJECTIVES

1. What do you know about "close reading" and providing evidence from the text?
2. Thinking in terms of "mentor texts," how might close reading support students' writing development?

Using Writing to Support Close Reading

Engagement and Evidence from the Text

Michelle Medlin Hasty and Kate Edwards Schrote

Close reading must raise engagement and joy, not diminish it.

(Lehman & Roberts, 2013, p. 5)

W riting has helped me to become a better reader," Keenan (all students' names are pseudonyms) wrote about his year spent in the Literacy Lab, a reading and writing support program for 12 eighth graders whose literacy skills were below grade level according to standardized tests.

We found that writing in literacy notebooks, alongside reading, increased engagement and improved understanding of texts. At the beginning of the year, Keenan, like most of his Literacy Lab peers, did not consider himself a reader or a writer. As teacher-researchers, we sought to investigate the origin of the students' admitted distaste for school-assigned texts, so we conducted paired interviews and asked students to complete Literate Learner profiles, eight-sectioned graphs we created to help us better understand students' reading and writing habits, interests, goals, and strengths in and out of school. From this data, we learned that most of the students consistently abandoned school-assigned texts. Reasons for not reading included characters not close to students' age, lack of interest in the story, and inability to follow plots that "bounced around."

The Shift from Not Reading to Close Reading

The problem that we faced is one we believe many language arts teachers share: How can we teach students who do not consider themselves readers to stick with

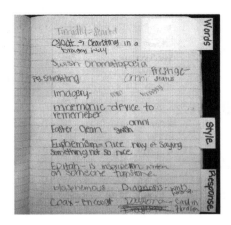

FIGURE 10.3.1   Sample Page from a
Student's Literacy Notebook.

texts, to read and reread, and to read closely? In this article, we show student examples of how literacy notebooks effectively supported close reading by helping students interact with and enjoy texts. We will explain the format of the Literacy Lab, describe the notebooks themselves, and show how using the notebooks helped the students read more closely.

Our literacy program was simply formatted; we read aloud and discussed the text, then wrote responses to the reading. We wanted the students to see reading and writing as reciprocally related: The depth and strength of reading could enhance writing and vice versa. We encouraged students to develop the habit of reading with notebooks open, pen in hand. Keeping a literacy notebook (shown in Figure 10.3.1) as we read helped us:

- Return to texts for second and third readings.
- Attend to the author's word choice, style, and purpose for writing.
- Interpret texts using evidence.
- Find joy in reading through engagement and connection.

The notebook included three sections: Words, Style, and Response. We asked the students to write in their Words section unfamiliar words that needed to be defined as well as words they especially liked and might use later in their own writing. At first we had to remind students to keep their notebooks open as we read, and to record unknown or interesting words, but by midsemester, most of the students were doing so on their own. At the conclusion of each reading portion of our workshop, students could share words they had recorded, and as we looked back at the sentences where the words appeared in the story, we often reread a small section of those passages.

The Style section provided a similar opportunity for close reading. For that section, students made note of phrases, sentences, or passages that stood out to them, skills required by the College and Career Readiness Anchor (CCRA) standards of the Common Core State Standards (CCSS) in Reading (National Governors Association Center for Best Practices & Council of Chief State School Officers, 2010). For example, in *Locomotion,* we explored Jacqueline Woodson's (2004) sensory details, considering how the author's word choice was significant to the meaning (NGA & CCSSO, 2010, R.4), to the text structure (R.5), and to main character Lonnie's point of view (R.6). In his notebook Deshawn recorded, "city so gray you'd think we live inside a big old gray box" (Woodson, 2004, p. 49). The students pointed out in discussion that these were ordinary words that an eleven-year-old boy would probably use, but they painted a picture in the reader's mind of how Lonnie viewed the city in "Just Nothing Poem." Lonnie is miserable in that part of the story, and the colors he describes are dark. Later in the book, as he spends time with his sister and is happier, the sensory details are brighter, reflecting his improved internal weather.

Students noticed this shift, and their habit of recording phrases in their notebooks helped them maintain an awareness of the author's language, style, and text structure that moved from gray to sunny as the narrator made peace with his life and began to enjoy it.

Following the read-alouds, students reacted to the story in the Response section of the notebook. They were free to respond personally, but they were required to cite evidence from the text (NGA & CCSSO, 2010, R.1). "I liked *Locomotion* because I liked how he [Lonnie] talked in the book," Santianna wrote. Jacinta agreed, writing

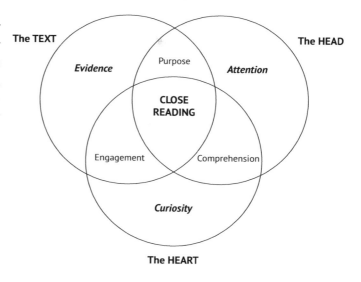

FIGURE 10.3.2   The Close Reading Connections.

"[*Locomotion*] came from a child's point of view." I pressed for specificity: How does Lonnie talk that makes his language seem like a child's? "He doesn't always use good grammar," Jacinta replied, pointing out Lonnie's use of "ain't" and double negatives. Again, students reread the text to find support for their ideas.

Close reading became a habit of the heart reinforced by written response. The literacy notebooks helped students read with curiosity and responsibility. What interesting words should be recorded? What words need definition or clarification? Curiosity and responsibility led to engagement. Engagement occurred because students read closely. They examined the author's word choice, the text structure, and the narrator's point of view. Far from a clinical dissection of the text, close reading coupled with space for personal response helped the students feel connected to the story because they knew the text. Figure 10.3.2 shows the connections between the reader's personal connections and the text evidence through close reading.

Close Reading as Cause and Effect of Engagement

Close reading seems both a cause and effect of engagement, a procedure and an outcome. The group read *No Crystal Stair* (Nelson, 2012), about Harlem bookseller Lewis Michaux. The book contains narrative passages and primary source data such as FBI memos and newspaper articles. Lewis's brother Lightfoot encourages a marriage that he hopes will change his brother's drinking and gambling habits. As we practiced a close reading of a prayer Lewis's fiancée writes just before the wedding, LaRae became interested in the arranged marriage. "If that was me, I would not do that," LaRae declared, and she later wrote about the difficulty of committing to someone "you rarely notice, barely recognize, and (are) not even close to being in love with." LaRae wanted to write about this section, so she knew she had to read closely. For *Locomotion,* it was the author's shift in word choice that engaged students more fully in close reading; for *No Crystal Stair,* it was the characters who emerged in close reading that engaged LaRae.

Our literacy notebooks helped the students become curious readers. A class discussion revealed that the students felt that Woodson created anticipation by hinting at how Lonnie's parents died and what had happened to his sister. "We didn't know a lot about Lonnie's life at first," Santianna wrote, explaining that she enjoyed *Locomotion* because it seemed suspenseful, and she wanted to keep reading. The students remarked that several mysteries surfaced early in the story, and they had to read on to solve them. Those unknowns are similar to the way students described other stories "bouncing around," as Lonnie moves from one setting to another and frequently goes back in time. However, because the students were intentionally recording words and phrases, they were able to follow *Locomotion* more easily. What might have seemed confusing in an earlier reading experience now was suspenseful and captivating.

Developing the habit of reading carefully to discover interesting individual words, phrases, and personal connections required attention and led to better comprehension. Understanding the texts led to emotional investment. The students stuck with the texts and kept reading. Table 10.3.1 provides further evidence of the connections detailed in students' notebooks.

TABLE 10.3.1   Connecting the Head, Heart, and Text: Student Notebook Examples

Book Title	The Head (words to clarify)	The Heart (personal response)	The Text (evidence from the book)
Locomotion (Woodson, 2004)	Vaporize–to disappear; the words "zapped" from Lonnie's head	Why does Lonnie use his writing and his voice?	Lonnie's voice helps him keep his parents' memory alive, like in the poem "Memory" on page 8 and the poem "Fire" on page 86.
No Crystal Stair (Nelson, 2012)	Power–controlling influence Caul–birth defect, means lucky	Lightfoot holds the power in Lewis's family, which is not fair.	Lightfoot was born with a caul over his face. His mother believed "he was destined to some high mission." He led the church, which made him more powerful. Page 20, power = Bible and religion.
Fire from the Rock (Draper, 2007)	Incredulous–not willing to believe	Why is this so unfair? I was so mad and sad! I was shocked! He was trying to save Sylvia, but he did not have a right to blow up Mr. Zucker's store.	It was Reggie who set off the fire-bombs! (page 180)

Conclusion

While our research does not suggest that a literacy notebook is a panacea for the problem of getting students who do not typically engage with or enjoy text to read closely, it does offer one solution. Writing supported close reading by meeting several CCRA standards:

- Reading "closely" and citing "specific textual evidence" (R.1)
- Reading closely with deep comprehension and critical thinking, analyzing the way that "ideas develop and interact" (R.3)
- Interpreting "words and phrases," evaluating "how specific word choices shape meaning" (R.4)
- Examining the "structure of texts" (R.5)
- Determining how "point of view shapes a text" (R.6)
  (NGA & CCSSO, 2010)

The literacy notebooks integrated these essential skills with personal connections as the students wrote in their Response sections. Whether close reading should entail readers' personal connections has been debated recently in the literacy education field (Pearson, 2013; Shanahan, 2012). Beers and Probst (2013) address this issue in their text on close reading, *Notice and Note:*

> Close reading, then, should not imply that we ignore the reader's experience and attend closely to the text and nothing else. It should bring the text and the reader *close* together. To ignore either element in the transaction, to deny the presence of the reader or neglect the contribution of the text, is to make reading impossible. (p. 36)

Beers and Probst contend that close reading and personal connection can and should coexist. Their argument is shaped by Rosenblatt's (1993) *transactional theory*, the idea that readers make meaning of the text by interacting with it, bringing their own ideas, connections, life experience, and knowledge.

The conflict over whether a reader's opinions or personal history should surface in reading is similar to a long-standing argument among those who research and teach written response to text. How much of the student's voice should be heard in written responses to text? Substantial research has shown that writing in response to text increases text comprehension (Graham & Hebert, 2010). Personal response to text yields higher comprehension than purely analytical writing. Often the personal connections allow a student to think critically and independently, whereas sometimes the analyses or interpretations without the personal connection can simply parrot the teacher's ideas or arguments (Marshall, 1987; Mulcahy-Ernt & Ryshkewitch, 1994; Newell, 1996; Wong, B., Kuperis, S., Jamieson, D., Keller, L., & Cull-Hewitt, R., 2002). However, it is easy to understand how personal response in writing can veer so far from the text itself that it becomes, as Stotsky (1995) warned, an exercise in "self-centered" writing (p. 773). In our study, literacy notebooks made it possible for students to connect personally with the texts while simultaneously requiring text evidence.

Our data show that the literacy notebooks effectively balanced personal response with close reading skills. Writing helped students to read curiously, attend to the text, and stick with stories instead of abandoning them in frustration. End-of-study Literate Learner profiles highlighted that students' perceptions of themselves as readers shifted from the beginning of the year. "I am a better reader now that I have been in this program," LaRae wrote, adding, "I understand what I read."

References

Beers, K., & Probst, R. E. (2013). *Notice and note: Strategies for close reading.* Portsmouth, NH: Heinemann.

Graham, S., & Hebert, M. (2010). Writing to read: Evidence for how writing can improve reading. A Report for the Carnegie Corporation. New York, NY: Carnegie Corporation.

Lehman, C., & Roberts, K. (2013). *Falling in love with close reading: Lessons for analyzing texts—and life.* Portsmouth, NH: Heinemann.

Marshall, J. (1987). The effects of writing in students' understanding of literary texts. *Research in the Teaching of English, 21*(1), 30–63.

Mulcahy-Ernt, P., & Ryshkewitch, S. (1994). Expressive journal writing for comprehending literature: A strategy for evoking cognitive complexity. *Reading and Writing Quarterly: Overcoming Learning Difficulties, 10*(4), 325–342.

National Governors Association Center for Best Practices & Council of Chief State School Officers. (2010). Common core state standards for English language arts and literacy in history/social studies, science, and technical subjects. Washington, DC: Author. Retrieved from http://www.corestandards.org/ela-literacy.

Newell, G. E. (1996). Reader-based and teacher-centered instructional tasks: Writing and learning about a short story in middle-track classrooms. *Journal of Literacy Research, 28*(1), 147–172. doi: 10.1080/10862969609547914.

Pearson, P. D. (TextProject). (2013). Research and the common core: Can the romance survive? [Web seminar]. Common Core State Standards Webinar Series. Available from http://textproject.org/events/common-core-state-standards-webinar-series/research-and-the-common-core-can-the-romance-survive/

Rosenblatt, L. M. (1993). The transactional theory: Against dualisms. *College English, 55*(4), 377–386.

Shanahan, T. (2012). The Common Core ate my baby and other urban legends. *Educational Leadership, 70*(4), 10–16.

Stotsky, S. (1995). The uses and limitations of personal or personalized writing in writing theory, research, and instruction. *Reading Research Quarterly, 30*(4), 758–776.

Wong, B., Kuperis, S., Jamieson, D., Keller, L., & Cull-Hewitt, R. (2002). Effects of guided journal writing on students' story understanding. *Journal of Educational Research, 95*(3), 179–191.

Literature Cited

Draper, S. M. (2007). *Fire from the rock.* NY: Speak.

Nelson, V. M. (2012). *No crystal stair.* Minneapolis, MN: Carolrhoda Lab.

Woodson, J. (2004). *Locomotion.* NY: Puffin Books.

Discussion Questions

1. Describe the effect that the use of close reading has on students' engagement with the text.
2. In the article, how were literacy notebooks to enhance students' writing development?

Conclusion

Chapter Activities

Activity 10.1
Read about the 6 + 1 writing traits using the link provided in the Online Resources section of this chapter. Select a children's picture book and examine it for each of the writing traits. Write a brief description of how the author used each trait of excellent writing in the book.

Activity 10.2
Write your own catalog poem following the directions given for the Read-Write-Think lesson found at the link in the Online Resources section of this chapter.

Online Resources

6 + 1 Writing Traits
http://educationnorthwest.org/traits/trait-definitions

Using Mentor Texts
https://iowareadingresearch.org/blog/mentor-texts-student-writing

Put That on the List: Independently Writing a Catalog Poem
http://www.readwritethink.org/classroom-resources/lesson-plans/that-list-independently-writing-895.html

Supporting Students with Literacy Challenges

Chapter Focus Questions

1. What are the roles of reading specialists in middle and secondary schools?
2. How are developmental reading programs different from remedial reading programs?
3. What is the role of the reading specialist in supporting content literacy instruction?

The overall literacy curriculum in middle and secondary schools must address three different facets:

- Developmental reading curriculum
- Content-area literacy instruction
- Literacy interventions for striving readers

Developmental Reading Curriculum

Many states require reading instruction through eighth grade, although it is often called "English Language Arts" (ELA) or a similar title. This instruction is the developmental reading curriculum intended for all students. Students who have not made adequate progress and who are reading below grade level may also receive remedial reading services or other support services, depending upon the school.

The goal of the developmental reading curriculum in the middle school is to support the students as they make the transition from *learning to read*, which was the focus in elementary school, to *reading to learn*, which increasingly becomes more of a focus as students move through the grades. In addition, the developmental reading curriculum supports students' development of higher-order thinking skills needed to read and comprehend increasingly difficult texts—both fiction and nonfiction.

The developmental reading curriculum should:

- support students' continued development of basic reading skills,
- build reading fluency and stamina,
- teach students new strategies for interacting with both fiction and nonfiction text,
- expand students' vocabularies,
- introduce students to new genre,
- encourage development of higher-order thinking skills, especially appreciation and evaluation,
- enhance students' abilities to meaningfully interact with digital media, and
- motivate students to view reading as a lifetime endeavor.

Developmental Reading Instruction in Middle Schools

ELA classes in many middle schools integrate the language arts into one course; there are not separate classes for reading, for writing, and for spelling as there tend to be in elementary schools. This integration allows teachers to take advantage of the interrelationships among the language arts. Instructional approaches that are effective in these classes include close reading, writing workshop, literature circles, book clubs, and SSR.

Content Area Literacy Instruction

As many educators have said repeatedly, "Every teacher is a teacher of reading." The math teacher, science teacher, computer teacher, industrial arts teacher—every teacher in the school must strive to support students' literacy development while teaching the subject matter in their courses. The problem with this is that many of them do not know how to do so, or they do not see literacy instruction as their responsibility.

It is the responsibility of the school's literacy specialists, reading specialists, literacy coaches, or curriculum director to provide guidance and support to the content area teachers so they can incorporate literacy instruction into each course. Through the use of the instructional plan described in Module 9, content teachers can effectively support students' literacy development during text-based lessons.

Professional development opportunities should be provided to content teachers so that they are familiar with the instructional goals and instructional strategies for pre-reading, during reading, and post-reading. In addition, support in identifying appropriate texts—including collateral readings—would help content teachers more effectively teach their own content material as well as supporting students' literacy development.

Literacy Interventions for Striving Readers

The reality of teaching in middle and secondary schools is that many of the students will not be reading on grade level. Teachers in middle and secondary schools can expect that the majority of the students in their classes will be unable to read grade-level texts effectively. The use of collateral readings and instructional strategies focusing on comprehension, vocabulary development, fluency, metacognition, and word recognition are obviously needed.

While almost all elementary schools have reading specialists on staff, only some middle and high schools do, although the number of middle and high school reading specialist positions grows annually. In addition, many middle and secondary schools are also hiring literacy coaches to work directly with content area teachers to improve student achievement in all subject areas.

Most often, only students with the most severe literacy difficulties receive direct additional remedial support in middle and high school settings. In middle school settings, the other students who are below grade level need to have their literacy skill development supported in developmental reading or ELA classes and through content literacy skills embedded in subject area courses. In secondary school settings, most students who read below grade level receive no additional support and must rely on content area teachers to teach content-specific literacy skills.

Reading specialists or coaches working in middle and secondary schools should strive for a comprehensive literacy curriculum to support the reading and writing development of all students. Many middle and secondary schools have established *literacy teams*—groups of faculty, parents, and administrators who are charged with organizing and evaluating the literacy curriculum in the school, planning professional development opportunities related to literacy, and using literacy-related assessment data to identify needs and to document progress. Often, a reading specialist or literacy coach is responsible for leading the literacy team.

Key Areas of Effective Adolescent Literacy Programs

Nancy E. Marchand-Martella, Ronald C. Martella, and Sheri L. Modderman

In this article, Marchand-Martella et al. present some eye-opening statistics regarding the literacy achievement of adolescents. They also describe critical instructional practices that are needed to improve this situation.

LEARNING OBJECTIVES

1. About what percentage of eight- and twelfth-grade students do you think read below grade level?
2. Based on your own experiences as either a student or a teacher in middle or secondary schools, list some issues that might keep adolescent students from reaching their full potential in literacy.

Key Areas of Effective Adolescent Literacy Programs

Nancy E. Marchand-Martella, Ronald C. Martella, and Sheri L. Modderman

At no other time in our history has the ability to read been so important to all members of society (Coyne, Kame'enui, & Carnine, 2011, p. 50). In fact, learning to read is the most important skill our students can learn in school, serving as the very foundation of all other academic subjects. Consider the following statistics noted by Brozo (2009)—about two-thirds of eighth and twelfth graders read below grade level; 32% of high school graduates are not prepared for college-level English composition courses; 40% of high school graduates do not have the literacy skills required by employers; and 1.2 million students drop out of high school every year with literacy skills lower than those in most industrialized nations. Ensuring adolescents become literate, productive members of society is an undertaking that may not only increase the number of students who graduate from high school, succeed in college, and work in jobs that support a healthy lifestyle, but may also save the nation billions of dollars.

According to Graham and Hebert (2010), $16 billion a year is spent by universities and businesses due to students' inadequate reading and writing skills. "Somewhere between one half to two thirds of new jobs in the future will require a college education and higher-level literacy skills" (Graham & Hebert, 2010, p. 7). With regard to the workplace, 40% of high school graduates lack the required literacy skills employers desire (National Governors Association for Best Practices [NGA], 2005). For students to be prepared for twenty-first century higher education and employment opportunities, literacy skills need to be explicitly taught throughout the adolescent years (NGA, 2005).

While some of the problems may stem from a lack of quality literacy instruction in the elementary grades, it is more likely that a lack of instruction to read complex text throughout the upper grades and beyond is the culprit (Greenleaf & Hinchman, 2009). The purpose of this paper is to discuss the research base of best practices for teaching adolescents the advanced literacy skills they need to succeed in high school, college, and the workplace (see Common Core State Standards for important information on college and career readiness literacy skills for students in grades K–5 and 6–12 at http://www. corestandards.org). Recommendations are made based on a review of this research base. This paper should not be considered a meta-analysis or research synthesis of all studies encompassing adolescent literacy.

The Importance of Academic Literacy

Academic literacy is the kind of reading proficiency needed to draw meaning from advanced narrative text and content-area text (Kamil et al., 2008; Kosanovich, Reed, & Miller, 2010; Torgesen et al., 2007). Academic literacy also requires reading proficiencies such as being able to make inferences from text, learning vocabulary from context, making intertextual links, and summarizing the main ideas within a text (Torgesen et al., 2007). Two results should occur from improvements in academic literacy (Torgesen et al., 2007). First, students should be able to respond to more complex questions, thereby demonstrating their deeper understanding of the material. Second, students should be able to master more information from content-area classes.

Similarly, Lee and Spratley (2010) used the term "disciplinary literacy" to describe the idea that adolescent readers typically require more specialized and complex literacy support and instruction in content areas. Beyond the elementary grades, students are expected not only to read and decode effectively but also to read for understanding. Snow and Moje (2010) described the widespread and misguided assumption that we should finish reading instruction by the end of third grade. They used the term "inoculation fallacy" to illustrate the notion that an early vaccination of reading instruction, especially in grades K–3, does not protect permanently against reading failure. Educators must continue to provide reading instruction beyond third grade. In sum, academic literacy goes beyond being able to read—a successful reader should be able to navigate advanced narrative and content-area text with ease and understanding.

Narrative Text

Narrative text describes events that occur through time that are "related through a causal or thematic chain" (Brewer, 1980, p. 223). In general, narrative text involves reading presented as nonfiction (e.g., biographies and memoirs) or fiction (e.g., novels and fables) that tells the reader *who did what to whom and why* (Dymock, 2007; Harris & Hodges, 1995). Research indicates that lower knowledge readers may benefit more from content delivered through narrative text that facilitates interest and builds better background knowledge (Wolfe & Mienko, 2007).

Adolescent students might struggle to read narrative text for a myriad of reasons. Narrative text encompasses a wide breadth of genres, in both fiction and nonfiction domains. As students progress through grade levels, the narrative text they are exposed to becomes increasingly complex (Dymock, 2007). Moreover, a lack of knowledge about narrative text structure, a skill generally acquired before or during early elementary education (Stein & Glenn, 1979), can broadly interfere with student comprehension across academic areas (National Institute for Child Health and Human Development [NICHD], 2000). Similarly, there may be fewer opportunities for struggling students to read narrative types of text at more advanced grade levels, and what narrative text they are exposed to will generally be comprised of content at a consistently advanced level. Finally, while lower knowledge readers may benefit more from content delivered via narrative text (Wolfe & Mienko, 2007), the majority of academic text for adolescent readers is expository in nature (Sáenz & Fuchs, 2002).

Content-Area/Expository Text

To be academically literate, the ability to read content-area text is an essential requirement. Content area is specific to certain subjects in a school setting. In general, most students can read and decode simple text but struggle with more complicated materials that are often present in middle and high school settings, namely science and social studies textbooks (Heller & Greenleaf, 2007). Therefore, literacy and learning within the content areas has become a critical feature of success for adolescent readers (Kosanovich et al., 2010). Research supports the notion that reading instruction should not end in the elementary grades but should continue throughout school. Adolescent readers need to develop more complex skills in order to learn from the increasingly specialized and complicated texts they will encounter in middle and high school (Fang & Schleppegrell, 2010).

Reading content-area text is difficult for several reasons. First, students typically have fewer experiences with expository text (Lenski, Wham, Johns, & Caskey, 2007). Second, the reading material in content-area text is often denser than the material in narrative text (Coyne et al., 2011). The organization is typically harder to follow (Abadiano & Turner, 2002; Sáenz & Fuchs, 2002), and the vocabulary is increasingly technical (Abadiano & Turner, 2002; Ediger, 2002; Fang, 2006; Sáenz & Fuchs, 2002). Third, reading the cumbersome multipart words found in and associated with science and social studies textbooks can be a significant stumbling block (Fang, 2006). Finally, the content in textbooks is based on the assumption that the readers have some previous knowledge of the topic at hand (Sáenz & Fuchs, 2002). In fact, Lee and Spratley (2010) stated that being able to comprehend written text is not a fixed ability but instead involves an interactive relationship between the text and prior knowledge and skills of the reader.

Adolescent Literacy

Adolescent literacy is focused reading instruction for students in grades 4 through 12. In a survey of reading experts conducted by the International Reading Association, adolescent literacy is considered a "very hot" topic. In fact, this topic "first appeared on the survey in 2001 and in 2006 attained 'very hot' status and has remained so ever since" (Cassidy, Ortlieb, & Schettel, 2010/2011, p. 1). Results of this survey illustrate a change in how "instructional business" is conducted in the primary grades (K–3). Instruction has been centered on teaching the basics of reading—*learning to read*. Reading instruction for older students has now shifted from the foundational focus of *learning to read* in grades K–3 to *reading to learn* for students in grades 4 and above. In 1997, Congress asked the NICHD to coordinate a panel to examine the research base and the efficacy of various instructional practices related to early reading (grades K–3). As a result, the National Reading Panel [NRP] was formed. In 2000, the NRP published the *Report of the National Reading Panel* and narrowed reading instruction to alphabetics, fluency, comprehension, teacher education and reading instruction, and technology and reading instruction. Armbruster, Lehr, and Osborn (2006) interpreted the NRP findings and made specific instructional recommendations for the classroom. Research-based practices for students in grades K–3 include phonemic awareness, phonics, fluency, vocabulary, and text comprehension (Armbruster et al., 2006).

Following on the heels of focused elementary-based reading instruction, Biancarosa and Snow (2006) developed guidelines for effective adolescent literacy instruction. *Reading Next* specifically addressed 15 components that best describe instructional practices for adolescent readers (Biancarosa & Snow, 2006). The components encompass instructional and infrastructure improvements necessary for effective literacy programs. The 15 elements include: (a) explicit comprehension instruction, (b) effective principles embedded in content, (c) motivation and self directed learning, (d) text-based collaborative learning, (e) strategic tutoring, (f) diverse texts, (g) intensive writing, (h) technology, (i) ongoing formative assessment, (j) extended time for literacy, (k) professional development, (l) ongoing summative assessments of students and programs, (m) teacher teams, (n) leadership, and (o) a comprehensive and coordinated literacy program. Research reviews and meta-analyses on adolescent literacy instruction followed (see Boardman et al., 2008; Kamil et al., 2008; Roberts, Torgesen, Boardman, & Scammacca, 2008; Scammacca et al., 2007; and Torgesen et al., 2007 for details). Funding on adolescent literacy initiatives became evident. For example, the Striving Readers program was developed. The Striving Readers program is funded and endorsed by the U.S. Department of Education and focuses comprehensive literacy support for students from birth to grade 12.

Achievement in Adolescent Literacy

The challenges of adolescent literacy are vast. The 2009 report of the *Nation's Report Card* (National Center for Education Statistics [NCES], 2009) showed that while scores exhibited a slight increase from 2007, there were still a disproportionate number of fourth- and eighth-grade students reading below grade level. The National Assessment of Educational Progress uses the term *basic* and *proficient* to describe levels of reading achievement. The *basic* level indicates only partial mastery of knowledge that is required for that grade level. The *proficient* level shows competence over grade-level material. For fourth grade, only 33% were at or above the proficient level, with 67% scoring at the basic level or below. The results for eighth grade showed only 32% at or above the proficient level, with 68% scoring at the basic level or below. Finally, in the twelfth grade, 38% scored at or above the proficient level, with 62% scoring at the basic level or below (National Center for Education Statistics [NCES], 2010). These numbers are staggering considering that the *basic* level denotes only partial mastery of prerequisite knowledge that is essential to performing at grade level. Students should be performing at proficient levels to handle the kinds of text they will encounter in the upper grades.

Further, about 8 million adolescent students experience difficulty reading at their appropriate grade level (ACT, 2006; Biancarosa & Snow, 2006). In fact, "some 70 percent of older readers require some form of remediation. Very few of these older struggling readers need help to read the words on a page; their most common problem is that they are not able to comprehend what they read" (Biancarosa & Snow, 2006, p. 3). Too often, reading instruction in middle and high schools is lacking and the curriculum is ill equipped to prepare students to comprehend the material (Greenleaf & Hinchman, 2009).

The Need for Explicit Instruction

When academic literacy skills are taught, explicit instruction should be provided. Explicit instruction involves direct teaching including teacher modeling, guided student practice with feedback, and independent student practice (Hock, Deshler, & Schumaker, 2000; Marchand-Martella & Martella, 2013; National Institute for Literacy [NIFL], 2007). Biancarosa and Snow (2006) and Kosanovich et al. (2010) list explicit instruction as the chief way to promote student learning. This systematic instructional process provides a framework for the gradual transfer of responsibility for student learning from the teacher to the student as the student becomes increasingly successful (Marchand-Martella & Martella, 2013). Each step of comprehension (i.e. strategies, monitoring and metacognition, teacher modeling, scaffolding, and apprenticeship) requires the use of explicit instruction by teachers in order to be successfully implemented by readers (Biancarosa & Snow, 2006). The key to explicit instruction is ongoing interaction and communication between the students and the teacher (Rupley, Blair, & Nichols, 2009). Only then can students learn to comprehend, understand, and interact with written text (Rupley et al., 2009).

Research almost universally supports explicit instructional practices (Archer & Hughes, 2011; Kirschner, Sweller, & Clark, 2006; Klahr & Nigam, 2004; Marchand-Martella, Slocum, & Martella, 2004). Explicit instructional approaches are considered more effective and efficient as compared to discovery-based approaches (Alfieri, Brooks, Aldrich, & Tenenbaum, 2010; Ryder, Tunmer, & Greaney, 2008), particularly when students are naïve or struggling learners.

Vaughn and Linan-Thompson (2003) answered the question, "So what is special about special education for students with LD?" Their answer, again based on a thorough review of the research literature, noted "students with LD benefit from explicit and systematic instruction that is closely related to their area of instructional need" (p. 145). Burns and Ysseldyke (2009) examined the frequency with which evidence-based practices were used with students with disabilities. They found explicit instruction was the most frequently used instructional methodology in their survey of special education teachers and school psychologists. No matter what research synthesis was reviewed, "the conclusions were clear: Explicit instruction should be a consistent mainstay of working with students both with and without learning difficulties" (Archer & Hughes, 2011, p. 17).

Five Areas of Effective Adolescent Literacy Programs

Based on the research reviews and meta-analyses on adolescent literacy instruction, recommendations can be organized into five general areas: word study, fluency, vocabulary, comprehension, and motivation (Boardman et al., 2008; Kamil et al., 2008; Roberts et al., 2008; Scammacca et al., 2007; Torgesen et al., 2007). Figure 11.1.1 illustrates these areas. Each of these areas is crucial to the reading improvement of older readers. Conspicuously absent from this list are phonemic awareness and phonics. If older students lack skills in phonemic awareness and phonics, these skills should be taught in an explicit and systematic fashion (see Armbruster et al., 2006 and Boardman et al., 2008 for a discussion on the importance of teaching these foundational skills).

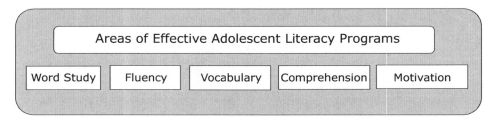

FIGURE 11.1.1   Five Areas of Effective Adolescent Literacy Programs.

Word Study

Instruction that focuses on reading at the word level is referred to as word study (Boardman et al., 2008). Deficits in word study negatively impact students' comprehension, vocabulary, and fluency (NIFL, 2007). Word study can benefit readers of any age and is best used when accompanied by materials appropriate to the age level of the student. It relies on word analysis and word recognition strategies in addition to identifying words that are irregular and unpredictable. By identifying words based on component elements that share certain commonalities such as the prefixes *un-*, *non-*, and *dis-*, students can learn groups of words and skills that no longer necessitate the memorization of individual words and meanings (Hennings, 2000). Instructional practices include teaching students how to use strategies to aid in reading words by breaking them into parts and identifying syllable types. Boardman et al. (2008) recommend teaching students: (a) to identify and break works into syllable types, (b) to read multisyllabic words, (c) to identify irregular words that do not follow typical patterns, (d) the meanings of word roots, bases, endings, prefixes and suffixes; and (e) when and how to use what they know about the structure of words to decode unknown words. Word study can be useful when content-area words are integrated and studied in a language arts classroom (Invernizzi, Abouzeid, & Bloodgood, 1997).

Decoding multipart or multisyllabic words is critical to success in reading content-area and narrative text in middle and high school. Many adolescent readers have basic decoding skills and can read simple texts; however, there is a significant population that struggles with decoding the more complex vocabulary (Boardman et al., 2008). Multisyllabic words are almost entirely responsible for understanding the meaning of most content-area text (Archer, Gleason, & Vachon, 2003). As previously noted, Boardman et al. (2008) suggested explicit teaching in breaking down words into their parts, blending the sounds in multisyllabic words, recognizing irregular words, suffixes, prefixes, endings and roots, and finally, teaching students how and when to use the above structural analysis skills when trying to decode unfamiliar words. Diliberto, Beattie, Flowers, and Algozzine (2009) suggested that since many struggling readers do not have the letter-sound correspondence mastered, explicitly teaching syllable chunking is an appropriate tool for struggling readers to use to decode multipart words.

Fluency

Fluency is the ability to read words "accurately, quickly, and with proper expression" (Malmgren & Trezek, 2009, p. 3). When students read fluently, they can devote their efforts toward understanding what is being read and spend less time decoding (Boardman et al., 2008). Fluency is a critical component of reading because it provides the connection between simply reading the words and actually understanding their meaning (Malmgren & Trezek, 2009). To improve fluency, Boardman et al. (2008) suggested (a) tracking students' progress in fluency and providing feedback on a frequent basis, (b) providing models of fluent reading and giving appropriate feedback, (c) allowing students to be proactive learners by letting them self-monitor their fluency, (d) using teacher-selected passages that include vocabulary that has been studied and previously taught or passages that can be read independently, (e) gradually increasing the difficulty of the passages as students demonstrate improved performance, and (f) using repeated oral reading with feedback.

The best method of improving reading fluency is through repeated oral reading (Hasbrouck, 2006; Hasbrouck & Tindal, 2006; Therrien, 2004). Fluency is a crucial element in adolescent literacy because if readers can devote less time and effort to decoding the words they are reading, they can spend more time understanding the words. Repeated reading typically requires students to read a particular passage several times until a desired goal is met (e.g., 100 correct words per minute [cwpm]) or for a certain length of time (e.g., 10 min). When using repeated oral reading, Boardman et al. (2008) recommended using passages with previously taught vocabulary that are at the students' reading level. In effect, repeated readings lead to increased vocabulary recognition with sight words and general vocabulary words, provide more practice opportunities for struggling readers, and are useful for fluency timings to monitor students' reading progress.

Vocabulary

Boardman et al. (2008) defined vocabulary development as knowing the meaning of words. When students understand the words they read and have strategies to figure out unknown words, they can make greater gains in understanding the meaning of what is being read. Many struggling students enter the classroom with grossly limited vocabularies compared to other classmates; without intervention these students are in danger of falling even further behind in the content areas (Rupley & Slough, 2010). However, when given the support and strategy-based vocabulary instruction, students are able to take previously unknown words and determine ways to glean the definition from the surrounding context or from other sources (Armbruster et al., 2006). Vocabulary knowledge is complex and multidimensional because it requires several layers of information including definitions, inter-word relationships, and differing connotations based on context (Lesaux, Kieffer, Faller, & Kelley, 2010). Students who struggle with reading often lack the "word consciousness" necessary to succeed and move forward (Boardman et al., 2008).

Specific-word and word-learning strategies are necessary for increasing students' vocabulary. Specific-word instruction teaches individual words to students. Words are divided into three different tiers (Beck, McKeown, & Kucan, 2002). Tier 1 words are words students are likely to already know (e.g., baby, happy). Tier 2 words are words that appear often in text and are more complex though not uncommon (e.g., coincidence, absurd). Tier 3 words are words that are specific to different content areas (e.g., spelunker, hydrogenous). Beck et al. (2002) suggest teachers focus vocabulary instruction on Tier 2 words while also explicitly teaching Tier 3 words to relevant content areas. McEwan (2007) offered several guidelines to teach vocabulary to mastery. First, teachers should post the vocabulary in the classroom to serve as a visual aid for those who may have trouble with the pronunciations. Second, teachers should provide student-friendly definitions of the words and suggest synonyms and antonyms of the words. Third, teachers should put the words into context and make connections to familiar aspects of students' lives. Fourth, teachers can use word games and concept maps to help students gain familiarity with the words and a conceptual framework to build around each word. Finally, teachers should ask questions and incorporate new vocabulary into everyday language.

Word-learning strategies, such as context clues and the use of references aids, are ways of accessing word meaning in an independent manner. Because teachers cannot teach students every word they need to know, it is vitally important students use strategies to learn the words themselves (Armbruster et al., 2006). Context clues involve defining unknown words using the surrounding words or sentences to derive their meaning (Carnine, Silbert, Kame'enui, & Tarver, 2010; Edwards, Font, Baumann, & Boland, 2004). Through careful and explicit teaching, a context clue strategy can be learned and vocabulary increased. Reference aids are helpful tools students use to determine word meaning (e.g., glossary, dictionary, or online dictionary) (Armbruster et al., 2006; Vaughn & Bos, 2009).

Comprehension

Comprehension is a skill that allows readers to understand and remember content that has been read. Previously mentioned areas of literacy—word study, fluency, and vocabulary—all serve as catalysts to remembering and understanding content on the written page (Boardman et al., 2008). Comprehension is "a complex cognitive endeavor and is affected by, at least, the reader, the text, and the context" (McKeown, Beck, & Blake, 2009, p. 218). At the secondary level, reading comprehension is arguably the most important component of reading instruction (Boardman et al., 2008). Readers who are successful at comprehending what they have read employ a variety of strategies before, during, and after they read. Therefore, more in-depth coverage of these comprehension strategies will be provided in this paper.

Activate Prior Knowledge

A key strategy for enabling readers to make connections with text is activating prior knowledge of the subject matter. Boardman et al. (2008) reported using strategies including previewing headings and concepts or making predictions and charting the results to increase students' interest. Students are encouraged to use their interest to make valuable connections with the text. To comprehend texts at deeper levels, students need to make inter-textual links connecting ideas from one text to another. Lenski (1998) surmised that when teachers plan and strategically compile texts with related issues or topics, they are giving the students the tools to make the necessary connections. Similarly, Lee and Spratley (2010) noted possessing prior knowledge of topics can influence what students comprehend, what attracts students' interest, and even what influences their opinions and perspectives.

Making connections through an activation of prior knowledge helps to foster motivation and reading engagement (Lenski et al., 2007; Tovani, 2000). Moreover, students who make connections during reading can better understand the relationship between the concepts being presented (Lenski et al., 2007). Many teachers provide students with structured text-connection activities to encourage better understanding of the material.

Monitor Comprehension

Another important comprehension skill that should be taught to adolescent learners is comprehension monitoring. By monitoring their own comprehension, students are able to oversee their understanding while they read, implementing corrective strategies when necessary (Boardman et al., 2008). Boardman et al. recommended teaching strategies that enable students to identify confusing or hard words and how to fix their misunderstandings when reading text. Slowing down when reading and rereading difficult texts are two more ways students can monitor their comprehension and improve their understanding (Robb, 1995; Schoenbach, Greenleaf, Cziko, & Hurwitz, 1999). For readers to become successful, employing these strategies and being aware of when to use them are essential skills.

Ask and Generate Questions

An effective tool for activating student engagement with text is asking questions before, during, and after reading (Boardman et al., 2008). When teachers develop comprehension questions and activities, Bloom's Taxonomy should be considered (Anderson et al., 2001). The Taxonomy of Education Objectives was originated by Benjamin S. Bloom in 1956 and is commonly called Bloom's Taxonomy (Krathwohl, 2002). Originally, Bloom's Taxonomy had its purpose in creating a common language with regard to goals in education and also lends itself to the decision-making process related to curriculum. Recently, Bloom's Taxonomy was revised and is divided into six categories of cognitive processes: remembering, understanding, applying, analyzing, evaluating, and creating. Bloom's Taxonomy is important because it can be helpful in creating questions that support or encourage higher order thinking in students.

Question generation requires students to develop and ask their own questions based on what they are reading (Hashey & Connors, 2003; Rosenshine, Meister, & Chapman, 1996; Vaughn

& Bos, 2009). When students generate questions, they are typically more motivated to read the text, clarify information they do not know, and exhibit inferential thinking (Tovani, 2000). Evidence also suggests that writing questions and answers makes the information easier to remember and provides more opportunity to interact with the content of the text (Graham & Hebert, 2010). Readers who struggle often fail to understand that deriving meaning from text requires active probing for meaning (Duffy, 2003).

Graphic Organizers

Graphic organizers are visual aids that help students remember, organize, and identify key information from their reading. Some examples of graphic organizers include Venn diagrams, concept maps, and story maps. Boardman et al. (2008) give several suggestions for the use of graphic organizers in the classroom. They can be used before reading to introduce information and to make predictions. During reading, they can be used to evoke discussions and to represent connections as well as to record information. After reading, they are useful for writing summaries and reviewing information. A research review (Vaughn & Edmonds, 2006) examined the effectiveness of graphic organizers for students with disabilities and noted improved reading comprehension.

Mnemonic Strategies

Mnemonic strategies are helpful comprehension strategies to teach to students; they are systematic procedures for enhancing memory and devices that aid students in remembering and retrieving important information (Lenski et al., 2007; Mastropieri & Scruggs, 1996). These strategies can help students take control of their learning (Glynn, Koballa, & Coleman, 2003). They can be useful scaffolding aids in content-area classrooms and serve to organize information into a systematic framework that is easy to remember (Glynn et al., 2003). The key to mnemonic strategies is to relate new information to what students have previously learned (Mastropieri & Scruggs, 1998). Mnemonic strategies have been found to be effective in bolstering students' story recall (Saczynski, Rebok, Whitfield, & Plude, 2007), vocabulary (Bryant, Goodwin, Bryant, & Higgins, 2003), and comprehension (Uberti, Scruggs, & Mastropieri, 2003).

For example, SQ3R is a questioning and mnemonic strategy that assists students in acquiring information from content-area text. SQ3R stands for Survey, Question, Read, Reflect, and Review, although other Rs are noted (e.g., Recite). The SQ3R strategy is one of the most prominent techniques for gleaning information from text (Vaughn & Bos, 2009). When students survey text, they should scan text features, looking at such parts as the beginning, the main part, and the end of a chapter, examining titles and subheads, sidebars, and visuals with captions. These features are components of a textbook that are added to enhance interest or understanding (Fisher, Frey, & Lapp, 2008).

Hedin and Conderman (2010) suggested using text features in rereading could be a useful tool. They argued that because the text is organized in a predictable way, using the text features can aid striving readers to reread paragraphs with greater understanding and, ultimately, greater meaning.

After scanning for text features, students should develop questions from the titles, subheads, or bold and highlighted words and read to answer these questions. Note taking helps students learn important information. When taking notes, students generally comprehend better because they are actively attending to the information. Writing about a text theoretically should enhance comprehension because it "provides students a tool" for recording, connecting, analyzing, and personalizing key ideas (Graham & Hebert, 2010, p. 13). Additionally, Graham and Hebert (2010) asserted that when students write about the material they read, their reading skills are enhanced. Also, when students are reviewing their notes, they are more likely to remember the material because they can spend more time with it (Robinson et al., 2006). Research suggests teaching strategic note taking is effective for aiding students with disabilities to recall and learn a greater amount of information (Boyle & Weishaar, 2001). Students then use these notes as study guides (Ogle, 1996; Santa, Havens, & Harrison, 1996). After students take notes, they should reflect on their written notes, making important text-to-text, text-to-self, and text-to-world connections (Tovani, 2000). Finally, students should review their written notes. This review serves as an important study strategy (Lenski et al., 2007).

Text Structure

An emphasis should be placed on text structure. Text structure refers to the way in which the text is organized (Montelongo, Berber-Jiménez, Hernández, & Hosking, 2006; National Education Association [NEA], 2006). Noting the text structures used by authors is one way for readers to organize information (Fisher et al., 2008). Expository text structure is usually organized in the following ways: (a) compare and contrast, (b) problem and solution, (c) cause and effect, (d) order or sequence, and (e) description/list. Recognizing text structure causes students to interact with the text to identify how the text structure and concepts are related (Montelongo et al., 2006; NEA, 2006). Authors use this text organization to communicate information to the reader. Additionally, Montelongo et al. (2006) found that identifying text structure helps students organize the most important information in science and social studies textbooks as well as identify the main ideas and help with recalling vital facts from the text.

Story grammar or story structure is "an attempt to construct a set of rules that can generate a structure for any story" (Rayner & Pollatsek, 1989, p. 307). In narrative text, the structural organization of the content contains common story elements—characters, settings, events, conflict, climax, and resolution (Duffy, 2003; Lapp, Flood, Brock, & Fisher, 2007). Faggella-Luby, Schumaker, and Deshler (2007) suggested narrative text structure analysis be introduced in a routine that includes three steps. First, students use self-questioning during pre reading. Next, students analyze the story structure during reading. Finally, after the reading, students summarize what they read.

Summarization

Summarization should be a key focus of instruction. In summarizing, students must identify, extract, and combine the most important information in the text (Schoenbach et al., 1999). Explicit instruction that teaches students how to summarize information is an important step in increasing students' comprehension. Graham and Hebert (2010) found that writing summaries about what was being read showed marked improvements in reading comprehension. They also stated that writing summaries about text is better than simply reading and rereading it. Teachers should provide examples and non-examples of quality summaries following instruction of how to write summaries of information. Summarization is a key strategy in getting students to remember and understand material they have read. Teaching students to summarize text ensures comprehension, given that students need to recall essential details encountered while reading (Carnine et al., 2010).

Reciprocal Teaching

Reciprocal teaching is a cooperative learning, scaffolded instructional procedure developed by Palincsar and Brown (1984) to bolster reading comprehension. Ideally, it is used with students at any grade level who score 35% or below on standardized reading assessments (Biancarosa & Snow, 2006). Reciprocal teaching consists of four strategies: questioning, clarifying, predicting, and summarizing. Questioning is the process of asking (silently, orally, or written) questions regarding recently read or reviewed text. Clarifying requires that the students clear up any questions about vocabulary or content in the text. When students guess what might happen next in the text, they are employing the predicting strategy. Finally, the summarizing strategy is a skill in which students take what they have read and condense the information identifying the gist of the content. The teacher models each skill then asks the students to implement the strategies in small groups. The students each take turns being the "teacher" and progressively work through each strategy with multiple texts (Biancarosa & Snow, 2006).

Metacognition

Metacognition is the process of thinking about one's own thinking. (Klingner, Vaughn, Dimino, Schumm, & Bryant, 2001). When students demonstrate metacognitive skills, they have the ability to discriminate between skills and strategies that are appropriate to use and under what conditions to use them. Ultimately, students need to think about what comprehension strategies they are using and if those strategies are necessary and useful. Biancarosa and Snow (2006) named metacognition instruction as an effective approach toward improving comprehension by saying that it is necessary to teach students to learn how they understand while they are reading. Successful learning in content-areas requires students be aware of how they understand a concept and how to "adjust their thinking to ensure learning" (Wilson, Grisham, & Smetana, 2009, p. 709). Wilson et al. (2009) also asserted that content learning and metacognition are executed by interactions with the text and through other experiences with the content.

Motivation

Struggling readers frequently lack the motivation to read (Boardman et al., 2008). Reading comprehension can be hindered by a lack of motivation and can limit the development of strategies that could make students more successful readers. An absence of motivation can have a spiraling and cyclical effect on struggling students. Students have difficulty reading and understanding advanced text and, as a result, lack the motivation to read (Boardman et al., 2008). Biancarosa and Snow (2006) listed motivation as one of the 15 critical elements of adolescent literacy. Based on a summary of research, Boardman et al. (2008) outlined four features that can bolster students' motivation to read. These include: (a) providing content goals for reading, (b) allowing and supporting student autonomy, (c) using text interesting to the student, and (d) increasing social interactions related to reading.

The main difference between motivation as compared to the other elements of reading instruction is that motivation is not taught explicitly; teachers promote motivation based on what and how they teach and the interactions they promote with text (see Boardman et al., 2008, Kamil et al., 2008, and Torgesen et al., 2007 for details). Therefore, motivation should not be seen as a stand-alone component of effective reading instruction but as an integrated part of an effective adolescent literacy program. Brozo and Flynt (2008) described six evidence-based principles for increasing motivation specifically in content-area classrooms. These include (a) elevating self-efficacy, (b) creating interest in new learning, (c) making an inside/outside literacy connection, (d) expanding choices and options, (e) offering an abundance of interesting texts, and (f) offering structured collaboration. With implementation of these six principles teachers can begin to create an engaging and motivating environment of learning for their students in content rich classes such as science and social studies.

Collaborative learning is a motivational method that allows students work in small groups to work out a problem or discuss a topic. All cooperative learning methods operate on the notion that students work together to learn the content and all are responsible for each other's learning (Slavin, 1996). The research supports the usefulness of collaborative learning at all grade levels because of increased student achievement as well as improved relationships and increased self-esteem (Slavin, 1996). The number of opportunities struggling students have to respond to text is increased when the students can collaborate with their peers. Similarly, when struggling students are grouped with successful classmates, their chance of success is greater (Boardman et al., 2008). Another important step in collaboration is the explicit teaching of how collaborative groups work—this is critical to the success of collaborative groups (Boardman et al., 2008). The *Reading Next* report (Biancarosa & Snow, 2006) lists text-based collaboration as one of the 15 essential elements of adolescent literacy instruction. Collaborative groups can be used across academic settings and across skill ranges. Collaborative groups can also be used to increase motivation thereby increasing understanding (Boardman et al., 2008).

Conclusion

A review of the research concerning content-area and narrative text reveals some critical instructional components of adolescent literacy achievement. Explicit instruction is key in teaching important skills and strategies in word study, vocabulary, comprehension, and fluency. Additionally, motivation must be an integral part of an effective adolescent literacy program. Educators have an enormous responsibility to create learning environments that are tailored to each student's needs and interests. It is required that the skills and strategies paramount to the enhancement of students' learning are applicable to authentic classroom scenarios where students will encounter challenging and unfamiliar content-area and narrative texts. Research has given educators the tools they need to bolster their instructional practices and they need only to review such documents to greatly increase students' academic achievement. If educators responsibly and reliably follow the 15 essential elements of effective literacy programs (Biancarosa & Snow, 2006) as well as focus their attention on the five areas of effective adolescent literacy instruction (Boardman et al., 2008), student achievement is likely to rise.

References

Abadiano, H., & Turner, J. (2002). Reading expository text: The challenges of students with learning disabilities. *New England Reading Association Journal, 38,* 49–55.

ACT, Inc. (2006). *Reading between the lines: What the ACT reveals about college readiness in reading.* Iowa City, IA: Author.

Alfieri, L., Brooks, P. J., Aldrich, N. J., & Tenenbaum, H. R. (2010). Does discovery-based instruction enhance learning? *Journal of Educational Psychology, 103,* 1–18.

Anderson, L., Krathwohl, D., Airasian, P. W., Cruikshank, K. A., Mayer, R. E., Pintrich, P. R., ... Wittrock, M. (2001). *A taxonomy for learning, teaching, and assessing: A revision of Bloom's taxonomy of educational objectives.* New York, NY: Longman.

Archer, A, L., Gleason, M. M., & Vachon, V. L. (2003). Decoding and fluency: Foundation skills for struggling older readers. *Learning Disability Quarterly, 26,* 89–101.

Archer, A. L., & Hughes, C. A. (2011). *Explicit instruction: Effective and efficient teaching.* New York, NY: The Guilford Press.

Armbruster, B. B., Lehr, F., & Osborn, J. (2006). *Put reading first: The research building blocks for teaching children to read* (3rd ed.). Jessup, MD: Center for the Improvement of Early Reading Achievement.

Beck, I. L., McKeown, M. G., & Kucan, L. (2002). *Bringing words to life: Robust vocabulary instruction.* New York, NY: Guilford.

Biancarosa, C., & Snow, C. E. (2006). *Reading next: A vision for action and research in middle and high school literacy. A report to Carnegie Corporation of New York* (2nd ed.). Washington, DC: Alliance for Excellent Education.

Boardman, A. G., Roberts, G., Vaughn, S., Wexler, J., Murray, C. S., & Kosanovich, M. (2008). *Effective instruction for adolescent struggling readers: A practice brief.* Portsmouth, NH: RMC Research Corporation, Center on Instruction.

Boyle, J. R., & Weishaar, M. (2001). The effects of strategic notetaking on the recall and comprehension of lecture information for high school students with learning disabilities. *Learning Disabilities Research and Practice, 16,* 133–141.

Brewer, W. F. (1980). Literary theory, rhetoric, and stylistics: Implications for psychology. In R. J. Shapiro, B. C. Bruce, & W. F. Brewer (Eds.), *Theoretical issues in reading comprehension* (pp. 221–239). Hillsdale, NJ: Erlbaum.

Brozo, W. G. (2009). Response to intervention or responsive instruction? Challenges and possibilities of response to intervention for adolescent literacy. *Journal of Adolescent Literacy, 53,* 277–281.

Brozo, W. G., & Flynt, E. S. (2008). Motivating students to read in the content classroom: Six evidence-based principles. *The Reading Teacher, 62,* 172–174.

Bryant, D. P., Goodwin, M., Bryant, B. R., & Higgins, K. (2003). Vocabulary instruction for students with disabilities: A review of research. *Learning Disability Quarterly, 26,* 117–128.

Burns, M. K., & Ysseldyke, J. E. (2009). Reported prevalence of evidence-based instructional practices in special education. *The Journal of Special Education, 43*(1), 3–11.

Carnine, D. W., Silbert, J., Kame'enui, E. J., & Tarver, S. G. (2010). *Direct instruction reading* (5th ed.). Columbus, OH: Pearson/Merrill.

Cassidy, J., Ortlieb, E., & Schettel, J. (2010/2011). What's hot for 2011. *Reading Today, 28*(3), 1, 6–7.

Coyne, M. D., Kame'enui, E. J., & Carnine, D. W. (2011). *Effective teaching strategies that accommodate diverse learners* (4th ed.). Boston, MA: Pearson.

Diliberto, J. A., Beattie, J. R., Flowers, C. P., & Algozzine, R. F. (2009). Effects of teaching syllable skills instruction on reading achievement in struggling middle school readers. *Literary Research and Instruction, 48,* 14–27. doi: 10.1080/19388070802226253

Duffy, G. G. (2003). *Explaining reading: A resource for teaching concepts, skills, and strategies.* New York, NY: Guilford Press.

Dymock, S. J. (2007). Comprehension strategy instruction: Teaching narrative text structure awareness. *The Reading Teacher, 61,* 161–167.

Ediger, M. (2002). Factors which make expository reading difficult. *Journal of Instructional Psychology, 29,* 312–316.

Edwards, E. C., Font, G., Baumann, J. F., & Boland, E. (2004). Unlocking word meanings: Strategies and guidelines for teaching morphemic and contextual analysis. In J. F. Baumann & E. J. Kame'enui (Eds.), *Vocabulary instruction: Research to practice* (pp. 159–176). New York, NY: Guilford.

Faggella-Luby, M. N., Schumaker, J. S., & Deshler, D. D. (2007). Embedded learning strategy instruction: Story structure pedagogy in heterogeneous secondary literature classes. *Learning Disability Quarterly, 30,* 131–147.

Fang, Z. (2006). The language demands of science reading in middle school. *International Journal of Science Education, 28,* 491–520.

Fang, Z., & Schleppegrell, M. J. (2010). Disciplinary literacies across content areas: Supporting secondary reading through functional language analysis. *Journal of Adolescent and Adult Literacy, 53,* 587–597. doi:10.1598/JAAL.53.7.6

Fisher, D., Frey, N., & Lapp, D. (2008). Shared readings: Modeling, comprehension, vocabulary, text structures, and text features for older readers. *The Reading Teacher, 61,* 548–556. doi: 10.1598/RT.61.7.4

Glynn, S., Koballa, T., & Coleman, D. (2003). Mnemonic methods. *The Science Teacher, 70*(9), 52–55.

Graham, S., & Hebert, M. A. (2010). *Writing to read: Evidence for how writing can improve reading. A Carnegie Corporation Time to Act Report.* Washington, DC: Alliance for Excellent Education.

Greenleaf, C. L., & Hinchman, K. (2009). Reimagining our inexperienced adolescent readers: From struggling, striving, marginalized and reluctant to thriving. *Journal of Adolescent and Adult Literacy, 53,* 4–13. doi:10.1598/JAAL.53.1.1

Harris, T. L., & Hodges, R. E. (Eds.). (1995). *The literacy dictionary: The vocabulary of reading and writing.* Newark, DE: International Reading Association.

Hasbrouck, J. (2006,). Drop everything and read—but how? *American Educator, 30,* 22–31, 46–47.

Hasbrouck, J., & Tindal, G. (2006). Oral reading fluency norms: A valuable assessment tool for reading teachers. *The Reading Teacher, 59,* 636–644.

Hashey, J. M., & Connors, D. J. (2003). Learn from our journey: Reciprocal teaching action research. *The Reading Teacher, 57,* 224–232.

Hedin, L. R., & Conderman, G. (2010). Teaching students to comprehend informational text through rereading. *The Reading Teacher, 63,* 556–565. doi: 10.1598/RT.63.7.3

Heller, R., & Greenleaf, C. (2007). *Literacy instruction in the content areas: Getting to the core of middle and high school improvement.* Washington, DC: Alliance for Excellent Education.

Hennings, D. G. (2000). Contextually relevant word study: Adolescent vocabulary development across the curriculum. *Journal of Adolescent and Adult Literacy, 44,* 268–279.

Hock, M. F., Deshler, D. D., & Schumaker, J. B. (2000). *Strategic tutoring.* Lawrence, KS: Edge Enterprises.

Invernizzi, M. A., Abouzeid, M. P., & Bloodgood, J. W. (1997). Integrated word study: Spelling, grammar, and meaning in the language arts classroom. *Language Arts, 74,* 185–192.

Kamil, M. L., Borman, G. D., Dole, J., Kral, C. C., Salinger, T., & Torgesen, J. (2008). *Improving adolescent literacy: Effective classroom and intervention practices: A Practice Guide* (NCEE #2008–4027). Washington, DC: National Center for Education Evaluation and Regional Assistance, Institute of Education Sciences, U.S. Department of Education. Retrieved from http://ies.ed.gov/ncee/wwc.

Kirschner, P. A., Sweller, J., & Clark, R. E. (2006). Why minimal guidance during instruction does not work: An analysis of the failure of constructivist, discovery, problem-based, experiential, and inquiry-based teaching. *Educational Psychologist, 41,* 75–86.

Klahr, D., & Nigam, M. (2004). The equivalence of learning paths in early science instruction: Effects of direct instruction and discovery learning. *Psychological Science, 15,* 661–667.

Klingner, J. K., Vaughn, S., Dimino, J., Schumm, J. S., & Bryant, D. (2001). *Collaborative strategic reading: Strategies for improving comprehension.* Longmont, CO: Sopris West.

Kosanovich, M. L., Reed, D. K., & Miller, D. H. (2010). *Bringing literacy strategies into content instruction: Professional learning for secondary-level teachers.* Portsmouth, NH: RMC Research Corporation, Center on Instruction.

Krathwohl, D. R. (2002). A revision of Bloom's Taxonomy: An overview. *Theory Into Practice, 41,* 212–218.

Lapp, D., Flood, J., Brock, C., & Fisher, D. (2007). *Teaching reading to every child* (4th ed.). Mahwah, NJ: Erlbaum.

Lee, C. D., & Spratley, A. (2010). *Reading in the disciplines: The challenges of adolescent literacy.* New York, NY: Carnegie Corporation of New York.

Lenski, S. D. (1998). Intertextual connections: Making connections across texts. *The Clearing House, 72,* 74–80.

Lenski, S. D., Wham, M. A., Johns, J. L., & Caskey, M. M. (2007). *Reading and learning strategies: Middle grades through high school* (3rd ed.). Dubuque, IA: Kendall/Hunt.

Lesaux, N. K., Kieffer, M. J., Faller, S. E., & Kelley, J. G. (2010). The effectiveness and ease of implementation of an academic vocabulary intervention for linguistically diverse students in urban middle schools. *Reading Research Quarterly, 45,* 196–228. doi.org/10.1598/RRQ.45.2.3

Malmgren, K. W., & Trezek, B. J. (2009). Literacy instruction for secondary students with disabilities. *Focus on Exceptional Children, 41*(6), 1–12.

Marchand-Martella, N. E., & Martella, R. C. (2013). Explicit instruction. In W. L. Heward (Ed.), *Exceptional children* (10th ed.) (pp. 166–168). Columbus, OH: Pearson/Merrill.

Marchand-Martella, N. E, Slocum, T. A., & Martella, R. C. (Eds.). (2004). *Introduction to Direct Instruction.* Boston, MA: Allyn & Bacon.

Mastropieri, M. A., & Scruggs, T. E. (1996). Reflections on "promoting thinking skills of students with learning disabilities": Effects on recall and comprehension of expository prose. *Exceptionality, 6,* 53–57.

Mastropieri, M. A., & Scruggs, T. E. (1998). Enhancing school success with mnemonic strategies. *Intervention in School & Clinic, 33,* 201–208.

McEwan, E. K. (2007). *Use and teacher content vocabulary daily.* Retrieved from: http://www.adlit.org/article/19792

McKeown, M. G., Beck, I. L., & Blake, R. (2009). Rethinking reading comprehension instruction: A comparison of instruction for strategies and content approaches. *Reading Research Quarterly, 44,* 218–253. doi.org/10.1598/RRQ.44.3.1

Montelongo, J., Berber-Jiménez, L., Hernández, A. C., & Hosking, D. (2006). Teaching expository text structures. *The Science Teacher, 73,* 28–31.

National Center for Education Statistics. (2009). *The nation's report card: Reading 2009* (NCES 2010–458). Washington, DC: Institute of Education Sciences, U.S. Department of Education.

National Center for Education Statistics. (2010). *The nation's report card: Grade 12 reading and mathematics 2009 national and pilot state results.* (NCES 2011–455). Washington, DC: Institute of Education Sciences, U.S. Department of Education.

National Education Association (NEA). (2006). *Using text structure.* Retrieved from http://www.nea.org/reading/usingtextstructure.html

National Governors Association for Best Practices. (2005). *Reading to achieve: A governor's guide to adolescent literacy.* Retrieved from: http://www.nga.org/Files/pdf/0510govguideliteracy.pdf.

National Institute of Child Health and Human Development (NICHD). (2000). Report of the National Reading Panel. Teaching children to read: *An evidence-based assessment of the scientific research literature on reading and its implications for reading instruction: Reports of the subgroups*

(NIH Publication No. 00–4754). Retrieved from http://www.nichd.nih.gov/publications/nrp/smallbook.cfm.

National Institute for Literacy (NIFL). (2007). *What content-area teachers should know about adolescent literacy.* Retrieved from http://www.nifl.gov/nifl/publications/adolescent_literacy07.pdf

Ogle, D. M. (1996). Study techniques that ensure content area reading success. In D. Lapp, J. Flood, & N. Farnan (Eds.), *Content area reading and learning instructional strategies* (2nd ed.) (pp. 3–14). Needham Heights, MA: Simon & Schuster.

Palincsar, A. S., & Brown, A. L. (1984). Reciprocal teaching of comprehension-fostering and comprehension-monitoring activities. *Cognition and Instruction, 1,* 117–175.

Rayner, K., & Pollatsek, A. (1989). *The psychology of reading.* Englewood Cliffs, NJ: Prentice Hall.

Robb, L. (1995). *Reading strategies that work: Teaching your students to become better readers.* New York, NY: Scholastic.

Roberts, G., Torgesen, J. K., Boardman, A., & Scammacca, N. (2008). Evidence-based strategies for reading instruction of older students with learning disabilities. *Learning Disabilities Research & Practice, 23,* 63–69.

Robinson, D. H., Beth, A., Odom, S., Hsieh, Y., Vanderveen, A., & Katayama, A.D. (2006). Increasing text comprehension and graphic note taking using a partial graphic organizer. *The Journal of Educational Research, 100,* 103–111.

Rosenshine, B., Meister, C., & Chapman, S. (1996). Teaching students to generate questions: A review of the intervention studies. *Review of Educational Research, 66,* 181–221.

Rupley, W., Blair, T., & Nichols, W. (2009). Effective reading instruction for struggling readers: The role of direct/explicit teaching. *Reading and Writing Quarterly, 25,* 125–138.

Rupley, W. H., & Slough, S. (2010). Building prior knowledge and vocabulary in science in the intermediate grades: Creating hooks for learning. *Literacy Research and Instruction, 49,* 99–112. doi: 10.1080/19388070902780472

Ryder, J. F., Tunmer, W. E., & Greaney, K. T. (2008). Explicit instruction in phonemic awareness and phonemically based decoding skills as an intervention strategy for struggling readers in whole language classrooms. *Reading and Writing, 21,* 349–369.

Saczynski, J. S., Rebok, G. W., Whitfield, K. E., & Plude, D. L. (2007). Spontaneous production and use of mnemonic strategies in older adults. *Experimental Aging Research, 33,* 273–294.

Sáenz, L. M., & Fuchs, L. S. (2002). Examining the reading difficulty of secondary students with learning disabilities: Expository versus narrative text. *Remedial and Special Education, 23,* 31–41.

Santa, C. M., Havens, L., & Harrison, S. (1996). Teaching secondary science through reading, writing, studying, and problem solving. In D. Lapp, J. Flood, & N. Farnan (Eds.), *Content area reading and learning instructional strategies* (2nd ed.) (pp. 3–14). Needham Heights, MA: Simon & Schuster.

Scammacca, N., Roberts, G., Vaughn. S., Edmonds, M., Wexler, J., Reutebuch, C. K., & Torgesen, J. K. (2007). *Interventions for adolescent struggling readers: A meta-analysis with implications for practice.* Portsmouth, NH: RMC Research Corporation, Center on Instruction.

Schoenbach, R., Greenleaf, C., Cziko, C., & Hurwitz, L. (1999). *Reading for understanding: A guide to improving reading in middle and high school classrooms.* San Francisco, CA: Jossey-Bass.

Slavin, R. E. (1996). Cooperative learning in middle and secondary schools. *The Clearing House, 69*, 200–204.

Snow, C. & Moje, E. (2010). Why is everyone talking about adolescent literacy? *Kappan, 91*(6), 66–69.

Stein, N., & Glenn, C. (1979). An analysis of story comprehension in elementary school children. In R. O. Freedle (Ed.), *Advances in discourse processing* (Vol. 2): *New directions in discourse processing* (pp. 53–120). Norwood, NJ: Ablex.

Therrien, W. J. (2004). Fluency and comprehension gains as a result of repeated reading: A meta-analysis. *Remedial and Special Education, 25*, 252–261.

Torgesen, J. K., Houston, D. D., Rissman, L. M., Decker, S. M., Roberts, G., Vaughn, S., ... Lesaux, N. (2007). *Academic literacy instruction for adolescents: A guidance document from the Center on Instruction.* Portsmouth, NH: RMC Research Corporation, Center on Instruction.

Tovani, C. (2000). *I read it, but I don't get it: Comprehension strategies for adolescent readers.* Portland, ME: Stenhouse.

Uberti, H. Z., Scruggs, T. E., & Mastropieri, M. A. (2003). Keywords make the difference! Mnemonic instruction in inclusive classrooms. *Teaching Exceptional Children, 10*(3), 56–61.

Vaughn, S., & Bos, C. S. (2009). *Strategies for teaching students with learning and behavior problems* (7th ed.). Upper Saddle River, NJ: Pearson.

Vaughn, S., & Edmonds, M. (2006). Reading comprehension for older readers. *Intervention in School and Clinic, 41*, 131–137.

Vaughn, S., & Linan-Thompson, S. (2003). What is special about special education for students with learning disabilities? *The Journal of Special Education, 37*, 140–147.

Wilson, N. S., Grisham, D. L., & Smetana, L. (2009). Investigating content area teachers' understanding of a content literacy framework: A yearlong professional development initiative. *Journal of Adolescent & Adult Literacy, 52*, 708–718.

Wolfe, M. B. W., & Mienko, J. A. (2007). Learning and memory of factual content from narrative and expository text. *British Journal of Educational Psychology, 77*, 541–564.

Discussion Questions

1. Research reported in the Marchand-Martella article identified five areas of importance in adolescent literacy programs and a number of critical instructional practices in each area. List the five areas and critical instructional practices identified in the article.

2. Why do you think that the literacy levels of many middle and secondary students are so far below expectations?

Making Complex Texts a Reality for All Students

Dynamic Scaffolding That Bridges the Gaps between Student and Text

Dan Reynolds and Amanda P. Goodwin

In this article, Reynolds and Goodwin provide ideas for teachers who are attempting to meet the Common Core State Standards by incorporating complex texts into the literacy curriculum.

LEARNING OBJECTIVES

1. In terms of literacy instruction, what is "scaffolding"? Name one instructional strategy you know that provides scaffolding for students.
2. In this article you will see the statement, "(Text) complexity can be found, and it can be made." What do you think this means? Brainstorm a list of factors that you believe make texts more "complex."

Making Complex Texts a Reality for All Students

Dynamic Scaffolding That Bridges the Gaps between Student and Text

Dan Reynolds and Amanda P. Goodwin

Introduction

The Common Core State Standards (CCSS) emphasize the role of text complexity in reading instruction. Under the CCSS, students are required to read texts at their grade levels "with scaffolding as needed at the upper end" of their grade level (National Governors Association for Best Practices, 2010, CCSS Appendix A, p. x).

This scaffolding is particularly important to CCSS reading success because only 34 percent of US eighth graders scored proficient or better on the 2015 NAEP test (National Center for Education Statistics, 2015). This means that many students are reading below grade level and will need teachers who are experts at scaffolding grade-level complex texts.

Quality reading instruction must continually strive to be ever more responsive to student needs—especially for diverse populations of readers. To better understand such responsive complex text scaffolding in practice, we designed a guided-reading intervention for small groups of middle schoolers, many of whom were struggling readers. Within a consistent lesson plan structure, the groups' tutors were encouraged to use a list of scaffolds whenever they felt necessary. After each lesson, the tutors documented their scaffolding. By analyzing how tutors scaffolded successful reading instruction, our study can help educators make the goal of reading complex texts a reality.

The Challenge of Complex Texts and the Role of the Teacher

To study scaffolding of reading, we use a reader-text-task framework (RAND, 2002) in which readers' skills and background knowledge affect text difficulty and the task's requirements affect a reader's approach to a text. In this view, the complexity of a text is more than just the words, but also includes the design of the reading task and the supports provided for the reader (Goldman & Lee, 2014). Thus, responsive teacher scaffolding can make a text more or less complex.

We define scaffolding as the teacher-initiated interactions during reading instruction where teachers notice a student need and respond with appropriate assistance to assist the student toward a curricular objective (Clark & Graves, 2005), and then the scaffold is removed when the student no longer needs it (Pressley, 2006). In addition, our scaffolds were developed with an interactive model of reading (Rumelhart, 1994) in mind. Tutors supported student thinking across many levels at the same time: word, sentence, paragraph, and text. Specifically, we designed scaffolds according to three levels from the National Reading Panel (National Institute of Child Health and Human Development, 2000): vocabulary (i.e., word level), fluency (i.e., phrase level) and comprehension (i.e., text level), along with social and motivational supports. Figure 11.2.1 presents a list of scaffolds used in this analysis.

In this intervention, the scripted lesson plan and the use of the same portions of the same texts provided a common frame within which to examine tutors' moment-to-moment scaffolding choices. Here is one example of tutor scaffolding. Scaffolds used in this transcript are labeled according to Figure 11.2.1. After the students read aloud from *To Space and Back* about the space shuttle lift-off, the tutor asked Sharon (all names are pseudonyms), a sixth-grade struggling reader and native speaker of Arabic, to choose a clue from the passage to answer the question *What is it like to be in space?*:

1. **TUTOR**: What are you connecting to? [Comprehension, #15]
2. **SHARON**: That their heads are like (waves hand) ... they feel that ... (continues waving)
3. **TUTOR**: Act it out for us. What do they feel like? [Comprehension, #15]
4. **SHARON**: (Pause) They feel light ...
5. **TUTOR**: Close! It says "Our heads are" what? [Comprehension, #16]
6. **SHARON**: Um ... (looks in text to find the word). Rattling ... around inside our helmets
7. **TUTOR**: What does that mean? [Vocabulary, #3]
8. **SHARON**: (Looks at tutor but does not respond)
9. **TUTOR**: (Shakes head side to side, mimicking the astronauts during liftoff) Can you imagine their helmets trying to stay on and there's so much roughness going on in the ride. Can they keep still? [Comprehension, #19]
10. **SHARON**: No. (Smiles)
11. **TUTOR**: No! (Smiles) So their heads are rattling—I like that—so the rocket blasts off, and there is lots of rattling.

	Scaffold	Example
Vocabulary [word-level support]		
1	Initiate students' metacognition about vocabulary.	Ask "Are there hard words we need to figure out?"
2	Prompt students to activate existing vocabulary strategies.	Ask, "What do you know that can help you figure out some of these words?"
3	Check specific word knowledge.	Ask a student what a specific word means.
4	Capitalize on students' morphological knowledge.	Check to see if students know any roots or affixes.
5	Point to (or ask students to point to) specific morphemes. Use them to pronounce a word or figure out its meaning.	Point out *mid* in midair.
6	Pre-teach words.	Before the lesson, select key vocabulary words and define them for students.
7	Write definitions on board.	Write "midair = suspended in the middle of the air" on the board.
8	Provide (or ask students to provide) examples.	Point out that "Bees can hover in *midair*."
9	Use context clues to figure out a word.	Ask, "What does it mean to be "weightlessly floating in midair?"
Fluency [phrase- and sentence-level support]		
10	Attend to punctuation as a clue to oral reading.	Have students read a passage with dramatic pauses at the commas.
11	Practice prosodic and tone-appropriate reading.	Suggest, "Let's read this like a conversation, like radio readers, or like tv announcers."
12	Help students' automatic word recognition.	Tell students to put their fingers under their text as they read.
13	Practice word-recognition and fluent reading with repeated readings.	Tell students "Let's pretend we are preparing for a show. Re-read this section to practice it."
Comprehension [text-level support]		
14	Initiate students' metacognition about comprehension.	Ask, "What can we do to figure this out?"
15	Prompt students to activate existing comprehension strategies.	Ask, "What strategies will help you understand the story? Is there anything you can make connections to or visualize?"
16	Encourage students to look for evidence in the text.	Have students point to text that supports their point. Ask, "Where did you see that point?"
17	Check for specific comprehension.	Ask, "What does this part mean?"
18	Check for general comprehension.	Ask students what is going on in the whole text.
19	Activate background knowledge about content.	Ask, "What do you already know about space?"
20	Activate background knowledge about text structure.	Inquire whether students have ever read this type of text before, and if so, what they expect to see.
21	Link the text to students' experiences and backgrounds.	Ask "How is this like your life?" or "Have you ever … ?"
22	Link text to real-world knowledge or to students' other classes.	Connect to students' history/science classes or reference current events.

FIGURE 11.2.1 List of Scaffolds with Illustrative Examples.

Prompted by Sharon's struggle to explain herself, the tutor steps in to scaffold at the comprehension level by inviting her to act out the passage and to check for specific textual evidence. When Sharon cannot explain the word "rattling," the tutor zooms in on the vocabulary level to help the student understand the g-forces astronauts experience during lift-off. The scaffolding helped the whole group's broad comprehension of the experience of life on the space shuttle, which was the purpose of the lesson. The sequence emerged dynamically: prompted by a broad concern for comprehension, the tutor probed for a scaffold that would work for Sharon, eventually settling on a vocabulary scaffold for "rattling" that the tutor then used as a piece of the overall comprehension puzzle. Here, the scaffolding emerges interactively across multiple levels as the tutor supports the student navigating challenging complex text.

Investigating Scaffolding

To find out what kinds of scaffolding were used to help struggling readers access complex texts, we analyzed the scaffolds used during our short four-lesson guided reading intervention for small groups of two to seven middle schoolers. Two members of our research team (including the second author) developed the lesson plans to use CCSS-type texts and meet CCSS objectives such as citing evidence, using grade-appropriate academic vocabulary, and determining the meaning of words within texts. The same sections of the same texts, *Rosa* (Lexile level 900; Giovanni & Collier, 2006) and *To Space and Back* (Lexile level 1090; Ride & Okie, 1986) were used for all students. Goodwin and Perkins (2015) describes the curriculum in more detail.

The diversity and ability of students in our study made it an ideal case to study emergent scaffolding with diverse learners. The 215 students were mostly fifth and sixth graders (96 percent), and 18 percent were White, 55 percent Black, 15 percent Hispanic, and 2 percent Asian. Their language backgrounds included 61 percent English-only speakers and 39 percent students who spoke a language other than English at home (11 different languages, mostly Spanish and Arabic). Since 74 percent of our students were below the 50th percentile for their grade level on the standardized reading comprehension pretest, this group of students is ideal to investigate how teachers scaffolded grade-level texts with students who were reading below grade level. Good instruction for this population could not have followed a one-size-fits-all model, and data suggests our tutors scaffolded within the lesson plans to bridge the gaps between students' understanding and the challenges of the complex texts.

After each lesson, the tutors marked the scaffolds they used on a common document, and these reports were collected and entered into a database, which was used to calculate the percentage of sessions in which each category of scaffolds was used (vocabulary, fluency, or comprehension). In addition, to find out whether teachers used scaffolding differently according to student ability, we compared percentages for the sessions with 50 percent or more struggling readers with the sessions of 49 percent or fewer struggling readers.

Our Findings

Tutors scaffolded dynamically across levels. We found that tutors used all three kinds of scaffolds regularly: vocabulary scaffolds in 84 percent of sessions, fluency in 57 percent of sessions, and comprehension in 90 percent of sessions. For vocabulary, it seems that the complex texts' vocabulary demands required extensive word-level support. For fluency, although oral reading practice is not as common in the middle grades, tutors still scaffolded fluency relatively often. Most frequently used were comprehension scaffolds, with which tutors helped students actively build understanding of the text. These results show educators sensing students' need for interactive support at all levels, then providing a range of supports to help students access the complex texts. It is likely that this scaffolding contributed to the overall success of the instruction, which supported word reading fluency, vocabulary knowledge, reading comprehension, and morphological awareness.

Here is another example of this dynamic multilevel scaffolding. After a group of three fifth-grade boys (two native Arabic speakers and one native Amharic speaker) read aloud from *To Space and Back* in their radio announcer voices [Fluency, #11], the tutor asked them to identify a key word to break down. When Aran mispronounces the word *midair* the tutor stepped in to scaffold:

1. **TUTOR**: Hmmm, what's this part say? [underlines "mid" on board] [Vocabulary, #5]
2. **ARAN**: Mid
3. **TUTOR**: Good, so say it again?
4. **ARAN**: Mid-midair
5. **TUTOR**: Nice! So anybody find a part that they know in "midair"? [Vocabulary, #5]
6. **AMIR**: Air and mid, and mid is like middle and air is like what you breathe in
7. **TUTOR**: Fantastic

In turn 1, the tutor highlighted morphology to help pronunciation. After making sure Aran could pronounce it, in turn 5 the tutor tried a morphology scaffold to help the group figure out the word's meaning. Immediately after this transcript, the tutor checked to see that the word made sense in context—for this text, the key concept about *midair* was not about respiration (as the student's explanation of the morpheme suggests in turn 6) but about weightlessness in the space shuttle. So the tutor had the students hold their pencils in midair to demonstrate the idea of weightlessness, effectively using the expanded understanding of this word to scaffold the students' comprehension [Comprehension, #22] of the whole text. The dynamic scaffolding sequence moved across levels, starting with the students' fluent reading practice, zooming in on a key vocabulary word, and finally placing that word within the broad context of the text.

Tutors differentiated, but not for all kinds of scaffolds. Figure 11.2.2 shows how scaffolding differed across low- and high-ability groups. In this case, we see that tutors used comprehension scaffolds in significantly more sessions with high percentages of struggling readers. On the other hand, vocabulary and fluency scaffolds do not show differentiated usage. Overall, even though the tutors did not know anything about their students before our study and had only two hours of instructional time, they were able to respond interactively in the moment-to-moment

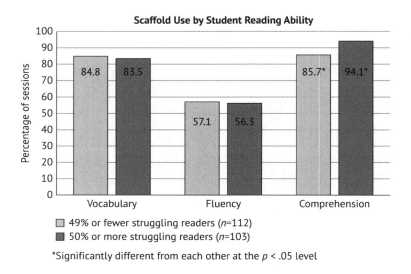

FIGURE 11.2.2   Frequency of Scaffold Uses According to Student Reading Ability.

scaffolding decisions to provide extra comprehension help to their struggling reading groups. This suggests that successful CCSS scaffolding involves educators identifying student needs during reading sessions and tailoring their support to meet those needs.

Equally interesting is that our tutors did *not* scaffold differentially in the vocabulary and fluency areas. The tutors appear to have felt that all students needed extensive vocabulary support and moderate fluency support. Perhaps the features of the texts—like rare and discipline-specific vocabulary words—may have outweighed student characteristics as the tutors selected these scaffolds.

Discussion

This investigation into quality teaching suggests that teachers need to be both flexible and consistent in their scaffolding practices to help students comprehend complex texts. Certainly the features of the complex texts were strong factors in driving tutors' scaffolding, and teachers did apply a consistent portfolio of scaffolds for all readers. Though, for many teachers, differentiation is often a required element at the lesson plan (i.e., curricular) level, many teachers may already be differentiating on a moment-to-moment level as they try to bridge the gaps between their students and complex texts. Figure 11.2.3 presents our scaffolding tips to help teachers toward that goal.

Tutors and teachers must remember to align their moment-to-moment scaffolding decisions with the lesson objective and the purpose for reading—which are key elements in determining a text's complexity (Goldman & Lee, 2015). The examples here show tutors stepping in to scaffold key concepts (e.g., g-forces and weightlessness) in the text about the space shuttle. When

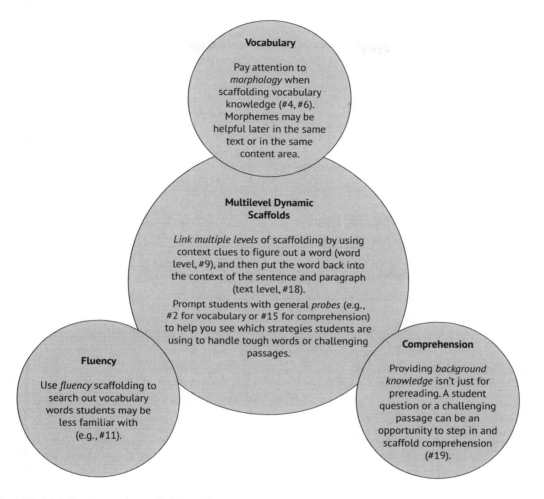

Vocabulary

Pay attention to *morphology* when scaffolding vocabulary knowledge (#4, #6). Morphemes may be helpful later in the same text or in the same content area.

Multilevel Dynamic Scaffolds

Link multiple levels of scaffolding by using context clues to figure out a word (word level, #9), and then put the word back into the context of the sentence and paragraph (text level, #18).

Prompt students with general *probes* (e.g., #2 for vocabulary or #15 for comprehension) to help you see which strategies students are using to handle tough words or challenging passages.

Fluency

Use *fluency* scaffolding to search out vocabulary words students may be less familiar with (e.g., #11).

Comprehension

Providing *background knowledge* isn't just for prereading. A student question or a challenging passage can be an opportunity to step in and scaffold comprehension (#19).

FIGURE 11.2.3 Dynamic Scaffolding Tips.

reading some complex and challenging texts, tutors and teachers could be perpetually scaffolding, interrupting students' process of comprehension! Tutors and teachers must remember that scaffolding is not an end in itself, but should be used in service of curricular objectives.

Providing diverse types of scaffolding is one way of showing students that there are multiple routes to comprehension. Though Sharon needed extensive scaffolding support in the example cited earlier, she also made great progress over the two-week intervention: she had scored in the 13th percentile on her standardized reading comprehension pretest, but scored at the 42nd percentile on the post-test. It appears that reading complex texts and being supported by intensive scaffolding resulted in significant improvement for Sharon.

This study illustrates dynamic scaffolding that responds to all kinds of readers. Recently, Hiebert and Pearson (2014) declared, "Understanding what makes texts complex for readers with particular profiles in particular contexts and tasks is a central one for the goal of a fully literate society" (p. 158). It is our hope that educators can use our list of scaffolds and our findings about how they were used to strengthen their instruction to meet the challenge of helping all students reading complex texts.

References

Clark, K. F., & Graves, M. F. (2005). Scaffolding students' comprehension of text. *The Reading Teacher, 58*(6), 570–580.

Giovanni, N., & Collier, B. (2006). *Rosa.* New York, NY: Square Fish.

Goldman, S. R., & Lee, C. D. (2014). Text complexity: State of the art and the conundrums it raises. *The Elementary School Journal, 115*(2), 290–300.

Goodwin, A. P., & Perkins, J. (2015). Word detectives: Morphological instruction that supports academic language. *The Reading Teacher, 68*(7), 510–523.

Hiebert, E. H., & Pearson, P. D. (2014). Understanding text complexity: Introduction to the special issue. *The Elementary School Journal, 115*(2), 153–160.

National Center for Education Statistics (2015). *The nation's report card.* Washington, DC: US Department of Education, Institute of Education Sciences. Retrieved from http://nces.ed.gov/nationsreportcard/reading/

National Governors Association Center for Best Practices & Council of Chief State School Officers. (2010). *Common Core State Standards for English language arts and literacy in history/social studies, science, and technical subjects.* Washington, DC. Retrieved from http://www.corestandards.org/assets/Appendix_A.pdf

National Institute of Child Health and Human Development. (2000). *Report of the National Reading Panel. Teaching children to read: An evidence-based assessment of the scientific research literature on reading and its implications for reading instruction* (NIH Publication No. 00-4769). Washington, DC: U.S. Government Printing Office. Retrieved from http://www.nichd.nih.gov/publications/nrp/upload/smallbook_pdf

Pressley, M. (2006). *Reading instruction that works: The case for balanced teaching.* New York, NY: Guilford.

RAND Reading Study Group. (2002*). Reading for understanding: Toward an R & D program in reading comprehension.* Santa Monica, CA: RAND. Retrieved from http://www.rand.org/pubs/monograph_reports/MR1465.html

Ride, S., & Okie, S. (1986). *To Space and Back.* New York, NY: Harper.

Rumelhart, D. E. (1994). Toward an interactive model of reading. In R. Ruddell, M. Ruddell, & H. Singer (Eds.), *Theoretical models and processes of reading.* (4th ed., pp. 864–894). Newark, DE: International Reading Association.

Discussion Questions

1. How do the authors define "dynamic scaffolding"? How does that approach support students' comprehension of complex texts?
2. Describe how the dynamic scaffolding approach could be used in a middle- or secondary-level classroom.

Conclusion

Chapter Activities

Activity 11.1

Select one of the instructional practices identified in the article. Research that instructional practice and develop a brief PowerPoint presentation that you could use to teach this practice to a group of middle or high school teachers who teach in the content areas, not literacy. Be sure to include all the information the teachers would need to incorporate this strategy into their own classrooms and include its theoretical support.

Activity 11.2

Interview a teacher who is responsible for teaching the developmental reading or English language arts curriculum in a middle school or secondary school. Focus your questions on what activities the students complete during the school year and what the teacher's goals are for the students.

CONCLUSION

21st Century Literacy for Middle and Secondary Students was designed to provide preservice and in-service teachers with a strong background in theory and best practices in instruction for tween and adolescent students. The chapter articles have provided the theoretical basis research basis that supports high-quality instructional approaches and strategies. The hands-on activities and resources serve to enhance and deepen the teachers' understanding of the presented content.

The information presented in the textbook elucidates concepts and approaches that are often included in state-mandated teacher-certification exams for middle- or secondary-level English language arts teachers and/or reading specialists. This text can be used as a handy study resource for those studying for these exams.

The most important factor in enhancing the literacy skills of adolescent and preadolescent students is an enthusiastic teacher who is able to effectively utilize the students' interests to enhance literacy instruction. It is hoped that this text has provided a toolkit with which teachers can accomplish this goal.

As said by the illustrious children's author Roald Dahl in his classic masterpiece, *Charlie and the Chocolate Factory*:

> *... Please, oh PLEASE, we beg, we pray,*
>
> *Go throw your TV set away,*
>
> *And in its place you can install,*
>
> *A lovely bookshelf on the wall.*